GCSE
French

Complete Revision
and Practice

Contents

Contents

Published by CGP

Editors:
Heather Gregson
Rachael Powers

Contributors:
Sarah Donachie
Jan Greenway
Alexandra Le-Guen Murray
Lynne Mold
Ian Sanderson

With thanks to Christine Bodin & Glenn Rogers for the proofreading.

Listening CD recorded, edited and mastered at Ferndale Studios by Marc Joy.
Additional editing and remastering by Neil Hastings.

ISBN: 978 1 84146 373 5
Website: www.cgpbooks.co.uk
Printed by Elanders Ltd, Newcastle upon Tyne.
Clipart from CorelDRAW®

Based on the classic CGP style created by Richard Parsons.

Numbers and Amounts

Wow — a book to make you a whizz at <u>French</u>. Here's a page about <u>numbers</u> to get you started.

Un, deux, trois — One, two, three...

① It all starts off easy enough. Learn <u>nought to ten</u> — no problem.

0	zéro
1	un
2	deux
3	trois
4	quatre
5	cinq
6	six
7	sept
8	huit
9	neuf
10	dix

② 11 to 16 all end in '<u>ze</u>'.
But 17, 18 and 19 are
'<u>ten-seven</u>' etc.

11	onze
12	douze
13	treize
14	quatorze
15	quinze
16	seize
17	dix-sept
18	dix-huit
19	dix-neuf

③ Most 'ten-type' numbers
end in 'nte' (except '<u>vingt</u>')
but <u>70</u> is '<u>sixty-ten</u>' and
<u>80</u> is '<u>four-20s</u>'. <u>90</u> is
'<u>four-20-ten</u>'.

20	vingt	60	soixante
30	trente	70	soixante-dix
40	quarante	80	quatre-vingts
50	cinquante	90	quatre-vingt-dix

Before words which are
<u>feminine</u>, like 'fille' or
'voiture', the 'un' or 'et un'
changes to '<u>une</u>' or '<u>et une</u>'.

21	vingt et un	71	soixante et onze	82	quatre-vingt-deux
22	vingt-deux	72	soixante-douze	95	quatre-vingt-quinze
23	vingt-trois	79	soixante-dix-neuf	98	quatre-vingt-dix-huit

④ The in-between numbers are like English — just remember '<u>et un</u>' for numbers
ending in 1. For the <u>70s</u> and <u>90s</u>, add the <u>teens</u> to soixante or quatre-vingt.

soixante-treize = seventy-three

100	cent
101	cent un
623	six cent vingt-trois
1000	mille
1 000 000	un million

⑤ When you get to hundreds and thousands, just put
"cent", "deux cent", "mille" (etc.) before the number.

mille neuf cent quarante - sept = <u>1947</u>

1900   40   7

The French put <u>full stops</u> or spaces between
digits in <u>long numbers</u>, rather than commas,
so ten thousand would be 10.000.

Add -ième to the number to get second, third, etc...

These are easy — just add '<u>ième</u>' to the number.
But '<u>1st</u>' is 'premier' (masc.) or 'première' (fem.).

Watch out for the <u>underlined</u> spellings. And words
ending in '<u>e</u>' (like quatre) lose the 'e' (quatrième).

1st is written 1er, or 1ère.
2nd is written 2ème, etc.

1st	<u>premier</u>, <u>première</u>	7th	septième
		8th	huitième
2nd	deuxième	9th	neu<u>v</u>ième
3rd	troisième	10th	dixième
4th	quatrième	20th	vingtième
5th	cin<u>q</u>uième	21st	vingt et unième
6th	sixième	100th	centième

Prenez la deuxième rue à gauche. = Take the <u>second</u> street on the left.

Start at the beginning, not with A, B, C but with 1, 2, 3

You're <u>bound</u> to know some of these numbers already. Don't get cocky and skip the page though —
you need to be able to say any one of these numbers <u>right off the top of your head</u>. Get revising.

Times and Dates

You <u>need</u> to be able to tell the <u>time</u> and understand what time things happen — so if you can't, <u>learn</u> it now.

Quelle heure est-il? — What time is it?

Just like there are <u>loads</u> of ways of saying the time in English, so there are in French too.
Of course, you have to <u>learn all</u> of them.

Quelle heure est-il?   = What time is it?

1) Something o'clock:

It's 1 o'clock:	Il est une heure
It's 2 o'clock:	Il est deux heures
It's 8 o'clock:	Il est huit heures

2) Quarter to and past, half past:

(It's) quarter past two:	(Il est) deux heures <u>et quart</u>
(It's) half past two:	(Il est) deux heures <u>et demie</u>
(It's) quarter to three:	(Il est) trois heures <u>moins le quart</u>

3) '... past' and '... to':

(It's) twenty past seven:	(Il est) sept heures <u>vingt</u>
(It's) twelve minutes past eight:	(Il est) huit heures <u>douze</u>
(It's) ten to two:	(Il est) deux heures <u>moins dix</u>

4) The <u>24-hour clock</u>:

They use it a lot in France
— and it's easier, too.

03:14:	(Il est) trois heures quatorze
20:32:	(Il est) vingt heures trente-deux
19:55:	(Il est) dix-neuf heures cinquante-cinq

Now is the time to learn this stuff

Being able to <u>say</u> or <u>recognise</u> the time is essential for your exams. This is the real <u>bread-and-butter</u> <u>stuff</u> that comes up again and again in all sorts of different topics — so you need to know it <u>inside out</u>.

Times and Dates

You need to be able to <u>recognise</u> the <u>days of the week</u>. You should learn how to <u>say</u> and <u>write</u> them too.

You use 'le' for all the days of the week

More '<u>vital basics</u>' — they'll gain you simple marks in the exams.

lundi	mardi	mercredi	jeudi	vendredi	samedi	dimanche
					1	2
3	4	5	6	7	8	9
10	11	12	13	14	15	16
17	18	19	20	21	22	23
24	25	26	27	28	29	30

Days of the week:

Monday:	lundi
Tuesday:	mardi
Wednesday:	mercredi
Thursday:	jeudi
Friday:	vendredi
Saturday:	samedi
Sunday:	dimanche

Days of the week are all <u>masculine</u>, with <u>no capital letters</u>. If you want to say '<u>on Monday</u>', it's '<u>lundi</u>' — but '<u>on Mondays</u>' is '<u>le lundi</u>'.

Je pars mardi . = I'm going away on <u>Tuesday</u>.

Je fais les courses le mardi . = I go shopping <u>on Tuesdays</u> (every Tuesday).

Some useful words about the week:

today:	aujourd'hui
tomorrow:	demain
yesterday:	hier
the day after tomorrow:	après-demain
the day before yesterday:	avant-hier
week:	la semaine
weekend:	le week-end
on Mondays:	le lundi

Janvier, février, mars, avril...

French months bear a striking resemblance to the English ones — make sure you <u>learn</u> what's <u>different</u>.

Il part en juillet . = He's leaving <u>in July</u>.

January:	janvier	*July:*	juillet
February:	février	*August:*	août
March:	mars	*September:*	septembre
April:	avril	*October:*	octobre
May:	mai	*November:*	novembre
June:	juin	*December:*	décembre

Months and seasons are <u>masculine</u>, with no capital letters.

winter:	hiver
spring:	printemps
summer:	été
autumn:	automne

You say '<u>au printemps</u>' for <u>in spring</u>. But you use '<u>en</u>' in front of all the other seasons.

Don't revise demain, do it aujourd'hui

It's really <u>important</u> to be able to say <u>when</u> you do things. You absolutely have to know how to say the <u>days of the week</u> and things like '<u>tomorrow</u>' or '<u>weekend</u>'. What are you waiting for?

4

Times and Dates

You can <u>bet</u> your bottom dollar you'll find this stuff on dates and times really useful. These essentials will make your sentences sound a whole lot more interesting. It's <u>guaranteed</u>.

You say "the 3 May" instead of "the 3rd of May"

Here's how to say <u>the date</u> in French. This is <u>bound to come up</u> in the <u>exam</u> — and the examiners won't be impressed if you can't do it.

Check out p.1 for help with the numbers.

1) In French, they don't say "the <u>third of</u> May" — they say "the <u>three</u> May".

   J'arrive le trois octobre. = I am coming on the 3rd of October.

2) The <u>first</u> is the odd one out, because it's like English. They say "<u>the first May</u>" ("<u>le premier mai</u>").

   Je suis né(e) le premier mars mille neuf cent quatre-vingt-treize. = I was born on the first of March 1993.

3) And this is how you <u>write the date</u> in a letter:

   Londres, le 5 mars 2009 = London, 5th March 2009

4) And here are some other useful bits:

   See p.14-15 for letters.

   | *in the year 2000:* | en l'an deux mille |
   | *in 2009:* | en deux mille neuf |

   ⬅ NOT 'deux mille <u>et</u> neuf'

Ce matin — This morning... Ce soir — This evening

You'll use these phrases <u>all the time</u> — they're <u>great</u> for making loads of <u>arrangements</u>.

Je fais souvent du ski. = I <u>often</u> go skiing.

See p.219 for how to say you <u>never</u> do something.

always:	toujours
sometimes:	quelquefois
(quite) often:	(assez) souvent
(quite) rarely:	(assez) rarement

this morning:	ce matin
this afternoon:	cet après-midi
this evening/tonight:	ce soir
tomorrow morning:	demain matin
this week:	cette semaine
next week:	la semaine prochaine
last week:	la semaine dernière
the weekend:	le week-end

Qu'est-ce que tu fais ce soir ? = What are you doing <u>tonight</u>?

Get learning — the date comes up all the time...

This is basic stuff, but it <u>will</u> get you more marks, so learn it. You can practise times and dates easily in your head by thinking 'How would I say that in French?' when you say the time or date in English.

Quick Questions

If you don't have a quick, thorough warm-up you might strain a brain cell or two when you do the exam questions. So take the time to run through these simple questions and get the basic facts straight before you leap into the real exam questions. Go on — you know it makes sense.

Quick Questions

1) Write down the French for the following numbers:

    a) 31   b) 28   c) 56   d) 63   e) 29   f) 41

2) Write down in words the French for the numbers 11-20.

3) How would you say the following numbers in French:

    a) 75   b) 85   c) 95

4) How would you say '101' in French?

5) How would you say '1011' in French?

6) Write down in words the French number for how many days are in a (non-leap) year.

7) Write out this French number in digits: quatre mille trois cent soixante-seize.

8) Say what the following mean in English:

    a) premier   b) dixième   c) troisième   d) vingt et unième.

9) Your friend says, "Ma chambre est au troisième étage." Which floor is their bedroom on?

10) You ask a stranger for directions to the bank and they reply, "Prenez la quatrième rue à gauche." Which street should you take?

11) In French, how would you say the time on each of these clocks?
    Use the 12-hour clock, e.g. for the first clock you'd write 'Il est cinq heures'.

    a)   b)   c)   d)   e)

12) Your friend tells you, "J'ai mangé du fromage mercredi." What day did your friend eat some cheese?

13) Write a sentence in French saying that on Mondays you play football and on Thursdays you go to the cinema.

14) Write down the date of your birthday in French, e.g. Mon anniversaire est... .

15) Write down these years in French:

    a) 1995   b) 2000   c) 2010

16) Say what the following mean in English:

    a) toujours   b) quelquefois   c) souvent   d) rarement

17) François tells you: "Hier j'ai fait mes devoirs, aujourd'hui je dois aller à l'école, mais demain je vais aller à la plage. J'arrive en Angleterre cet automne, vers le cinq novembre."

    a) When did he do his homework?   c) When is he coming to England?

    b) When is he going to the beach?   d) What does he have to do today?

18) Ask your French friend what they are doing tonight.

Being Polite

You won't get far with a French speaker if you're rude — try opening with these superb gems of <u>politeness</u>.

Bonjour — Hello

Learn these phrases — they're <u>crucial</u>.

Hello:	Bonjour
Hi:	Salut
Welcome:	Bienvenue
Good evening:	Bonsoir
Good night:	Bonne nuit
Goodbye:	Au revoir

Have a good trip:	Bon voyage
Happy birthday:	Bon anniversaire
Have a good weekend:	Bon week-end
Have a good party:	Bonne fête
Happy New Year:	Bonne année
Good luck:	Bonne chance

Comment ça va? — How are you?

Keeping a <u>conversation</u> going is <u>easy</u> if you use a few of these <u>lil' sparklers</u>.

Comment ça va? = How are you?　　　***Et toi?*** = And you? (Informal)

Comment allez-vous? = How are you? (Formal)　　　***Et vous?*** = And you? (Formal)

'<u>Tu</u>' and '<u>vous</u>' both mean '<u>you</u>' in French. If you're talking to <u>someone older</u> than you, or to a <u>stranger</u>, you <u>usually</u> use '<u>vous</u>'. <u>Only</u> use '<u>tu</u>' if you're talking to <u>friends</u>, <u>family</u> or <u>other young people</u>.

Ça va bien, merci. = (I am) fine, thanks.

You <u>can</u> just say 'Bien, merci' (you might get more <u>marks</u> for the whole thing, though).

See p.39 if you're not well and you need to explain why.

Not good:	Ça ne va pas bien.
Not bad:	Pas mal.
I don't know:	Je ne sais pas.
Great!:	Super!
I feel fantastic:	Je me sens fantastique.
I feel good:	Je me sens bien.
I feel awful:	Je ne me sens pas bien du tout.
So so:	Comme ci comme ça.

Voici Pierre — This is Pierre

Other <u>useful stuff</u> you should know...

Est-ce que je peux vous présenter Pierre? = May I introduce Pierre?

Enchanté(e). = Pleased to meet you. (Literally 'enchanted')

Entre. Assieds-toi. = Come in. Sit down. (Familiar, singular)

Entrez. Asseyez-vous. = Come in. Sit down. (Formal or plural)

Merci bien. C'est très gentil. = Thank you. That's very kind.

Being polite is very very important...

These bad boys will help you out lots when it comes to your <u>exams</u>. They're absolutely <u>vital</u> — they make you sound like you <u>really</u> know how to speak great French. And examiners like that.

Being Polite

You'll be expected to use <u>appropriate</u> language in your assessments, so learn this page really well.

Je voudrais — I would like

It's more polite to say '<u>je voudrais</u>' (I would like) than '<u>je veux</u>' (I want).

Here's how to say you would like <u>a thing</u>:

Je voudrais **du pain.** = <u>I would like</u> some bread.

See p.8-9 for other ways to ask questions, p.220-221 for more info on the conditional, and p.24-25 for help on asking for things at the dinner table.

Here's how to say you would like <u>to do</u> something:

Je voudrais **voyager en Europe.** = <u>I would like</u> to travel in Europe.

She would like: Elle voudrait

S'il vous plaît — Please... Merci — Thank you

Easy stuff — maybe the first French words you ever learnt. Don't forget them.

s'il vous plaît = please (formal)   **merci** = thank you   **de rien** = you're welcome

This is for when you're calling the person 'vous'. If you call them 'tu', you need to say: '<u>s'il te plaît</u>'. See p.6.

Je suis désolé(e) — I'm sorry

Here are a couple of ways to <u>apologise</u> — learn them both, and how they're used.

Je suis désolé(e). = I'm sorry.

Use this one if you're talking to a friend or someone you know well.

Pardon. = I'm sorry.

Add an 'e' here if you're female.

Est-ce que je peux...? — May I...?

'<u>Est-ce que je peux</u>' is another way of saying '<u>May I</u>'.

Excusez-moi... = Excuse me... (Formal)

You can also use this if you want to ask someone the way.

have something to drink: avoir quelque chose à boire   *go to the toilet:* aller aux toilettes

...est-ce que je peux **m'asseoir ?** = ...may I <u>sit down</u>?

Knowing when to be polite is just as important...

A really common mistake is to say '<u>s'il vous plaît</u>' to someone who you're calling '<u>tu</u>'. Tsk. That kind of thing is <u>crucial</u> to get right in your speaking and writing assessments.

Asking Questions

Whatever grade you're hoping for in your GCSE you'll <u>need</u> to be able to <u>understand</u> and <u>ask questions</u>.

Quand — When... Pourquoi — Why... Où — Where

Learn these question words — they're pretty important.

These are interrogative adverbs.

when?:	quand?
why?:	pourquoi?
where?:	où?
how?:	comment?
how much/many?:	combien de...?
at what time...?:	à quelle heure...?
who/whom?:	qui?
which...?:	quel(le)...?

'Quel' is a tricky question word. It has different meanings in English <u>and</u> has to agree with the object it's talking about. It has masculine, feminine, singular and plural forms.

which...? what...?:	
quel...?	quels...?
quelle...?	quelles...?

Quand est-ce que tu rentres?   = <u>When</u> are you coming back?

Qui a cassé la fenêtre?   = <u>Who</u> broke the window?

Quelle est la date?   = <u>What</u> is the date?

Quels vêtements allez-vous porter?   = <u>Which</u> clothes are you going to wear?

Où est la salle de bains?   = <u>Where</u> is the bathroom?

Comment y es-tu allé?   = <u>How</u> did you get there?

You MUST be able to ask basic questions PROPERLY

The vocab on this page is <u>essential</u> for understanding what you're being asked during your speaking assessment. It's also the sort of stuff you'll use <u>all</u> the time if you're in France — so it's worth knowing.

Asking Questions

Just like in English, there are a few different ways to ask questions in French. Learn to recognise them.

1) Use **Est-ce que** to start questions

To turn a statement into a yes-no question, put 'Est-ce que' onto the beginning of the sentence.

Est-ce que tes bananes sont jaunes? = Are your bananas yellow?

To answer yes to a question containing a negative, use 'si'.

Est-ce que tu n'as pas soif? = Aren't you thirsty? *Si.* = Yes.

If your question starts with 'What...', use 'Qu'est-ce que'.

Qu'est-ce que tu manges le soir? = What do you eat in the evening?

OR... *Que manges-tu le soir?*

You can start the question with 'Que' — but the verb (manger) and the subject (tu) switch places in the question and you add a hyphen.

2) Ask a question by putting the verb first

In English, you change 'I can go' to 'Can I go?' to make it a question (swapping the subject and verb) — it's exactly the same in French except you need to add a hyphen between the subject and the verb.

Est-elle partie? = Has she gone?

Peux-tu m'aider? = Can you help me?

3) Ask a question by changing your tone of voice

You can say a normal sentence but just raise your voice at the end to show it's a question.

Tu as des frères ou des sœurs? = Do you have any brothers or sisters?
(Literally: You have brothers or sisters?)

Using these different techniques looks really impressive

Start by learning all the question words at the top of the last page. Shut the book and keep writing them all out until you know them. Then, learn to use the three main ways to ask a question.

Opinions

It pays to have an opinion. <u>Learn how</u> to say what you think... in many different ways. Genius.

Say what you think — it'll sound impressive...

You'll often be asked what you <u>think</u> of stuff. So get learning these handy phrases.

J'aime le tennis de table, mais le football ne me plaît pas . = <u>I like</u> table tennis, but <u>I don't like</u> football.

<u>Liking things</u>
I love...: J'adore...
I like/love...: J'aime...
I like...: ...me plaît
I'm interested in...: Je m'intéresse à...
I find ... great: Je trouve ... chouette
I like ... a lot: J'aime beaucoup...

<u>Disliking things</u>
I don't like...: Je n'aime pas...
I don't like...: ...ne me plaît pas
...doesn't interest me: ...ne m'intéresse pas
I find ... awful: Je trouve ... affreux/affreuse

See p.218-219 for more on negatives.

<u>Watch out</u> — 'J'aime Pierre' can mean 'I love Pierre'. To say you like him, try 'Je trouve Pierre sympathique' (I think Pierre's nice).

<u>Other useful phrases</u>
It's all right: Ça va
I don't mind / care: Ça m'est égal
I prefer...: Je préfère...

Quelle est ton opinion sur...? — What's your opinion of...?

<u>All</u> these nifty phrases mean pretty much the <u>same thing</u> — 'What do you think of...?'.
If you can use all of them, your French will be <u>wildly fascinating</u> — and that means <u>more marks</u>.

<u>Finding out someone's opinion</u>
What do you think of...?: Qu'est-ce que tu penses de...?
What's your opinion of...?: Quelle est ton opinion sur...?
What do you think?: Qu'est-ce que tu penses?
How do you find...?: Comment trouves-tu...?

<u>I think...</u>
I think that... : Je pense que...
I think that... : Je crois que...
I think ... is ... : Je trouve ... ...

Qu'est-ce que tu penses de mon petit ami? = <u>What do you think of</u> my boyfriend?

Je pense qu'il est fou. = <u>I think that</u> he's mad.

Quelqu'un — Someone

You might need to know the word '<u>someone</u>', at some point, somewhere, in something. So here it is...

J'ai vu quelqu'un dans le jardin. = I saw <u>someone</u> in the garden.

The examiner wants to know you have your own opinions
Never underestimate the power of <u>opinions</u>. It might seem hard to believe, but they <u>do want</u> you to say what you think. Make sure you learn one way to say '<u>I like</u>' and '<u>I don't like</u>' first. They're the basics.

Opinions

Don't just say that you like or hate something — really bowl your teacher over by explaining why.

Use these words to describe things

Here's a whole load of words to describe things you like or don't like. They're dead easy to use, so it really is worth learning them.

Describing words are adjectives. See p.170-174 for more on this.

good:	bon(ne)	brilliant:	génial(e) / super
great:	super / chouette	nice (person):	sympa / sympathique
beautiful:	beau/belle	nice / kind:	gentil(le)
friendly:	amical(e)	marvellous:	merveilleux / merveilleuse
splendid:	magnifique	bad:	mauvais(e)
fantastic:	formidable / fantastique	awful:	affreux / affreuse
interesting:	intéressant(e)		

Bob est **super** .

= Bob is great.

Les filles sont **affreuses** .

= The girls are awful.

For 'because' say 'parce que'

To make your opinion more convincing, give a reason for it. The best way to do that is to use the handy phrase 'parce que' — 'because'.

J'aime bien ce film, **parce que** les acteurs sont formidables.

= I like this film a lot, because the actors are fantastic.

Je trouve ce film affreux, **parce que** l'histoire est ennuyeuse.

= I think this film is awful, because the story is boring.

J'adore jouer du violon, **parce que** je trouve la musique classique très belle.

= I love playing the violin, because I find classical music very beautiful.

Le rugby me plaît beaucoup, **parce que** l'ambiance dans mon équipe est amicale.

= I really like rugby, because the atmosphere in my team is friendly.

If you hear the word 'car', it means 'because'

Elle est très fatiguée, **car** elle travaille tout le temps.

= She is very tired, because she works all the time.

Learn all this, especially 'parce que'

It's not much cop only knowing how to ask someone else's opinion, without being able to say what YOU think and why. All these phrases are easy — just stick them together to get a sentence.

What do you think of...?

To boost your grade, you need to give your opinions. Learn this, do well and boost away.

Use 'je trouve...' to give your opinion

Giving opinions is really important in French. It shows that you can be creative with the language.

Je trouve **ce groupe** **magnifique** .   = I think this group is splendid.

this team:	cette équipe
this magazine:	ce magazine
this music:	cette musique

bad:	mauvais(e)
boring:	ennuyeux/ennuyeuse
quite good:	assez bon(ne)

Use these adjectives and the others on page 11 to give your opinion.

Est-ce que tu aimes...? — Do you like...?

You'll also need to be able to understand other people's opinions.

Est-ce que tu aimes **ce groupe** ?   = Do you like this group?

this film:	ce film
this newspaper:	ce journal
this book:	ce livre
this programme:	cette émission

it: le/la

For more on object pronouns, see p.188-189.

Je n'aime pas ce groupe. Je **le** *trouve* **mauvais** .   = I don't like this group.
I think they're bad.

These are linked. If the first bit is masculine, then the second bit must be masculine too. If the thing was feminine, it would be 'la' and mauvaise.

Je trouve ce journal **ennuyeux** . *Et toi?*   = I think this newspaper is boring.
What do you think?

Use any of the adjectives at the top of p.11.

This is a good way of asking informally whether somebody agrees with what you've just said.

Moi aussi, je le trouve ennuyeux.   = I think it's boring too.

You don't have to tell the truth, just make sure the French is correct

Giving your opinion about things gets you big marks in the assessments. It's quite easy to say why you like something, so you've got no excuses — you've just got to learn these phrases.

Quick Questions

Take a deep breath and go through these Quick Questions one by one. These are the really important basics that you need for your exams, so make sure you know them like the back of your hand.

Quick Questions

1) Write down two ways of saying "hello" in French.

2) It's Friday night. Tell your friend to have a good weekend in French.

3) How would you say "how are you?" in French to:

a) your teacher   b) your best friend?

4) Your teacher tells you, "Comme ci comme ça." Your best friend tells you, "Je me sens bien." How does each of them feel?

5) How would you say "Come in. Sit down." in French to:

a) your best friend   b) the Queen   c) a group of your classmates?

6) You want to introduce your friend Paul to your friends. How would you say, "May I introduce Paul?" in French?

7) How would you politely say that you would like some water in French?

8) Write down the French for:

a) please (formal)   b) thank you   c) you're welcome

9) How would you say "I'm sorry" to:

a) your friend for bumping into her   b) your teacher for forgetting your homework?

10) You want to ask a stranger in France for directions. How would you say "Excuse me"?

11) Marie says, "Est-ce que je peux avoir quelque chose à boire?" What is she asking?

12) Write down the French for the following words:

a) how?   b) when?   c) why?   d) who?   e) where?

13) Turn these sentences into questions using "Est-ce que...":

a) Tu aimes le football.   b) Vous avez vu ce film.

14) Turn the following phrases into questions using "Qu'est-ce que...":

a) Tu manges pour le petit déjeuner.   b) Tu as fait en vacances.

15) Turn these sentences into questions by putting the verb first:

a) Tu as mangé mon sandwich.   b) Elle est allée à l'école.

16) Chantal says, "J'aime bien ton pantalon, mais je trouve tes chaussures affreuses." What is she saying about your clothes?

17) Translate the following questions into French:

a) What do you think of my house?   b) What's your opinion of football?

18) What is the French word for "someone"?

19) In French, write down the masculine singular form of each adjective:

a) friendly   b) beautiful   c) interesting   d) bad   e) awful

20) What are the two French words for "because"?

21) Your friend Marc says, "Je n'aime pas ce livre. Je le trouve affreux. Est-ce que tu aimes ce livre?" Translate what Marc said into English.

Informal Letters

I just know you're going to be <u>chuffed</u> to bits when I tell you that you'll probably have to write a letter in French at some point — it could very easily be in your written assessment.

Start a letter with 'Cher Bob' — 'Dear Bob'

Learn the <u>layout</u> of letters, and how to say 'Dear Blank...' and all that stuff. It's essential. This letter's short on content, but it shows you how to <u>start</u> and <u>end</u> it properly, and where to put the <u>date</u>.

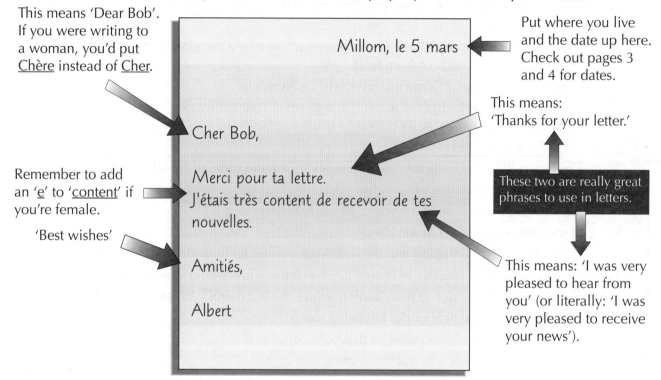

This means 'Dear Bob'. If you were writing to a woman, you'd put <u>Chère</u> instead of <u>Cher</u>.

Put where you live and the date up here. Check out pages 3 and 4 for dates.

Millom, le 5 mars

Cher Bob,

Merci pour ta lettre.
J'étais très content de recevoir de tes nouvelles.

Amitiés,

Albert

This means: 'Thanks for your letter.'

These two are really great phrases to use in letters.

This means: 'I was very pleased to hear from you' (or literally: 'I was very pleased to receive your news').

Remember to add an '<u>e</u>' to '<u>content</u>' if you're female.

'Best wishes'

Use these phrases in your letters

Here's a lovely <u>one-size-fits-all</u> phrase for all your informal letters.

Ça va? = How are you?

You can use it at the start of a letter, just after 'Dear whoever'.

<u>Just before</u> you <u>sign off</u> you might want to <u>stick in</u> this sentence.

J'espère recevoir bientôt de tes nouvelles.

= I hope to hear from you soon.

<u>Don't panic</u> if you have to write a postcard — just do the same as for a short letter.

Another way to sign off...

À bientôt = See you soon.

Learn how to write decent letters to get easy marks

For once, some fairly <u>easy</u> stuff — hurrah. It's all really useful stuff for your written work. Make sure you know the French <u>stock phrases</u> really well — then your letter will sound dead smart and <u>authentic</u>.

Formal Letters

You may be asked to write a formal letter instead — it's a bit mean, but sadly you've no choice. Study the basic format below and practise creating some formal correspondence of your own.

Put your name and address at the top left

Letters — they really are just as simple as this...

The name and address of who you're writing to goes here.

It looks impressive if you put your name and address at the top. (In French, the addresses go the opposite way round to in English — sender on the left, recipient on the right.)

Put this if you don't know the person's name or gender. If you know it's Monsieur Claude Terrier, put that above his address and write 'Monsieur' here.

This little lot simply means: I spent two nights at the Saint Michel Hotel between the 12th and the 14th of April. The employees were great, very kind and welcoming and the room was clean.

Unfortunately, I'm not at all satisfied with my stay because the shower didn't work, the TV was broken and there was too much noise everywhere, so I didn't sleep very well.

Aleesha Thompson
16 Rusland Drive
Manchester
M14 7ZN
Grande-Bretagne

Hôtel Saint Michel
16, rue des Papillons
Paris
France

le 20 avril 2010

Put the date here.

Monsieur / Madame,

J'ai passé deux nuits à l'Hôtel Saint Michel entre le 12 et le 14 avril. Les employés étaient super, très agréables et accueillants, et la chambre était propre.

Malheureusement, je ne suis pas du tout satisfaite de mon séjour parce que la douche ne fonctionnait pas, la télévision était cassée et il y avait trop de bruit partout, donc je n'ai pas très bien dormi.

Veuillez agréer, Monsieur/Madame, l'expression de mes sentiments distingués.

A. Thompson

Aleesha Thompson

Yours sincerely

Check out page 92 for problems vocab and page 153 for help writing a job application letter.

Learn these ways to end a letter

This set ending is quite long, I'm afraid — just learn it and churn it out.

to a woman: Madame

Je vous prie d'agréer, Monsieur,
l'expression de mes sentiments distingués.   = Yours faithfully / sincerely

Another useful phrase: ***Je vous remercie d'avance.***   = Many thanks in advance.

You really will be throwing away marks if you can't write a good letter

All these things are important. The whole point of the writing assessment is to test that you can WRITE to people. If you learn the basic format of a letter, you're already halfway there.

Quick Questions

It's your lucky day — you've almost reached the end of Section 1 and you also have a set of wonderful questions about writing letters to help you on your way. Go through these questions and make sure you can answer them all. This stuff could well come up in your exams.

Quick Questions

1) How would you start an informal letter to:

a) your friend Barbara

b) your friend Dave?

2) How would you say "Thanks for your letter" in French?

3) In a letter, your penfriend Lisette writes, "J'étais très contente de recevoir de tes nouvelles." What does this mean in English?

4) Write down the word for "Best wishes" in French.

5) Where do you put the date in an informal letter?

6) You read this sentence in a letter: "J'espère recevoir bientôt de tes nouvelles." What does this mean in English?

7) Pick the correct translation of "À bientôt" from the following options:

a) I am well.

b) Bye for now.

c) Yours sincerely.

8) In a formal letter, where would you write:

a) your name and address

b) the name and address of the person you're writing to?

9) You want to write a letter of complaint to a hotel, but you don't know the name of the manager or whether it's a man or a woman. How would you start the letter in French?

10) Translate these handy little sentences into English:

a) J'ai passé cinq nuits dans votre hôtel.

b) Les employés étaient gentils.

c) Ma chambre était propre.

11) How would you say "Unfortunately, I'm not satisfied" in French?

12) Choose the correct translation of "Yours sincerely" from the following options:

a) Je vous prie d'agréer, Monsieur, l'expression de mes sentiments distingués.

b) Je te prie d'agréer, Monsieur, l'expression de mes sentiments distingués.

c) Je vous prie d'agréer, Monsieur, l'expression de mes sentiments affreux.

13) How would you say "Many thanks in advance" in French?

Listening Questions

Listen to these people saying when their birthday is and put the information in the table.

Example	Louise	**7th**	**June**
1	Marc		
2	Élodie		
3	Sylvie		

Track 2

You're planning a trip to the cinema. When is your friend free?

	Day	When?
Example	**Wednesday**	**evening**
4		
5		

Track 3

Example   The film starts at .... **five past three / 3:05** ....

6   (a)   The film finishes at ....

      (b)   Pierre should arrive at the cinema at ....

Reading Question

1   Read this email from Michel.

Salut Tom,

Hier soir, je suis allé au stade voir le match entre PSG et Auxerre.
C'était ⬚1⬚ ! Moi je suis ⬚2⬚ du PSG donc j'étais très content du
résultat. Est-ce que tu as vu le match à la ⬚3⬚ ? Nous avons marqué deux
⬚4⬚ avant la fin de la première mi-temps! Le mois dernier le PSG a
acheté un nouveau joueur et je l'aime beaucoup. Je trouve qu'il a une
connaissance incroyable du jeu.

Je vais au ⬚5⬚ chaque samedi. J'y vais avec un groupe de ⬚6⬚ et c'est
toujours génial. Le football, c'est ma passion. Quand je ne suis pas en
train de regarder un match, je suis dehors en train de jouer. Le lundi soir,
je vais au centre sportif pour jouer avec d'autres garçons.

Toi aussi, tu aimes le football? Est-ce que tu veux venir voir un match
avec nous quand tu seras ici en septembre? Je crois que le PSG va jouer
un match samedi vingt et un septembre. Si ça t'intéresse je peux acheter
un ⬚7⬚ pour toi et tu peux me donner l'⬚8⬚ quand tu arriveras.

À bientôt,

Michel

Choose a word from the table to fill each of the gaps above. Write the correct number in the
box beside each word:

		match
		billet
Example:	1	formidable
		buts
		fana
		copains
		argent
		télé

Speaking Question

This is your first speaking test. You'll need to get someone to help you out here, or it just won't work. Try getting a friend to read the teacher's role, so you can pretend it's a real assessment. Think about what you're going to say before the conversation starts.

Task: Television

You are going to have a conversation with your teacher about television.

Your teacher will start the conversation and ask you the following questions:

- What is your favourite television programme? Why?
- Who's your favourite actor on television? Describe him/her.
- How much television do you watch a week?
- Would you like to be the star of a TV show? Why/why not?
- Do you think people watch too much television?
- Do you like the same programmes as your friends?
- !

! Remember that the exclamation mark means you'll have to answer a question that you won't have prepared an answer to.

The whole conversation should last about five minutes.

Teacher's Role

You need to ask the student the following questions. You should speak first.

1 Quelle est ton émission préférée? Pourquoi?

2 Qui est ton acteur préféré à la télé? Décris le/la.

3 Combien d'heures de télévision regardes-tu chaque semaine?

4 Est-ce que tu aimerais être vedette de télévision? Pourquoi/pourquoi pas?

5 Crois-tu que les gens regardent trop de télévision?

6 Est-ce que tu aimes les mêmes émissions que tes ami(e)s?

7 !

! The unpredictable question could be:

Qu'est-ce que tu vas regarder ce week-end?

Writing Questions

Task 1: General Stuff

You are replying to an email from your French penfriend asking you about the cinema. You should write 250-300 words.
You could include:

- How often you go to the cinema and who you go with,
- What the cinemas are like near where you live,
- The sorts of films you like, and your favourite actors,
- A description of a film you have enjoyed recently,
- The sorts of films you hate,
- When you are next going to the cinema and what you are going to see.

Remember that to score the highest marks you need to answer the task as fully as possible, expanding on the points above when it is relevant to do so.

Task 2: General Stuff

You have a terrible meal at a restaurant in France. Write a formal letter of complaint to the restaurant owner. You should write 250-300 words.
You could include:

- When you went to the restaurant and if it was a special occasion,
- Who you were with,
- Any problems you had when you arrived,
- What you ate and problems with the food,
- What the staff were like,
- What you would like the owner to do about your complaint.

Remember that to score the highest marks you need to answer the task as fully as possible, expanding on the points above when it is relevant to do so.

Revision Summary

These questions are here to make sure you know your stuff. Work through them all and check which ones you couldn't do. Look back through the section to find out the answers, then have another go at the ones you got stuck on. Then look up any you still can't do. Keep going till you can do all of them — so you know you've really learnt it.

1)   Count out loud from 1 to 20 in French.

2)   How do you say these numbers in French? a) 22   b) 35   c) 58   d) 71   e) 112   f) 2101

3)   What are these in French?   a) 1st   b) 4th   c) 7th   d) 19th   e) 25th   f) 52nd

4)   Ask 'What time is it?' in French.

5)   Say all the days of the week in French, from Monday to Sunday.

6)   How do you say these in French?   a) yesterday   b) today   c) tomorrow

7)   Say all of the months of the year in French, from January to December.

8)   How do you say the date of your birthday in French?

9)   'Qu'est-ce que tu fais ce soir?' means 'What are you doing this evening?'
     How would you say, 'What are you doing: a) this afternoon?' b) this morning?'
     c) next week?'

10) 'Tu chantes' means 'You sing' or 'You are singing'. What do these questions mean?
     a) Pourquoi tu chantes? b) Où est-ce que tu chantes? c) Qu'est-ce que tu chantes?
     d) Chantes-tu bien? e) Quand est-ce que tu chantes? f) Est-ce que tu chantes?

11) What's the French for? a) Please   b) Thank you   c) How are you? d) I'm sorry e) May I...

12) How would you ask someone what they think of Elvis Presley? (In French.)
     Give as many ways of asking it as you can.

13) How would you say these things in French? Give at least one way to say each of them.
     a) I like Elvis Presley. b) I don't like Elvis Presley.   c) I find Elvis Presley interesting.
     d) I love Elvis Presley.   e) I find Elvis Presley awful.   f) I think that Elvis Presley is fantastic.

14) You like the group 'The Sheep Shearers', but you think 'James and the Infinite Monkeys' are
     brilliant. How would you tell someone that in French? (Leave the band names in English.)

15) Write a letter to your friend Marie-Claire. Write your address, say hello and tell her
     something you've done. You would like to hear from her soon — how would you say
     that in your letter?

16) How would you end a formal letter in French?

Food

You need to learn the vocab for all the basic food, especially the things you like and eat often. There's a lot of information to digest here, but the more you know, the better.

L'épicerie et la boucherie — greengrocer's and butcher's

This is basic, meat and two veg vocab.
You really do need to know it.

Meats: les viandes (fem.)

pork:	le porc	lamb:	l'agneau (masc.)	chicken:	le poulet
sausage:	la saucisse	beef:	le bœuf	turkey:	la dinde
salami:	le saucisson	steak:	le bifteck	duck:	le canard
ham:	le jambon	veal:	le veau	goose:	l'oie (fem.)

Fruits: les fruits (masc.)

apple:	la pomme
banana:	la banane
strawberry:	la fraise
raspberry:	la framboise
pineapple:	l'ananas (masc.)
grapefruit:	le pamplemousse
cherry:	la cerise
apricot:	l'abricot (masc.)
peach:	la pêche
pear:	la poire
lemon:	le citron

Vegetables: les légumes (masc.)

potato:	la pomme de terre
carrot:	la carotte
tomato:	la tomate
cucumber:	le concombre
onion:	l'oignon (masc.)
cauliflower:	le chou-fleur
French beans:	les haricots verts
lettuce:	la salade / la laitue
mushroom:	le champignon
cabbage:	le chou
pea:	le petits pois

Sea food: les fruits de mer (masc.)

fish:	le poisson	oyster:	l'huître (fem.)
salmon:	le saumon	mussel:	la moule
trout:	la truite	crab:	le crabe
tuna:	le thon	prawn / shrimp:	la crevette

Les boissons et les desserts — drinks and desserts

Every decent meal needs a dessert and a drink.

Drinks: les boissons (fem.)

tea:	le thé
coffee:	le café
beer:	la bière
cider:	le cidre
wine:	le vin
coke®:	le coca
fruit juice:	le jus de fruit
lemonade:	la limonade
mineral water:	l'eau minérale (fem.)

Desserts: les desserts (masc.)

cake:	le gâteau
biscuit:	le biscuit
ice cream:	la glace
pancake:	la crêpe
yogurt:	le yaourt
honey:	le miel
jam:	la confiture
chocolate:	le chocolat
sweets:	les bonbons (masc.)

These pages of vocab aren't easy, but make sure you learn them

You know what you have to do. All of this vocabulary is very important, as there's no way to predict what will actually come up in the exam. You need to learn ALL of it.

Food

Here's some more lovely _food vocab_ including the important basics like bread, milk and butter.
It's a good idea to learn some of France's famous _speciality dishes_ in case you're tested on them too.

D'autres aliments — Other foods

Here are some more _basic foods_ to learn.

bread:	le pain
milk:	le lait
cream:	la crème
butter:	le beurre
cheese:	le fromage
egg:	l'œuf (masc.)

sugar:	le sucre
salt:	le sel
pepper:	le poivre
vinegar:	le vinaigre
flour:	la farine
rice:	le riz

mustard:	la moutarde
soup:	le potage / la soupe
pasta:	les pâtes (fem.)
cereals:	les céréales (fem.)
chips:	les pommes frites (fem.)
crisps:	les chips (fem.)

Les spécialités — Specialities

Have a look at these French _specialities_ that you
might want to try too — _learn_ them really well.

croissant:	le croissant
snails:	les escargots (masc.)
salad starter:	les crudités (fem.)
cheese and ham toastie:	le croque-monsieur
potatoes with cheese topping:	le gratin dauphinois
leg of lamb:	le gigot d'agneau

Don't forget, you need to know if each word is masculine or feminine

A lot of foods aren't that easy to remember — you _just have to learn them really well_. Make sure you
can _spell_ them too. Have a good look at the French specialities, in case they ask you to _order food_.

Mealtimes

You can use the vocab on this page to be polite in French, at <u>any time</u>, in <u>any situation</u>.

Voudriez-vous...? — Would you like...?

This is another form of that useful verb '<u>vouloir</u>'.

'Voudriez' is in the conditional — p.220-221.

Voudriez-vous **le sel** *?* = Would you like <u>the salt</u>?

the pepper: le poivre   *the wine:* le vin   *the butter:* le beurre

Est-ce que je peux vous passer **une serviette** *?* = Can I pass you <u>a napkin</u>?

to drink: boire

Voudriez-vous **manger** *?* = Would you like <u>to eat</u>?

Either 'Oui, je veux bien' or 'Oui, merci' sound more French than 'Oui, s'il vous plaît'.

Oui, je veux bien. = Yes please.   *Non, merci.* = No thanks.

Est-ce que tu as faim ou soif? — Are you hungry or thirsty?

Questions like these are <u>important</u>. Make <u>sure</u> you understand them, or you may go hungry... or lose marks.

Est-ce que tu as **faim** *?* = Are you <u>hungry</u>?   *J'ai* **faim** *.* = I'm <u>hungry</u>.

thirsty: soif

thirsty: soif

Non, merci. Je n'ai pas **faim** *.*

= No thanks. I'm not <u>hungry</u>.

Pourriez-vous...? — Could you...?

Here are two <u>dead nifty</u> phrases to <u>learn</u>. Use them <u>properly</u> and you'll be the soul of politeness.

Est-ce que je peux avoir **le sel** *, s'il vous plaît?* = May I have <u>the salt</u>, please?

a napkin: une serviette   *the sugar:* le sucre

Pourriez-vous me passer **le poivre** *, s'il vous plaît?*

= Could you pass me <u>the pepper</u>, please?

Showing that you know these polite phrases will get you top marks

This page covers a <u>load</u> of phrases to help you out with any mealtime situation that comes up in your French exam. There are some really <u>useful verbs and phrases</u> on this page so learn them <u>properly</u>.

Mealtimes

Je ne mange pas de... — I don't eat...

Je ne mange pas de petits pois. = I don't eat peas.

See p.22-23 for more foods.

no longer: plus
never: jamais

meat: viande (fem.)
dairy: produits laitiers (masc.)

Je suis végétarien(ne) / végétalien(ne). = I'm a vegetarian / vegan.

Vous dînez en famille? — Do you eat with your family?

See p.31 for more family members.

On mange toujours en famille. = We always eat as a family.

at the same time: en même temps   *separately:* séparément

Mon père travaille tard, donc il n'est pas possible de manger ensemble.

My mother: Ma mère
My sister: Ma sœur

goes to the gym: va au gymnase
has a football match: a un match de foot

= My dad works late, so it's not possible to eat together.

If you only want a little, ask for 'un peu'

a bit: un peu

Je voudrais beaucoup de sucre, s'il vous plaît. = I would like lots of sugar, please.

Je voudrais un gros morceau de gâteau. = I would like a big piece of cake.

J'ai assez mangé, merci. = I've eaten enough, thanks.

a lot: beaucoup   *trop:* too much

Ça suffit. = That's enough.

For more quantities, see page 64.

Est-ce que ça vous a plu? — Did you like it?

Le repas était bon.
= The meal was good.

very bad: (très) mauvais
delicious: délicieux
very good: très bon

Le repas n'était pas bon.
= The meal wasn't good.

Que c'est bon, que c'est bon

I for one seriously love French food. They're really big on high-quality, fresh produce. You can see that just by going round a French market. The fruit stalls look like a beautiful Renoir painting.

Daily Routine

Chores and revision — two peas from the same pod. But unlike ironing, once done, <u>revision</u> is <u>done for ever</u>.

Décris-moi une journée typique — Describe a typical day

Daily <u>routine</u>. <u>Learn</u> it. <u>Work</u> it. <u>Know</u> it like it's... um... <u>routine</u>.

Je me réveille à **sept heures**.

= <u>I wake up</u> at <u>seven o'clock</u>.

I get up:	Je me lève	*I work:*	Je travaille
I shower:	Je me douche	*I relax:*	Je me détends
I get dressed:	Je m'habille	*I go to bed:*	Je me couche

See page 2 for more info about time.

Est-ce que tu fais le ménage? — Do you do the housework?

Even if you <u>never</u> help at home, <u>learn</u> these words.

Je **fais la vaisselle** à la maison.

= I <u>wash up</u> at home.

I make my bed:	Je fais mon lit
I do the laundry:	Je fais la lessive
I do the shopping:	Je fais les courses
I tidy my room:	Je range ma chambre
I lay the table:	Je mets la table
I wash the car:	Je lave la voiture
I do some gardening:	Je fais du jardinage
I walk the dog:	Je promène le chien

Je dois **faire la vaisselle**.

= I have to <u>wash up</u>.

make my bed:	faire mon lit
do the laundry:	faire la lessive
do the shopping:	faire les courses
tidy my room:	ranger ma chambre
lay the table:	mettre la table
wash the car:	laver la voiture
do some gardening:	faire du jardinage
walk the dog:	promener le chien

These verbs are all in the <u>infinitive</u> (see page 195).

Je gagne de l'argent de poche quand j'aide à la maison .

= I earn pocket money for <u>helping at home</u>.

This all seems a bit like hard work to me

Examiners just love hearing all about your daily routine. Learn the important vocab on this page really well then you can tell them all about what time you get up in the morning. It's exciting stuff.

Daily Routine

As-tu besoin de quelque chose? — Do you need anything?

In your listening exam, you might hear someone <u>asking</u> for <u>something</u> or <u>offering to help out</u>...

Est-ce que vous avez du dentifrice ? = Do you have <u>any toothpaste</u>?

a towel: une serviette   *an aspirin:* une aspirine

Est-ce que je peux prendre une douche ? = Can I <u>take a shower?</u>

have a towel: avoir une serviette

Est-ce que je peux faire la vaisselle ? = Can I <u>wash up?</u>

vacuum: passer l'aspirateur
lay the table: mettre la table

Peux-tu m'aider à faire la lessive ? = Can you help me do <u>the washing</u>?

the washing-up: la vaisselle

Est-ce que je peux vous aider à faire la lessive ?

= Can I help you do <u>the washing</u>?

It's always useful to know how to ask for help

You never know when you might need to ask someone to <u>help you out</u> — you could even learn how to ask someone to <u>test</u> you on all these lovely questions about daily routine. Now that would be <u>good</u>.

Quick Questions

These questions are designed to test your knowledge of all kinds of food-related situations, with some daily routine stuff thrown in for good measure. When you've finished and you can answer all the questions, you can reward yourself with a well-earned snack.

Quick Questions

1) Your French friend Nadia has left you a shopping list. What does she want you to buy?

   a) des abricots

   b) du thé

   c) des pommes de terre

   d) du beurre

   e) un gigot d'agneau

   f) des crevettes

   g) un citron

   h) du vin

2) Write down the French for these words:

   a) puddings

   b) vegetables

   c) seafood

   d) drinks

3) Write down the French word for each of these traditional dishes:

   a) snails

   b) cheese and ham toastie

   c) potatoes with a cheese topping

4) What is French for "Would you like the water?"

5) How would you say, "Can I pass you the butter?" in French?

6) The waiter in a restaurant asks you, "Voudriez-vous manger?" What is he asking you?

7) How would you ask your French friend, "Are you hungry?"

8) What does "J'ai faim mais je n'ai pas soif" mean?

9) You're in a posh French restaurant. How would you ask someone to pass the following items in French:

   a) the salt   b) a napkin?

10) You don't eat fruit or vegetables but you love hamburgers. How would you say this in French?

11) How would you say, "I often eat apples but I never eat mushrooms"?

12) Your French friend tells you, "Je suis végétarien". What are they telling you?

13) In a letter from your French penfriend, it says, "On mange toujours en famille sauf le mardi parce que mon père va au gymnase." What does this mean?

14) Your friend has made a chocolate cake. How would you say that you would like:

   a) a bit of cake   b) a big piece of cake?

15) What does "Est-ce que ça vous a plu?" mean in English?

16) You're telling your French friend about your daily routine. Write a sentence saying what time you:

   a) get up   b) shower   c) get dressed   d) go to bed

17) Write a sentence saying that on Mondays you lay the table and on Fridays you do the washing up. Say you earn pocket money for helping at home.

18) What does "Peux-tu m'aider à laver la voiture?" mean in French?

19) How would you say "Do you need anything?" to a friend in French?

About Yourself

You might already know some of this stuff, but it's <u>ultra-important</u>, so make sure you know it back to front. Talking about yourself in your speaking or writing assessment — it's almost certain to come up.

Parle-moi de toi-même — Tell me about yourself

These are the <u>basics</u>. <u>Learn</u> them <u>all</u>.

What are you called?: Comment tu t'appelles?

Je m'appelle Angela . = I'm called <u>Angela</u>.

How old are you?: Quel âge as-tu?

J'ai quinze ans . = I'm <u>15 years old</u>.

When is your birthday?: Quand est ton anniversaire?

Mon anniversaire est le douze décembre .

= My birthday is the <u>12th of December</u>.

See pages 117-119 for where you live, page 1 for more numbers and pages 3-4 for more dates.

Where do you live?: Où habites-tu?

J'habite à Lancaster .

= I live in <u>Lancaster</u>.

What do you like?: Qu'est-ce que tu aimes?

J'aime le football .

= I like <u>football</u>.

You can use this to say you like anything, but be careful: 'Je t'aime' means 'I love you'.

Comment es-tu? — What are you like?

You have to <u>describe</u> how gorgeous you are as well.

Je suis grand(e) . = I am <u>tall</u>.

medium height: de taille moyenne

short: petit(e)
fat: gros(se)
thin: maigre
slim: mince

J'ai les yeux marron . = I have <u>brown</u> eyes.

For more colours, see page 66.

blue: bleus
green: verts

'Marron' is a strange adjective — it doesn't need an 's' on the end even though 'yeux' is plural.

J'ai les cheveux longs . = I have <u>long</u> hair.

short: courts
shoulder-length: mi-longs
quite long: assez longs

dark: foncés   *red:* roux
light: clairs   *black:* noirs
blond: blonds   *brown:* bruns

Describing yourself (or someone else) crops up often

Learn how to <u>ask</u> and <u>answer</u> questions about yourself, and make sure you can say lots of <u>wonderful</u> things about yourself in French. You <u>need</u> to be able to talk about yourself in your assessments.

The Alphabet

You may have to <u>spell</u> your name and home town letter by letter in your <u>speaking assessments</u>. So learn the French alphabet and then practise spelling things like the name of your pet or your town.

Comment ça s'écrit? — How do you spell that?

Here's how to <u>pronounce</u> the letters of the French <u>alphabet</u>. Practise going through it <u>out loud</u> — yes, you'll sound daft, but you'd sound dafter getting it wrong.

A	— ah (like in 'car')
B	— bay
C	— say
D	— day
E	— eu (like in 'peu')
F	— eff
G	— jay ('j' like 'g' in 'beige')
H	— ash
I	— ee (like in 'me')
J	— jee ('j' like 'g' in 'beige')
K	— kah
L	— ell
M	— em
N	— en
O	— oh
P	— pay
Q	— kue ('ue' like in 'tu')
R	— air
S	— ess
T	— tay
U	— ue (as in 'tu')
V	— vay
W	— dooble vay
X	— eex
Y	— ee-grek
Z	— zed

Ma mère s'appelle Julia. 'Julia' ça s'écrit: jee, ue, ell, eeh, ah .

= My mother is called Julia. 'Julia' is spelt: <u>J, u, l, i, a</u>.

For letters with accents, you just say the letter followed by the accent, so 'â' would be 'ah circonflexe'.

é	—	aigu
è	—	grave
ê	—	circonflexe
ç	—	cédille
ï	—	tréma

It's really worth taking the time to get comfortable with the alphabet

There's only one thing to say about this page — just make <u>darn sure</u> you know the French alphabet back to front and inside out. It's the kind of thing that could crop up in the <u>listening</u> exam.

Family and Pets

You might have to talk or write about your <u>family</u> situation and your <u>pets</u> — it's best to be prepared...

J'ai une sœur — I have one sister

To <u>describe</u> your family structure, use these sentences:

J'ai deux frères et une sœur .   = I have two <u>brothers</u> and one <u>sister</u>.

Ils s'appellent Jack, Henry et Charlotte.   = They are called Jack, Henry and Charlotte.

'Ils' is used for a group of <u>males</u> or a <u>mixture</u> of males and females.

a girlfriend: une petite amie

Je suis célibataire.   = I am single.

J'ai un petit ami .   = I have <u>a boyfriend</u>.

J'habite avec... — I live with...

Remember, <u>detail</u> is key in the assessments — especially when it comes to talking about your family.

J'habite avec mes parents .   = I live with <u>my parents</u>.

My father:	Mon père	*My male cousin:*	Mon cousin
My brother:	Mon frère	*My female cousin:*	Ma cousine
My sister:	Ma sœur	*My stepmother:*	Ma belle-mère
My mother:	Ma mère	*My stepfather:*	Mon beau-père
My aunt:	Ma tante	*My grandmother:*	Ma grand-mère
My uncle:	Mon oncle	*My grandfather:*	Mon grand-père
My niece:	Ma nièce	*My wife:*	Ma femme
My nephew:	Mon neveu	*My husband:*	Mon mari

Je viens d'une famille monoparentale.   = I come from a single-parent family.

Est-ce que tu as des animaux domestiques?
— Have you any pets?

a cat:	un chat	*a guinea pig:*	un cochon d'Inde
a bird:	un oiseau	*a rabbit:*	un lapin
a fish:	un poisson	*a mouse:*	une souris
a horse:	un cheval	*a hamster:*	un hamster

<u>Animals</u>. Always <u>useful vocab</u> to know.

J'ai un chien .   = I have <u>a dog</u>.   **Je n'ai pas d'animaux.**   = I <u>don't</u> have <u>any animals</u>.

Mon chien s'appelle Max.   = My dog is called Max.   **Il est marron .**   = He is <u>brown</u>.

If you don't have any pets you can just make some up

This stuff is pretty <u>straightforward</u>. You learn the sentence, learn the words, and just <u>slot in</u> whichever words you need. There's no excuse for not being able to do this stuff — <u>learn it</u>.

Personality

It helps you <u>connect</u> to other people, makes or breaks that job interview, could win you a spot on X Factor or in the hearts of the nation, and it's <u>who you are</u>. It's <u>personality</u>, and it's <u>important</u>.

Comment es-tu? — What are you like?

You might be asked to <u>talk about your personality</u> in the speaking tasks, so here goes...

nice:	agréable / sympa		*friendly:*	amical(e)
funny:	amusant(e) / drôle		*kind:*	aimable / gentil(le)
lively:	plein(e) de vie / animé(e)		*well-behaved:*	sage
chatty:	bavard(e)		*generous:*	généreux / généreuse
honest:	honnête		*hard-working:*	travailleur / travailleuse

He is: Il est   *She is:* Elle est

Je suis magnifique .

= <u>I am</u> <u>amazing</u>.

impatient:	impatient(e)		*jealous:*	jaloux / jalouse
impolite:	impoli(e)		*selfish:*	égoïste
mean:	méchant(e)		*proud:*	fier / fière
boring:	ennuyeux / ennuyeuse		*shy:*	timide
lazy:	paresseux / paresseuse		*sad:*	triste

quite: assez

Je suis un peu idiot(e) .

= I am <u>a bit</u> <u>stupid</u>.

J'ai une attitude positive — I have a positive attitude

J'ai toujours une attitude positive .   = <u>I</u> always <u>have</u> a <u>positive</u> attitude.

He has: Il a...   *She has:* Elle a...

negative: négative

Je sais comment faire rire les gens.   = <u>I know</u> how to make people <u>laugh</u>.

He knows: Il sait...
She knows: Elle sait...

cry: pleurer

in a bad mood: de mauvaise humeur

Je suis souvent de bonne humeur .   = I'm often <u>in a good mood</u>.

There's plenty of vocab here — so you know what you need to do

This <u>personality</u> vocab isn't just useful for GCSE French — it could also come in handy to describe the man or woman of your dreams if you're ever a contestant on Blind Date in France...

Personality

Ma sœur / Mon frère est... — My sister / brother is...

Mon frère a douze ans. Il est *amusant et bavard mais il est* *un peu paresseux et impoli .*

= My brother is twelve years old. He's <u>funny</u> and <u>chatty</u> but he's a bit <u>lazy</u> and <u>impolite</u>.

= My sister's <u>lively</u>, <u>generous</u> and <u>friendly</u>. She's often <u>in a good mood</u>.

Ma sœur est pleine de vie, *généreuse et amicale . Elle* *est souvent de bonne humeur .*

Il est marié . = He's <u>married</u>.

single:	célibataire
separated:	séparé(e)
divorced:	divorcé(e)
widowed:	veuf / veuve

Elle a les yeux bleus . = <u>She</u> has <u>blue</u> eyes.

| My girlfriend: | Ma petite amie/ma copine |
| My boyfriend: | Mon petit ami/mon copain |

La personnalité des autres — Other people's personalities

Talking about other people's <u>personalities</u> is simple — just use these celeb <u>examples</u> as <u>guidelines</u>...

J'ai beaucoup de respect pour Reese Witherspoon. *Elle a le sens de l'humour. Elle est travailleuse ,* *optimiste et pleine de vie . Elle est une bonne mère.*

= I have lots of respect for Reese Witherspoon. She has a sense of humour. She is <u>hard-working</u>, <u>optimistic</u> and <u>lively</u>. She is a good mother.

= I have lots of respect for Lewis Hamilton. He always has a positive attitude. He is <u>hard-working</u>, <u>chatty</u> and <u>kind</u>. He is also a good driver.

J'ai beaucoup de respect pour Lewis Hamilton. Il a *toujours une attitude positive . Il est travailleur ,* *bavard et aimable . Il est aussi un bon pilote.*

You can't just talk about yourself all the time, you know

Even though you're <u>probably</u> the most interesting person you know, you might have to talk about other people's personalities, like your <u>family</u> or a <u>celebrity</u>. You need to learn this page for the assessments.

Relationships and Future Plans

This page is <u>particularly useful</u> if you want to send a letter to a French <u>agony aunt</u>.

Un bon ami doit être... — A good friend must be...

It's good to know the <u>qualities</u> you're looking for...

a good partner: un(e) bon(ne) partenaire

À mon avis, un(e) bon(ne) ami(e) doit ... = In my opinion, <u>a good friend</u> must...

be honest:	être honnête
be trustworthy:	être fidèle
be kind:	être sympa
be understanding:	être compréhensif / compréhensive
be chatty:	être bavard(e)
be like me:	être comme moi
be fun:	être amusant(e)

Mon partenaire idéal devrait être amusant et bavard , comme moi.

= My ideal partner should <u>be fun and chatty</u>, like me.

On s'entend bien ensemble... — We get on well together...

<u>Relationships</u> aren't always plain sailing. Painful, but here's <u>how to tell</u> a French person all about it:

Je m'entends bien avec mon ami(e). = I get on well with <u>my friend</u>.

my mother: ma mère *my sister:* ma sœur *my brother:* mon frère

Nous sommes meilleur(e)s ami(e)s. = We are best friends.

Il me plaît. = I fancy him.

Je suis tombé(e) amoureux / amoureuse. = I've fallen in love.

I think I'm in love with GCSE French

This page is full of <u>nice things</u> to say about your friends and family. Even though it might seem a bit <u>weird</u> talking about your friends in your French exam, it's got to be done — so learn it <u>well</u>.

Relationships and Future Plans

On ne s'entend pas bien ensemble...
— We don't get on well together...

On ne se comprend pas.   = We don't understand each other.

| She doesn't listen to me: | Elle ne m'écoute pas |
| They don't listen to me: | Ils ne m'écoutent pas |

Il ne m'écoute pas .   = He doesn't listen to me.

On se dispute toujours.
= We argue all the time.

Elle est trop égoïste.   = She's too selfish.

Il est trop jaloux.   = He's too jealous.

Je voudrais me marier... — I'd like to get married...

It's good to have a <u>plan</u>. If you're not sure of your <u>relationship plans</u> then <u>learn</u> how to say so...

À l'avenir, je voudrais ...   = In the future, I'd like...

... to fall in love:	tomber amoureux / amoureuse
... to get engaged:	me fiancer
... to get married:	me marier
... to have children:	avoir des enfants

Je vais attendre un(e) partenaire idéal(e).   = I'm going to wait for an ideal partner.

Je peux très bien me débrouiller seul(e) — je n'ai pas l'intention de me marier tout de suite.   = I can get along fine on my own — I don't intend to get married right away.

Je ne suis pas prêt(e) à y penser.   = I'm not ready to think about it.

This topic could easily come up — so think about what you'd say

Take another look over this page so it all comes <u>trippingly off the tongue</u>. It's a bit weird having to talk about relationships in French lessons, but you'll just have to get <u>used to it</u> because it might come up.

Quick Questions

There's no denying it — the last few pages were super important. There's a good chance you'll have to talk about what you're like or listen to someone else saying what they're like in your exams. The best way to get this learnt is to work your way through these questions until you can answer them all.

Quick Questions

1) A French person asks you, "Où habites-tu?" What are they asking?

2) How would you say, "I am 15 years old"?

3) How would you say, "I have blue eyes and long blonde hair"?

4) Your French penfriend writes a letter telling you about himself. He says, "Je suis grand et j'ai les yeux verts. J'ai les cheveux courts et roux." What does this mean?

5) You are booking a hotel room in France. The receptionist asks, "Comment vous appelez-vous? Et comment ça s'écrit?". What two questions does she ask?

6) Spell your name out loud using the French alphabet.

7) You want to tell your French friend about your family. You have two brothers and one sister. They are called John, James and Kathryn. Write this out in French.

8) What does "J'ai une petite amie" mean?

9) Write down the French for the following members of the family:

   a) father   b) sister   c) grandmother   d) aunt   e) stepfather

10) You're talking about home life with your penfriend.

    a) What does your friend mean when he asks you, "Est-ce que tu as des animaux domestiques?"?
    b) How would you say, "I have a brother and he is ten years old"?
    c) Your penfriend says, "J'ai des cousins et des cousines." What does he mean?

11) Your friend tells you, "Mon petit ami est amusant, bavard et généreux." What is her boyfriend like?

12) You're reading a lonely hearts column in a French paper. One advert reads, "Je suis sage et sympa mais un peu paresseuse." What does this mean?

13) Your brother is thirteen years old. He's really mean and selfish. Write this in French.

14) You hear an interview with a French celebrity on the radio. They say, "J'ai toujours une attitude positive et je suis souvent de bonne humeur. Je suis fantastique." Translate what they said into English.

15) How would you say, "I know how to make people laugh"?

16) Translate the following phrases into English:

    a) être fidèle   b) être sympa   c) être comme moi

17) How would you say, "In my opinion, a good friend must be fun" in French?

18) How would you say, "We get on well together"?

19) Nadine is telling you all about her friends. What does she mean when she says:

    a) "Je m'entends bien avec Camille"?
    b) "Michel me plaît"?

20) You're reading some letters to an agony aunt in a French magazine. Translate the following phrases into English:

    a) Je suis tombé amoureux.
    b) On se dispute toujours.
    c) Elle ne m'écoute pas.

21) How would you say, "In the future I'd like to get married and have children"?

Social Issues and Equality

Unemployment, equal opportunities, gender and race issues — it's enough to make you want to wave around a big banner. Learn this page so you can fight for your rights.

Notre société n'est pas égale — Our society isn't equal

I am a girl / a boy:	je suis une fille / un garçon
I am younger / older:	je suis plus jeune / plus âgé(e)
I am Jewish / Muslim / Christian:	je suis juif / juive / musulman(e) / chrétien(ne)

Certains **me traitent différemment** parce que **je viens d'Afrique** .

= Some people <u>treat me differently</u> because <u>I come from Africa</u>.

are violent:	sont violents
are racist:	sont racistes
are mean:	sont méchants

C'est **raciste** . = It's <u>racist</u>.

sexist: sexiste	*unfair:* injuste

of race: de la race	*of religion:* de la religion

Ce n'est pas juste de discriminer à cause **de l'âge** .

= It's not fair to discriminate because <u>of age</u>.

Le racisme , c'est affreux. = <u>Racism</u> is awful.

Inequality: L'inégalité

Je pense que les droits de l'homme sont importants.

= I think that human rights are important.

This stuff is really important for your French GCSE

Examiners <u>love</u> testing you on this stuff so you <u>need</u> to learn this page. You might have to read a newspaper article on <u>social issues</u> or listen to someone's views on <u>racism</u>, so it's best to be prepared.

Social Issues and Equality

Violence, vandalism and unemployment are big issues too — so make sure you've got an opinion on them so you can talk about them in French.

La violence et le vandalisme — Violence and vandalism

Il y a beaucoup de **violence** *dans ma ville.* = There is lots of <u>violence</u> in my town.

> *poverty:* pauvreté   *vandalism:* vandalisme

> *bullied:* brutalisé(e) *hit:* battu(e)

En rentrant à la maison une fois j'ai été **menacé(e)** *.*

= On the way home once I was <u>threatened</u>.

C'est effrayant.   = It's terrifying.

> *violence:*   violence
> *threats:*   menaces

Je voudrais vivre sans **crainte** *.*   = I'd like to live without <u>fear</u>.

Les effets du chômage — The effects of unemployment

Il y a beaucoup de **chômeurs** *dans ma ville.*

= There are lots of <u>unemployed people</u> in my town.

> *homeless people:*   *disadvantaged people:*
> SDF   personnes défavorisées

Il est au chômage depuis deux ans.   = He's been out of work for two years.

Sans argent, il est difficile de trouver un logement.

= Without money, it's difficult to find housing.

On commence à se sentir déprimé(e).   = You start to feel depressed.

Sorry, a bit bleak, this page

Hardly a barrel of laughs, was it, and quite a <u>tricky</u> one to boot. Try to learn some of the more complex sentences <u>off by heart</u>. You'll be surprised how this will help you in the <u>assessments</u>.

Feeling Unwell

Here's everything you need to know about feeling ill in France.

Comment ça va? — How are you?

Je suis malade.   = I am ill.

Je ne me sens pas bien.   = I don't feel well.

Je dois aller voir le médecin .

| to the hospital: | à l'hôpital (masc.) |
| to the chemist's: | à la pharmacie |

= I need to go <u>to see the doctor</u>.

Où as-tu mal? — Where does it hurt?

Here's how you say what bit hurts...

J'ai mal à l'estomac .   = I have <u>stomach ache</u>.

You can use '<u>j'ai mal à</u>' with any part of your body that's hurting...

a headache:	mal à la tête
a sore throat:	mal à la gorge
backache:	mal au dos
an earache:	mal à l'oreille

Use 'au' for 'le' words, 'à la' for 'la' words, 'à l'' for words starting with a vowel or a silent 'h', and 'aux' for plurals.

the nose:	le nez
the eye:	l'œil (masc.)
the eyes:	les yeux (masc.)
the ear:	l'oreille (fem.)
the mouth:	la bouche
the teeth:	les dents (fem.)
the lips:	les lèvres (fem.)
the hair:	les cheveux (masc.)

hurt (plural): font mal

Mon doigt me fait mal .

My head:	Ma tête
My arms:	Mes bras (masc.)
My ears:	Mes oreilles (fem.)

= <u>My finger hurts</u>.

the head:	la tête
the neck:	le cou
the throat:	la gorge
the back:	le dos
the foot:	le pied
the knee:	le genou
the leg:	la jambe
the finger:	le doigt
the hand:	la main
the arm:	le bras
the shoulder:	l'épaule (fem.)

Je me suis cassé le bras.   = I've broken my arm.

J'ai un rhume .

a cough:	une toux
flu:	la grippe
seasickness:	le mal de mer
a temperature:	de la fièvre

= I have <u>a cold</u>.

Pouvez-vous me donner quelque chose?
— Can you give me something?

Pouvez-vous me donner un médicament ?   = Can you give me <u>some medicine</u>?

some plasters:	des sparadraps (masc.)
some tablets:	des comprimés (masc.)
some aspirin:	de l'aspirine (fem.)

Ça va mieux.   = I feel better.

Ça va bien.   = I feel well.

This stuff's fairly straightforward, but really important

This vocab might come up in one of your speaking or listening tasks — so make sure you know how the words are pronounced as well as how they're spelt, and you'll be well on your way to a top grade.

Health and Health Issues

These next two pages are a bit like PSHE in French — you lucky, lucky people. You probably have an <u>opinion</u> on this stuff already. Some of the French vocab and expressions are a bit tricky though.

Qu'est-ce que tu fais pour rester en bonne santé?
— What do you do to stay healthy?

Pour rester en bonne santé ...

= To stay healthy ...

I eat lots of vegetables:	je mange beaucoup de légumes.
I rarely eat chocolate:	je mange rarement du chocolat.
I drink water often:	je bois souvent de l'eau.

Je fais beaucoup de sport pour ...

= I play a lot of sport to ...

stay fit:	rester en forme.
lose weight:	perdre du poids.

Je ne fais rien parce que ...

= I do nothing because ...

exercising is boring:	faire de l'exercice, c'est ennuyeux.
I don't have time:	je n'ai pas le temps.
I'm already perfect:	je suis déjà parfait(e).

Je suis au régime. Je ne mange que de l'alimentation saine.

= I'm on a diet. I only eat healthy food.

La drogue dans le sport — Drugs in sport

Often a big talking point for the French, this. Especially when the <u>Tour de France</u> is on.

La drogue est un problème dans le cyclisme .   = Drugs are a problem in <u>cycling</u>.

athletics: l'athlétisme (masc.)	*football:* le football

Ce n'est pas juste pour la majorité des cyclistes *qui ne trichent pas.*

= It's not fair for the majority of <u>cyclists</u> who don't cheat.

athletes: athlètes	*players:* joueurs

This stuff's fairly straightforward, but really important

There's loads you might want to say about these <u>exciting</u> topics, but learning the stuff on this page is a <u>good</u> start. <u>Think</u> about what else you might want to say, write it down and <u>practise</u> it.

Health and Health Issues

Health issues keep <u>cropping up</u> in the news and the examiners love them too. Have a think about these things so if you're asked for your opinion on <u>obesity</u> or <u>size-zero models</u>, you'll have loads to talk about.

L'obésité est devenue un grand problème
— Obesity has become a big problem

Here's how to give your opinion on <u>expanding waistlines</u>...

Il est triste *de voir des enfants* très *gros.*   = It's <u>sad</u> to see <u>very</u> fat children.

extremely: extrêmement   *really:* vraiment

It's awful: C'est affreux   *It's depressing:* C'est déprimant

À mon avis, c'est la faute de la publicité *.*   = In my opinion, it's the fault <u>of advertising</u>.

of society: de la société   *of the parents:* des parents

Beaucoup de gens ne mangent pas suffisamment
—A lot of people don't eat enough

...and on <u>tiny</u> waistlines. Have a look at this:

"Il y a beaucoup de pression pour être maigre comme les mannequins. Il y a des filles qui pensent à leur poids tout le temps, mais franchement ce n'est pas sain. Il faut bien manger, et surtout il faut mener une vie active. Comme ça, les gens auraient moins de problèmes de santé."

= There's a lot of pressure to be as thin as models. There are girls who think about their weight all the time, but frankly it's not healthy. You have to eat well, and above all you have to lead an active life. That way people would have fewer health problems.

For this topic, go back and brush up on food as well
There's loads of stuff on this page that could <u>easily</u> come up somewhere in the assessments. Some of the 'opinions' stuff is quite tricky, but you need to be ready for <u>anything</u>.

Health and Health Issues

Here are some more key phrases — this time about <u>smoking</u>, <u>drinking</u> and <u>drugs</u>.

Qu'est-ce que tu penses du tabagisme?

What do you think of smoking?

This stuff's relevant for <u>drugs</u> and <u>alcohol</u> so learn the <u>vocab</u> in the pale boxes too.

Je ne fume pas.   = I don't smoke.

| Alcohol: L'alcool (masc.) |

Fumer , c'est dégoûtant. Je déteste quand les autres fument , c'est vraiment impoli. Je ne sortirais jamais avec un fumeur / une fumeuse .

| drink: boivent |

= <u>Smoking</u> is disgusting. I hate it when others <u>smoke</u>, it's really impolite. I'd never go out with <u>a smoker</u>.

| alcoholic: un/une alcoolique |

| would never drink: | ne boirais jamais |
| would never smoke: | ne fumerais jamais |

| drink: bois |

Je fume mais je ne deviendrais jamais toxicomane . C'est trop dangereux.

= I <u>smoke</u> but I <u>would never become a drug addict</u>. It's too dangerous.

J'aime fumer.   = I like smoking.

Quand je fume, je me détends. Je sais que ce n'est pas sain, mais je pense que c'est cool.

= When I smoke, I relax. I know it's unhealthy, but I think it's cool.

Heureusement il est interdit de fumer dans les lieux publics.

= Thankfully it's forbidden to smoke in public places.

J'ai arrêté de fumer il y a un an

— I stopped smoking a year ago

Pourquoi avez-vous décidé d'arrêter?   = Why did you decide to stop?

Je commençais à avoir des problèmes de santé.   = <u>I was starting to have health problems</u>.

| *I had trouble breathing, especially when doing sport:* | J'avais du mal à respirer, surtout en faisant du sport. |
| *I couldn't afford it. There's too much tax on tobacco:* | Ça me coûtait trop cher. Il y a trop de taxe sur le tabac. |

Whether or not you smoke, you might need an opinion on it

Whatever you think about the issues on these pages, it's well worth spending some time writing a couple of sentences summing up your ideas — then, if you need them, you can simply reel them off

Quick Questions

The last few pages were pretty intense, which means it's even more important that you get your head around these health and social issues. You need to be able to talk about this stuff so if you don't have an opinion then just make one up — but make sure you can say something.

Quick Questions

1) You've been told you're too young for a job at your local supermarket. How would you say in French that it's not fair to discriminate because of age?

2) You read an interview with a French person in the newspaper. The title of the article is "Certains sont méchants parce que je suis musulman." What does the title mean?

3) How would you say that there is a lot of poverty in your town?

4) Your French penfriend writes a letter about her town and she says, "En rentrant à la maison une fois j'ai été menacée. C'était effrayant." Translate what she said into English.

5) Translate the following words into French:

   a) unemployed people

   b) fear

   c) homeless people

6) Your uncle has been out of work for three years. Write this in French.

7) Your aunt tells you, "Il est difficile de trouver un logement sans travail". What is she telling you?

8) Translate into English:

   a) "Où as-tu mal?"

   b) "Pouvez-vous me donner quelque chose?"

9) You're taking part in a French exchange when you start feeling ill. Tell your friend that you've got a stomach ache and you need to go to the doctor.

10) What is the French for the following medical conditions:

   a) an earache

   b) a sore throat

   c) a headache?

11) Your French friend's grandma says to you, "J'ai un rhume et je tousse. Et j'ai de la fièvre aussi." What has she said to you?

12) Translate these body parts into French:

   a) nose   b) foot   c) arm   d) finger   e) teeth   f) shoulder

13) How would you say that to stay healthy you only eat healthy food?

14) How would you say that you don't play sport because exercising is boring?

15) In French, write that you think drugs are a problem in football and it's not fair because the majority of players don't cheat.

16) In an article in a French newspaper you read a sentence that says, "Il est déprimant de voir des enfants vraiment gros. C'est la faute de la publicité." What does this mean?

17) Your friend Lise has sent you an email about her boyfriend Alain. She says, "Alain fume toujours et je trouve que fumer est dégoûtant. Je n'aime pas quand Alain fume." What is she telling you?

18) How would you say that you stopped smoking a year ago?

Listening Questions

Track 4

These people are having a meal together. What items do they want passing to them?

Example: <u>**Salt**</u> and <u>**pepper**</u>

1 .... and ....

2 .... and ....

3 .... and ....

Track 5

Thierry is talking about being unemployed. Complete the sentences below.

Example: He was unemployed for <u>**one year**</u>.

4 a) When he left university he didn't have any ....

   b) He decided to ....

   c) Six months later ....

Reading Question

1   Read this letter from your French penfriend.

Marseille, le 5 mai

Salut!

Comment ça va? En octobre je vais commencer mes études de droit à l'université de la Sorbonne à Paris. Je suis très content de pouvoir faire mes études à l'université la plus prestigieuse en France!

Le seul souci c'est que je vais devoir quitter ma famille et les amis que j'ai ici. Récemment j'ai trouvé un appartement que je vais partager avec un autre étudiant qui s'appelle Enzo. L'appartement est assez petit mais au moins nous avons chacun notre chambre même si elles sont petites.

D'un côté j'ai hâte d'emménager parce que je vais enfin pouvoir être indépendant et faire ce que je veux quand je le veux. Et puis surtout je pourrai inviter mes amis à dîner et faire la fête toute la nuit. Je pourrai aussi sortir le soir et rentrer tard sans être interrogé par mes parents. Mais d'un autre côté il faudra que je me débrouille avec Enzo pour le ménage et pour les courses.

En plus je pense que le confort de la maison de mes parents va me manquer. Et puis ma mère est un vrai cordon bleu, je ne sais pas cuisiner comme elle. Par conséquent il faudra souvent que je mange des plats préparés ou que j'aille au Quick.

Enfin, je suis un peu nerveux de quitter la maison mais je pense que je vais vite m'y habituer, et puis je reviendrai chez mes parents un week-end sur deux et aussi pour les vacances scolaires.

Amitiés,

Guillaume

Write T (true), F (false) or ? (don't know) for the following statements.

1.   Guillaume is not happy about going to the Sorbonne.

2.   Guillaume will have to share a room with his flatmate.

3.   Guillaume is looking forward to a busy social life.

4.   Guillaume is looking forward to inviting his brother to Paris.

5.   Enzo will do the housework and Guillaume will do the shopping.

6.   Guillaume is anxious about leaving home.

Reading Question

2 Read each of these paragraphs about unemployment.

1. À l'école je portais des vêtements à la mode. Quand j'étais à l'université, j'avais une belle voiture que j'avais achetée avec mon propre argent. Mais ces temps-ci les choses ont changé. J'ai de plus en plus de mal à parler aux gens et ça m'inquiète parce que je me dis que je ne pourrai pas trouver la femme de ma vie parce que je suis sans emploi.

2. J'ai toujours aimé les meilleures choses dans la vie. J'adore aller au restaurant avec mes amis. Habituellement, on va au restaurant tous les week-ends mais en ce moment c'est difficile parce que je n'ai pas les moyens de sortir si souvent. C'est gênant et j'en ai honte. Je dois maintenant me contenter de manger au fast-food.

3. Pendant dix ans tout allait bien dans mon entreprise. Mais avec la crise économique nous n'avons pas reçu autant de commandes. J'ai dû licencier la plupart de mon équipe et demander à ceux qui restent de travailler à mi-temps. Toutes les entreprises de la région ont dû faire la même chose et cela a augmenté le taux de chômage.

4. J'ai perdu mon emploi de caissière il y a cinq ans. Au début je partageais un logement avec une amie mais je dormais dans une petite chambre. J'ai dû partir parce qu'elle a déménagé. Heureusement il y a un immeuble en ville où je loue une chambre. Je reçois une allocation immobilière et une allocation chômage.

Choose a title for each paragraph. Write the correct letter in each box.

1. ☐

2. ☐

3. ☐

4. ☐

A. Housing

B. Loss of confidence

C. Looking for a job

D. Lack of money

E. How to help reduce unemployment

F. Falling demand

Speaking Question

It might seem weird discussing your health with your teacher, but there's a chance they will ask you about it, so best to practise now and be prepared.

Task: Health

You are going to have a conversation with your teacher about health issues.

Your teacher will start the conversation and ask you the following questions:

- What do you do to stay healthy?
- What is your favourite sport? Why?
- When was the last time you were ill? What was wrong?
- What do you eat at lunchtime at school?
- What are you going to have for dinner tonight?
- Do you think there are some models who are too thin?
- !

! Remember that the exclamation mark means you'll have to answer a question that you won't have prepared an answer to.

The whole conversation should last about five minutes.

Teacher's Role

You need to ask the student the following questions. You should speak first.

1   Qu'est-ce que tu fais pour rester en bonne santé?

2   Quel est ton sport préféré? Pourquoi?

3   Quand as-tu été malade pour la dernière fois? Qu'est-ce que tu avais?

4   Qu'est-ce que tu manges à midi au collège?

5   Qu'est-ce que tu vas manger ce soir?

6   Penses-tu qu'il existe des mannequins qui sont trop maigres?

7   !

!   The unpredictable question could be:

    Qu'est-ce que tu penses du tabagisme?

Writing Questions

Task 1: Relationships

Your best friend has just told you that they're getting engaged. You think they're too young. Write them an email expressing your views. You should write 250-300 words.

You could include:

- Congratulations on their news,
- How you feel about the engagement,
- Why you feel that way,
- What you think they should do,
- Your views on marriage in general,
- What you would do if you were in their situation,
- Concerns that your other friends have about their engagement.

Remember that to score the highest marks you need to answer the task as fully as possible, expanding on the points above when it is relevant to do so.

Task 2: Homelessness

Your teacher has asked your local Big Issue seller to speak to your class. You have been asked to write up a report for the e-magazine you send to your twin school in France. You should write 250-300 words.

You could include:

- What his daily life is like and where he lives,
- What happened to cause him to be homeless,
- Good and bad things that have happened to him while being homeless,
- What he would like his life to be like in the future,
- Your opinions about homeless people and what you think society could do to help them.

Remember that to score the highest marks you need to answer the task as fully as possible, expanding on the points above when it is relevant to do so.

Revision Summary

These questions are here to make sure you <u>know your stuff</u>. Work through them and look up the answers to any tough ones you're struggling with. Keep practising them <u>all</u> again and again. Do I sound like a <u>broken record</u> yet... Hope so. I've always wondered what that might be like.

1) You're making fruit salad for a party. Think of as many different fruits as you can to put in it — and write down at least 5 in French. Make a list (in French) of 5 drinks for the party too.

2) Your hosts are offering you more chocolate cake. Decline politely, thank them for the meal, and say it was delicious. Offer to pass your hostess the milk for her coffee.

3) Write down how you'd say that you like vegetables but don't like sausages. You don't eat meat any more and you're hungry.

4) Décris-moi une journée typique.

5) You're telling your host family all about your home life. Say that you make your bed, do the shopping and lay the table. Tell them that you earn pocket money for helping out at home.

6) How would you tell your name, age and birthday to someone you've just met?

7) Describe three of your friends and say how old they are. Comment on the colour of their eyes and their marital status, and spell their names out loud.

8) Tell your penfriend what relations you have — including how many aunts, cousins etc.

9) Your animal-loving friend has six rabbits, a bird, a guinea pig and two cats. How could she say what these are in French?

10) Imagine that you are a boring, impolite, wise, funny, lively person who has a sense of humour and knows how to make people laugh. How would you say all this in French?

11) Write three sentences about the personalities of two of your favourite celebrities.

12) In your opinion, what three qualities should a good friend have? Finish the following sentence — "À mon avis, un bon ami / une bonne amie doit..."

13) Isabelle says: "J'ai un petit ami qui s'appelle François. On s'entend bien. Nous sommes les meilleurs amis du monde. On ne se dispute jamais. François est honnête, fidèle et compréhensif, et il est toujours là pour moi. Je pense que je suis tombée amoureuse." (Sickening.) What did she say in English?

14) Write a short paragraph to explain your views on equal opportunity.

15) Do the same as in Q.14 but for unemployment... Sorry.

16) How would you say you have each of these ailments in French?
a) stomach ache b) headache c) a cold d) flu e) a broken arm f) seasickness

17) Est-ce que tu es en bonne santé? Pourquoi? Pourquoi pas?

18) Il y a un an tu fumais, mais maintenant tu ne fumes plus. Pourquoi?

Sports and Hobbies

There's always loads in the exams about <u>sports</u> and whether you like playing them or not.

Est-ce que tu fais du sport? — Do you do any sport?

<u>Sports</u> and <u>hobbies</u> are a popular choice for speaking and writing assessments.

<u>Verbs for sports</u>

to go fishing:	aller à la pêche
to run:	courir
to cycle:	faire du cyclisme
to swim:	nager
to ski:	faire du ski
to play:	jouer
to walk, hike:	faire une randonnée
to ice skate:	patiner

<u>Names for sports</u>

basketball:	le basket
football:	le foot(ball)
tennis:	le tennis
table tennis:	le ping-pong
horse riding:	l'équitation (fem.)
skateboarding:	le skate
swimming:	la natation
ice skating:	le patinage
snowboarding:	le surf des neiges
water sports:	les sports nautiques
winter sports:	les sports d'hiver

<u>Places you can do sports</u>

sports centre:	le centre sportif	*gymnasium:*	le gymnase
leisure centre:	le centre de loisirs	*park:*	le parc
swimming pool:	la piscine	*ice rink:*	la patinoire
sports field:	le terrain de sport	*mountains:*	les montagnes (fem.)

Tu aimes regarder le sport? — Do you like watching sport?

Je préfère participer parce que ...   = I prefer to participate because...

I love training:	j'adore m'entraîner.
I like working in a team:	j'aime travailler en équipe.
I love the stadium atmosphere:	j'adore l'ambiance du stade.

I'm injured and I can't play any more:
je me suis blessé(e) et je ne peux plus jouer.
it's expensive to play: ça coûte cher de jouer.

Je préfère regarder le jeu parce que ...   = I prefer to watch the game because...

Know your sports

Not only do you have to do sport in PE, you have to talk about it in French. Even if you hate sport, you'll have to <u>pretend</u> you do something. And you'll need to recognise the others.

Sports and Hobbies

You need to know the vocab for all different kinds of <u>hobbies</u> too.

Est-ce que tu as un passe-temps?
— Do you have a hobby?

There are <u>other things</u> to do apart from sports.

<u>General but vital</u>

hobby:	le passe-temps
interest:	l'intérêt (masc.)
club:	le club (de...)
member:	le membre

<u>Verbs for indoor activities</u>

to dance:	danser
to sing:	chanter
to collect:	collectionner
to read:	lire

<u>Other important words</u>

chess:	les échecs (masc.)
film:	le film
performance:	le spectacle
play (in a theatre):	la pièce de théâtre
reading (activity):	la lecture

Est-ce que tu joues d'un instrument?
— Do you play an instrument?

If music's what you're into, see page 57.

<u>Musical words</u>

band, group:	le groupe
CD:	le CD, le disque compact
instrument:	l'instrument (masc.)
concert:	le concert

<u>Musical instruments</u>

flute:	la flûte
drum kit:	la batterie
clarinet:	la clarinette
guitar:	la guitare
trumpet:	la trompette
piano:	le piano
violin:	le violon
cello:	le violoncelle

Revising this page is my favourite hobby

It's a <u>valid</u> point that learning about all these hobbies in French is not as <u>fun</u> as actually doing them — but you've got to know them so <u>learn</u> these vocab lists and <u>test</u> yourself until you know them all.

Sports and Hobbies

What you do in your <u>free time</u> comes up somewhere in the assessments <u>every year</u>.

Qu'est-ce que tu fais pendant ton temps libre?

<u>Sport</u> and <u>music</u> are big topics. — What do you do in your free time?

Je joue au football le week-end . = I play <u>football</u> <u>at weekends</u>.

badminton: au badminton
tennis: au tennis

every day: chaque jour
every week: chaque semaine
twice a month: deux fois par mois

chess club: club d'échecs
squash club: club de squash

Je joue du piano . = I play <u>the piano</u>.

Je suis membre d'un club de tennis .

= I'm a member of a <u>tennis club</u>.

<u>Handy hint</u>: To talk about any sports club, just put '<u>club de</u>' and the name of the sport.

If you're talking about games, use '<u>jouer à</u>', but with instruments, it's '<u>jouer de</u>'.
à + le = au   de + le = du
à + la = à la   de + la = de la
à + l' = à l'   de + l' = de l'
à + les = aux   de + les = des
Je joue au badminton.   Je joue de la clarinette.

Est-ce que tu aimes le football? — Do you like football?

Here's how to say what you <u>think</u> of different hobbies.

the cinema: le cinéma
hiking: les randonnées

exciting: passionnant(e)(s)
interesting: intéressant(e)(s)

Oui, j'adore le football .

= Yes, I love <u>football</u>.

Je trouve le football fantastique .

= I think <u>football</u> is <u>fantastic</u>.

I agree: Je suis d'accord.
I don't agree: Je ne suis pas d'accord.

For <u>agreeing</u> and <u>disagreeing</u>
you can use these phrases.

Pourquoi est-ce que tu penses cela? = Why do you think that?

Je n'aime pas courir *, parce que c'est* difficile . = I don't like <u>running</u>, because it's <u>difficult</u>.

music: la musique

boring: ennuyeux

Always use the <u>masculine</u>
form after "<u>c'est</u>".

You need to have an opinion about sports and hobbies

There's important stuff on this page — you <u>need</u> to be able to say <u>what</u> you do in your <u>free time</u>
and <u>why</u>. Make sure you remember when it's 'jouer <u>à</u>' and when it's 'jouer <u>de</u>'.

Television

You might have to listen to people talk about television in the exam, or you may need to talk about it in the speaking assessment. You never know, so make sure this is part of your <u>repertoire</u>.

Qu'est-ce que tu aimes regarder à la télé?
— What do you like to watch on TV?

Basically, this stuff's all really handy.

to read: lire

Quelles émissions *est-ce que tu aimes* **regarder** *?*

Which books: Quels livres

= <u>Which TV programmes</u> do you like <u>to watch</u>?

to listen to: écouter   *to read:* lire

Put what you like to watch, listen to or read here.

J'aime **regarder** **Westenders** *.*   = I like <u>to watch</u> <u>Westenders</u>.

documentaries:	des documentaires
soaps:	des feuilletons
films:	des films
plays:	des pièces de théâtre
shows:	des spectacles
advertisements:	des publicités
the news:	les actualités (fem.)

For more about giving opinions, see pages 10-12.

This one's always plural, like in English.

a documentary:	un documentaire
a soap:	un feuilleton
a film:	un film
a play:	une pièce de théâtre
a show:	un spectacle
an advertisement:	une publicité

Je voudrais regarder ...   = I would like to watch ...

This is all vital stuff so learn it well

You might well face a <u>television-related</u> question in your assessments so you <u>need</u> to know this vocab.
Then you can practise talking about your <u>favourite</u> television programmes and why you like them.

Television

À quelle heure commence l'émission?
— When does the programme start?

L'émission commence à vingt heures
et finit à vingt et une heures trente .

> For more information about telling the time, see page 2.

= The programme starts at <u>8pm</u> and finishes at <u>9:30pm</u>.

Qu'est-ce que tu as fait récemment?
— What have you done recently?

This bit of <u>past tense</u> looks really impressive — try to use it when you're talking about films or television programmes.

> For more about times and dates, see pages 2-4.

J'ai vu *Amélie* récemment . = I <u>saw</u> <u>Amélie</u> <u>recently</u>.

heard:	écouté
read:	lu

the radio:	la radio
the new song by Take This:	
la nouvelle chanson de Take This	

last week:	la semaine dernière
two weeks ago:	il y a deux semaines
a month ago:	il y a un mois

J'ai lu, J'ai vu, J'ai entendu... — I read, I saw, I heard...

Je viens de lire un livre impressionnant . = I've just <u>read</u> an <u>impressive</u> <u>book</u>.

listened to:	d'écouter
watched:	de regarder
seen:	de voir

a play:	une pièce de théâtre
a show:	un spectacle
a film:	un film
a cartoon:	une bande dessinée

interesting:	intéressant(e)
surprising:	surprenant(e)
funny:	drôle

Le titre était 'Le Mariage de mon meilleur ennemi'.

= The title was 'My Best Enemy's Wedding'.

Make sure you've got plenty to say on this topic

This is a <u>great</u> chance to show the examiner that you can use the <u>past tense</u> so you need to be able to use it properly. <u>Practise</u> the sentences and phrases on this page and you won't be <u>lost for words</u>.

Talking About the Plot

Books, films, TV programmes — you may have to discuss things you've read, seen or heard recently. It sounds quite daunting, even in English, but it's really simple if you learn these easy phrases...

Parle-moi de ce qui s'est passé...
— Tell me about what happened...

woman:	une femme	*boy:*	un garçon
girl:	une fille	*actor:*	un acteur
actress:	une actrice	*star:*	une vedette
singer:	un chanteur / une chanteuse		

Il s'agit d' un homme qui portait des lunettes et un manteau invisible.

= It's about a man who wore glasses and an invisible coat.

had lots of money:	avait beaucoup d'argent
loved to travel:	adorait voyager
was very handsome but a bit stupid:	
était très beau mais un peu stupide.	

You can make up anything you like here. (Maybe don't mention robots if you're talking about a classical novel...) Just make sure you use the imperfect tense. For more info, see pages 209-212.

Qu'est-ce que tu en pensais? — What did you think of it?

Opinions go down really well at GCSE French — so you need to learn this stuff.

Je l'ai trouvé(e) génial(e) .

= I thought it was great.

For more about giving opinions, see pages 10-11.

informative:	instructif / instructive
entertaining:	amusant(e)
interesting:	intéressant(e)
boring:	ennuyeux / ennuyeuse
fantastic:	fantastique

This is quite tricky — remember to add an 'e' to the past participle and the adjective (if necessary) if the thing you are referring to is feminine, e.g. une émission, une publicité, une pièce de théâtre.

You need an opinion — so if you don't have one, make one up

Examiners love it when you can give your opinion on something, especially if it's done in perfect French. And remember — you need the imperfect tense to talk about the plot in the past.

Quick Questions

Quick Questions

1) How would you say in French that you do these sports?

 a)   b)   c)

2) Your friend Eric tells you, "Je voudrais aller au centre de loisirs ce soir." Where does he want to go tonight?

3) You like watching sport but you prefer to participate because you love training. How would you say this in French?

4) Your French penfriend writes to you and asks, "Est-ce que tu as un passe-temps?" What are they asking you?

5) Marc says, "Je joue de la batterie chaque jour."

    a) What does he play?   b) How often does he play?

6) Stephen tells you, "Je suis membre d'un club de natation." What has he told you?

7) Write down in French "I don't like playing chess because it's boring".

8) Read this letter from your penfriend, then answer the questions below in English.

> J'adore le tennis, et je joue au rugby le week-end. J'aime bien nager, mais je n'aime pas faire du ski parce que c'est difficile. Je fais du ski chaque année près de Chamonix, et c'est tellement ennuyeux — je préfère faire du patinage.

    a) Which sport doesn't she like?

    b) Which sport does she play at weekends?

    c) Which sport does she like to do when she's near Chamonix?

9) How would you say the following sentences:

    a) I find hiking interesting.

    b) I find snowboarding exciting.

10) Your friend Claudine tells you, "J'aime regarder les documentaires mais je n'aime pas regarder les publicités." What has she told you?

11) Your favourite TV programme starts at 7.30pm and finishes at 8.15pm. Write this as a sentence in French.

12) "J'ai écouté la nouvelle chanson de John Bonne il y a deux semaines." What does this mean in English?

13) Translate the following words into English:

    a) une pièce de théâtre

    b) un spectacle

    c) une bande dessinée

14) Your friend has just seen the latest French blockbuster at the cinema. He says, "Il s'agit d'une femme qui avait beaucoup d'argent et adorait voyager." Translate what he said about the film into English.

Music

Learn how to say what music you're into and whether you play a musical instrument.

Qu'est-ce que tu aimes comme musique?

You need to find <u>interesting</u> ways of talking about your musical tastes.

— What kind of music do you like?

Mon genre musical préféré , c'est la musique jazz.

= <u>My favourite type of music</u> is <u>jazz</u>.

pop   rock   danse   classique   rap

J'aime toutes les chansons qu'on entend en boîte.   = I like all the songs you hear in clubs.

Je trouve les symphonies de Beethoven incroyables .

= I find <u>Beethoven's symphonies</u> <u>incredible</u>.

| *songs by Take This:* | les chansons de Take This |
| *musicals:* | les comédies musicales |

| *very good:* | très bons / bonnes |
| *really great:* | vraiment chouettes |

Où est-ce que tu aimes écouter de la musique?

— Where do you like listening to music?

J'écoute de la musique en voiture sur mon lecteur mp3 .

= I listen to music <u>in the car</u> <u>on my MP3 player</u>.

on the bus:	en autobus
at home:	à la maison
while I'm walking:	en marchant

on the radio:	à la radio
on my mobile phone:	sur mon téléphone portable
on my hi-fi system:	sur ma chaîne hi-fi

You can also say 'baladeur mp3' for 'MP3 player'.

To play an instrument is **'jouer d'un instrument'**

Je joue du piano . Je m'entraîne tous les jours . = I play <u>the piano</u>. I practise <u>every day</u>.

the guitar:	de la guitare
the keyboard:	du clavier
the drums:	de la batterie

| *once a week:* | une fois par semaine |
| *at weekends:* | le week-end |

See page 51 for more musical instruments.

Je fais partie d'un groupe de rock.   = I play in a rock band.

Music is a really important topic

If music comes up in one of the assessments, and you haven't got much to say, you could try: '<u>J'aimerais</u> jouer du piano' (= '<u>I'd like to...</u>'), and then give a reason. It's better than nothing.

Famous People

The next couple of pages are all about the lifestyles of the <u>rich</u> and <u>famous</u>. Think about your favourite celebrity and make sure you can say lots of things about how <u>fabulous</u> they are in French.

Quelles célébrités aimes-tu? — Which celebrities do you like?

This is the same <u>straightforward</u> stuff that you use to talk about you and your family.

Je trouve Beyoncé Knowles fantastique.   = I think Beyoncé Knowles is fantastic.

C'est une chanteuse américaine célèbre.   = She is a famous American singer.

Beyoncé est très mignonne et je pense qu'elle chante comme un ange, aussi.   = Beyoncé is very cute and I think that she sings like an angel, as well.

La vie des célébrités... — Celebrity life...

My dad:	Mon père
Elvis:	Elvis

his clothes were so cool: ses vêtements étaient si cools.

... m'a beaucoup influencé(e) parce que ...   = ... has influenced me a lot because ...

Ma plus grande réussite est ...

= My greatest achievement is ...

the support I've been able to give to international organisations: le soutien que j'ai pu donner aux organisations internationales.
my platinum disc: mon disque de platine.

J'ai l'ambition de ... = My ambition is to ...

Je voudrais ... = I would like to ...

travel: voyager.   *help out:* donner de l'aide.   *win an Oscar:* gagner un Oscar.

Learn these phrases so you can talk about your favourite celebrity

This page gives <u>you</u> the freedom to give <u>your opinion</u> on <u>celebrities</u> and their <u>influence in society</u> — all in a <u>foreign language</u>. It's tricky stuff, but master this and your French will be fabulous.

Famous People

Vous aimez être célèbre? — Do you like being famous?

If you're asked to write an <u>interview</u> with a celeb, here are some useful phrases:

Oui, j'aime la vie de vedette parce que ...

= Yes, I love life as a celebrity because ...

I am successful:	j'ai du succès.
I have lots of money:	j'ai beaucoup d'argent.
I am able to travel:	je peux voyager.

Je gagne beaucoup donc je peux donner de l'argent aux organisations caritatives.

= I earn a lot so I can give money to charity.

Est-ce que vous avez beaucoup de fans ?

= Do you <u>have</u> lots <u>of fans</u>?

like having:	aimez avoir

of hit records:	de tubes	*of money:* d'argent

Oui, j'en ai beaucoup.   = Yes, I have lots of them.

Je n'aime pas être célèbre... — I don't like being famous

Je déteste la vie de vedette car ...

= I hate life as a celebrity because ...

I don't have a normal life:	je n'ai pas une vie normale.
people follow me everywhere:	les gens me suivent partout.

Je ne suis jamais chez moi parce que je dois voyager beaucoup.

= <u>I'm never at home</u> because I have to travel a lot.

I miss my family:	Ma famille me manque
I'm always tired:	Je suis toujours fatigué(e)

Les journalistes racontent ma vie dans les journaux et je n'aime pas ça.

= Journalists write about my life in the newspapers and I don't like it.

It's so tiring being famous and fabulous

There are <u>good</u> and <u>bad</u> points about being famous, and you <u>need</u> to know how to talk about them in French. It'll come in handy if you want to talk about <u>a day in the life</u> of your fave celebrity.

New Technology

Ah, computers. What a lovely topic for your French GCSE — make sure you have plenty to say.

Je suis toujours sur l'ordinateur

— I'm always on the computer

It's good to be able to give details about what you use computers for.

J'ai créé **un site internet pour** **mon club d'échecs** .

= I have created a website for my chess club.

a home page: une page d'accueil

my band: mon groupe
my orchestra: mon orchestre

Here's some vocab that might come in handy in the assessments.

camera:	un appareil photo	*touch screen:*	un écran tactile
blogger:	un bloggeur / une bloggeuse	*link:*	un lien
button:	un bouton	*monitor:*	un moniteur
camcorder:	un caméscope	*battery:*	une pile
games console:	une console de jeux	*CD drive:*	un lecteur CD
internet café:	un cybercafé	*network:*	un réseau

Je vais télécharger mes photos sur mon ordinateur.
Avant de les mettre en ligne, je vais les imprimer.

= I am going to upload my photos onto my computer. Before putting them online, I am going to print them.

Je vais bloguer ça — I'll put it on my blog

They might ask you to imagine you're writing a blog for your written assessment.

Manchester   25/02/2009   19h20

Je viens de passer une journée très agréable. Nous sommes allés en famille rendre visite à des amis au pays de Galles.

On a très bien mangé — du rôti d'agneau — et l'après-midi on s'est promené dans le petit village près de chez eux.

Il y avait des vues superbes des montagnes galloises. Je pense que j'aimerais vivre là-bas à l'avenir.

Regardez les photos en cliquant sur cette icône:

Je vous invite à laisser vos commentaires!

I've just had a very nice day. We went with the family to visit some friends in Wales.

We ate very well — roast lamb — and in the afternoon we went for a walk in the little village near their house.

There were wonderful views of the Welsh mountains. I think I'd like to live there in the future.

Look at the photos by clicking on this icon:

I invite you to leave your comments!

The blogger describes what he/she has done today in the perfect tense. See pages 204-208.

You might need to read or write a blog in the exam

Everyone's blogging nowadays, so the examiners reckon that it's good practice to be able to write a blog in your French exam. Make sure you learn all the computer vocab — that's important stuff too.

Email and Texting

Je voudrais envoyer un courrier électronique
— I would like to send an email

Est-ce que je peux envoyer un email à mon ami(e) d'ici? = Can I send <u>an email</u> to my friend from here?

a fax: un fax

email: un email un courrier électronique un courriel	*from:* de *to:* à / pour *send:* envoyer *subject:* sujet / objet	*(cc) copy to:* copier à *reply (to all):* répondre (à tous) *forward:* transférer

Je vérifie ma boîte email régulièrement.   = I check <u>my inbox</u> regularly.

If you're asked to write an email to someone you know, use <u>informal</u> language:

1) Use '<u>tu</u>' (and 's'il <u>te</u> plaît'). <u>DON'T</u> switch between 'tu' and 'vous'.
2) Start a text with '<u>Salut</u>' or '<u>Bonjour</u>'. End it with '<u>À plus tard</u>', '<u>À tout à l'heure</u>' or '<u>À bientôt</u>'.
3) Imagine you're <u>actually</u> writing to someone you <u>know</u>. Think of things you would <u>actually</u> say.

Envoyer un texto — To send a text message

Who knows, you might be asked to read a <u>text message</u> in the reading exam. Here's an example of the kind of thing you should expect to see:

Hi Pierre. Do you want to come to the cinema tonight? Jean and I will be there around 7pm. We don't know yet which film we're going to watch. See you later, Steve

15:04

Salut Pierre. Tu veux venir au cinéma ce soir? Jean et moi y serons vers 19h00. On ne sait pas encore quel film on va regarder. À plus tard, Steve

J'aime parler au téléphone — I like to talk on the phone

You need an opinion on emails and text messages.

Je préfère ne pas passer trop de temps sur l'ordinateur — ce n'est pas très sain. = I prefer not to spend too much time on the computer — it's not very healthy.

Les courriels ne sont pas très personnels. Je préfère écrire une lettre. = Emails aren't very personal. I prefer to write a letter.

Les enfants devraient faire du sport au lieu d'être devant un moniteur tout le temps. = Children should be playing sport instead of being in front of a monitor all the time.

You could see an email or a text message in your exam

Emails and text messages could <u>well</u> come up in your exam. If you're asked to write one to someone you <u>know</u>, make sure you use the informal '<u>tu</u>' form — if you don't know the person, use '<u>vous</u>'.

Quick Questions

These questions are here to make sure you learnt the last few pages really well. You could be asked to talk about different kinds of music or your favourite celebrity, so it's a good idea to revise these pages properly. Blogs, emails and texts are pretty vital stuff too.

Quick Questions

1) How would you ask your French friend Frédéric what kind of music he likes?

2) Your friend Claudine is telling you about her favourite music:

> Mon genre musical préféré, c'est la musique pop. J'aime les chansons qu'on entend en boîte. Je trouve les chansons de Club Brothers vraiment chouettes.

   a) What is Claudine's favourite kind of music?

   b) What does she think about songs that you hear in clubs?

   c) What does she say about Club Brothers?

3) What are the two ways of saying 'MP3 player' in French?

4) How would you say in French that you play the drums in a rock band?

5) Translate the following phrases into English:

   a) C'est une chanteuse anglaise célèbre.

   b) Elle chante comme un ange.

   c) Ses vêtements sont si cools.

6) How would you say in French that your mum has influenced you a lot?

7) You're reading an interview with a celebrity in a French magazine when you read this sentence: "Ma plus grande réussite est le soutien que j'ai pu donner aux organisations internationales." What does this mean in English?

8) Pretend that you're a famous French celebrity. Write a sentence saying that you like life as a celebrity because you can travel and you have lots of money.

9) Write down the French for the following words:

   a) website   b) games console   c) touch screen   d) battery   e) network

10) Your brother is always on the computer. He has created a website for his orchestra. How would you write this in French?

11) You are telling your French friend about a funny thing that happened to you last week. He says, "Je vais bloguer ça." What does this mean?

12) What are the three ways of saying 'email' in French?

13) Translate the following verbs into English:

   a) envoyer   b) répondre   c) copier   d) transférer

14) How would you say that you check your inbox every day?

15) If you were writing an email to someone you know, would you use 'tu' or 'vous'?

16) Your penfriend's grandma is talking about how much she hates new technology. She tells you, "Les enfants devraient faire du sport au lieu d'être devant un moniteur tout le temps — ce n'est pas très sain." Translate what she's told you into English.

Shopping

Make sure you know <u>everything</u> there is to know about shopping in French.

Où est...? — Where is...?

Où est la boulangerie *, s'il vous plaît?*   = Where is the <u>baker's</u>, please?

the till point: la caisse

You'll need to know the names of all the other shops too:

grocer's:	l'épicerie (fem.)	*bookshop:*	la librairie
hypermarket:	l'hypermarché (masc.)	*cake shop:*	la pâtisserie
department store:	le grand magasin	*sweet shop:*	la confiserie
newsagent:	le kiosque à journaux	*fishmonger's:*	la poissonnerie
perfume shop:	la parfumerie	*delicatessen:*	la charcuterie
jeweller's:	la bijouterie	*butcher's:*	la boucherie

À quelle heure...? — What time...?

You need these useful sentences to talk about when shops are <u>open</u> or <u>closed</u>.
For times, see page 2.

À quelle heure est-ce que le magasin ouvre *?*   = What time does the shop <u>open</u>?

close: ferme

Le supermarché ouvre à neuf heures *.*   = The supermarket opens at <u>nine o'clock</u>.

Tous les magasins ferment à six heures *.*   = All the shops shut at <u>six o'clock</u>.

Allons faire les magasins! — Let's go shopping!

Il y a des soldes au centre commercial *.*   = There are <u>sales</u> <u>at the shopping centre</u>.

discounts: des réductions (fem.)   *on the internet:* sur internet

in town: en ville

Je préfère faire du shopping sur internet *.*

= I prefer to shop <u>on the internet</u>.

easier:	plus facile	*cheaper:*	moins cher
more difficult:	plus difficile	*less fun:*	moins drôle

Faire des achats sur internet, c'est plus rapide *que dans les magasins.*

= Buying things on the internet is <u>faster</u> than in the shops.

try on: essayer

Je préfère voir *les choses avant de les acheter.*   = I prefer <u>to see</u> things before buying them.

Shopping is a really important topic

You might have to talk about <u>where things are</u> and <u>when they open</u> in your speaking assessment — you'd be daft not to learn it. Get these sentences learnt along with the names of <u>all</u> the shops too.

Shopping

Est-ce que je peux vous aider? — Can I help you?

Say what you'd like using '<u>Je voudrais...</u>'

> *1kg:* un kilo   *a litre:* un litre   *a packet:* un paquet

Je voudrais cinq cents grammes **de sucre, s'il vous plaît.**

= I'd like <u>500g</u> of sugar, please.

The <u>shop assistant</u> might say: <u>You</u> could reply:

Autre chose?   = Anything else?   **Non, merci.**   = No, thank you.

C'est tout?   = Is that everything?   **Non, je voudrais aussi** une pomme de terre **, s'il vous plaît.**

> *two apples:* deux pommes (fem.)
> *three pears:* trois poires (fem.)

= No, I'd like <u>a potato</u> as well, please.

Est-ce que vous avez...? — Do you have...?

It's useful to know this vocab in case it pops up in your listening or speaking assessments.

Excusez-moi, avez-vous du pain **?**   = Excuse me, do you have any <u>bread</u>?

> *milk:* du lait   *cheese:* du fromage   *eggs:* des œufs (masc.)   *bananas:* des bananes (fem.)

Oui, le **voilà.**   = Yes, there <u>it</u> is.   **Non, nous n'en avons pas.**   = No, we don't have any.

> *it:* le / la

Je voudrais un peu de **fromage.**   = I'd like <u>a little bit of</u> cheese.

> *lots of:* beaucoup de   *a slice of:* une tranche de

> *several:* plusieurs

> For more food,
> see page 22-23.

Je voudrais quelques **pommes.**   = I'd like <u>some</u> apples.

This page covers loads more vocab for shopping

<u>Money</u> and <u>shop talk</u> are pretty important, especially for those speaking assessments. This page features <u>loads</u> of useful phrases for shopping in France too — make sure you know <u>everything</u> here.

Shopping

You might need to ask how much something <u>costs</u> in a shop.

Ça fait combien? — How much is that?

There are <u>100 cents</u> in a <u>euro</u>, like there are 100 pence in a pound.

This is what you'd <u>see</u> on a French <u>price tag</u>:

€ 5,50

This is how you <u>say</u> the price.

Ça fait **cinq euros cinquante** .

= That'll be <u>5 euros 50 cents</u>.

> *by credit card:* par carte (de crédit)

Est-ce que je peux payer en espèces ?

= Can I pay <u>with cash</u>?

Je fais des économies... — I'm saving up...

<u>Knowing</u> this useful vocab about <u>pocket money</u> will make your shop talk more <u>interesting</u>.

On me donne dix euros d'argent de poche par mois . = I get <u>ten euros</u> pocket money a <u>month</u>.

> *£5:* cinq livres

> *week:* semaine

> *I'd like to buy:*
> Je voudrais acheter

> *make-up:* du maquillage
> *computer games:* des jeux électroniques (masc.)

J'achète des vêtements de sport avec mon argent de poche.

= <u>I buy</u> <u>sports clothes</u> with my pocket money.

This page is all about money, money, money... and shopping

Money is important stuff — if you don't have any then you can't go shopping. <u>Practise</u> all this lovely French vocabulary and make sure you know this page <u>really well</u>. You'll be glad you did.

Shopping

Shopping for a bunch of bananas is all well and good, but shopping for clothes could well pop up in your exams. It's useful if you ever need to buy clothes in France too.

Les vêtements — Clothing

Most of these clothes are everyday items — so you need to know them.

J'aime **cette paire de chaussures** . = I like this pair of shoes.

Je n'aime pas **ce manteau** . = I don't like this coat.

shirt:	la chemise	sock:	la chaussette	handbag:	le sac à main
blouse:	le chemisier	shoe:	la chaussure	purse:	le porte-monnaie
trousers:	le pantalon	trainer:	la basket	wallet:	le portefeuille
jeans:	le jean	sandal:	la sandale	pyjamas:	le pyjama
shorts:	le short	hat:	le chapeau	raincoat:	l'imperméable (masc.)
dress:	la robe	scarf:	le foulard	hoody:	le pull à capuche
jacket:	la veste	tie:	la cravate	casual jacket:	le blouson
skirt:	la jupe	glove:	le gant	swimming costume:	le maillot de bain
jumper:	le pull	watch:	la montre		

They might ask what colour you want — quelle couleur...?

Colours crop up all over the place. Remember, the colour goes after the noun, and has to agree with it.

Colours: les couleurs (fem.)

black:	noir(e)	brown:	marron
white:	blanc(he)	orange:	orange
red:	rouge	pink:	rose
yellow:	jaune	purple:	violet(te)
green:	vert(e)	light blue:	bleu clair
blue:	bleu(e)	dark blue:	bleu foncé

Je voudrais un pantalon **bleu** . = I'd like a pair of blue trousers.

Je voudrais une jupe **verte** . = I'd like a green skirt.

There are some handy lists to learn on this page

It's common sense — just don't forget your clothes. Some of them are dead easy — le pyjama, le pull, le short etc. Others need a bit more effort. It'll be worth it though, so learn these words.

Shopping

Here's another <u>pretty important</u> page of lovely French shopping stuff — and it's not too tricky.

Je voudrais... — I would like...

Make sure you're really comfortable with '<u>Je voudrais</u>' — you'll be needing it <u>all the time</u>.

Je voudrais *un pantalon, s'il vous plaît. Je prends la taille* **quarante-quatre** *.*

= <u>I'd like</u> a pair of trousers, please. I'm size <u>44</u>.

> Another good way to say 'I would like' is 'J'aimerais...'.

> Continental sizes:
>
>   *size:* la taille
> *dress size 8 / 10 / 12 / 14 / 16:* 36 / 38 / 40 / 42 / 44
> *shoe size 5 / 6 / 7 / 8 / 9 / 10:* 38 / 39 / 41 / 42 / 43 / 44

> For clothing, see page 66.

> *a receipt:*   un reçu
> *an exchange:*   un échange

Je voudrais *un remboursement , s'il vous plaît.*

= I'd like <u>a refund</u>, please.

Est-ce que vous le prenez? — Will you be taking that?

To buy or not to buy — that is the question. <u>Learn</u> these useful phrases too:

> *it:* le / la

Je **le** *prends.*   = I'll take <u>it</u>.

> *It's too small:*   C'est trop petit
> *It's a bit old-fashioned:*   C'est un peu démodé

Je ne le prends pas. **Je n'aime pas la couleur** *.*

= I'll leave it. <u>I don't like the colour.</u>

More super shopping vocab to learn

There's loads of shopping language here that'll come in really <u>handy</u>. Learn as much of this as you can. And <u>remember</u> — as long as you <u>know</u> your stuff, you'll do <u>fine</u> in your GCSE.

Shopping

This page is all about adding a bit more detail to your shopping conversations
— and that's how you'll bag those <u>extra marks</u>.

Je cherche... — I'm looking for...

Details are good — try to memorise these easy phrases.

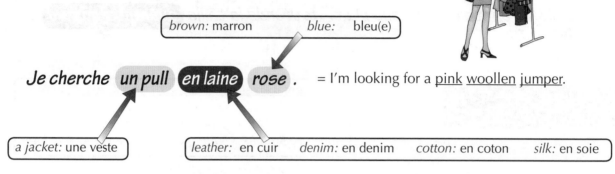

| *brown:* marron | *blue:* bleu(e) |

Je cherche **un pull** **en laine** **rose** . = I'm looking for a <u>pink</u> <u>woollen</u> <u>jumper</u>.

| *a jacket:* une veste |

| *leather:* en cuir | *denim:* en denim | *cotton:* en coton | *silk:* en soie |

The 'en' means 'of them'. See page 190.

Est-ce que vous en avez **un** *?*   = Do you have <u>one</u>?

Use '*une*' if the item requested is feminine or '*d'autres*' if you want to say 'other ones'.

C'est à la mode — It's in fashion

It's good to talk about the <u>latest trends</u> too...

| *This summer:* Cet été | *This season:* Cette saison |

Cet automne tout le monde porte **un pull à capuche** .

= <u>This autumn</u> everyone is wearing <u>a hoody</u>.

Cette saison toutes les filles portent une jupe.

= This season all the girls are wearing skirts.

Les vêtements des années soixante sont à la mode cette année.

= The clothes of the sixties are fashionable this year.

These phrases will help make your sentences more interesting

The examiners will love it if you can add a bit of <u>extra detail</u> to your sentences — it'll win you those <u>all-important</u> bonus marks. Learn this stuff so you can talk about the latest <u>fashions</u> and <u>trends</u>.

Inviting People Out

You'll need the right phrases for inviting people out in French.

Sortons — Let's go out

These are all really <u>useful</u> phrases for the assessments, so get them <u>learnt</u>.

Using the 'nous' form here means 'let's' — see p.222.

Allons **à la piscine** . = Let's go <u>to the swimming pool</u>.

to the theatre: au théâtre	to the park: au parc

Oui, je veux bien. = Yes, I'd love to.

Good idea!:	Bonne idée!
Great!:	Super!

Non, merci . = No, thank you.

I'm sorry, I can't:	Je suis désolé(e), je ne peux pas
I don't have enough money:	Je n'ai pas assez d'argent

Je préférerais nager — I'd prefer to go swimming

To suggest an alternative activity or to talk about your dream hobby, use the <u>conditional</u>.

Si j'étais riche, **je ferais du ski** *tous les week-ends.*

I'd buy clothes: j'achèterais des vêtements
I'd go clubbing: j'irais en boîte (de nuit)

= If I was rich, <u>I would go skiing</u> every weekend.

If you learn this and use it in the right way you'll score loads more marks — worth it, even though it's a bit tricky.

For more on the conditional, see page 220-221.

J'organise une surprise-partie...
— I'm organising a surprise party...

This stuff will be extra-useful if you're planning a surprise party.

On va **écouter de la musique** *et manger* **une pizza** .

= We're going <u>to listen to music</u> and eat <u>a pizza</u>.

to watch movies: regarder des films		sweets:	des bonbons
to dance:	danser	popcorn:	du pop-corn

For more foods, see page 22-23.

Veux-tu venir? = Do you want to come?

Il nous faudra **du chocolat** . = We'll need <u>some chocolate</u>.

some films: des films	some CDs: des CD

Est-ce que tu peux amener **du pop-corn** ? = Can you bring <u>some popcorn</u>?

Saying "Je préférerais..." + activity is very impressive

Now you've got that <u>sorted</u> you'll be perfectly set for any invitation or social event that comes your way. If you're still unsure, then <u>go back</u> over it until you know it all without looking at the page.

Going Out

This stuff about <u>buying tickets</u>, <u>opening times</u> and <u>where things are</u> is essential — you need to be able to <u>talk</u> about it for your speaking assessments, or <u>understand</u> it in the listening exam.

...près d'ici? — ...near here?

Est-ce qu'il y a un théâtre près d'ici? = Is there <u>a theatre</u> near here?

a *sports field:* un terrain de sport
a *bowling alley:* un bowling
a *cinema:* un cinéma

play tennis: jouer au tennis   *go for walks:* se promener

Peut-on nager près d'ici? = Can we <u>swim</u> near here?

Je voudrais un billet, s'il vous plaît. = I'd like one ticket, please.

Qu'est-ce qu'il y a à l'affiche? — What's on?

À quelle heure commence le spectacle ? = When does <u>the performance</u> <u>start</u>?

finish: finit

the film: le film   *the match:* le match

Il commence à huit heures et finit à dix heures .

= It starts at <u>8.00</u> and finishes at <u>10.00</u>.

Est-ce que c'est un film d'horreur ? = Is it a <u>horror</u> film?

romantic:	d'amour	*comedy:*	comique
adventure:	d'aventures	*war:*	de guerre
sci-fi:	de science-fiction	*police:*	policier

Learn all the questions and answers on this page

This stuff could come up in your <u>speaking assessment</u> or <u>listening exam</u> — you need to be able to <u>understand</u> it all... So don't just sit there, let's get to it — <u>get into gear</u> and get down to it.

Going Out

Ask how much it costs — 'Combien ça coûte?'

Combien coûte l'entrée **à la piscine** *?*   = How much does it cost to go <u>swimming</u>?

> *bowling:* au bowling
> *to the cinema:* au cinéma

Ça coûte **deux euros** *l'heure.*   = It costs <u>2 euros</u> per hour.

Combien coûte **un billet** *?*   = How much does <u>one ticket</u> cost?

Un billet coûte cinq euros.   = One ticket costs 5 euros.

> *How much do two tickets cost?:*
> Combien coûtent deux billets ?
>
> Plural endings.

> *two tickets:* deux billets

Je voudrais **un billet** *, s'il vous plaît.*   = I'd like <u>one ticket</u>, please.

Quand est-ce que la piscine est ouverte?
— When is the swimming pool open?

For other places, see p. 111-112.

À quelle heure est-ce que **la piscine** *est* **ouverte** *?*   = What time is <u>the swimming pool</u> <u>open</u>?

> *the sports centre:* le centre sportif

> *closed:* fermé(e)

> 'Il' for a masculine place.

Elle ouvre à **neuf heures et demie** *et ferme à* **cinq heures** *.*

= It opens at <u>half past nine</u> and closes at <u>five o'clock</u>.

Knowing when places open and close is really useful

This is vital stuff for your exams right here on this page. Learn how to ask <u>how much</u> tickets cost for things, and when places <u>open</u> and <u>close</u>. You'll be <u>stuck</u> if you don't know it.

Going Out

Je suis allé(e) au cinéma — I went to the cinema

There's a chance you'll have to mention what you did last weekend. Make sure you have an answer.

my parents: mes parents *some friends:* des ami(e)s	*in the evening:* le soir *later:* plus tard

J'ai regardé un film avec un ami et après nous avons mangé au restaurant.

= I watched a film with a friend and afterwards we ate in a restaurant.

I went shopping: J'ai fait du shopping *I went clubbing:* Je suis allé(e) en boîte (de nuit)

Est-ce que le film était bon? — Was the film good?

You've got to be able to say whether you thought the film was any good.

Qu'est-ce que tu penses du film ? = What do you think of the film?

of the performance:	du spectacle
of the play:	de la pièce (de théâtre)
of the concert:	du concert

Il était assez bon . = It was quite good.

very good:	très bon(ne)
bad:	mauvais(e)

To find out more about giving opinions, see pages 10-12.

If you're asked about something feminine, you need 'Elle' here. But 'le film' is masculine — so this is 'Il'.

Le film était bon, mais on était trop proche de l'écran . = The film was good, but we were too close to the screen.

too far from the stage: trop loin de la scène

Qui a gagné le match? — Who won the match?

It looks really good if you can give some details in the past tense about what you've seen.

J'étais très content(e) du résultat. = I was really pleased with the result.

I wasn't: Je n'étais pas

jumped: a sauté *passed the ball:* a passé le ballon

lost: a perdu

Mon joueur préféré a marqué deux fois.

= My favourite player scored twice.

Mon équipe a gagné .

= My team won.

Learn all this and you won't be stuck for things to say

There's a lot to learn on this page but I'm afraid that's no excuse for not revising it. Get stuck in and it won't be long before you're giving your opinion on the latest rom-com in perfect French.

Quick Questions

Here's another set of quick questions to test your knowledge of the last few pages. First, have a go at answering them all so you can work out which bits you know and which bits you don't. Then go back over the bits you couldn't remember until you can answer every question without hesitating.

Quick Questions

1) Ask where each of the following shops is:
   a) the newsagent   b) the bookshop   c) the butchers

2) You're staying at a French hotel and you ask the receptionist about the shops in the town. She tells you, "Tous les magasins ferment à sept heures sauf le supermarché. Le supermarché ferme à neuf heures." What has she said to you?

3) Your French friend wants to go shopping. Tell her that you prefer to shop on the internet because it's faster and there are always sales.

4) How would you say "to try on clothes" in French?

5) You're in a shop in Paris. The shop assistant says, "Est-ce que je peux vous aider?" What has she asked you?

6) Write a sentence in French saying that you would like a litre of water and a kilo of potatoes. Then ask the shop assistant if they have any cheese.

7) "Je voudrais quelques cerises et une tranche de jambon." What does this mean?

8) What is the French for:
   a) cash   b) credit card?

9) Tell your friend in French that you get £15 pocket money a month.

10) Your friend Chantelle tells you, "Je fais des économies. Je voudrais acheter un sac à main." What has she said to you?

11) Write down the words for the following items of clothing in French:
   a) hat   b) trousers   c) jumper   d) dress   e) raincoat   f) tie

12) You're writing your Christmas list to give to your French grandma. Write a sentence for each item of clothing, saying that you would like it:
   a) a red wallet
   b) a light blue shirt
   c) a dark purple scarf

13) How would you say, "I'm size 42" in French?

14) You're flicking through a French fashion magazine and you find a page about the latest fashion trends. It says, "Cet été toutes les filles portent un short et un chemisier blanc. En ce moment, les cravates sont très à la mode pour les garçons." Translate this into English.

15) How would you say "Let's go to the cinema tonight" in French?

16) Tell your French friend that you're organising a surprise party. Ask them to bring some films and some sweets.

17) What does, "Est-ce qu'il y a un terrain de sport près d'ici?" mean?

18) Ask when the swimming pool opens and how much it costs to go swimming.

19) Your French friend went to the cinema last night. He says, "J'ai regardé un film avec ma petite amie. C'était un film comique et il était très bon." Translate what he said into English.

20) You've just been to a football match. Your friend Monique asks you, "Qui a gagné le match?" What has she asked you?

Listening Questions

Track 6

These people are going out. Where are they meeting and at what time?

	Where?	What time?
Example	**in front of the swimming pool**	**2 o'clock / 14:00**
1		
2		
3		

Track 7

4   You're on the phone listening to the information about film times at the Rex Cinema this afternoon. Complete the following sentences.

a)   The first film starts at ....

b)   The film ends at ....

c)   It costs .... for an adult.

d)   It costs .... for a young person.

Track 8

A group of French teenagers are talking about their hobbies. What activities do they like to do and when? Complete the table.

	Activity	When
Example	**swimming**	**at the weekend**
5		
6		
7		

Listening Questions

Track 9

8 You'll hear someone talking about a concert they went to recently.

a) When was the concert? ....

b) Where did she meet her friends? ....

c) Was the concert good? ....

d) What did she like about the concert? ....

Track 10

These people are talking about hobbies. Fill in the table.

	Name	Activity	When?
Example	**Nasser**	**computer games**	**after school**
9	Myriam		
10	Simone		
11	Davy		

Track 11

How much pocket money do these French teenagers get? What do they spend their money on? Fill in the table.

	How much?	What do they buy?
Example	**8 euros a week**	**CDs and magazines**
12		
13		

Reading Question

1   Read each person's opinion on new technology, then answer the question below.

Camille, 17 ans

Je suis étudiante à l'université et je passe beaucoup de temps à la bibliothèque. J'ai beaucoup d'amis et je fais des efforts pour les voir. Pour moi le contact humain est très important et les machines ne peuvent pas remplacer cela. Je dois dire que je suis assez technophobe, je n'aime envoyer ni courriers électroniques ni textos.

Jérôme, 14 ans

Mes parents ne sont pas contents de moi. Je suis dans mon nouveau collège depuis seulement deux mois et j'ai déjà eu trois heures de retenue. Le problème c'est que les copains de mon ancien collège m'envoient des textos quand je suis en classe. Mon portable est très important pour moi car il me permet de rester en contact avec mes copains.

Mathilde, 16 ans

Ça ne me dérange pas d'utiliser l'ordinateur pour communiquer avec mes amies parce que c'est très facile de s'en servir. En fait je peux vivre avec ou sans mon ordinateur. Je ne pense pas qu'il soit nécessaire pour les étudiants d'en avoir mais c'est vrai que ça peut aider quelquefois.

Brice, 19 ans

J'ai toujours été fana de nouvelles technologies. Quand j'étais plus jeune, mes parents avaient un ordinateur et je passais mon temps à jouer sur la console Nintendo®. Je suis toujours sur l'ordinateur. J'ai même mon propre site où je blogue et je reçois des emails de mes amis ainsi que de mes professeurs.

Write whether the students are for (F), against (A) or have no strong opinion (N) about technology.

1. Camille   [ ]

2. Jérôme   [ ]

3. Mathilde   [ ]

4. Brice   [ ]

Reading Question

2   Read each paragraph, then answer the questions below.

Je me sers toujours de l'internet pour mes achats. En ce moment je suis en terminale, et je vais bientôt passer mon bac donc je n'ai pas beaucoup de temps libre pour faire les magasins. Par conséquent l'internet m'aide beaucoup. On peut surfer sur internet et faire des achats à n'importe quelle heure ou même le dimanche quand la plupart des magasins sont fermés. — **Élodie, 18 ans.**

L'internet, ce n'est pas mon truc. Il y a à peu près deux mois maintenant j'ai essayé de télécharger de la musique, car il y avait quelques chansons que je voulais acheter. Malheureusement, j'ai dû appuyer sur une mauvaise touche parce que j'ai fini par acheter trois albums, ce qui m'a coûté presque trente euros au lieu de trois! Franchement je n'étais pas contente. — **Naomie, 19 ans.**

L'internet, c'est simple, je ne peux pas m'en passer! J'achète tout en ligne, mes vêtements, mes livres, ma musique, mes entrées de cinéma. N'importe qui peut naviguer sur internet, nous habitons à la campagne et ma mère ne peut plus s'empêcher de tout commander sur internet. Le seul problème pour moi c'est que je finis toujours par dépenser tout mon argent de poche très rapidement. — **Marc, 18 ans.**

En ce qui me concerne les achats sur internet c'est terminé! Plusieurs fois j'ai commandé des vêtements et à chaque fois j'ai été déçue et j'ai dû tout renvoyer parce que rien ne me va jamais! Les vêtements sont toujours soit trop petits soit trop grands, ou ils sont moches. — **Amélie, 21 ans.**

Write the correct person's name next to each question.

1.   Who never buys the right clothes sizes online?   ....

2.   Who is able to go online whenever they want?   ....

3.   Who spends all their money by shopping online?   ....

4.   Who will need to go on an ICT refresher course?   ....

5.   Who cannot live without the internet?   ....

Speaking Question

This speaking assessment is all about your favourite music and what musical instruments you can play. Don't forget that you'll need a friend to help you out and take the teacher's role.

Task: Music

You are talking about music with your French friend. Your teacher will play the part of your friend and will ask you the following questions:

- Do you listen to music a lot?
- Where do you like listening to it?
- What kind of music do you like?
- Where do you buy your music?
- Do you listen to music on the radio?
- Do you play a musical instrument?
- !

! Remember that the exclamation mark means you'll have to answer a question that you won't have prepared an answer to.

The whole conversation should last about five minutes.

Teacher's Role

You need to ask the student the following questions. You should speak first.

1 Est-ce que tu écoutes souvent de la musique?

2 Où est-ce que tu aimes l'écouter?

3 Quelle genre de musique aimes-tu?

4 Où est-ce que tu achètes ta musique?

5 Tu écoutes de la musique à la radio?

6 Est-ce que tu joues d'un instrument?

7 !

! The unpredictable question could be:

Quel genre de musique est-ce que tu n'aimes pas?

Writing Questions

Task 1: Pocket Money

Your French teacher has asked you to write a short piece about money for the school magazine. You should try to write 250-300 words.

You could include:

* how much pocket money you get,
* whether or not you have to help at home to earn your pocket money,
* your views on saving your pocket money,
* whether you have a part time job or plan to get one in the future,
* the sorts of things you usually buy with your pocket money,
* your opinion on whether parents should give their children money,
* advice to other students on what to do with their money.

Remember that to score the highest grades you need to answer the task as fully as possible, expanding on the points above when it is relevant to do so.

Task 2: Leisure Activities

You're writing a piece for your French blog about the activities available for teenagers in Britain today. You should try to write 250-300 words.

You could include:

* what hobbies you have and why you like them,
* what you usually do at the weekends,
* an activity you'd like to do during the holidays,
* the films you've seen at the cinema,
* whether you can afford to do all the activities you'd like to,
* your views on the activities available in your town,
* whether you think there's enough for teenagers to do in the UK.

Remember that to score the highest grades you need to answer the task as fully as possible, expanding on the points above when it is relevant to do so.

Revision Summary

These questions are here to make sure you <u>know your stuff</u>. Work through them <u>all</u>, check the ones you couldn't do, <u>look back</u> through the section for the answers, then have another go. And (eventually) <u>voilà</u>.

1) What is the French for each of these sports? What's the French for the place where you would do them? a) football b) swimming c) snowboarding d) ice skating

2) Write down as many French words as you can to do with playing or listening to music.

3) Say that you go swimming at the weekend and that you're a member of a badminton club.

4) You like watching films and soaps on TV. Tonight you'd like to watch a documentary that starts at nine o'clock. How would you say this in French?

5) Think of a film you saw recently and one you saw a month ago, and say this in French. (You don't have to translate the film titles into French.)

6) You have just watched an interesting and surprising show. Say this in French. Remember to tell me its title and tell me what happened.

7) Your friend Paul is music mad. Ask him in French whether he listens to music on the radio, or on his MP3 player. Now pretend to be Paul and answer the question, giving a reason.

8) Nadine thinks she's fallen in love with Robbie Williams. Write her a short email in French saying what you think about celebrities and what you think about him in particular.

9) Aimerais-tu être célèbre? Pourquoi? (Give <u>two</u> reasons.)

10) Your French uncle wants to find out the UK weather forecast on the web, but he's not very internet savvy. Tell him there's a link on the homepage of the BBC website.

11) You check your email inbox every day. Tell the French-speaking world.

12) You're out of bread. How do you ask where the baker's is and whether it's open?

13) What are the French names for: a) a newsagent b) a cake shop c) a butcher's d) a bookshop e) a sweet shop f) a supermarket g) a department store?

14) Est-ce que tu préfères faire les courses sur internet ou en ville? Pourquoi?

15) A shop assistant asks you 'Est-ce que je peux vous aider?' and later 'Voulez-vous autre chose?' What do these two questions mean in English? How would you answer them?

16) You want to buy a brown jumper, size 38, and some cotton pyjamas. How do you say this to the shop assistant?

17) Describe your perfectly planned surprise party in no more than 3 French sentences.

18) Tu veux aller au concert. Le concert commence à vingt et une heures et finit à vingt-deux heures trente. Un billet coûte cinq euros. Comment est-ce qu'on dit ça en anglais?

19) Décris-moi un spectacle, un film ou un match que tu as vu récemment. (3 phrases max.)

Holiday Destinations

You need to know about <u>countries</u> and <u>nationalities</u> for describing yourself or your <u>holiday</u> plans.

D'où viens-tu? — Where do you come from?

Learn this phrase <u>off by heart</u> — if the country you're from isn't here, check in a dictionary.

Je viens **d'Angleterre** . *Je suis* **anglais(e)** . = I come <u>from England</u>. I am <u>English</u>.

from Wales:	du pays de Galles
from Northern Ireland:	d'Irlande du Nord
from Scotland:	d'Écosse

Welsh:	gallois(e)
Northern Irish:	irlandais(e) du nord
Scottish:	écossais(e)

> <u>IMPORTANT BIT:</u>
> You must add '<u>e</u>' on the end for <u>women and girls</u> (see page 170).
> *Je suis anglaise.*

Je suis **anglophone** .

French-speaking: francophone

= I am <u>English-speaking</u>.

J'habite en **Angleterre** . = I live in <u>England</u>.

Où habites-tu? = Where do you live?

or 'Où est-ce que tu habites?'

Use 'en' for feminine countries and masculine ones beginning with a vowel, and 'au' for all other masculine countries. For plural countries, it's 'aux'.

Learn these foreign countries

You also need to <u>understand</u> where <u>other people</u> come from.

Algeria:	l'Algérie (fem.)
America:	l'Amérique (fem.) / les États-Unis (masc.)
Australia:	l'Australie (fem.)
Austria:	l'Autriche (fem.)
Belgium:	la Belgique
Canada:	le Canada
China:	la Chine
France:	la France
Germany:	l'Allemagne (fem.)
Greece:	la Grèce
Holland:	la Hollande
Netherlands:	les Pays-Bas (masc.)
India:	l'Inde (fem.)
Italy:	l'Italie (fem.)
Japan:	le Japon
Morocco:	le Maroc
Poland:	la Pologne
Portugal:	le Portugal
Spain:	l'Espagne (fem.)
Switzerland:	la Suisse

African:	africain(e)
Algerian:	algérien(ne)
American:	américain(e)
Australian:	australien(ne)
Austrian:	autrichien(ne)
Belgian:	belge
Canadian:	canadien(ne)
Chinese:	chinois(e)
French:	français(e)
German:	allemand(e)
Greek:	grec/grecque
Dutch:	néerlandais(e)
Indian:	indien(ne)
Italian:	italien(ne)
Japanese:	japonais(e)
Moroccan:	marocain(e)
Polish:	polonais(e)
Portuguese:	portugais(e)
Spanish:	espagnol(e)
Swiss:	suisse

Map labels: L'Écosse, L'Irlande du Nord, La Grande-Bretagne, L'Angleterre, La République d'Irlande, La Pologne, Le pays de Galles, L'Allemagne, La Belgique, La France, La Suisse, Le Portugal, L'Espagne, L'Italie

England:	l'Angleterre (f.)
Northern Ireland:	l'Irlande du Nord (f.)
Scotland:	l'Écosse (f.)
Wales:	le pays de Galles
Great Britain:	la Grande-Bretagne
Republic of Ireland:	la République d'Irlande

English:	anglais(e)
Irish:	irlandais(e)
Scottish:	écossais(e)
Welsh:	gallois(e)
British:	britannique

IMPORTANT: <u>Don't</u> use a capital letter for all these adjectives.

You need to know how to spell these countries and nationalities

These <u>countries</u> and <u>nationalities</u> aren't too hard, so <u>learn them all</u>. With the ones where the French word is <u>a bit like the English</u>, check you've got the <u>spelling</u> right — e.g. <u>Italy</u> and <u>Italie</u>.

Catching the Train

This page gives you a few of the <u>basics</u> you might come across in the exam.

Je veux y aller en train — I want to go there by train

Here's how to buy a <u>ticket</u>. You'd be <u>nuts</u> not to learn this.

Est-ce qu'il y a un train **pour Paris** *?*   = Is there a train <u>to Paris</u>?

> *second class:* deuxième classe

Un **aller simple** *pour Paris, en* **première classe** *.*

> Two: Deux
> Three: Trois

> *single(s):*   aller(s) simple(s)
> *return(s):*   aller-retour(s)

= <u>One</u> <u>single</u> to Paris, <u>first class</u>.

Un aller-retour pour Paris, s'il vous plaît.   = One return ticket to Paris, please.

Vous voyagez quand? — When are you travelling?

Here are a few more <u>details</u> about rail travel.

> *today:*   aujourd'hui
> *next Monday:*   lundi prochain
> *on the tenth of June:* le dix juin

Je voudrais aller à Caen, **samedi** *.*   = I would like to travel to Caen <u>on Saturday</u>.

Quand est-ce que le train **part pour** *Caen?*   = When does the train <u>leave for</u> Caen?

> *arrive at:* arrive à

\\\\\\\\\\\\\\\\\\///////
For more info on
times and dates,
see pages 2-4.
///////////\\\\\\\\\

Le train **part de** *quel quai?*   = Which platform does the train <u>leave from</u>?

And this is how to ask <u>where stuff is</u>.

> *the waiting room:* la salle d'attente   *the left luggage:* la consigne

> *the ticket windows:* les guichets (masc.)

Où est **le quai** *, s'il vous plaît?*

= Where is <u>the platform</u>, please?

Où sont **les toilettes** *, s'il vous plaît?*

= Where are <u>the toilets</u>, please?

Excusez-moi Monsieur, je cherche **le wagon-restaurant** *.*   = Excuse me sir, I'm looking for <u>the restaurant car</u>.

> *the sleeping car:* le wagon-lit

You might need this railway vocabulary in your exam

Get on and revise this <u>train vocabulary</u> so you know all about <u>buying tickets</u> and <u>catching the train</u>. This could come up in the listening exam so you need to be <u>prepared</u> for any station situation.

Catching the Train

You'll need to know a bit about the French rail network too.

On prend l'Eurostar™ — We're taking Eurostar™

You could get passages like the ones below in the reading or listening parts of the exam.

"J'habite dans le Kent, mais je travaille une journée par semaine en France. Avant je prenais le bateau de Douvres à Calais mais maintenant je préfère prendre l'Eurostar™. C'est pratique."

= "I live in Kent, but I work one day a week in France. Before, I used to take the ferry from Dover to Calais but now I prefer to take the Eurostar™. It's practical."

"Je suis Parisienne, et je fais souvent des voyages à Nottingham. Je prends l'Eurostar™ et je change à St Pancras. Le trajet dure environ quatre heures et demie."

= "I am Parisian, and I make a lot of trips to Nottingham. I take the Eurostar™ and I change at St Pancras. The journey takes about four and a half hours.

Le chemin de fer — The railway

There are a few different types of trains and stations in France, and you'll need to know them.

La SNCF — Société Nationale des Chemins de fer Français — wow, no wonder they shortened it. This is the normal French train network. A train station in French is une gare SNCF.

Le TGV — Train à Grande Vitesse — the pride of the French railway system, these provide high-speed links between big cities.

Le RER — Réseau Express Régional — express regional network. The type of train that commuters use to get into Paris.

Le Métro — Métropolitain — the underground. A tube station is une station de métro (not une gare...).

You might have to listen to a Railway Announcement...

Le train à destination de Bordeaux part du quai numéro huit à quinze heures quarante-cinq.

= The train to Bordeaux leaves from platform 8 at 15:45.

And to finish, more vocab...

to depart:	partir	to get on:	monter dans	timetable:	l'horaire (masc.)
departure:	le départ	to get off:	descendre de	reclining seat:	la couchette
to arrive:	arriver	to change (trains):	changer (de train)	coming from:	en provenance de
arrival:	l'arrivée (fem.)	compartment:	le compartiment	going to:	à destination de

---

Learn all about the French railway network on this page

Examiners can ask loads of different things about travelling. So you'd better make sure you can answer all the questions they could throw at you about it. When it gets to the exam, you'll be glad you did.

All Kinds of Transport

Here's what you need to <u>know</u> about other forms of <u>transport</u>. This is another one of those topics that you'll need to know <u>really well</u> — and you need to know loads of <u>vocab</u> for it, too.

Comment y vas-tu? — How do you get there?

You might need to say <u>how</u> you <u>get about</u>.

J'y vais à pied. = I go there on foot.

to school:	à l'école / au collège

D'habitude, je vais **en ville** **en bus** .

= I normally go <u>into town</u> <u>by bus</u>.

by bus:	en bus / en autobus
on the underground:	en métro
by car:	en voiture
by coach:	en car / en autocar
by boat:	en bateau
by plane:	en avion
by Eurostar:	en Eurostar
by bike:	à vélo
by motorbike:	à moto

J'y vais **en train** .

= I go there <u>by train</u>.

Le départ et l'arrivée — Departure and arrival

These are the kinds of questions which could come up when <u>travelling</u>. Or in your <u>exam</u>, perhaps.

Est-ce qu'il y a **un bus** *pour Toulouse?* = Is there <u>a bus</u> to Toulouse?

a flight: un vol	*a coach:* un car	*a train:* un train

Quand part **le prochain bus** *pour Amiens?* = When does <u>the next bus</u> to Amiens leave?

the (next) coach: le (prochain) car	*the (next) flight:* le (prochain) vol

Quand est-ce que **l'avion** *arrive à Marseille?* = When does <u>the plane</u> arrive in Marseilles?

Quel bus...? — Which bus...?

No doubt about it — you need to be able to ask <u>which bus</u> or <u>train</u> goes <u>where</u>. Just learn <u>this</u>.

Quel bus *va* **au centre-ville** *, s'il vous plaît?* = <u>Which bus</u> goes <u>to the town centre</u>, please?

Which train... : Quel train...

to the station:	à la gare
to the airport:	à l'aéroport (masc.)
to the harbour / port:	au port

C'est bien le bus pour **l'aéroport** *?* = Is this the right bus for <u>the airport</u>?

Learn the names for different kinds of transport

There's a chance this <u>lovely lot</u> will come up in your listening exam, so <u>revise</u> this page until there's not an exam question that could catch you out. You certainly won't <u>regret</u> it.

Holiday Accommodation

This page has all the words you need to know about <u>hotels</u>, <u>hostels</u>, <u>camping</u> and <u>foreign exchanges</u>.

Je cherche un logement — I'm looking for somewhere to stay

Learn these different <u>places to stay</u>...

hotel: l'hôtel (masc.)

campsite: le camping

self-catering cottage: le gîte

youth hostel: l'auberge de jeunesse (fem.)

host family: la famille d'accueil

Learn this vocabulary for Hotels and Hostels

<u>Verbs used in hotels:</u>

to recommend:	recommander	*to stay:*	rester
to reserve:	réserver	*to leave:*	partir
to confirm:	confirmer	*to cost:*	coûter

<u>Things you might want to ask for:</u>

full board (room + all meals): la pension complète
half board (room + some meals): la demi-pension

<u>Parts of a hotel or youth hostel:</u>

restaurant:	le restaurant
dining room:	la salle à manger
dormitory:	le dortoir
lift:	l'ascenseur (masc.)
stairs:	l'escalier (masc.)
car park:	le parking

<u>Things about your room:</u>

key:	la clé, la clef
balcony:	le balcon
bath:	le bain
shower:	la douche
washbasin:	le lavabo

<u>Paying for your stay:</u>

bill:	la note
(set) price:	le prix (fixe)

Je fais un échange — I'm going on a school exchange

If you get a question about exchange visits, <u>don't panic</u>.

Je reste chez une famille française.

with a host family: en famille d'accueil

= I'm staying <u>with a French family</u>.

<u>Useful exchange vocab:</u>

to write to:	correspondre (avec)
to get to know:	faire la connaissance de
to invite:	inviter
hospitality:	l'hospitalité (fem.)
present / gift:	le cadeau

J'aurai ma propre chambre. = I'll have <u>my own room</u>.

the chance to speak French every day: l'occasion de parler français tous les jours

---

There's so much useful vocab on this page

There are some <u>crucial</u> words on this page which could crop up in lots of <u>different</u> exam situations.
You could <u>hear</u> a hotel reservation, <u>read</u> a hotel review or have to <u>talk</u> about your last holiday.

Booking a Room

It's crucial when you're <u>planning</u> a holiday to be able to talk about everything on this page.

Avez-vous des chambres libres?

— Do you have any rooms free?

double:
pour deux personnes

Je voudrais une **chambre** **pour une personne** . = I'd like a <u>single</u> <u>room</u>.

room with a bath: chambre avec bain
room with a balcony: chambre avec balcon

You could be a bit more specific and use these.

For more numbers, see page 1.

Je voudrais rester ici **deux nuits** . = I'd like to stay here <u>two nights</u>.

one night: une nuit

If there's more than one person, use deux personne<u>s</u>, trois personne<u>s</u> etc.

C'est combien par nuit pour **une personne** ? = How much is it per night for <u>one person</u>?

Je **la** *prends.* = I'll take <u>it</u>.

If the 'it' you're talking about is masculine (e.g. 'le gîte') then use 'le'.

it: le / la

Je ne **la** *prends pas.* = I won't take <u>it</u>.

You'll need a holiday after all this revision

Even if you think you'll <u>never</u> go on holiday or book a hotel room in France, there's <u>no excuse</u> for not learning everything that's on this page. Make sure you know the <u>example sentences</u> and the <u>vocab</u> too.

Booking a Pitch

Est-ce qu'on peut camper ici? — Can I camp here?

It's a good idea to get familiar with this camping vocab for your exams.

Je voudrais un emplacement pour une nuit. = I'd like <u>a pitch</u> for <u>one night</u>.

two weeks: deux semaines

pitch (place for a tent): un emplacement

sleeping bag: un sac de couchage

caravan: une caravane

tent: une tente

You may have to book ahead. See page 15 for how to write formal letters.

You might need these phrases too:

Est-ce qu'il y a de l'eau potable ici? = Is there drinking water here?

Est-ce que je peux allumer un feu ici? = Can I light a fire here?

Où est-ce que je peux trouver...? = Where can I find...?

Learning camping vocab is no picnic, that's for sure

This might seem like a <u>mini topic</u> compared to all the stuff about booking hotels, but it's <u>important</u> to know it. That way, if a question comes up about something on this page, you'll be <u>ready</u> for it.

Planning Your Holiday

Money transactions, excursions and hiring stuff... all extremely important aspects of effective holiday planning. If you want to get great marks, you'd better get learning these unbelievably useful phrases.

Le bureau de change — The currency exchange

Well, you won't get far without money — so learn this stuff carefully.

Je voudrais changer *de l'argent* .   = I would like to change <u>some money</u>.

> £50: cinquante livres sterling

Je voudrais encaisser *ce chèque de voyage* .   = I would like to cash <u>this traveller's cheque</u>.

> *these traveller's cheques:* ces chèques de voyage

Voulez-vous voir *une pièce d'identité* ?   = Do you want to see <u>proof of identity</u>?

> *my passport:*   mon passeport
> *my driving licence:*   mon permis de conduire

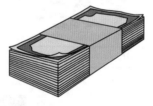

Le syndicat d'initiative — The tourist office

Here's how you <u>find out</u> what a town's got to offer...

Pouvez-vous me donner des renseignements sur *le zoo* , *s'il vous plaît?*

    = Can you give me information about <u>the zoo</u>, please?

> *the town:* la ville

Où est *le musée* , *s'il vous plaît?*   = Where is <u>the museum</u>, please?

> *the church:*   l'église

It's important to know what happens in the bureau de change

The <u>currency exchange</u> and the <u>tourist office</u> are both popular topics for the assessments. You'll also find this stuff useful if you're on <u>holiday</u> in France and you want to find out <u>what's going on</u> in the area.

Planning Your Holiday

Peut-on partir en excursion?

— Can we go on an excursion?

the museums in Metz:
les musées de Metz

Avez-vous des brochures sur **les excursions autour de Lyon** ?

= Do you have any brochures about <u>excursions around Lyons</u>?

Je voudrais **visiter Versailles** . = I'd like <u>to visit Versailles</u>.

to go to a museum:	aller au musée
to visit the palace / castle:	visiter le château

from the church: de l'église (fem.)
from the market: du marché

Ce car va à Versailles. **Le car** part **de l'hôtel de ville** à **une heure et demie** .

The train: Le train

2 o'clock: deux heures   *3:15:* trois heures quinze

= This coach goes to Versailles. <u>The coach</u> leaves <u>from the town hall</u> at <u>half past one</u>.

Je voudrais louer des skis — I'd like to hire some skis

one week: une semaine

Je voudrais louer **un vélo** pour **deux jours** .

sleeping bags: des sacs de couchage

= I'd like to hire <u>a bike</u> for <u>two days</u>.

You might need to find out about an excursion too

There's more stuff to learn here that will be <u>useful</u> in any French exam or tourist information centre in France. Make sure you know the <u>questions</u> to ask and the <u>answers</u> to reply, just in case you need them.

Quick Questions

This is the first set of quick questions for this section and there's a fair bit to learn here. There's really nothing for it, so get stuck in with the first question and make your way down to the end — by then you should have a pretty good grasp of all the French vocab on the last few pages.

Quick Questions

1) Fabien asks you: "D'où viens-tu?" Tell him you're from Wales and you're Welsh.

2) Write down the French for:

   a) an Irish girl   b) a French boy   c) an Italian girl   d) a German girl

3) What does "Je suis anglophone" mean?

4) Write down the French for the following countries:

   a) Germany   b) Spain   c) Switzerland   d) England   e) Scotland

5) What does 'Est-ce qu'il y a un train pour Lyon?' mean in English?

6) Write down these words in French:

   a) a single ticket, first class

   b) two return tickets

   c) a single ticket, second class

7) Translate these questions into English:

   a) Où est le quai, s'il vous plaît?

   b) Quand est-ce que le train part pour Paris?

   c) Vous voyagez quand?

8) What is the SNCF?

9) What is the French word for 'train timetable'?

10) Your penfriend tells you, "D'habitude je vais en ville en bus, mais le week-end j'y vais en métro. Je vais au collège à pied."

    a) How does she normally go into town?

    b) What does she do differently at the weekends?

    c) How does she go to school?

11) You're at a busy French bus station. Ask the nearest stranger which bus goes to the airport.

12) Your French teacher is telling you about the accommodation arrangements for your school trip to France. He says: "En Bretagne, on va rester chez des familles d'accueil, mais à Paris nous serons dans une auberge de jeunesse." Where will you be staying?

13) Translate these words into French:

    a) dining room   b) bill   c) lift   d) stairs   e) half board

14) You need a room for one night. How would you ask a hotel receptionist if they have any rooms free?

15) Write down the French for, "I'd like to stay here for a week, please."

16) You're camping in France. How would you ask the following questions:

    a) Can I camp here?

    b) Can I light a fire here?

    c) Where can I find a sleeping bag?

17) You're in the currency exchange in France and you hear the person in front of you in the queue ask, "Voulez-vous voir une pièce d'identité?" What does this mean?

18) What does "Je voudrais louer des sacs de couchage" mean in English?

Where / When is...?

Here's how French people ask <u>where</u> and <u>when things are</u>. It's all pretty important stuff for you to know.

Ask where things are — use 'Où est... ?'

Knowing how the French ask <u>where</u> things are is supremely important — get these <u>learnt</u>.

Où est **la salle à manger** *, s'il vous plaît?* = Where is <u>the dining room</u>, please?

the car park:	le parking
the games room:	la salle de jeu
the telephone:	le téléphone

Où sont **les toilettes** *?* = Where are <u>the toilets</u>?

If the place you're looking for is plural, remember to use 'Où sont...' instead of 'Où est...'

Use 'Elle' for 'la' words, 'Elles' and 'Ils' for plural words and 'Il' for 'le' words.

Elle est **au** **troisième étage** *.* = <u>It's</u> on the <u>third floor</u>.

Use 'au' here because 'étage' is masculine.
Use 'à la' for feminine words, e.g. 'elle est à la piscine'.

fourth floor:	quatrième étage
second floor:	deuxième étage
first floor:	premier étage
ground floor:	rez-de-chaussée

For higher floor numbers, see page 1.

<u>Other words you might need:</u>

straight on:	tout droit	*outside:*	à l'extérieur
upstairs:	en haut	*on the left / right:*	à gauche / à droite
downstairs:	en bas	*at the end of the corridor:*	au bout du couloir

À quelle heure est... ? — At what time is... ?

When you've understood <u>where</u> everything is, you'll need to know <u>when</u> things happen, too...

À quelle heure est-ce que **le petit déjeuner** *est servi, s'il vous plaît?*

= At what time is <u>breakfast</u> served, please?

lunch:	le déjeuner
evening meal:	le dîner

For more times, see page 2.

Il est servi entre six heures et huit heures. = It's served between six and eight o'clock.

You'll need to learn this page really well

This stuff will really help you out in your exams if you're asked to listen to some <u>directions</u> or talk about <u>where</u> something is. Make sure you know your <u>right</u> from your <u>left</u> in French too.

Problems with Accommodation

You've got to know how to talk about problems with your accommodation for your French exam.

Il y a un problème... — There's a problem...

Make sure you can write about at least two problems.

glasses: verres (masc.)

Il n'y a pas de serviettes dans la chambre.

= There aren't any towels in the room.

cold: froid

Il fait trop chaud . = It's too hot.

La télévision est cassée. = The TV is broken.

The chair: La chaise

The phone: Le téléphone

cold: froide

L'eau est trop chaude .

= The water is too hot.

'Eau' is feminine, so remember to add an extra 'e' onto 'chaud(e)' and 'froid(e)'.

La douche ne fonctionne pas. = The shower doesn't work.

Pouah, c'est dégoûtant! — Yuck, it's disgusting!

Il y a de l'eau partout. = There is water everywhere.

mud: de la boue

The bath: Le bain

La chambre est sale. = The room is dirty.

Il y a trop de bruit — je ne peux pas dormir. = There is too much noise — I can't sleep.

Est-ce que vous pouvez faire quelque chose?
— Can you do something?

beds: des lits (masc.)

Il nous faut des serviettes supplémentaires. = We need some extra towels.

Je voudrais une autre chambre. = I would like a different room.

You'll need this page if you want to complain

Fingers crossed, you'll never need to complain about this stuff when you're on holiday in France. But you may well have to complain about an imaginary holiday during your assessments, so learn this well.

At a Restaurant

If you've <u>been</u> to <u>France</u>, a lot of these <u>signs</u> and <u>phrases</u> could be <u>familiar</u> to you. Knowing what to do in a French restaurant is really useful, and it can also come up in your exam — so this is <u>important</u> stuff.

Au restaurant... — In the restaurant...

Here are some <u>words and phrases</u> you'll find useful when talking about <u>restaurants</u>.

Ouvert

= Open

Fermé

= Closed

Plat du jour
Spécialités

= Dish of the day
Specialities

Service
compris

= Service included

Pourboire

= Tips

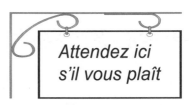

Attendez ici
s'il vous plaît

= Wait here, please

À la carte

À prix fixe

À la carte:
= Individually priced items
Menu à prix fixe:
= Fixed price menu

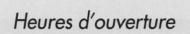

Heures d'ouverture

= Opening hours

Défense
de fumer

= No smoking

Learn the signs

These are all signs that you might <u>well</u> find in a French restaurant, or even your exam. There's n[...]
<u>many</u> words to learn on this page so there's <u>no excuse</u> for not knowing them. Get it done.

At a Restaurant

Est-ce que vous avez une table libre?

This part's <u>easy</u> — definitely worth learning.

— Do you have a table free?

Je voudrais réserver une table pour quatre *personnes, s'il vous plaît.*

> two: deux   three: trois

= I would like to reserve a table for <u>four</u>, please.

Nous sommes quatre *.*   = There are <u>four</u> of us.

Nous voudrions nous asseoir à l'extérieur *.*   = We'd like to sit <u>outside</u>.

> on the terrace: sur la terrasse

Est-ce que je peux avoir la carte, s'il vous plaît?   = May I have the menu, please?

Où sont les toilettes *, s'il vous plaît?*   = Where <u>are</u> <u>the toilets</u>, please?

> is: est

> the phone: le téléphone

> See page 91 for help asking where things are.

Je voudrais... — I would like...

Now it's time for that all-important part... <u>ordering</u>.

> See page 22-23 for food vocab.

> the steak: le bifteck
> the chocolate cake: le gâteau au chocolat

Comme plat principal *, je voudrais* la pizza au poulet *, s'il vous plaît.*

= <u>I'd like</u> <u>the chicken pizza</u>, please.

> ...tarter: hors d'oeuvre (masc.)
> ...ssert: dessert (masc.)

a "MUST LEARN" page

...ve an <u>opinion</u> about the kinds of food you'd like or want to taste. You might need to ...you'd <u>prefer</u> and whether there were any <u>problems</u> with a meal. It's all <u>useful</u> stuff.

HOLIDAYS

At a Restaurant

Désolé, il n'y a plus de porc — Sorry, there's no more pork

You may need to understand changes if they <u>haven't got</u> your order or if a <u>mistake</u> is made.

Je prendrai l'agneau à la place du porc.   = I'll have the lamb instead of the pork.

> *the lamb:* l'agneau   *the pork:* le porc

Il y a une erreur. Je n'ai pas commandé ceci .

= There's been a mistake. I didn't order <u>this</u>.

Je ne suis pas satisfait(e) — I'm not satisfied

Je voudrais me plaindre.   = I'd like to make a complaint.

> *The pork:*   Le porc

> *is too hot:*   est trop chaud
> *is too cold:* est trop froid

Le bœuf n'est pas assez cuit .   = <u>The beef</u> <u>is underdone</u>.

J'ai trouvé une mouche dans ma soupe.   = I found <u>a fly</u> in my soup.

> *a snail:* un escargot *a hair:* un cheveu

Le service ici est affreux.   = The service here is awful.

Est-ce que vous avez fini? — Have you finished?

There's <u>no</u> getting away from having to know <u>this</u>. You can't leave without paying.

Est-ce que je peux payer? = May I pay?   *L'addition, s'il vous plaît.*   = The bill, please.

Est-ce que le service est compris?   = Is service included?

Asking about the service charge will really impress the examiners

When a <u>restaurant bit</u> comes up in the exam, you'll be <u>kicking yourself</u> if you haven't revised it.
And if you're after a <u>top grade</u>, you'll really need to <u>impress</u>. So you have to learn <u>all</u> of it.

Quick Questions

Learning the facts and practising the exam questions is the only recipe for success. That's what the questions on these pages are all about. All you have to do — is do them.

Quick Questions

1) You're staying in a hotel in France. How would you ask where the games room is?

2) You're in a restaurant and you want to know where the toilets are. How would you ask this in French?

3) What does "Le téléphone est au rez-de-chaussée" mean in French?

4) You ask where the dining room is and you're told, "Elle est au quatrième étage, au bout du couloir". Where is the dining room?

5) What is the French for:

   a) on the right

   b) on the left

   c) straight on?

6) Write down how to ask when breakfast is served in French.

7) You want to complain about your hotel room. Write down in French that there aren't any towels in the room and the water is too cold.

8) What does "La douche ne fonctionne pas" mean in English?

9) In the reception of your hotel, you hear another guest complaining loudly in French. He says, "Il y a trop de bruit et je ne peux pas dormir. Je voudrais une autre chambre." Translate what he said into English.

10) Write down the French for "I need some extra beds".

11) You see the following signs on your holiday in France. What does each one mean?

   a) Service compris   b) Attendez ici   c) Pourboire

12) How would you ask if there's a table free in the restaurant?

13) Your French friend tells the waiter in a restaurant, "Nous sommes deux et nous voudrions nous asseoir à l'extérieur." What has she said?

14) How would you say "May I have the menu, please?" in French?

15) How would you say the following sentences in French:

   a) I would like the chocolate cake.

   b) I would prefer the pork.

   c) I would like to taste the snails.

16) Your waiter tells you, "Désolé, il n'y a plus d'agneau." What is the problem?

17) How would you say that you'll have the soup instead of the chips?

18) Tell your waiter that the beef is undercooked in French.

19) You read a restaurant review. It says, "Le service ici est affreux et j'ai trouvé un cheveu dans ma soupe." Translate this into English.

20) Write down how you would ask if the service is included in French.

Talking About Your Holiday

Où es-tu allé(e)? — Where did you go?

This is <u>where</u> you went: ...and this is <u>when</u> you went:

Je suis allé(e) **aux États-Unis** , **il y a deux semaines** .

= I went <u>to the USA</u>, <u>two weeks ago</u>.

to Spain:	en Espagne
to France:	en France
to Ireland:	en Irlande

a week ago:	il y a une semaine
last month:	le mois dernier
in July:	en juillet
in the summer:	en été

Avec qui étais-tu en vacances?
— Who were you on holiday with?

J'étais en vacances avec **ma famille** *pendant* **un mois** .

= I was on holiday with <u>my family</u> for <u>a month</u>.

For past tenses, see pages 204-212.
For more on family, see page 31.

a fortnight:	quinze jours
two weeks:	deux semaines

my brother:	mon frère
my friends:	mes ami(e)s
my classmates:	mes camarades de classe

Qu'est-ce que tu as fait? — What did you do?

You need to be able to say what you <u>did</u> on holiday — <u>learn</u> it well.

Je suis allé(e) **à la plage** .   = I went <u>to the beach</u>.

For sports and activities, see page 50-52.

This is a reflexive verb — see pages 216-217 for more on these.

Je me suis détendu(e) .   = <u>I relaxed</u>.

to the disco:	en discothèque
to the museum:	au musée

I enjoyed myself:	Je me suis amusé(e)
I played tennis:	J'ai joué au tennis

Comment tu y es allé(e)? — How did you get there?

Remember the little word '<u>y</u>', which means '<u>there</u>'.

Nous y sommes allé(e)s **en voiture** .   = We went there <u>by car</u>.

by plane:	en avion	*by train:*	par le train / en train
by boat:	en bateau	*by bike:*	à vélo

For more types of transport, see page 84.

This page has loads of "MUST LEARN" vocab

You need to <u>understand</u> other people talking about their holidays and <u>talk</u> about your own holidays too. <u>Cover the page</u>, <u>scribble</u>, <u>look back</u> etc. Keep going till you've <u>learnt everything</u> on this page.

Talking About Your Holiday

Opinions and tales of woe — the examiners love them. So plough on and learn this stuff as well...

Comment était le voyage? — How was the trip?

Comment étaient tes vacances? = How was your holiday?

Je les ai aimées. = I liked it.

Je ne les ai pas aimées. = I didn't like it.

Les vacances étaient formidables. = The holiday was great.

Comme ci comme ça. = So-so.

Il a plu tous les jours — It rained every day

For more on weather, see page 102-103.

If they ask you to compare different holidays, the weather's a good place to start...

En Italie, il faisait plus chaud qu' en Écosse. = In Italy it was hotter than in Scotland.

En France, il pleuvait moins qu' en Espagne. = In France, it rained less than in Spain.

This is the comparative. For more examples, see pages 179-181.

Il faisait aussi froid en Suisse qu' en Autriche. = It was as cold in Switzerland as in Austria.

Ça t'a plu? — Non, il a fait très beau

Watch out for the verbs on this page — some of them, like 'pleuvoir' (to rain), are irregular.
If you don't get the verb in the right form and tense, your sentence just won't make any sense.

Talking About Your Holiday

Quelle catastrophe — What a disaster

Sometimes things don't quite go to plan when you're on holiday.

"Nous avons fait du ski. Ma sœur est tombée, et s'est cassé la jambe."

= We went skiing. My sister fell, and broke her leg.

a ski resort: une station de ski

"Nous sommes allés à une station balnéaire, mais mes parents détestent la plage."

= We went to <u>a seaside resort</u>, but my parents hate the beach.

"J'ai eu mal de la route. Nous avons dû nous arrêter pendant une heure dans une aire de repos."

= I was carsick. We had to stop for an hour at <u>a motorway rest area</u>.

service station: une station-service

For more on the <u>perfect tense</u>, see pages 204-208.

"Ma mère a laissé son passeport à l'hôtel. Elle n'a pas pu prendre l'avion."

= My mother left her passport at the hotel. She couldn't take the plane.

"Mon père s'est fâché parce qu'on nous avait promis une vue de mer, mais notre gîte n'en avait pas."

= My father got annoyed because they'd promised us a sea view, but our cottage didn't have one.

If your holiday was perfect, make something up

You might be one of those <u>lucky</u> people who always has a super <u>relaxing holiday</u> with no mess-ups. Make sure you can talk about and understand potential holiday <u>disasters</u>, just in case they come up.

Talking About Your Holiday

Here's some more on holidays — this time about where you're <u>planning</u> on going. You need to be totally <u>ready</u> to answer any of the questions that come your way in the exams.

Où iras-tu l'année prochaine?

— Where will you go next year?

<u>Tricky</u> stuff now — learn to talk about things you <u>will do</u> in the <u>future</u>...

These are the future tense...

Où est-ce que tu iras?　　= Where will you go?

> For more info about the future tense, see pages 200-201.

J'irai en Amérique dans deux semaines.

= I will go to America in two weeks.

These are the easy future tense...

Comment vas-tu y aller?　　= How are you going to get there?

Je vais y aller en avion.　　= I'm going to go there by plane.

Qu'est-ce que tu vas prendre?　　= What are you going to take?

Je vais prendre des vêtements, mes lunettes de soleil et des livres.

= I'm going to take some clothes, my sunglasses and some books.

You've got to be able to talk about the future too

There are loads of <u>holiday-type questions</u> that could crop up in the exams. You might be asked about a <u>past</u> holiday, a holiday <u>disaster</u> or where you're going <u>next year</u>. You need to be prepared for <u>anything</u>.

Talking About Your Holiday

Here's your chance to talk about the holiday of your dreams.

Mes vacances de rêve — My dream holiday

This bit's all about what you <u>would</u> do if you <u>could</u>. This uses the <u>conditional</u> (see pages 220-221).

Comment seraient tes vacances de rêve?   = What would your dream holiday be like?

Mes vacances de rêve seraient de...

= My dream holiday would be to...

stay in a five-star hotel:	rester dans un hôtel cinq étoiles
visit a city like... :	visiter une grande ville comme...
spend a month in the country:	passer un mois à la campagne
go away with my friends:	partir avec mes ami(e)s
go away with my family:	partir avec ma famille

You might like to start with a fancy "if" — which examiners <u>love</u>, if you get the tenses right.

Si j'avais beaucoup d'argent ... / Si j'étais riche ...

= If I had a lot of money ... / If I were rich ...   *...je ferais le tour du monde.*

...I would take a trip round the world.

À ton avis, est-ce que les vacances sont importantes?
— In your opinion, are holidays important?

If your speaking assessment's on <u>holidays</u>, you might need to give your <u>opinion</u> on holidays <u>in general</u>.

Bien sûr que oui — il faut prendre le temps de se détendre.   = Of course. It's essential to take time to relax.

Est-ce qu'on prend trop de vacances?   = Do we take too many holidays?

Oui — tous ces vols sont mauvais pour l'environnement.

trips abroad: voyages à l'étranger   = Yes — all these <u>flights</u> are bad for the environment.

Holidays — always a tense time...

Like lots of things in GCSE French, talking about holidays comes down to which <u>tense</u> you use.
Think of how to say the activity in the <u>infinitive</u> (e.g. 'partir'), and then put it into the correct tense.

The Weather

The weather could come up in <u>loads</u> of exam situations — especially if you're talking about what rubbish weather you had on your last <u>holiday</u>.

Quel temps fait-il? — What's the weather like?

These <u>short sentences</u> are the ones you definitely <u>can't do without</u> — and they're <u>easy</u>.

It's snowing:
il neige

Aujourd'hui, **il pleut** . = <u>It's raining</u> today.

It doesn't <u>always</u> rain, so here are a few others you could use:

Il fait froid . = It's <u>cold</u>.

warm:	chaud
sunny:	du soleil
hot:	très chaud

You can use any of these words after 'Il fait...'.

Literally translated, this means 'There is wind.'

Il y a du vent . = It's <u>windy</u>.

icy:	de la glace	*thundery:*	du tonnerre
rainy:	de la pluie	*stormy:*	des tempêtes (fem.)
cloudy:	des nuages (masc.)		/ des orages (masc.)

Quel temps faisait-il? — What was the weather like?

This is quite easy, and it sounds <u>dead impressive</u>:

for three days:	pendant trois jours
all week:	toute la semaine

It snowed: Il a neigé

Il a plu **tous les jours** .

= <u>It rained</u> <u>every day</u>.

Il faisait froid . = It was <u>cold</u>.

nice:	beau
bad:	mauvais
foggy:	du brouillard

Il y avait des vents forts . = There were <u>strong winds</u>.

showers:	des averses (fem.)
sunny intervals:	des éclaircies (fem.)
lightning:	des éclairs (masc.)

You'll need to know types of weather, so learn this well

This stuff on weather <u>nearly always</u> comes up in the exam, so you've got to know it. Still, all you need to do is <u>learn</u> the <u>main sentences</u> on this page and the bits of vocab, and you'll be just <u>fine</u>.

The Weather

Don't panic if you hear the <u>future tense</u> in a weather forecast — learn this page and you'll be <u>OK</u>.

You might hear the future tense in a weather forecast

Make sure you can recognise important weather verbs when they're in the future tense.

Il fera du soleil . = It will be <u>sunny</u>.

nice:	beau	*cold:*	froid
bad:	mauvais	*warm:*	chaud
foggy:	du brouillard		

Il pleuvra / Il va pleuvoir . = <u>It will rain</u>.

It will snow: Il neigera / Il va neiger

Il y aura des averses. = There will be showers.

La météo — The weather forecast

<u>*La météo aujourd'hui*</u>
Aujourd'hui il fera chaud en France. Demain il y aura du vent dans le sud et des nuages dans le nord . Il va pleuvoir sur la côte.

in the east: dans l'est
in the west: dans l'ouest

= <u>*Today's Weather Forecast*</u>
Today it will be warm in France. Tomorrow it will be windy <u>in the south</u> and cloudy <u>in the north</u>. It will rain on the coast.

Tomorrow: Demain   *The day after tomorrow:* Après-demain

<u>*La météo en Angleterre*</u>
Aujourd'hui il pleuvra dans le nord. Il y aura des averses dans l'ouest, mais il y aura des éclaircies dans l'après-midi.

= <u>*The Weather Forecast in England*</u>
<u>Today</u> it will rain in the north. There will be showers in the west, but there will be sunny intervals in the afternoon.

Make sure you can understand a weather forecast

'<u>Le temps</u>' can either mean '<u>time</u>' or '<u>weather</u>', but you should always be able to tell from the <u>context</u> which one it is. Weather's a favourite with examiners, so you need to <u>learn</u> the <u>examples</u> on this page.

Quick Questions

Et voilà... another set of questions to test your knowledge of the last few pages. You'll soon know if you've got to grips with this topic — you should be able to answer every question before you move on. Make sure you go back over the bits you don't know until you can do all these questions.

Quick Questions

1) Translate this dialogue into English:

   A: Où es-tu allé en vacances? Es-tu allé à l'étranger?

   B: Bien sûr, je suis allé en Espagne le mois dernier.

   A: Et avec qui étais-tu en vacances?

   B: Avec mes amis. Nous sommes allés à la plage tous les jours. Je me suis bien amusé.

   A: Super! En été je suis allée en Irlande pendant quinze jours avec ma famille. Les vacances étaient formidables.

2) What is French for "I relaxed"?

3) Write down in English: "Nous y sommes allées en bateau."

4) How would you ask someone how their journey was in French?

5) Your penfriend has sent you this email about her recent holiday:

   > Salut. Tu m'as demandé comment étaient mes vacances. Eh bien, quelle catastrophe! Nous avons fait du ski pendant une semaine en Italie. J'étais en vacances avec ma famille mais mes parents détestent faire du sport. Le premier jour, mon père est tombé et s'est cassé le bras.

   a) How long did she go for?   c) Who did she go with?

   b) Where did she go?   d) What happened on the first day?

6) What is the French for "a seaside resort"?

7) What does this mean in English?: "En France, il faisait plus du soleil qu'en Angleterre. En Italie, il pleuvait moins qu'en Suisse."

8) Translate these questions into English:

   a) Où est-ce que tu iras?   b) Qu'est-ce que tu vas prendre?

9) How would you say, "I'm going to Scotland by train and I'm going to take a magazine and lots of clothes" in French?

10) What does this mean?: "Mes vacances de rêve seraient de rester dans un hôtel cinq étoiles à la campagne"?

11) Imagine you are writing the French weather forecast. Write a sentence for each picture describing the weather for tomorrow:

   a)    b)    c)

12) What is the French for "today's weather forecast"?

13) How would you ask someone what the weather will be like tomorrow?

14) What does "Il a plu tous les jours" mean in French?

Listening Questions

Track 12

You're on holiday and you're listening to the weather forecast for Europe. What will the weather be like today and tomorrow in the following countries?

	Country	Today	Tomorrow
Example	France	hot	very hot
1			
2			

Track 13

3   The manager of your hotel is telling you about your room and about the hotel. Answer the following questions in English.

a)   What floor is your room on? ....

b)   How much does it cost per room per night? ....

Track 14

You're going to listen to a conversation about holidays. Where did these people stay? Who with? For how long? Complete the table below.

	Where?	Who with?	For how long?
Example	hotel	family	10 days
4			
5			

Listening Questions

Track 15

These people are talking about their holidays. For each person, choose the correct phrase.

A   I went to Austria.

B   I went to London.

C   I went round the world.

D   I won a trip to the United States.

6  Françoise: ☐   **7**  Vincent: ☐

Track 16

8   Listen to this conversation about transport, then write "true" or "false" for each statement.

a)   She relies on her car to travel everywhere.   ....

b)   She's freer to go out because she has a car.   ....

c)   She thinks that cars don't cause pollution.   ....

d)   She can do more exercise because she has a car.   ....

Track 17

You're in a restaurant and you're deciding what to have.
Listen to the waiter's suggestions and fill in the gaps.

Example:

Vegetables: a) **potatoes**   b) **cauliflower**   c) **carrots**

9 Meat: a) pork   b) ....   c) beef

10 Fruit: a) ....   b) apple(s)   c) ....

11 Crêpes: a) jam   b) ....   c) ....

Reading Question

1   Read this restaurant review.

La Plage aux Galets, par Charles Boucher.

Hier soir, nous sommes allés – c'est-à-dire, ma femme, mes deux filles (quatorze et dix-huit ans) et moi – au restaurant La Plage aux Galets. Le restaurant a ouvert il y a deux semaines. Le chef de cuisine, Jean-Pierre Dupont, vient d'un autre restaurant assez connu, Le Chat Doré. On s'attendait à des merveilles!

Nous avons réservé une table pour huit heures. Nous sommes arrivés à huit heures dix et on ne pouvait pas trouver notre table. Heureusement, il y avait deux autres tables libres. L'une des tables était près de la fenêtre: on avait une belle vue sur la mer. Il y avait une bonne ambiance dans le restaurant. Tant mieux! On a dû attendre une heure avant d'être servi.

 Alors, il y a eu d'autres problèmes. Ma fille aînée a commandé des frites. Elles n'étaient pas tellement bien préparées. Ma femme n'avait pas de serviette. Ma fille cadette est végétarienne, mais il n'y avait pas beaucoup de choix pour elle...

J'ai commandé un bifteck saignant et il est arrivé trop cuit. Comme dessert, j'ai choisi du gâteau au chocolat, mais on m'en a servi un tout petit morceau. Et enfin, le café était froid! Nous n'y retournerons pas!

Read the following sentences. If you think the sentence is true, write **T** in the box. If you think it's false, write **F** in the box.

a)   La Plage aux Galets has been open for many years.

b)   Nobody had ever heard of the chef before.

c)   The Boucher family weren't expecting the food to be very good.

d)   The Boucher family arrived late at the restaurant.

e)   Monsieur Boucher liked the atmosphere in the restaurant.

f)   One of Monsieur Boucher's daughters doesn't eat meat.

g)   Monsieur Boucher ordered a medium-cooked steak.

Speaking Question

This speaking assessment is about past holidays. Don't forget that you'll need a friend or parent to help you out and take the teacher's role.

Task: Holidays

You are being interviewed for a TV show called "Les vacances affreuses". Your teacher will ask you the following:

- Where did you go on holiday last year?
- How did you get there? How was the journey?
- Did you stay in a hotel? What was it like?
- Did you have any problems during your holiday?
- Did you complain? What happened?
- Would you go back there one day?
- !

! Remember that the exclamation mark means you'll have to answer a question that you won't have prepared an answer to.

The whole conversation should last about five minutes.

Teacher's Role

You need to ask the student the following questions. You should speak first.

1 Où êtes-vous allé(e) en vacances l'année dernière?

2 Vous y êtes allé(e) comment? Comment était le voyage?

3 Est-ce que vous êtes resté(e) dans un hôtel? C'était comment?

4 Est-ce que vous avez eu des problèmes pendant votre séjour?

5 Vous vous êtes plaint(e)? Qu'est-ce qu'il s'est passé?

6 Est-ce que vous y retourneriez un jour?

7 !

! The unpredictable question could be:

Comment était la nourriture?

Writing Questions

Task: Holidays

You're on holiday and you're writing an email to your French penfriend all about your experiences. You should try to write 250-300 words.
You could include:

- where you are and how you travelled there
- what your first impressions of the country were
- an account of a disastrous experience or problem you've had
- your favourite meal so far
- what you think of the hotel or campsite where you're staying
- what activities you would like to do during the rest of your holiday
- when you'll be going home

Remember that to score the highest grades you need to answer the task as fully as possible, expanding on the points above when it is relevant to do so.

Task: Tourist Information

You've been asked to write a short article in French for your town's Tourist Information website about a local tourist attraction. You should try to write 250-300 words.

You could include:

- what the attraction is
- where it is and how to get to it
- what you can do there
- where you can have a meal
- which groups of people would find it most interesting
- how to find out more information

Remember that to score the highest grades you need to answer the task as fully as possible, expanding on the points above when it is relevant to do so.

Revision Summary

It's that time again folks... another dreaded revision summary. Don't dread it. Work in harmony with it, so that by the time you've answered all of these questions (several times), you'll feel like you're a fully-fledged Frenchified person, and ready to take on that exam.

1) Write down four countries in the UK and five other countries, in French. How would you say that you came from each of these places?

2) Write down the nationality to go with each of the places above (but in French).

3) You're at a French train station. Ask for three return tickets to Tours, second class. Ask when and what platform the train leaves from and where the left luggage office is.

4) How do you say these in French?
a) the platform   b) the waiting room   c) the timetable   d) the ticket window   e) the departure

5) How would you do these in French?
a) Say that you'd like to travel to Marseilles on Sunday.   b) Ask if there are any trains going there.

6) Say that you go to school by car, but your friend walks.

7) You've missed the bus to Pont-Audemer. Ask when the next bus leaves and when it'll arrive.

8) What are these in French? a) hotel b) youth hostel c) campsite d) cottage e) host family

9) How do you say these in French? a) key   b) bill   c) stairs   d) tent   e) sleeping bag

10) Your friend announces: "Je reste chez une famille d'accueil et j'aurai l'occasion de parler beaucoup de français." What have they just told you about the school exchange they are set to go on?

11) You arrive at a French hotel. Say you want one double room and two single rooms. You want to stay five nights. Say you'll take the rooms.

12) You've arrived in France without any euros. Tell the assistant at the bureau de change that you want to change £100 and cash some traveller's cheques.

13) Imagine that you are a first class impersonator. Impersonate a tourist in France. Ask if the tourist office has any brochures about the Alps. Then ask if you can hire skis for two weeks.

14) Ask when breakfast is served, out loud and in French.

15) You've just arrived at a grotty hotel. The floor in your room is completely flooded and, randomly, there are snails everywhere. How would you complain to the lady at reception?

16) You're in a restaurant. It's all gone wrong — you want to complain. The lamb isn't cooked properly and there's a fly in your soup. How would you say all this in French?

17) How would you ask someone how their holiday was, what they did, how they got there, and how the journey was? Imagine you now have to answer these questions in French.

18) Describe your dream holiday in three French sentences.

19) You've just listened to the weather forecast. Say that tomorrow it will be hot and the sun will shine.

Names of Buildings

If you're going to talk about your town, you need to know the names for buildings.
Yes, it's a bit dull, but you absolutely <u>have</u> to learn them.

Learn all these **bâtiments** — buildings

These are the basic, bog-standard '<u>learn-them-or-else</u>' buildings.

the bank:
la banque

the butcher's:
la boucherie

the church:
l'église (fem.)

the theatre:
le théâtre

the railway station:
la gare

the market:
le marché

the baker's:
la boulangerie

the cinema:
le cinéma

the supermarket:
le supermarché

the castle / palace:
le château

the post office:
la poste

the library:
la bibliothèque

Any of these could come up in your exams

These are the most <u>basic</u> buildings that are likely to come up in the exams. If you don't at least <u>know</u> these words, you'll be completely <u>stumped</u>. That can only mean one thing — <u>knuckle down</u> and learn.

Names of Buildings

D'autres lieux — Other places

OK, I'll come clean. There are absolutely <u>loads</u> of buildings you need to <u>know</u>. Here's the rest:

Some shops

shop:	le magasin
bookshop:	la librairie
newsagent:	le tabac
chemist's:	la pharmacie
cake shop:	la pâtisserie

See page 63 for more shops.

Touristy bits

hotel:	l'hôtel (masc.)
youth hostel:	l'auberge de jeunesse (fem.)
travel agent:	l'agence de voyages (fem.)
tourist information office:	le syndicat d'initiative
museum:	le musée

Other important bits

cathedral:	la cathédrale	*bus station:*	la gare routière
park:	le parc	*town hall:*	l'hôtel de ville (masc.), la mairie
swimming pool:	la piscine	*sports ground:*	le terrain de sport
airport:	l'aéroport (masc.)	*recycling centre:*	le centre de recyclage
stadium:	le stade	*police station:*	le commissariat
town centre:	le centre-ville	*university:*	l'université (fem.)
hospital:	l'hôpital (masc.)	*school:*	le collège, l'école (fem.)

Have a little patience and you'll get all these learnt

Learning vocab is <u>dull</u>, but it's pretty likely that this stuff will come up. <u>Turn over</u> the page and try to <u>write down</u> all the words. Then <u>look back</u> and have <u>another go</u> at the ones you got wrong. Do it <u>now</u>.

Asking Directions

It's pretty likely you'll get at least <u>one</u> question about <u>asking</u> or <u>understanding directions</u>. If you <u>don't</u> learn this stuff, that's one question you <u>won't</u> be able to answer. That's a good enough reason to learn it.

Où est... ? — Where is... ?

Asking <u>where something is</u> is dead easy — 'Où est...' plus the place name:

> See pages 111-112
> for more buildings.

Où est la poste , s'il vous plaît?   = Where is <u>the post office</u>, please?

Est-ce qu'il y a une bibliothèque près d'ici?   = Is there <u>a library</u> near here?

Le cinéma est... — The cinema is...

this way:	par ici	*behind the bank:*	derrière la banque
that way:	par là	*in front of the school:*	devant l'école
here / there:	ici / là-bas	*on the corner:*	au coin
next to the park:	à côté du parc	*above the bar:*	au-dessus du bar

Le cinéma est entre la banque et le parc .

= The cinema is <u>between the bank and the park</u>.

opposite the bank:	en face de la banque
below the café:	au-dessous du café
at the end of the road:	au bout de la rue
at the end of the garden:	au fond du jardin

You need to have these at your fingertips for top marks

Just reading this page <u>isn't</u> enough I'm afraid — you need to actually <u>learn</u> this stuff. You'll be glad you did when a directions question <u>pops up</u> in the exam or when you're hopelessly <u>lost</u> in France.

Asking Directions

C'est loin d'ici? — Is it far from here?

It's a good idea to check <u>distance</u>, before letting yourself in for a 3-hour trek:

Est-ce que le cinéma est loin d'ici?   = Is <u>the cinema</u> far from here?

the post office:	la poste
the park:	le parc

C'est à deux kilomètres d'ici.   = It's <u>two kilometres</u> from here.

a few kilometres: à quelques kilomètres	*not far:* à deux pas	*far:* loin	*near:* près

Use 'pour aller à...?' to ask the way

You'll probably hear people asking directions in your <u>listening test</u>.

(to a woman): madame

to the castle: au château   *to the hospital:* à l'hôpital

Pardon monsieur , pour aller à la banque , s'il vous plaît?   = Excuse me <u>sir</u>, how do I get <u>to the bank</u>, please?

Use '<u>au</u>' for 'le' words, '<u>à la</u>' for 'la' words, and '<u>à l'</u>' for words starting with a vowel and most words which start with an 'h'. See page 167.

Look at page 1 for more stuff on 1st, 2nd, etc.

Learn this important vocab for directions:

go straight on:	allez tout droit	go / turn right at the traffic lights:	tournez à droite aux feux
go right:	tournez à droite	go straight on, past the church:	allez tout droit, devant l'église
go left:	tournez à gauche	take the first road on the left:	prenez la première rue à gauche

Learn this and you won't be lost for words

<u>Cover</u> it up, <u>scribble</u> it down, <u>check</u> what you got wrong, and try it again. That's the way to learn this stuff. Keep at it until you know it <u>all</u> — then you'll be really ready for <u>anything</u> in the exam.

Quick Questions

You must be getting used to the routine by now — these quick questions run over the basic facts of the section so far. If you struggle with any of them, you need to look back over the pages and learn the bits you're not sure about. Then try the questions again until you can do them all.

Quick Questions

1) Write the French words for:
   a) the railway station
   b) the butcher's
   c) the baker's
   d) the library
   e) the church

2) What is the French word for 'buildings'?

3) Translate each of these words into English:
   a) le magasin
   b) l'agence de voyages
   c) l'hôtel de ville
   d) le syndicat d'initiative

4) Someone asks you, "Où est la gare routière?" What does this mean?

5) Ask a stranger where the recycling centre is in French.

6) How would you ask if there is a police station near here in French?

7) You've asked a passer-by for directions to the swimming pool. They tell you, "La piscine est au bout de la rue, à côté du marché." What have they told you?

8) In French, tell your friend that the sports ground is opposite the bank.

9) Write a sentence in French for the following directions:
   a) the cathedral is between the cake shop and the newsagent
   b) the bank is above the post office
   c) the chemist's is this way, on the corner
   d) the youth hostel is in front of the school

10) After you've given someone directions to the airport, they ask you, "C'est loin d'ici?" What have they asked you?

11) Your French friend asks you if your school is far from here. How would you tell them that it's not far?

12) How would you ask someone how to get to the university in French?

13) You're trying to find the police station in Nice. You stop several strangers to ask the way, but they each give you different directions. Translate each answer into English:
   a) Le commissariat? Allez tout droit et prenez la première rue à gauche.
   b) Je pense que le commissariat est près d'ici. Tournez à droite aux feux et passez devant la boucherie.
   c) Bien, tournez à gauche. Le commissariat est au-dessous de la banque.

Where You're From

This page deals with <u>regions</u> and <u>cities</u> that you'll be expected to know the name of in French. Don't just worry about where <u>you</u> come from — you might come across these in <u>any</u> part of the exams.

Tu es de quelle région? — Which region are you from?

You'll definitely need to recognise lots of regions of France and French-speaking places:

Je viens de Bretagne .   = I come <u>from Brittany</u>.

Remember that 'de + le = du'. See page 167.

from the Massif Central:	du Massif Central	*from Quebec:*	du Québec
from Corsica:	de Corse	*from Normandy:*	de Normandie
from the south of France:	du Midi	*from Provence:*	de Provence

The counties of Britain have a 'le' or a 'du' in front of them.

J'habite dans le Surrey .   *Je viens du Surrey .*

= I live <u>in Surrey</u>.   = I come <u>from Surrey</u>.

Les grandes villes — Cities

Normally the names of <u>cities</u> are the same in French and English, but there are a few <u>exceptions</u> you're expected to <u>know</u>.

Brussels:	Bruxelles	*London:*	Londres
Dover:	Douvres	*Lyons:*	Lyon
Edinburgh:	Édimbourg	*Marseilles:*	Marseille

J'habite au bord de la mer — I live by the sea

There are a few names of <u>seas</u> and <u>mountains</u> you need to know.

the Atlantic:	l'Atlantique (masc.)	*the mountain(s):*	la montagne
the Mediterranean:	la Méditerranée	*the Pyrenees:*	les Pyrénées (fem.)
the English Channel:	la Manche	*the Alps:*	les Alpes (fem.)

Mon village se trouve au pied des Pyrénées.   = My village lies at the foot of the Pyrenees.

You might need to say you live near a <u>river</u>:

Une rivière   = A river

J'habite dans une ville située sur le Severn .   = I live in a town situated on <u>the Severn</u>.

the Thames:	la Tamise
the Seine:	la Seine
the Rhone:	le Rhône

You've got to be able to say something about where you live

There's not an awful lot to learn here, but it is the kind of stuff that can <u>catch you out</u> if you haven't seen it before. Have another <u>quick look</u> at this page before you move on to the next page.

Talking About Where You Live

You'll have to understand and answer questions about where you <u>live</u>.
If you've <u>learnt</u> this, you'll be able to understand and answer. Simple as that.

Où est-ce que tu habites? — Where do you live?

You <u>won't</u> get through GCSE French without using this <u>vocab</u> — so make sure you learn it well.

J'habite à **Barrow** *.*   = I live in <u>Barrow</u>.

Barrow se trouve dans **le nord-ouest** *de l'Angleterre.*

= Barrow's in <u>the north-west</u> of England.

> *the north:* le nord   *the west:* l'ouest (masc.)
> *the south:* le sud   *the east:* l'est (masc.)

See page 81 for more countries.

You have to write about life 'dans ta ville' — 'in your town'

Practise writing a description of <u>your town</u>, your <u>favourite</u> town or a <u>dream</u> town.

Qu'est-ce qu'il y a dans ta ville?

= What is there in your town?

Il y a **un marché** *.*   = There's <u>a market</u>.

See pages 111-112 for more buildings and places.

Est-ce que tu aimes vivre à Barrow?   = Do you like living in Barrow?

J'aime *vivre à Barrow.*   = <u>I like</u> living in Barrow.

> *I don't like:* Je n'aime pas

Vivre à Barrow, ce n'est pas mal.   = Living in Barrow is not bad.

You need to say why you like or dislike where you live

Here's another chance to give your <u>opinion</u>, and this time it's about where you live. You need to say <u>where</u> you live and what there is in your town or area. You've got to have <u>something</u> to say.

Talking About Where You Live

Comment est Barrow? — What is Barrow like?

Descriptions of <u>towns</u> could come up in any of your <u>assessments</u> — it's need-to-know stuff.

La ville est **très intéressante** . = The town is <u>very interesting</u>.

boring:	ennuyeuse
great:	chouette
dirty:	sale
clean:	propre
quiet:	tranquille

Il y a **beaucoup** *à faire.* = There's <u>lots</u> to do.

enough: assez   *always something:* toujours quelque chose

Il n'y a rien à faire. = There's nothing to do.

<u>Longer descriptions</u> may seem tough at first but they're simply <u>all the bits you already know</u> put together.

J'aime vivre à **Barrow** *, parce qu'il y a toujours quelque chose à faire.*

= I like living in <u>Barrow</u>, because there's always something to do.

Je n'aime pas vivre à **Bogville** *, parce qu'il n'y a rien à faire.*

= I don't like living in <u>Bogville</u>, because there's nothing to do.

Add more detail about where you live

J'habite au numéro quatre, rue Tub, à Lancaster. = I live at 4 Tub Street, Lancaster.

Le paysage autour de Lancaster est très beau et vert.

= The countryside around Lancaster is very beautiful and green.

a town: une ville   *a village:* un village

Lancaster est **une grande ville** *de quarante-six mille habitants et il y a beaucoup d'industrie.*

= Lancaster is <u>a city</u> with 46 000 inhabitants and there is a lot of industry.

This page is all about adding extra detail to your answers

If you come from a dreary place which has <u>nothing</u> going for it, you can <u>make things up</u> (within reason) — chances are there'll be <u>something</u> to say about a place near you. Make sure you're prepared.

Talking About Where You Live

This page isn't too bad — even the tricky stuff is really just a case of 'learn the sentences and learn what words you can change around in them'. If you spend the time on it, it'll become super easy.

Tu habites avec qui? — Who do you live with?

J'habite avec **mes grands-parents** *.*   = I live with my grandparents.

my parents:	mes parents	*my father:*	mon père	*my boyfriend:*	mon petit ami
my friends:	mes ami(e)s	*my mother:*	ma mère	*my girlfriend:*	ma petite amie

J'aime habiter en famille parce que **...**   = I like living with family because...

I don't need to cook: je n'ai pas besoin de cuisiner.
I can talk about my troubles with someone:
je peux parler de mes inquiétudes avec quelqu'un.

Je n'aime pas habiter en famille parce que **...**   = I don't like living with family because...

my brother annoys me all the time:
mon frère m'énerve tout le temps.
I don't have any privacy: je n'ai pas de vie privée.

Chez toi — At your home

Being able to write about where you live and understanding others talking about their home is really important too...

semi-detached house: maison jumelée   *detached house:* maison individuelle

J'habite une **petite** **maison** **moderne** *.*   = I live in a small, modern house.

big:	grande
pretty:	jolie

old:	ancienne
green:	verte

You don't need 'dans' when you say where you live. Literally, you say, 'I live a house'. It's easiest if you think 'habiter' = 'inhabit'.

the motorway: de l'autoroute (fem.)
the shops: des magasins (masc.)

Mon appartement *se trouve près* **du parc** *.*

= My flat is near the park.

My house: Ma maison

on the ground floor: au rez-de-chaussée

Mon appartement est *au premier étage* *.*   = My flat is on the first floor.

Everyone needs to be able to say this stuff

You need to be able to say where you live — just say "J'habite au numéro..." and then the number of the house or flat, followed by the street name. Easy really. But only if you bother to learn it.

Inside Your Home

You've got to be able to <u>describe</u> your home. Luckily, you don't need to say <u>everything</u> that's in it — just some things.

Comment est ta maison? — What's your house like?

It'll look <u>impressive</u> if you can give <u>details</u> about your home. <u>Details</u> are the <u>answer</u>...

Comment est la cuisine *?*   = What's <u>the kitchen</u> like?

Est-ce que la cuisine *est* grande *?*   = Is the <u>kitchen</u> <u>big</u>?

the dining room: la salle à manger

comfortable: confortable	*great:* chouette	*ugly:* laide /
tiny: toute petite	*beautiful:* belle	moche

La cuisine est jolie *.*   = <u>The kitchen</u> is <u>nice</u>.

It's not: Ce n'est pas

C'est *ma pièce préférée.*   = <u>It's</u> my favourite room.

Est-ce que tu as un jardin? — Have you got a garden?

Ma maison *a un jardin.*   = <u>My house</u> has a garden.

My flat: Mon appartement

a tree: un arbre	*a balcony:* un balcon
a lawn: une pelouse	*a swimming pool:* une piscine

Nous avons des fleurs *dans notre jardin.*

= We have <u>flowers</u> in our garden.

Even if you make it up, just get the words right

If you get a question in the assessments about where you live, you might have to say what's <u>in</u> your home. Try to give as much <u>detail</u> about your home as you can, even if it's not strictly true.

Inside Your Home

Est-ce que tu as une chambre à toi?
— Have you got your own room?

You'll pick up more <u>marks</u> with these...

J'ai une chambre à moi. = I have my own room.

OR

J'ai ma propre chambre. = I have my own room.

Je partage une chambre avec **mon frère** *.* = I share a room with <u>my brother</u>.

ma sœur: my sister

Décris-moi ta chambre... — Describe your room to me...

<u>Remember</u>, if these aren't in your room, you can be <u>creative</u> (lie) — get the <u>vocab spot on</u>, though.

Il y a quels meubles dans ta chambre? = What furniture is there in your bedroom?

Dans ma chambre, il y a **...** = In my bedroom there is / there are...

a wardrobe:	une armoire	*a mirror:*	un miroir
a bed:	un lit	*some curtains:*	des rideaux (masc.)

Le fauteuil est *rouge et* **les murs sont** *gris.* = <u>The armchair is</u> red and <u>the walls are</u> grey.

'<u>Le fauteuil</u>' is <u>singular</u>, so the verb 'être' is too = <u>est</u>   '<u>Les murs</u>' is <u>plural</u>, so the verb 'être' is too = <u>sont</u>

You'll need to learn this page really well

It's all about <u>the little details</u> here. Once you've <u>learnt</u> these <u>phrases</u>, you can go into great detail about everything that's in your room and <u>wow</u> the examiners with your descriptive brilliance.

Quick Questions

It's easy to think that you know everything on the last few pages, but there's probably something you've missed, and that might cost you important exam marks. Make sure you've learnt these pages properly by testing yourself with these questions — that way no exam question can catch you out.

Quick Questions

1) You're asking a group of French teenagers where they're from. Translate each of their answers into English:

   a) Laurence: "Je viens du Midi."

   b) Hugh: "Moi? Je viens de Corse."

   c) Sara: "Je viens du Massif central."

2) Write down in French that you live in Cumbria.

3) Write down the French version of the following cities:

   a) London   b) Edinburgh   c) Dover

4) Write down the French for the English channel.

5) Say that you live in a town situated on the river Avon.

6) Your new French friend asks you where you live. Write down in French that you live in Bristol and say that Bristol is in the south-west of England.

7) What does "Est-ce que tu aimes vivre à Manchester?" mean in English?

8) Your penfriend Jean has written you a letter about where he lives.

   > J'habite à Superville dans l'ouest de la France. La ville est chouette — il y a beaucoup de restaurants et une belle rivière dans le centre-ville. Cependant, la ville est un peu sale parce qu'il y a beaucoup d'industries.

   a) Where is Superville?

   b) Give two good things Jean says about living in Superville.

   c) Why does Jean say the town is a bit dirty?

9) Write in French that you live with your parents, sister and grandparents.

10) Say you like living with your family because you don't need to cook, but your brother annoys you.

11) Write down in French that you live in a pretty semi-detached house near the shops.

12) Your friend Monique lives in a flat. She tells you, "Mon appartement est au rez-de-chaussée." What has she told you?

13) How would you ask your penfriend what their house is like in French?

14) Write in French that your kitchen is big and ugly. Say that the dining room is your favourite room because it's big.

15) Your friend tells you, "Nous avons une pelouse, une piscine et beaucoup de fleurs dans notre jardin." Write down what this means in English.

16) Write that you have your own room in French.

17) Clara tells you: "Dans ma chambre, il y a une armoire, un fauteuil rouge, un lit et des rideaux blancs." Translate what she said into English.

18) How would you say that the walls in your bedroom are blue in French?

Festivals and Special Occasions

You might be asked to talk about how you celebrate <u>special occasions</u> like your birthday or cultural celebrations like Christmas. Here's <u>everything</u> you'll need to know.

Quand est-ce que vous fêtez? — When do you celebrate?

You'll need to be able to talk about <u>what</u> is celebrated and <u>when</u>...

Christmas Eve / Day:	la veille / le jour de Noël	*a bank holiday:*	un jour férié
New Year's Eve:	le réveillon	*Easter:*	Pâques

On fête **le jour de l'An** **le premier janvier** .

= We celebrate <u>New Year's Day</u> <u>on 1st January</u>.

Put the <u>time of year</u> here.

Put a <u>specific date</u> here.

Valentine's day: la Saint-Valentin

Le 14 février , *on se réunit pour fêter* **mon anniversaire** .

= <u>On 14th February</u>, we get together to celebrate <u>my birthday</u>.

For more dates, see page 3-4.

Où est-ce que vous fêtez, et avec qui?
— Where do you celebrate, and who with?

my family: ma famille	*my colleagues:* mes collègues	*everybody:* tout le monde

Je vais célébrer avec **mes amis** . = I'm going to celebrate with <u>my friends</u>.

See page 69 for more on parties.

On va organiser une fête **chez nous** . = We're going to organise a party <u>at home</u>.

at the restaurant: au restaurant	*in a hotel:* dans un hôtel

You might need to talk about special occasions

Once your exams are over, then you can think about <u>celebrating</u> — but until then you'll have to <u>learn</u> how to talk about celebrations in French. You'll be <u>glad</u> you know this stuff when you're in the exam.

Festivals and Special Occasions

Qu'est-ce que vous faites pour célébrer?
— What do you do to celebrate?

Pour célébrer, **on mange de la nourriture festive** . = To celebrate, <u>we eat festive foods</u>.

we have fun:	on s'amuse
we dance:	on danse
we give presents:	on offre des cadeaux
we receive presents:	on reçoit des cadeaux
we sing together:	on chante ensemble
we eat as a family:	on dîne en famille

For how to say 'I am Christian / Muslim etc.' see pages 37.

Pour Noël ...

For Christmas ...

we go to midnight mass:
on va à la messe de minuit.
we have a Christmas tree:
on a un sapin de Noël.
we play games as a family:
on fait des jeux en famille.

we light 8 candles — one per day, for 8 days:
on allume huit bougies — une par jour, pour huit jours.
we play games and we give presents:
on fait des jeux et on offre des cadeaux.

Pour la Hanoukka ...

For Hanukkah ...

we fast for 30 days:
on jeûne pendant trente jours.
we go to the mosque to pray:
on va prier à la mosquée.

Pour le Ramadan ...

For Ramadan...

Learn all these — whether you celebrate them or not

It's important that you can <u>give details</u> about some sort of <u>celebration</u>, <u>who</u> you celebrate it with and <u>what you do</u> to celebrate. So, the sooner you start learning this page, the sooner it'll be done.

The Environment

If the environment comes up, you'll need to have an opinion. It's a chance for you to write or say what you <u>think</u> about something real and <u>important</u>.

Il y a de graves problèmes...
— There are some serious problems...

Start with the <u>problems</u>...

Il y a trop de **pollution** *.* = There's too much <u>pollution</u>.

deforestation:	déboisement (masc.)
consumption:	consommation (fem.)
light:	lumière (fem.)
noise:	bruit (masc.)

On consomme trop de ressources naturelles et d'énergie.

= We use too many natural resources and too much energy.

La pollution de l'air par les gaz d'échappement *est un danger pour l'environnement.*

= <u>Air pollution from exhaust fumes</u> endangers the environment.

the hole in the ozone layer:	le trou dans la couche d'ozone
global warming:	le réchauffement de la terre
the greenhouse effect:	l'effet de serre (masc.)
overpopulation:	la surpopulation
deforestation:	le déboisement

On ne fait pas assez attention aux espèces en voie de disparition.

= We don't pay enough attention to endangered species.

Think about what you can say about the environment
The environment's a really <u>important</u> topic. There's <u>loads</u> you can say about the environment — just make sure you have the <u>vocab</u> to say what you want. The only way to make sure is to <u>learn</u> this page.

The Environment

Est-ce que l'environnement est important pour toi?
— Is the environment important to you?

Then talk about <u>your opinions</u>...

OUI!

> *I think the environment is very important:*
> je pense que l'environnement est très important

Oui, **je m'intéresse beaucoup à l'environnement** .

= Yes, <u>I'm very interested in the environment</u>.

Il y a de la pollution partout parce qu'il y a trop d'embouteillages .

= There is pollution everywhere
<u>because there are too many traffic jams</u>.

> *we don't recycle as much as we should:*
> on ne recycle pas comme on le devrait
> *we use too much packaging:*
> on utilise trop d'emballage

NON!

> *I'm not worried about the environment:*
> je ne m'inquiète pas au sujet de l'environnement

Non, **ça ne m'intéresse pas du tout** .

= No, <u>I'm not interested in it at all</u>.

Nous n'avons pas le temps de recycler — on travaille tout le temps .

= We don't have time to recycle
— <u>we work all the time</u>.

> *there are other more important things:*
> il y a d'autres choses plus importantes
> *the government should find solutions:*
> le gouvernement devrait trouver des solutions

Have your opinions about the environment at the ready

There are so many <u>different aspects</u> of the environment you could <u>choose</u> to talk about —
there's bound to be at least one that interests you. As always, <u>be wise</u> and learn the <u>basics</u>.

The Environment

Here's some stuff you can do <u>in the home</u> and in the <u>local area</u> to help the environment.

À la maison... — In the home...

On pourrait ... = We could...

turn off the light / television / heating:
éteindre la lumière / la télévision / le chauffage
use less water / packaging:
utiliser moins d'eau / d'emballage

sort our rubbish:
trier nos déchets
recycle packaging instead of throwing it away:
recycler les emballages au lieu de les jeter
grow vegetables in the garden:
cultiver des légumes dans le jardin

Here are some things you can <u>recycle</u>:

box / tin:	la boîte
cardboard box:	le carton
plastic bag:	le sac en plastique
rubbish:	les ordures (fem.) / les déchets (masc.)
packaging:	les emballages (masc.)
bottles:	les bouteilles (fem.)

Dans les environs... — In the local area...

On devrait ... = We should...

share the journey to work with friends:
partager le voyage au travail avec des ami(e)s
use public transport to travel to school:
utiliser les transports en commun pour aller au lycée
create more pedestrian zones:
créer plus de zones piétonnes
build more cycle lanes: construire plus de pistes cyclables

buy products with recyclable packaging:
acheter des produits aux emballages recyclables
find the nearest recycling centre:
trouver le centre de recyclage le plus proche

Don't be put off by all the words on this page — just learn them

These pages are <u>hard</u> — there's loads of <u>vocab</u>, and most of it isn't everyday stuff. Still, just think how you'll kick yourself if it comes up in the exam and you haven't learnt it. That would be <u>sad</u>.

The Environment

You need to be able to talk about what you think will happen to the environment in the future too.

À l'avenir... — In the future...

Who knows what the future holds...

À l'avenir, **il n'y aura plus de pétrole** . = In the future, <u>there will be no more oil</u>.

> *we will not have any more natural resources:*
> on n'aura plus de ressources naturelles
> *we will use renewable energy sources (wind and solar):*
> on utilisera des énergies renouvelables (éolienne et solaire)
> *the world will be even more overpopulated:*
> le monde sera encore plus surpeuplé

These sentences are written in the future tense. See pages 200-201 for more on this.

Il faudra réduire les émissions de gaz carbonique.

= We will have to reduce carbon dioxide emissions.

Nous devons protéger l'environnement.
Sinon, nos enfants souffriront terriblement.

animals: les animaux

= We must protect the environment. Otherwise, <u>our children</u> will suffer terribly.

You can also talk about the future using the <u>conditional tense</u>:

Si on conduisait moins, il y aurait moins d'émissions, et moins de pluies acides.

= If we drove less, there would be fewer emissions and less acid rain.

See pages 220-221 for more on the conditional tense.

Learn how to talk about the future of the planet

Even though you can't <u>predict</u> the future, you can still talk about what you think <u>will</u> happen or what <u>could</u> happen. You'll <u>really</u> impress the examiners if you can get your head around this lot.

Quick Questions

Well done... you've made it to the Quick Questions at the end of a tricky section. There's more to be done though because you've got to make sure that all that information is going to stay in your brain for the exam. And there's only one way to do that — test yourself until you can answer every question.

Quick Questions

1) Write down the French for:

   a) Christmas Eve   b) New Year's Eve   c) Easter

2) What does this mean: "On fête la Saint-Valentin le 14 février."

3) How would you ask where someone celebrates Christmas in French?

4) What does, "Je vais célébrer mon anniversaire avec mes amis" mean?

5) You'd like to organise a party at a restaurant. How do you say that in French?

6) Write down the French for the following phrases, using 'on':

   a) we have fun

   b) we give presents

   c) we sing together

   d) we dance

7) At Christmas you go to midnight mass and have a Christmas tree. How would you write this in French?

8) Your French friend is talking about how she celebrates Hanukkah. She tells you, "Pour la Hanoukka, on allume huit bougies et on fait des jeux. On dîne en famille." How does she celebrate?

9) Write down the French for the following words:

   a) overpopulation   b) global warming   c) the greenhouse effect

10) You read a newspaper article in French about the environment. It says, "On ne fait pas assez attention aux espèces en voie de disparition. Il y a trop de déboisement et c'est un danger pour l'environnement." Translate this into English.

11) You believe that the environment is very important and you think that we don't recycle as much as we should. How would you say this in French?

12) You're not interested in the environment because there are other more important things. Write down your opinion in French.

13) Your French friend tells you, "Je m'inquiète au sujet de l'environnement. On pourrait éteindre la lumière et le chauffage. On devrait trier nos déchets et acheter des produits aux emballages recyclables." Translate this into English.

14) Translate the following phrases into English:

    a) On devrait utiliser les transports en commun pour aller au lycée.

    b) On peut recycler les bouteilles, les cartons et les sacs en plastique.

    c) On devrait construire plus de pistes cyclables.

15) Turn these sentences into French:

    a) In the future, we will not have any more oil.

    b) The world will be overpopulated.

    c) We will have to reduce our carbon dioxide emissions.

Listening Questions

Track 18

Someone gives you directions in French to some buildings in town.
Write down the name of each building you are given directions to and which
letter it corresponds to on the map.

Example   cinema ....   B ....

1   ....

2   ....

3   ....

you are here

Track 19

These French teenagers are talking about whether or not they like their town.
For each person, write yes or no, and give **one** reason why or why not.

Example   YES ....   there's a cinema ....

4   ....

5   ....

6   ....

Track 20

You're going to listen to a conversation about travelling around town. Do these people live near
to or far from their destination? Where are they going? How do they get there? Fill in the table.

	Near/Far?	Destination?	Transport?
Example	**near**	**university**	**on foot**
7			
8			
9			

Reading Question

1 Read this article about forest fires.

LES INCENDIES DE FORÊT

Il semble que partout dans le monde les forêts soient menacées par le feu. En Australie, il y a des incendies graves presque tous les ans et plus récemment ils sont devenus un danger dans les pays chauds de la Méditerranée aussi. On dit qu'il existe peut-être un lien entre l'augmentation du nombre des incendies et le réchauffement de la planète.

Ces incendies entraînent beaucoup de problèmes. Par exemple, ils sont responsables pour énormément de déboisement, ils détruisent beaucoup de maisons et ils contribuent à la pollution de l'air aussi. En plus, il y a des gens pour qui cette pollution mène à des problèmes de respiration ou des maladies de peau ou des yeux.

Malheureusement, même si nous arrêtions tout de suite de produire du gaz carbonique, il y aurait toujours des incendies. Cependant, il y aura moins de risque si on ne fume pas dans les forêts et si on n'y fait pas du feu quand on fait du camping.

Choose **four** sentences which are correct according to the article and write the letters in the boxes.

A	Forest fires aren't a problem in Europe.
B	There are often forest fires in Australia.
C	Some people think forest fires are linked to global warming.
D	The fires are caused by people building houses in the forest.
E	Deforestation is one way of preventing fires.
F	Forest fires affect people's health.
G	If we stop emitting carbon dioxide, there would be no more fires.
H	There are things people can do to reduce the risk of forest fires.

☐ ☐ ☐ ☐

Reading Question

2   You're reading a blog set up by a group of students at a French school. They're talking about where they'd like to live when they leave home.

Juliette

Je n'ai pas du tout envie de quitter la maison familiale. Je crois que ma famille va me manquer beaucoup, surtout mes sœurs, qui sont comme mes meilleures amies. Alors je prendrai un appartement tout près de chez moi, et je partagerai avec une autre fille. Comme ça je me sentirai moins seule.

Florence

Je vais partir de chez moi cet été, après avoir passé mon bac. J'ai toujours habité dans une toute petite ville, où il n'y a rien à faire et où tout le monde se connaît. Je rêve d'habiter une grande ville au bord de la mer, comme Nice ou Marseille, et de rencontrer plein de gens avec qui je peux faire la fête tous les week-ends! Vive la liberté!

Henri

J'adore inviter mes amis à dîner, donc je me vois dans une ville où il est facile d'acheter de la bonne nourriture. Je déteste faire mes courses au supermarché – je préfère aller à la boulangerie, la boucherie et la poissonnerie. Ce qui m'inquiète, c'est que je n'aurai pas suffisamment d'argent pour louer une maison avec une grande cuisine!

Arnaud

Le village où j'habite actuellement se trouve au pied des Alpes, et bien qu'il soit très joli il est aussi très isolé donc j'ai du mal à sortir en ville avec mes amis. À l'avenir, je voudrais m'installer dans une ville avec de bons transports en commun. Cependant, si j'apprenais à conduire, je serais très content de rester ici.

For each blog, choose the correct heading from the list below.

Juliette ☐

Florence ☐

Henri ☐

Arnaud ☐

A   Worries about moving out

B   Being near work

C   New friends

D   Getting about

E   Buying a house

F   Entertaining at home

Speaking Question

This speaking question is going to test whether you can talk about environmental issues in French. Sounds tricky — but you just need to have the key vocab sorted and you'll be fine. Try these questions for size and make sure you have someone who can play the role of the teacher.

Task: Environment

You are being interviewed for a radio programme about the environment.
Your teacher will start the conversation and ask you the following questions:

- Is the environment important to you?
- What do you think are the main problems where you live?
- Do you recycle?
- How do you think recycling could be increased?
- How could we reduce pollution caused by vehicles?
- What could you do in your home to help the environment?
- !

! Remember that the exclamation mark means you'll have to answer a question that you won't have prepared an answer to.

The whole conversation should last about five minutes.

Teacher's Role

You need to ask the student the following questions. You should speak first.

1 Est-ce que l'environnement est important pour toi?

2 À ton avis, quels sont les problèmes les plus graves dans ta région?

3 Est-ce que tu recycles?

4 Comment est-ce que tu penses qu'on pourrait améliorer les taux de recyclage?

5 Comment penses-tu qu'on pourrait réduire la pollution entraînée par les transports?

6 Qu'est-ce que tu pourrais faire chez toi pour aider l'environnement?

7 !

! The unpredictable question could be:

À ton avis, quel est l'avenir de l'environnement?

Writing Questions

Task 1: Promoting Your Town

You've got a summer job at your local tourist office. They've asked you to produce a page on their website for French visitors. You should write 250-300 words. You could include:

- Where your town is and what it's like,
- Reasons why people should visit,
- Opinions of other satisfied tourists,
- The best places to eat,
- Reasons why your town is well-known,
- Details about events that usually take place over the summer,
- Other must-see attractions.

Remember that to score the highest marks you need to answer the task as fully as possible, expanding on the points above when it is relevant to do so.

Task 2: Festivals and Celebrations

You have been asked to write an article about a festival you celebrate to send to your exchange school in France. You should write 250-300 words. You could include:

- What happens in the lead-up to your chosen festival,
- The roles of different members of your family,
- The traditions involved in the festival,
- A description of special food associated with the festival,
- An account of what happens on the main day of the festival,
- How you feel about the festival.

Remember that to score the highest marks you need to answer the task as fully as possible, expanding on the points above when it is relevant to do so.

Revision Summary

These questions really do check what you <u>know</u> and <u>don't know</u> — which means you can spend your time learning the bits you're shaky on. Make sure you work through all the questions.

1)   You're in France and are writing to your penfriend about the sights. How do you say there's a castle, a swimming pool, a university, a cinema, a cathedral and a theatre?

2)   Write down five shops and five other buildings you might find in a town (not the ones above).

3)   You need to go to the chemist's. How do you ask where it is, and if it's far away?

4)   What do these directions mean?: "La pharmacie est à un kilomètre d'ici. Tournez à droite, prenez la première rue à gauche et allez tout droit, devant l'église. La pharmacie est à droite, entre la banque et le cinéma."

5)   A French tourist has come to see your home town and is looking for the youth hostel. Tell him to go straight on, turn left at the traffic lights and the youth hostel is on the left.

6)   Tell your French penfriend Jean-Jacques where you live, whereabouts it is (which country and whether it's north-east etc.) and what it's like...

7)   Say that you like living in your town — there's loads to do and it's quite clean.

8)   Say your address and describe the place where you live — is it a town or a village, is the landscape nice, how many people live there, and who do you live with?

9)   Your French friend Marie says: "J'habite avec mes parents et mon frère. J'aime habiter en famille parce que je peux parler de mes inquiétudes avec quelqu'un." What does she mean?

10) Marie-Françoise lives in a big, modern house. It's near the town centre, shops and a motorway. How would she say this in French?

11) Write down the names of four rooms, and four describing words. Use these words to create at least four sentences to describe the rooms in your house, e.g. La cuisine est jolie.

12) Tom has his own room. He has red walls and a brown wardrobe. He has a bed, a mirror and some curtains. He doesn't have an armchair. How will he say all this in French?

13) Quels festivals fêtes-tu? Quand est-ce que tu les fêtes? Où est-ce que tu les fêtes, et avec qui? Qu'est-ce que tu fais pour célébrer?

14) Est-ce que l'environnement est important pour toi? Pourquoi?

15) Sofie's worried about global warming. Give your views on the problems facing the environment.

16) There's no stopping Sofie — she's just told you she'd like to live in a remote wooden hut and be at one with nature. Suggest some more realistic options for saving the environment. You'll need to mention at least six — she's very set on the wooden hut idea.

School Subjects

There's no way to avoid <u>schools</u> and <u>jobs</u>, no matter how much they <u>stress you out</u>.
Learn this section <u>well</u> and you should hopefully stress less.

Tu fais quelles matières? — What subjects do you study?

Go over these subjects until
you know them <u>all</u> really well...

Numbers and Stuff
maths: les mathématiques (fem.),
les maths (fem.)
IT: l'informatique (fem.)

Arts and Crafts
art: le dessin
music: la musique
drama: l'art dramatique (masc.)

Sciences
science: les sciences (fem.)
physics: la physique
chemistry: la chimie
biology: la biologie

Physical Education
PE: l'éducation physique (fem.) / le sport / l'EPS (fem.)

Languages
French: le français
German: l'allemand (masc.)
Spanish: l'espagnol (masc.)
Italian: l'italien (masc.)
English: l'anglais (masc.)

Humanities
history: l'histoire (fem.)
geography: la géographie
D&T: les travaux manuels (masc.)
religious studies: l'éducation religieuse (fem.)
PSHE: l'instruction civique (fem.)

> *I study:* J'étudie   →   **J'apprends** le français.   = <u>I'm learning</u> French.

Quelle est ta matière préférée?

— What's your favourite subject?

OK, school stuff may not be exciting,
but you <u>definitely</u> need to know it.

> *I don't like:* Je n'aime pas
> *I hate:* Je déteste   →   **J'aime** les maths .   = <u>I like</u> <u>maths</u>.

There's more on how to say
what you like and don't
like on pages 10–12.

> **Je préfère** la biologie .   = I prefer <u>biology</u>.

You can put any
school subject in
the green boxes.

> **Ma matière préférée est** le sport .   = <u>PE</u> is my favourite subject.

Depuis quand...? — How long...?

This isn't here because I like it. It's here because it could be in <u>your assessments</u>. So <u>learn it</u>.

> **Depuis quand apprends-tu le français?**   = How long have you <u>been learning</u> French?

Be careful to use the present tense — you don't
say 'I have been' as in English. See pages 196-199.

> **J'apprends le français depuis trois ans.**   = <u>I've been learning</u> French for three years.

You need to know all this school vocabulary

Play around with this page until you've got it firmly lodged in your brain. Make sure you <u>know</u> all the
subjects you do really well, and <u>understand</u> the ones you don't do when you see or hear them.

The School Routine

Not the most exciting of pages ever, but it's <u>worth</u> all the effort when you get <u>tricky questions</u> on <u>school routine</u>. Go for <u>short</u> snappy sentences — that way, they're easier to <u>remember</u>.

Comment vas-tu au collège? — How do you get to school?

This bit's <u>basic</u> — know the basics...

by bus: en bus   *by bike:* à vélo

*Je vais au collège **en voiture** .* = I go to school <u>by car</u>.

Use 'au lycée' or 'au collège' for 'to school'. For more on forms of transport, see page 84.

Je vais au collège à pied. = I go to school on foot.

L'emploi du temps — The timetable

It's important you know how to describe a <u>school day</u> — une <u>journée scolaire</u>.

*Les cours **commencent** à neuf heures.* = Lessons <u>begin</u> at 9.00.

finish: finissent

For more on times, see page 2.

Nous avons huit cours par jour. = We have 8 lessons per day.

Chaque cours dure trente minutes. = Each lesson lasts 30 minutes.

Nous faisons une heure de devoirs par jour. = We do one hour of homework a day.

La récréation est à onze heures. = <u>Break</u> is at 11.00.

Lunch break: La pause déjeuner

I talk with friends: Je parle avec mes ami(e)s
I do my homework: Je fais mes devoirs
I play football: Je joue au football
I go in the computer room: Je vais dans la salle d'informatique

*Je **mange un fruit** dans la cour pendant la récré.*

= <u>I eat a piece of fruit</u> in the playground at break time.

School routine — routinely dull

This stuff isn't the <u>most</u> exciting page you'll ever read but it's one of the most <u>important</u>. Make sure you've already <u>thought</u> about what you could say about your school — it's best to be <u>prepared</u>.

The School Routine

L'année scolaire — The school year

This is all a bit more <u>tricky</u> but, if you want a top mark, you need to <u>learn it</u>.

Il y a trois trimestres.   = There are three terms.

Nous avons six semaines **de vacances** en été .   = We have <u>six weeks'</u> holiday <u>in the summer</u>.

eight weeks: huit semaines	*five days:* cinq jours	*at Christmas:* à Noël *at Easter:* à Pâques

J'adore **la rentrée parce que** ...   = <u>I love</u> the start of the new school year because...

I hate: Je déteste

I can't wait to see my friends:	j'ai hâte de voir mes ami(e)s.
I feel ready to go back to school:	je me sens prêt(e) à revenir au lycée.
I have no desire to study again:	je n'ai aucun désir de recommencer mes études.

Portez-vous un uniforme? — Do you wear a uniform?

You might hear people talking about the <u>differences</u> between <u>schools</u> in the UK and in France...

D'habitude les élèves anglais portent un uniforme à l'école.

= English students usually wear a uniform to school.

See page 66 for more on clothes and colours.

Notre uniforme est un pull rouge, un pantalon gris, une chemise blanche et une cravate verte.

= Our uniform is a red jumper, grey trousers, a white shirt and a green tie.

we go to nursery school from the age of 3 to 6:	on va à la maternelle de trois à six ans
we go to secondary school from the age of 11 to 15:	on va au collège de onze à quinze ans
we study for the 'baccalauréat' at a 'lycée':	on étudie pour le bac au lycée
we have to go there on Saturday mornings:	on doit y aller le samedi matin
the school day is longer:	la journée scolaire est plus longue

En France, on ne va pas au collège le mercredi après-midi .

For more information on times, see page 2.

= In France, <u>we don't go to school on Wednesday afternoons</u>.

Be prepared to talk about your school routine

Don't forget the phrases for your exciting <u>school routine</u>, and the sentences for saying how you <u>go</u> to school. Remember the handy phrase '<u>par jour</u>' — you can stick it in loads of sentences.

More School Stuff

OK, I know this school stuff is a bit close to home and it's a bit boring. (Well, properly boring actually.)
But at the end of the day, you need to know it — so power through and you'll reap exam rewards.

Les règles sont strictes — The rules are strict

On n'a pas le droit de parler dans les couloirs .   = We're not allowed to talk in the corridors.

to go in the staff room:	d'entrer dans la salle des profs
to write on the (interactive) whiteboard:	d'écrire sur le tableau blanc (interactif)
to wear jewellery:	de porter des bijoux
to eat in the lab:	de manger au laboratoire

En France , on doit passer un examen à l'âge de quinze ans .   *16:* seize ans

In Great Britain: En Grande-Bretagne   = In France, we have to take an exam at the age of 15.

On appelle cet examen le brevet.   = This exam's called the 'brevet'.

French students take
the 'brevet' at the
age of 15, and the
'baccalauréat' at 18.

Mes affaires — My stuff

Learn this list of stuff you find in your school bag — and I'm not talking about half-eaten sandwiches,
an unwashed PE kit, or the crumpled-up newsletter you should have given your mum last week.

biro:	un bic	*felt-tip pen:*	un feutre	*pen:*	un stylo
pencil:	un crayon	*scissors:*	des ciseaux (masc.)	*calculator:*	une calculatrice
rubber:	une gomme	*ruler:*	une règle	*exercise book:*	un cahier

School rules — not as far as I'm concerned
Details, details — they're vital for this section. Close the book and see how many you can remember
— the more, the better. Examiners will be impressed if you know a bit about French schools too.

Problems at School

You might need to talk about some of the <u>problems</u> that people have at school, like <u>bullying</u> or <u>peer pressure</u>. Learn the stuff on these pages and then you'll be <u>prepared</u>.

J'en ai assez... — I've had enough of it...

Est-ce que tout se passe bien au lycée?   = Is everything going well at school?

Oui, tout va bien.   = Yes, everything's going well.

Non, j'ai beaucoup de problèmes à l'école...   = No, I've got lots of problems at school...

J'ai de bonnes notes mais je ne peux pas sortir avec mes ami(e)s parce que je n'ai jamais le temps.   = I get good marks, but I can't go out with my friends because I never have time.

> *I have difficulties understanding:*
> j'ai des difficultés à comprendre
> *I'm under pressure:* je suis sous pression

Au collège, il faut toujours se dépêcher et les explications sont toujours trop rapides pour moi .

= At school, we always have to rush and <u>the explanations are always too quick for me</u>.

> *failing:* d'échouer

Je crains de devoir redoubler .   = I fear <u>having to repeat a year</u>.

On doit porter un uniforme démodé et on n'a pas le droit de porter de maquillage.

= We have to wear an old-fashioned uniform and we aren't allowed to wear make-up.

Make sure you learn the phrases on this page

Even if you're not having any <u>difficulties</u> at school, you might have to listen to someone else talking about their <u>problems</u>. Either way, you'll <u>need</u> this vocab so make sure you <u>really</u> know this stuff.

Problems at School

Je suis stressé(e) — I'm stressed

Je travaille dur mais ce n'est jamais assez pour mes parents *.*

| my teachers: mes profs |

= I work hard, but it's never enough for <u>my parents</u>.

Mes parents sont stricts. Je dois étudier tout le temps.

= My parents are strict. I have to study all the time.

Les profs ne m'aiment pas et me mettent toujours en retenue.

= The teachers don't like me and always put me in detention.

Je ne peux pas être moi-même — I can't be myself

Il n'y a personne à qui je peux parler.   = There's nobody I can talk to.

Je connais beaucoup de gens mais je n'ai pas de vrai(e)s ami(e)s.

= I know lots of people but I don't have any real friends.

| a boyfriend: un copain |

On me brutalise.   = I get bullied.   *Tout le monde a* une copine *sauf moi.*

= Everyone has <u>a girlfriend</u> except me.

Il faut toujours porter des vêtements de marque et ça coûte vraiment cher.

= You always have to wear brand-name clothes and it's really expensive.

J'ai commencé à manquer les cours.   = I've started to play truant.

Assez 'stressed', you say 'out' — Stressed, out, stressed, out

Frankly, it would be <u>dull</u> if everyone said everything was great all the time. This stuff's <u>tricky</u>, but really <u>worth learning</u>. There's quite a lot to learn here, but make sure you don't <u>skip</u> over any of it.

Quick Questions

There's just no point in skimming over this section because it's all really important. Make sure you've learnt the section properly and then test yourself with these quick questions. If you struggle with any of the questions, go back over those pages again until you're sure that you know your stuff.

Quick Questions

1) Write down the French words for the following school subjects:

   a) art

   b) chemistry

   c) D&T

   d) PE

2) Your French friend asks you, "Quelle est ta matière préférée?" What does this mean?

3) In French, write that you hate maths but you love English.

4) How would you say that your favourite subject is geography?

5) a) What does "Depuis quand apprends-tu le français?" mean?

   b) How would you answer it in French?

6) You travel to school by car. Write this down in French.

7) At break you play football or go to the computer room. You always eat a piece of fruit. Write this down in French.

8) Your friend tells you, "Au collège, chaque cours dure cinquante minutes et nous avons six cours par jour. La récréation est à onze heures et demie. Nous avons trois trimestres." What does this mean?

9) You want to tell your friend that you like the start of the school year because you can't wait to see your friends, but you don't want to wear the uniform. Write this down in French.

10) Your school uniform is a white shirt, red tie, green jumper and black trousers. Describe it to your penfriend in French.

11) Analise is telling you about the school system in France. Translate what she tells you:

> En France, on ne porte pas d'uniforme. On ne va pas au collège le mercredi après-midi mais on doit y aller le samedi matin et la journée scolaire est très longue.

12) Tell Analise that the rules in your school are strict. You're not allowed to talk in the corridors or wear jewellery.

13) What do these words mean in English?:

   a) une gomme   b) un cahier   c) un feutre

14) Translate these phrases into French:

   a) I get good marks

   b) I'm under pressure

   c) I don't want to fail

   d) I get bullied

15) Your friend Pierre is having a rant about his school in an email. He says, "Je travaille assez dur mais je parle avec mes copains quand je suis en classe et les profs ne m'aiment pas. Ils me mettent toujours en retenue." Translate what he says into English.

Work Experience

These pages might encourage you to think about your <u>future</u> or think <u>back</u> to a time when you've done some <u>work experience</u>. Either way, you'll <u>need</u> the stuff on these pages.

As-tu fait un stage? — Have you done work experience?

Work experience is <u>great</u> — except for when it isn't...

J'ai fait mon stage en entreprise chez Peugeot .

> *Put any company name here*

= I did my work experience at <u>Peugeot</u>.

J'y ai travaillé pendant une semaine, du deux au sept mars.

= I worked there for a week, from 2nd to 7th March.

Je n'ai jamais *fait de stage.*

> *haven't yet:* n'ai pas encore

= I <u>have never</u> done work experience.

Est-ce que tu as aimé le travail? — Did you like the work?

More <u>opinions</u> wanted here...

Le travail était amusant . = The work was <u>fun</u>.

> *stressful:* stressant
> *interesting:* intéressant

> *comfortable:* confortable

Je me suis senti(e) seul(e) . = I felt <u>lonely</u>.

> *were friendly:* étaient sympathiques
> *were interesting:* étaient intéressants

Mes collègues de travail n'étaient pas sympa . = My colleagues <u>were unfriendly</u>.

Make sure you have something to say about this stuff

Work experience is a <u>funny old thing</u>... If you haven't done any then either tell the <u>truth</u> in perfect French or use your imagination and <u>make something up</u>. Either way, make sure your French is <u>right</u>.

Work Experience

C'est une journée très longue... — It's a very long day...

Imagine that your work experience job is your <u>career</u> for life. Does that change your <u>opinions</u>?

Les conditions sont terribles .   = The <u>conditions</u> are <u>terrible</u>.

hours: horaires (masc.)

comfortable: <u>co</u>nfortables   *fantastic:* fantastiques

It is: C'est

Ce n'est pas très bien payé .   = <u>It's not</u> very well paid.

Le travail est ennuyeux .   = The work is <u>boring</u>.

difficult: difficile

J'ai un emploi à mi-temps — I have a part-time job

Make these easier by choosing <u>easy-to-say</u> jobs and <u>simple</u> values — if only the rest of life was like that.

J'ai un travail à mi-temps .   = I've got <u>a part-time job</u>.

a holiday / temporary job: un emploi temporaire

£15 per week: quinze livres par semaine

Je gagne cinq livres par heure .   = I earn <u>£5 per hour</u>.

Je suis boucher/bouchère .   = I am <u>a butcher</u>.

You can find plenty more jobs on page 147.

What a way to make a living
You might have to comment on your <u>work experience</u> or <u>part-time jobs</u> in the speaking assessment.
Talk about anything work-related that you've done in your life, and give your <u>opinions</u> about it too.

Plans for the Future

If your idea of future plans is what you're doing next weekend, then try thinking a bit further ahead...

La vie après les examens... — Life after the exams...

There are loads of things to do <u>after GCSEs</u>. Here's the <u>basic vocab</u>.

Je voudrais **préparer le bac** .

= I would like <u>to do A-levels</u>.

'Bac' is short for 'baccalauréat', the French equivalent of A-levels — except that they do more subjects than we do.

to study geography: étudier la géographie.
to continue my studies: continuer mes études.

I already have some good friends there:
j'ai déjà de bon(ne)s ami(e)s là.
I'll be able to concentrate on my favourite subjects:
je pourrai me concentrer sur mes matières préférées.

J'ai choisi d'entrer en première au lycée parce que ...

= I've chosen to go into the Sixth Form because...

J'ai pris la décision de quitter l'école. = I've made the decision to leave school.

Je voudrais **faire un stage en entreprise** . = I'd like <u>to do a placement at a company</u>.

to take a year out: prendre une année sabbatique
to get married and have children: me marier et avoir des enfants

Je vais chercher un emploi. = I'm going to look for a job.

If you'd like to do a particular job after school, use some of the vocabulary from page 150.

Je voyagerai. = I will travel.

Here's your chance to think about life after exams

This kind of stuff crops up <u>year after year</u>, so make sure you're prepared to talk about it. Learn how to say what <u>you</u> want to do in the future but also think about what <u>other people</u> might want to do too.

Plans for the Future

Always say **Why** you want to do something

When you're commenting on your future plans, give a <u>reason</u> for them each time.
For example, 'I want to take a year out so that I can travel'.

> Remember to get the gender (le or la) right for the school subjects. Refresh your memory on page 136.

Je voudrais étudier la musique *, parce que je veux devenir* musicien(ne) *plus tard.*

= I would like to study <u>music</u>, because I want to be <u>a musician</u> afterwards.

an accountant: comptable   *a teacher:* prof(esseur)

Je voudrais préparer le bac car après je veux étudier la biologie à l'université.

= I would like to do A-levels because afterwards I want to study biology at university.

Je ne veux pas aller à l'université après le bac parce que je veux chercher un emploi *tout de suite.*

= I don't want to go to university after A-levels because I want <u>to look for a job</u> straight away.

to travel:	voyager
to take a year out:	prendre une année sabbatique
to be an apprentice:	être apprenti(e)

Je voudrais faire un stage en entreprise dans une banque *pour gagner de l'expérience.*

= I would like to do a work placement in <u>a bank</u> to get some experience.

a bakery:	une boulangerie	*a post office:*	une poste
a library:	une bibliothèque	*a police station:*	un commissariat

Je ne veux pas penser à l'avenir. Ça m'inquiète parce que j'ai peur d'être au chômage.

= I don't want to think about the future. It worries me because I'm afraid of being unemployed.

Life after GCSE — hard to imagine

I know GCSE French seems like a <u>scary mystery</u>, but this might come up in your GCSEs...
Learn all this and you'll be <u>laughing</u>. Use words like '<u>je voudrais</u>' and '<u>parce que</u>' for extra marks.

Types of Job

There are more jobs here than you can shake a stick at — and you do need to recognise them all.

Female versions of jobs can be tricky

Often, job titles in French are different for men and women. You need to recognise both versions...

Watch out for the feminine versions of jobs — although there are lots which just add an 'e' in the feminine, some follow different rules. For example, '-er' often becomes 'ère', '-teur' often becomes '-trice' (but watch out for chanteur/chanteuse), and '-eur' often becomes '-euse'.

Le musicien (masc.)   **La musicienne (fem.)**   = Musician

Le boucher (masc.)   **La bouchère (fem.)**   = Butcher

L'acteur (masc.)   **L'actrice (fem.)**   = Actor / actress

Le coiffeur (masc.)   **La coiffeuse (fem.)**   = Hairdresser

The gender of a job depends on who is doing it

To be on the safe side, best learn to recognise these too...

The gender of the job is masculine (le) for a man and feminine (la) for a woman — except for 'médecin', 'plombier', 'pompier' and 'mannequin', which are always masculine.

Professional jobs

accountant:	le/la comptable
secretary:	le/la secrétaire
architect:	l'architecte (masc./fem.)
lawyer/solicitor:	l'avocat(e)
manager:	le/la gérant(e)

Manual jobs

mechanic:	le mécanicien, la mécanicienne
electrician:	l'électricien, l'électricienne
plumber:	le plombier
chef:	le cuisinier, la cuisinière
baker:	le boulanger, la boulangère
farmer:	le fermier, la fermière
gardener:	le jardinier, la jardinière
labourer:	l'ouvrier, l'ouvrière
engineer:	l'ingénieur(e)

Medical jobs

dentist:	le/la dentiste
chemist:	le pharmacien, la pharmacienne
nurse:	l'infirmier, l'infirmière
doctor:	le médecin
vet:	le/la vétérinaire

A load more jobs

salesperson:	le vendeur, la vendeuse
waiter/waitress:	le serveur, la serveuse
journalist:	le/la journaliste
head teacher:	le directeur, la directrice
policeman/woman:	le/la gendarme / le policier, la policière
fireman/woman:	le pompier
soldier:	le soldat, la soldate
postman/woman:	le facteur, la factrice
primary teacher:	l'instituteur, l'institutrice
air hostess/	l'hôtesse de l'air (fem.),
air steward:	le steward de l'air
receptionist:	l'hôte d'accueil (masc.), l'hôtesse d'accueil (fem.)
computer scientist:	l'informaticien(ne)
cashier:	le caissier, la caissière
model:	le mannequin

Arty jobs

writer:	l'écrivain, l'écrivaine
designer:	le dessinateur, la dessinatrice

Good job you've learnt all this

Start with the jobs you find easiest — then learn the rest. Make sure you know all the female versions too — ooh, I don't envy you. But think how knowledgeable you'll be at the end of it all.

Jobs: Advantages and Disadvantages

What a page title... It pretty much sums up what's <u>important</u> here, I think.

Say what job you'd like to do and why

State the job you'd like to do with a <u>short</u> and <u>simple</u> reason why.

Use 'devenir' (to become) to say what job you'd like to do.

I hope: J'espère → **Je voudrais devenir médecin, ...** = <u>I would like</u> to become a doctor, ...

varied: varié
fun: amusant

IMPORTANT: In French you DON'T use 'un'/'une' when you're talking about a job you have or want to have.

... parce que le travail serait intéressant . = ... because the work would be <u>interesting</u>.

Dans mon travail, je voudrais résoudre des problèmes .

to work with people/numbers: travailler avec les gens/les chiffres = In my job, I'd like <u>to solve problems</u>.

Je n'aimerais pas être... — I wouldn't like to be...

Je n'aimerais pas être avocat(e) . = I wouldn't like to be <u>a lawyer</u>.

Je serais toujours fatigué(e) .

You can put any job from page 147 here.

= I'd always be <u>tired</u>.

unhappy: malheureux(euse)   *stressed:* stressé(e)   *under pressure:* sous pression

Les heures au bureau seraient trop longues. = The hours <u>in the office</u> would be too long.

at work: au travail   *in the classroom:* dans la salle de classe   *in the operating theatre:* dans la salle d'opération

Je préférerais travailler comme... — I'd prefer to work as...

Je préférerais devenir docteur . = I would prefer to become <u>a doctor</u>.

You can put any job from page 147 here.

J'aurais l'occasion de voyager . = I'd have the chance <u>to travel</u>.

to be creative: d'être créatif / créative   *to work with animals:* de travailler avec des animaux
to be myself: d'être moi-même   *to work in a hospital:* de travailler dans un hôpital

I'll take the pros and leave the cons...
Saying what job you <u>want</u> to do and <u>why</u> is pretty essential. If the truth's <u>too hard</u> to say, e.g. you want a job in inverse-polarity-dynamo maintenance, then say something simpler. Just say <u>something</u>.

Working Abroad

Fed up of working in the same old country? Why not try another...

Tu voudrais travailler à l'étranger?

The world's your oyster...

— Would you like to work abroad?

J'aimerais faire un stage en entreprise en France.

= I would like to do a work placement <u>in France</u>.

Je vais travailler chez un fleuriste à Aix-en-Provence.
Ce métier m'intéresse beaucoup.

= I'm going to work at a florist's in Aix-en-Provence. I'm really interested in this kind of work.

> See page 81 for a list of countries. Remember 'au' for masculine countries ('en' if starting with a vowel), and 'aux' when it's plural.

Je voudrais prendre une année sabbatique en France

...or should I say your huître...

— I'd like to take a gap year in France

Après le bac, je veux aller en France pour ... .   = After A-levels, I want to go to France to ...

study at university:	étudier à l'université
do some professional training:	faire une formation professionnelle
work in a bar:	travailler dans un bar
work in a ski resort:	travailler dans une station de ski
be an au pair:	être au pair
see the country and meet people:	voir le pays et rencontrer des gens

Je voudrais voir le monde avant de continuer mes études.

= I would like to see the world before continuing my education.

J'ai passé une année magnifique — I had a brilliant year

travel around: voyager	*buy a car:* acheter une voiture

Je n'avais pas de salaire, donc je n'avais pas d'argent pour m'amuser .

= I didn't get paid, so I didn't have any money <u>to enjoy myself</u>.

C'était une très belle expérience. Et ce sera une bonne chose pour ma carrière, je pense.

= It was a really good experience. And it will be a good thing for my career, I think.

Never have a gap year in a leap year

A gap year may not be for you, but have a think about it and make sure you have an <u>opinion</u> one way or the other. Also, it might come up in the <u>listening</u> or <u>reading exams</u>, so you can't ignore it.

Quick Questions

There's only one way to do well in the exam — learn the basics and then test yourself using these questions. If there are any you can't answer, go back over the last few pages until you're sure that you know it all.

Quick Questions

1) How would you ask your French friend if they've done work experience?

2) How would you say that you've never done work experience?

3) Your friend tells you, "J'ai travaillé chez Renault à Paris pendant un mois." What does this mean in English?

4) A group of French teenagers are talking about their work experience. You hear the following phrases. What do they each mean?

a) le travail était stressant

b) je me suis sentie seule

c) ce n'est pas très bien payé

d) les horaires sont fantastiques

5) Write in French that you have a part-time job and you earn six pounds an hour.

6) Write in French that you would like to do A-levels and you want to go to university.

7) Your friend Lise tells you, "J'ai pris la décision de quitter l'école parce que je voudrais prendre une année sabbatique et voyager." What does this mean?

8) How would you say in French that you're going to look for a job?

9) Tell your French friend that you'd like to study maths because you want to be a maths teacher.

10) Translate the following jobs into French, giving the male and female form for each:

a) actor   c) accountant

b) butcher   d) receptionist

11) Give the English translation for the following jobs:

a) le coiffeur   c) l'infirmier

b) le plombier   d) l'écrivain

12) You're talking about your ideal job to your French penfriend. Tell them in French that you want to work with people. Say you wouldn't want to be a lawyer because the hours would be too long. You'd prefer to be a journalist because you'd have the chance to travel.

13) Your friend Nicolas asks you, "Est-ce que tu voudrais travailler à l'étranger?" What does this mean?

14) You're telling your French teacher all about your future plans. Write in French how you would say that you want to go to France to work in a ski resort or in a bar. Say that you would like to see the country and meet people.

15) What is the French word for a gap year?

16) How would you say that a year in France will be good for your career?

17) Your French friend tells you, "Je voudrais faire une formation professionnelle parce que je voudrais être avocat." What does this mean?

Getting a Job

These pages cover loads of <u>key phrases</u> you'll need if you want to talk about getting a job.

Je cherche un emploi... — I'm looking for a job...

Je cherche un emploi dans un hôtel . = I'm looking for a job in <u>a hotel</u>.

See page 1 for more numbers.

a restaurant:	un restaurant	*an office:*	un bureau
a leisure centre:	un centre de loisirs	*a shop:*	un magasin

a holiday / temporary job: un emploi temporaire

Je veux un emploi à mi-temps . = I want <u>a part-time job</u>.

Je voudrais ce poste parce que...
— I would like this job because...

J'ai déjà deux *ans d'expérience.* = I already have <u>two</u> years' experience.

I speak English / French / Italian / Spanish:
je parle anglais / français / italien / espagnol.

Je serais idéal(e) pour ce poste parce que je suis bilingue . = I'd be ideal for this job because <u>I'm bilingual</u>.

animals: les animaux   *the public:* les gens

J'aime travailler avec les enfants . = I like working with <u>children</u>.

I am practical:	je suis pratique
I am always full of life:	je suis toujours plein(e) de vie
I am never impolite:	je ne suis jamais impoli(e)

J'ai beaucoup d'expérience et je suis travailleur / travailleuse .

= I have lots of experience and <u>I'm hard-working</u>.

Use 'parce que' to say why you want a job

It's <u>not</u> enough to say that you want a job — you need to be able to say <u>why</u> you would be good at it. If you're <u>struggling</u>, look back over the <u>personality words</u> on pages 32-33 for some <u>inspiration</u>.

Getting a Job

On cherche... — We are looking for...

Offre d'emploi:
On cherche un serveur ou
une serveuse
Lundi et vendredi soir
19.00 - 21:00

= Wanted:
We're looking for a waiter/waitress.
Monday and Friday evening.
7 - 9pm.

See pages 32-33 for more character traits.

Vous aimez travailler avec les animaux?
On cherche un(e) assistant(e).
20 heures par semaine.
Appelez Jean au
033 12-24-38-42

= Do you like working with animals?
We're looking for an assistant.
20 hours per week.
Call Jean on 033 12-24-38-42

On cherche quelqu'un de pratique,
travailleur(euse), honnête et aimable
pour vendre et organiser.
Entrez pour plus d'infos.

= We're looking for someone
practical, hard-working, honest and
nice to sell products and organise.
Come in for more info.

J'aimerais poser ma candidature — I'd like to apply

Imagine you've <u>applied</u>. Hopefully they'll <u>call back</u> and say something like this:

Est-ce que vous pouvez venir pour un entretien ...

= Can you come <u>for an interview</u>...

and meet us: nous rencontrer

... lundi, le 14 février à 10h?

= ... on Monday, 14th February at 10am?

the boss: le / la patron(ne)

... avec Monsieur LeBrun ...

= with <u>Mr LeBrun</u>

a photo:	une photo
your passport:	votre passeport (masc.)
your driving licence:	votre permis de conduire (masc.)

Apportez une copie de votre CV , s'il vous plaît.

= Please bring <u>a copy of your CV</u>.

This is the sort of topic that the examiners love to ask about

You might be faced with a <u>job advert</u> in your reading assessment so it's good to be <u>familiar</u> with the kind of phrases that could <u>pop up</u>. That way you won't get a nasty <u>shock</u> when it comes to exam time.

Getting a Job

Good <u>covering letter</u>, dazzling <u>CV</u>, nice <u>tie</u>, job's <u>yours</u>.

J'ai lu votre annonce — I read your advertisement

Every job application needs a good letter...

See p.15 for more on writing formal letters.

Rachael Johnson
46 Loxley Road,
Ambridge,
Borsetshire. BO12 2AM

Madame de Villiers
Commerce Tapisserie,
19 rue du Conquérant,
14066 Bayeux
le 30 octobre 2010

Madame,

J'ai lu votre annonce dans *Le Monde* hier, et je voudrais poser ma candidature pour le poste de Chef de Projet.

Vous verrez dans mon CV ci-joint que ma carrière a été variée, puisque j'ai travaillé dans les secteurs privés et publics. Je pense que j'ai l'expérience nécessaire pour ce rôle.

Ce poste m'intéresse beaucoup, et je suis disponible pour un entretien dès que vous le souhaiterez.

Je vous prie d'agréer, Madame, l'expression de mes sentiments distingués.

Rachael Johnson

I read your advertisement in *Le Monde* yesterday, and I would like to apply for the position of Project Manager.

You will see in my attached CV that my career has been varied, as I have worked in the private and public sectors. I think that I have the necessary experience for this role.

I am very interested in this position, and I am available for an interview as soon as you wish.

Vous verrez dans mon CV ci-joint... — You will see in my CV attached...

And every applicant needs a good CV...

CURRICULUM VITAE

Rachael Johnson
46 Loxley Road, Ambridge, Borsetshire. BO12 2AM
Téléphone 02 40 54 10 66
Nationalité anglaise

ÉDUCATION
1998:   Licence d'Histoire (mention très bien)
1995:   A-levels (équivalence Baccalauréat):
            Histoire (B), Anglais (B), Mathématiques (C)

EXPÉRIENCE PROFESSIONNELLE
Depuis 2005:   Gérante de ventes chez 'Sales Albion', Loxley.
1998-2005:   Fonctionnaire

AUTRES RENSEIGNEMENTS
Programme de formation d'informatique (mars 2007)
Permis de conduire
Je parle couramment anglais, français et gallois.

EDUCATION
1998: History degree (first class)
1995: A-levels (equivalent to Bac)
            History (B), English (B), Maths (C)

PROFESSIONAL EXPERIENCE
Since 2005: Sales manager
at 'Sales Albion', Loxley
1998-2005: Civil servant

OTHER INFORMATION
Training course in IT (March 2007)
Driving licence
I speak fluent English, French and Welsh.

Et une belle cravate

Make sure you read through the <u>covering letter</u> and <u>CV</u> on this page so you know all the vocab. If you <u>really</u> want to practise this stuff, have a go at writing <u>your own CV</u> down in French.

Telephones

You have to know <u>French phone vocab</u> and understand <u>messages</u> and stuff — it's <u>simple</u>. No. Really it is.

Un coup de téléphone — A phone call

Use 'ton' for someone you know well. If you need to be more formal, use 'votre'.

*Quel est **ton** numéro de téléphone?*   = What is <u>your</u> telephone number?

*Mon numéro de téléphone est le **vingt-huit, dix-neuf, cinquante-six**.*   = My telephone number is <u>28 19 56</u>.

Phone numbers are always given in 2-digit numbers, e.g. <u>twenty-eight</u> rather than <u>two-eight</u>. And don't ask me why they stick a 'le' in front of it — they <u>just do</u>.

When you make a call, say 'ici Bob' — 'It's Bob here'

You <u>need</u> to be able to <u>understand</u> the general phone vocab used in France...

You might hear this when someone <u>answers</u> the phone: *Allô! C'est **Philippe** à l'appareil.*   = Hello! <u>Philippe</u> speaking.

You might hear these <u>common phrases</u> on the phone:

*Est-ce que **Bob** est là?*   = Is <u>Bob</u> there?

*Est-ce que je peux parler à **Joanie**?*   = Can I speak to <u>Joanie</u>?

*Je vous **le** passe.*   = I'll put you through <u>to him</u>.

to her: la

This is a common conversation <u>closer</u>:   *À plus tard.*   = See you later.

Je veux laisser un message — I want to leave a message

You have to be able to understand phone <u>messages</u>. This is a typical <u>run-of-the-mill</u> one:

Hello, this is <u>Nicole Smith</u>.

The caller's name should go here.

I have a message for <u>Jean-Claude</u>.

This is who needs to call back.

This is what time he should call back.

*Allô, ici **Nicole Smith**. J'ai un message pour **Jean-Claude**. Est-ce qu'il peut me rappeler vers **dix-neuf heures ce soir?** Mon numéro de téléphone est le **cinquante-neuf, dix-huit, quarante-sept**. Merci beaucoup. Au revoir.*

Can he call me back at around <u>7pm tonight</u>?

My phone number is <u>59 18 47</u>.

This is the phone number he should return the call to.

Thanks a lot. Goodbye.

Le téléphone — sounds phoney to me

Make sure you learn the stuff on this page <u>really</u> well. You might hear a <u>telephone conversation</u> or somebody leaving an <u>answerphone message</u> in your listening exam. <u>Be prepared</u> and learn this page.

The World of Business

Examiners quite like listening and reading scenarios in which people discuss goods and services they need, or are providing. Don't ask me why — just read on and learn the examples.

Je vais me renseigner — I'll make some enquiries

Knowing how to ask for information is really important. As is understanding the answer.

Est-ce que vous savez où je peux trouver un plombier ?

a dentist	un dentiste
a doctor	un médecin
a hairdresser	un coiffeur

= Do you know where I can find a plumber?

Je vous conseille de chercher dans l'annuaire .

in the yellow pages:	dans les pages jaunes
in the post office:	à la poste
on the internet:	sur internet
at the tourist information office:	à l'office de tourisme

= I advise you to look in the phone book.

To 'advise someone to do something' is 'conseiller quelqu'un de faire quelque chose'. See page 199 for more verbs that work in this way.

Il y a un problème avec ma commande
— There's a problem with my order

Here's a phone conversation between a customer and a supplier.

Le vendeur:

"Ordi-vendeur, bonjour."
Hello, this is Ordi-vendeur.

Remember: nom = surname, prénom = first name.

"Alors, est-ce que je peux prendre votre nom, s'il vous plaît?"
Right, can I take your name please?

"Merci. J'ai trouvé votre commande. Quel est le problème, monsieur?"
Thank you. I've found your order. What is the problem, sir?

"Je suis désolé, monsieur. On a eu des problèmes avec notre fournisseur. On peut vous l'envoyer demain après-midi."
I'm sorry, sir. We've been having some problems with our supplier. We can send it to you tomorrow afternoon.

"Merci monsieur. Bonne journée."
Thank you sir. Have a good day.

Le client:

"Bonjour monsieur. J'ai commandé un ordinateur la semaine dernière, mais il y a un problème avec la commande."
Hello sir. I ordered a computer last week, but there's a problem with the order.

See page 60 for more technical vocab.

"Oui, c'est Césaire, Henri Césaire."
Yes, it's Césaire, Henri Césaire.

"Vous m'avez envoyé l'ordinateur, l'écran et la souris, mais je n'ai pas encore reçu le clavier."
You've sent me the computer, the screen and the mouse, but I haven't yet received the keyboard.

"Donc je l'aurai après-demain... D'accord, ça ira."
So I'll have it the day after tomorrow... OK, that'll be all right.

For more on the future tense, see pages 200-201.

"Merci monsieur. Au revoir."
Thank you sir. Goodbye.

Order? Chaos, more like

In the exams you're likely to come across vocab and phrases that you've seen before in a completely different context. The important thing is not to let the different scenarios throw you. Good luck...

Quick Questions

Section Six is jam-packed full of so much really useful information — and you need to know it all. Test yourself with these quick questions so you know where the gaps in your knowledge are, then read back over those pages. Pretty soon you'll be able to cope with anything that crops up in the exam.

Quick Questions

1) How would you say in French that you're looking for a job in an office?

2) What is the French for:

a) a part-time job?   b) a holiday job?

3) You're applying for a job as a language assistant in a French school and you're writing a cover letter. Say that you would be ideal for this job because you like working with children and you speak French.

4) Translate the following phrases into English:

a) je suis bilingue

b) je suis plein de vie

c) je ne suis jamais impoli

5) You're looking for jobs in a local French newspaper. Translate this job advert:

> Vous aimez travailler avec les gens? Vous parlez anglais? On cherche un serveur ou une serveuse. 15 heures par semaine. Appelez Pierre au 034 23-34-12-34.

6) You've applied for a job in a leisure centre and you get a phone call from the company. The secretary says to you, "Allô, est-ce que vous pouvez venir pour un entretien lundi 31 janvier à 9h avec le patron? Apportez une copie de votre CV et votre permis de conduire, s'il vous plaît." Translate this into English.

7) You're putting together a CV to send to companies in France. Translate the following words that you might need into French:

a) French degree

b) professional experience

c) training course in IT

d) other information

8) Translate this answerphone message into English:

> Allô, ici Jean Paul. J'ai un message pour Marie. Est-ce qu'elle peut me rappeler vers vingt heures ce soir? Mon numéro de téléphone est le cinquante-trois, vingt et un, quarante-quatre. Merci beaucoup. Au revoir.

9) a) What does "Est-ce que vous savez où je peux trouver un coiffeur?" mean?

b) What does "Je vous conseille de chercher dans l'annuaire" mean?

10) When working in a call centre for a clothing company in France, a customer calls to say there is a problem with their order. Tell them that you've found their order and that your company has been having some problems with their supplier. Say that you're sorry and you can send their order out next week.

Listening Questions

Track 21

Some people are discussing the jobs their family members do. Fill in the gaps in the table.

	Father	Mother	Brother	Sister	Person speaking
Example	**Hairdresser**	**X**	**X**	**Student**	**Secretary**
1	X	X		Policewoman	
2	X		Teacher	X	

Track 22

These teenagers are talking about the school day. Fill in the gaps.

Example   Lessons start at ...**8:05**... and finish at ...**4:55**... .

On Monday morning, she has ...**Spanish**... , History , ...**Maths**... and French.

Her favourite subject is ...**French**... because it's ...**easy**... .

3   Lessons start at .... and finish at ....

On Monday morning, he has .... , English , ... and Maths.

His favourite subject is .... because it's ....

4   Lessons start at .... and finish at ....

On Monday morning, she has .... , Geography , ... and IT.

Her favourite subject is .... because it's ....

Track 23

These people are talking about their part-time jobs. Complete the table.

	Place of work	How much do they earn?
Example	**shop**	**9 euros an hour**
5		
6		
7		

Listening Questions

Track 24

8 Answer these questions:

a) What is his favourite subject? ....

b) Why? ....

c) What does he want to do immediately after leaving school? ....

Track 25

9 Nicole is talking about her plans for the future. Write the correct letter in each box.

a) She wants to be:

    A   a nurse

    B   a singer

    C   a teacher

    D   a doctor

b) Her mother wants her to be:

    A   a doctor

    B   a pharmacist

    C   a waitress

    D   an accountant

Track 26

Xavier and Marie are talking about school. Find the sentence which best matches what they say and write the correct letter in the box.

10 Xavier

11 Marie

    A   I get too much homework.

    B   I prefer science and I hate history.

    C   Science teachers are horrible.

    D   I don't like Wednesday evenings.

    E   I prefer history and I hate science.

Reading Questions

1   Read this article from a French school newsletter.

Tu es en seconde? Tu as pensé à ce que tu vas faire plus tard? Quel métier te fait rêver? Nous avons interviewé Leïla, de la classe 2FT, au sujet de son avenir:

Quelle est ta matière préférée?
J'aime surtout la biologie, la physique et la chimie. Je trouve ces matières faciles et les profs sont sympas. Je fais des progrès en maths et en informatique aussi et j'aime bien l'allemand et l'anglais. À mon avis, il est important de pouvoir parler une autre langue.

Tu t'es décidée sur ce que tu vas faire l'année prochaine?
Pour moi, pas de problème! Je voudrais préparer le bac et j'ai choisi une option scientifique.

Et quel métier t'intéresse le plus?
J'aimerais être médecin. Mon père est médecin et il m'a beaucoup encouragée, mais je sais que c'est un boulot difficile et que je devrai travailler très dur pour réussir aux examens. J'aimerais travailler quelques mois dans un autre pays, en Allemagne ou aux États-Unis peut-être, parce que j'aime voyager et je m'intéresse aux autres cultures.

Tu as un petit emploi à mi-temps?
Oui, le samedi je travaille dans un magasin de chaussures. C'est un emploi qui n'est pas du tout intéressant, mais je gagne €7,00 par heure et ça, ce n'est pas mal!

Answer the questions in English:

a)   What does Leïla think about speaking more than one language?

....

b)   Leïla would like to work as a ....

c)   Is Leïla's father happy about her career plans?

....

d)   What does Leïla need to do in order to become a doctor?

....

e)   What is Leïla's Saturday job?

....

Reading Questions

2 These French teenagers are talking about some of the problems they have at school. Read each paragraph then answer the questions below.

> Je viens d'avoir encore une mauvaise note en maths. Hier c'était en biologie. J'essaie de mon mieux, mais pourtant j'ai du mal à comprendre le programme cette année. Les explications vont toujours trop vite pour moi, surtout en maths. Je crains de devoir redoubler à la fin de l'année.

Christophe 16 ans

> J'ai hâte de terminer les examens parce que je suis très stressée en ce moment. Je passe toutes mes soirées à réviser, par conséquent je ne peux pas sortir avec mes amis et ça me manque beaucoup. Vivement les vacances!

Laëtitia 17 ans

> Ma famille et moi venons de déménager alors j'ai changé d'école. Je dois dire que j'ai du mal à m'habituer au nouveau système. C'est une école privée et malheureusement on doit porter un uniforme démodé et on n'a pas le droit de porter de maquillage. C'est barbant les règles!

Aline 15 ans

> J'aime bien le lycée, ça marche bien, j'ai de bons résultats et beaucoup de copains. Ce que j'aime bien c'est qu'on peut s'exprimer et les profs nous traitent comme des adultes. Par contre ce qui m'ennuie c'est le conformisme. Pour être accepté par les autres il faut toujours porter des vêtements de marque, ça coûte vraiment cher et je n'ai pas les moyens de m'acheter beaucoup de vêtements.

Yasmine 16 ans

Choose the correct person. Write C (for Christophe), L (for Laëtitia), Y (for Yasmine) or A (for Aline) next to each question.

a) Who is struggling to get used to a new school system? ....

b) Who is scared of having to retake a year? ....

c) Who has good marks at school? ....

d) Who can't spend time with friends because of school work? ....

e) Who is not allowed to wear make-up at school? ....

f) Who is annoyed with having to spend a lot of money on clothes? ....

Speaking Question

This speaking question is all about school.
Make sure you get someone to play the role of the teacher.

Task: School

You are going to have a conversation with your teacher about school.
Your teacher will start the conversation and ask you the following questions:

- How do you get to school?
- What are your favourite subjects? Why?
- What was your primary school like?
- Do you have any problems at school?
- If you could change one thing about school, what would it be?
- What would you like to do next year?
- !

! Remember that the exclamation mark means you'll have to answer a question that you won't have prepared an answer to.

The whole conversation should last about five minutes.

Teacher's Role

You need to ask the student the following questions. You should speak first.

1 Comment vas-tu au collège?

2 Quelles sont tes matières préférées? Pourquoi?

3 Comment était ton école primaire?

4 Est-ce que tu as des problèmes au collège?

5 Si tu pouvais changer une chose au collège, qu'est-ce que tu changerais?

6 Qu'est-ce que tu voudrais faire l'année prochaine?

7 !

! The unpredictable question could be:

Qu'est-ce que tu voudrais faire après avoir quitté l'école?

Writing Questions

Task 1: Work and Education

While on work experience, you are asked to email the organisers of a conference in France to book managers from your company onto the conference. You should write 250-300 words.

You could include:

*   The dates and subject of the conference,
*   The number and names of the people attending and their job titles,
*   Information about your company,
*   A question asking for details of where the conference is,
*   A question asking about the accommodation and meal arrangements.

Remember that to score the highest marks you need to answer the task as fully as possible, expanding on the points above when it is relevant to do so.

Task 2: School in France and in the UK

You have been asked to write an article about the differences between the British and French school systems. You should write 250-300 words. You could:

*   Compare the length of the school day and break times,
*   Compare the subjects that are studied,
*   Compare school rules and school uniform,
*   Compare the exam systems,
*   Say which system you think is better and why,
*   Include any changes you would make to the British school system.

Remember that to score the highest marks you need to answer the task as fully as possible, expanding on the points above when it is relevant to do so.

Revision Summary

This revision summary covers everything from Section Six. Try to answer all the questions <u>without looking back</u> over the pages in this section. <u>Don't panic</u> if you can't answer every question — just find out what you don't know and <u>learn those pages</u> until you <u>know it all</u>.

1) Say what all your GCSE subjects are in French. I guess one of them will be 'le français'...

2) What's your favourite subject? What subject(s) don't you like? Answer in French.

3) Depuis quand apprends-tu le français? Translate the question. And then answer it in French.

4) How would you say that your lunch break begins at 12.30pm and that you eat salad and then play volleyball?

5) How would you say that you have six lessons every day and each lesson lasts 50 minutes?

6) Pete is describing his school to his French penfriend Christophe. How would he say that there are three terms, that he wears a school uniform and that the rules are very strict?

7) "Au collège, on n'a pas le droit de porter un pull à capuche et on ne peut pas parler dans les couloirs." Your French friend has just told you this in her latest email. What does she say?

8) Décris-moi ton uniforme.

9) Stéphanie says, "J'ai des difficultés à comprendre au collège — les explications sont toujours trop rapides pour moi et je crains de devoir redoubler." What does she mean?

10) Write a full French sentence explaining where you did your work experience. If you didn't do work experience anywhere then write that down. Also answer: "As-tu un emploi à mi-temps?"

11) Qu'est-ce que tu voudrais faire après les examens?

12) Tell a French passer-by what you look for in a job, what job you'd most like to do and why.

13) Write down in French that you would like to have a gap year in France in order to see the country and meet people.

14) Translate into French: "He's looking for a job in a restaurant. He has two years' experience."

15) Quel est ton numéro de téléphone? (No cheating and writing it in numerals — do it in French. And say it out loud.)

16) Impress your French teacher by telling them in French that they should look online for a dentist.

Nouns

Stop — before you panic, this stuff is a lot less scary than it looks. It's all pretty simple stuff about words for people and objects — nouns. This is really important.

Every French noun is masculine or feminine

Whether a word is masculine, feminine, singular or plural affects a heck of a lot of things. All 'the' and 'a' words change and, if that wasn't enough, the adjectives (like 'new' or 'shiny') change to fit the word.

EXAMPLES:

> an interesting book: <u>un</u> livre intéressant (masculine)
> an interesting programme: <u>une</u> émission intéressant<u>e</u> (feminine)

It's no good just knowing the French words for things — you have to know whether each one's masculine or feminine too...

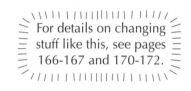

For details on changing stuff like this, see pages 166-167 and 170-172.

The Golden Rule:
Each time you learn a word, remember a le or la to go with it — don't think 'dog = chien', think 'dog = le chien'.

le and la
LE in front of a noun means it's masculine. LA in front = feminine.

These rules help you guess what gender a word is

If you have to guess whether a word is masculine or feminine, these are good rules of thumb:

Rules of Thumb for Masculine and Feminine Nouns

MASCULINE NOUNS:
most nouns that end:

-age	-er	-eau	-ing	-ment	-ou
-ail	-ier	-et	-isme	-oir	-eil

also: male people, colours, languages, days, months, seasons

FEMININE NOUNS:
most nouns that end:

-aine	-ée	-ense	-ie	-ise	-tion
-ance	-elle	-esse	-ière	-sion	-tude
-anse	-ence	-ette	-ine	-té	-ure

also: female people

Learn these rules but don't let them put you off

This section does have quite a lot of scary-looking grammar in it, but it's all got to be learnt I'm afraid. So take a deep breath and go through this section slowly and carefully. You'll be fine.

Making Nouns Plural

Making Nouns Plural

1) Nouns in French are usually made plural by adding an 's' — just like English, really.

> e.g.: une orange → des oranges
> *an orange* → *oranges*

2) But there are always <u>exceptions</u> to the rule in French.
Nouns with the endings in the table below have a
<u>different</u> plural form — and this lot are just the beginning.

Noun ending	Irregular plural ending	Example
-ail	-aux	travail → travaux
-al	-aux	journal → journaux
-eau	-eaux	bureau → bureaux
-eu	-eux	jeu → jeux

> **Top tip for plurals**
> Each time you <u>learn</u> a new word, make sure you know <u>how</u> to make it into a plural too.

3) Some nouns ending in -ou take the plural -oux.

> e.g.: un bijou → des bijoux
> *a jewel* → *jewellery*

4) Some nouns have completely irregular plurals. You'll have to learn these nouns by practising over and over.

> e.g.: un œil → des yeux
> *an eye* → *eyes*

5) Some nouns <u>don't change</u> in the plural.
These are usually nouns that end in <u>-s</u>, <u>-x</u> or <u>-z</u>.

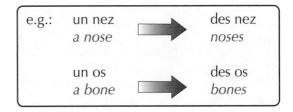

> e.g.: un nez → des nez
> *a nose* → *noses*
>
> un os → des os
> *a bone* → *bones*

6) When you make a noun plural, instead of 'le' or 'la' to say 'the', you have to use '<u>les</u>' — see page 166.

Learn all these plural endings

The bottom line is — <u>every time</u> you learn a word in French, you <u>have</u> to learn whether it's <u>le</u> or <u>la</u>, and how to make it <u>plural</u>. If you get it wrong, you'll <u>lose marks</u> for accuracy — don't say I didn't warn you.

Articles

'The' and 'a' — you use these words more than a mobile phone. They're tricky. Revise 'em well.

'A' — un, une

Grammar Fans: these are called 'Indefinite Articles'.

1) In English we don't have genders for nouns — simple.
2) In French, you need to know whether a word is masculine or feminine.

masculine	feminine
un	une

EXAMPLES:

Masculine

J'ai un frère.

= I have a brother.

Feminine

J'ai une sœur.

= I have a sister.

'The' — le, la, l', les

Grammar Fans: these are called 'Definite Articles'.

1) Like the French for 'a', the word for 'the' is different for masculine and feminine. This one has a plural form as well, though.

2) For words starting with a vowel (a, e, i, o, u) the 'le' or 'la' are shortened to l', e.g. l'orange.

3) Some words starting with an 'h', also take 'l'' instead of 'le' or 'la'. Sadly there's no rule for this — you just have to learn which ones take 'l'' and which ones take 'le' or 'la'.

masculine singular	feminine singular	in front of a vowel / some words beginning with 'h'	masculine or feminine plural
le	la	l'	les

EXAMPLES:

Le garçon. = The boy.

La fille. = The girl.

L'homme. = The man.

Les hommes. = The men.

Le hamster. = The hamster.

Les hamsters. = The hamsters

Articles come into almost every sentence you'll ever use

You'll need this stuff for your GCSE — you really won't get far without it. Luckily this stuff isn't too tricky, so as long as you learn this page thoroughly, you shouldn't have any problems at exam time.

Articles

'De' and 'à' + le, la, l', les = 'to the' and 'of the'

1) Weird stuff happens with '<u>à</u>' (to) and '<u>de</u>' (of).
2) You <u>can't</u> say 'à le', 'à les', 'de le' or 'de les'.
3) '<u>À</u>' and '<u>de</u>' combine with '<u>le</u>' and '<u>les</u>' to make new words — '<u>au</u>', '<u>aux</u>', '<u>du</u>' and '<u>des</u>'.

	le	la	l'	les
à +	au	à la	à l'	aux
de +	du	de la	de l'	des

EXAMPLES :

Je vais <u>à</u>   +   *<u>le</u> café*   =   *Je vais <u>au</u> café.*   = I go to the café.

Je viens <u>de</u>   +   *<u>le</u> Canada*   =   *Je viens <u>du</u> Canada.*   = I come from Canada.

'Some' or 'any' — du, de la, de l', des

Grammar Fans: these are called '<u>Partitive Articles</u>'.

These don't just mean '<u>of the</u>' — they can also mean '<u>some</u>' or '<u>any</u>'.

masculine singular	feminine singular	in front of a vowel / 'h' which takes 'l''	masculine or feminine plural
du	de la	de l'	des

EXAMPLES:

Avez-vous <u>du</u> pain?   *J'ai <u>des</u> pommes.*

  = Have you got <u>any</u> bread?   = I have <u>some</u> apples.

N.B. In <u>negative</u> sentences, like 'I don't have any apples', you just use '<u>de</u>' — 'Je n'ai pas <u>de</u> pommes'.

A page on 'the' — not the most fun

There's no getting around it — you <u>need</u> this stuff to get your <u>French right</u> in the <u>assessments</u>.
<u>Cover up</u> the page and write out the <u>tables</u> — keep on scribbling till you can do it in your sleep.

Quick Questions

You're going to need every bit of grammar in this section when the big day comes around. If you don't learn it now, you'll be stuck when you try to answer those exam questions in French. Go over the last few pages then answer every question on this double page before moving on. That should do the trick.

Quick Questions

1) Write down whether each of these words is masculine or feminine:
   a) chien   b) souris   c) chat   d) oiseau
   e) lapin   f) vache   g) père   h) mère
   i) sœur   j) frère   k) pomme   l) orange
   m) maison   n) hôpital   o) école   p) collège

2) Translate these words into French, then write down whether they're masculine or feminine:
   a) airport   b) music   c) cake   d) cinema
   e) beach   f) egg   g) strawberry   h) tennis
   i) rugby   j) biology

3) For each of the following word endings, say whether words which end that way are usually masculine or feminine:
   a) -tion   b) -ière   c) -ment   d) -esse
   e) -ou   f) -ée   g) -sion   h) -ail
   i) -er   j) -elle   k) -isme   l) -ise
   m) -té   n) -ure   o) -et

4) Are colours, months, days and seasons usually masculine or feminine?

5) Turn these words from the singular to the plural:
   a) fromage   b) poire   c) homme   d) enfant
   e) maison   f) poisson   g) table   h) chaise
   i) crayon

6) Now turn these from the singular to the plural — they're a bit more tricky:
   a) journal   b) tableau   c) os   d) cheval
   e) oiseau   f) œil   g) nez   h) jeu
   i) château   j) drapeau

7) Try and turn these plural nouns back into singular ones (and write down whether they are masculine or feminine):
   a) travaux   b) choux   c) bureaux   d) cadeaux
   e) femmes   f) yeux   g) feux   h) bras
   i) gâteaux   j) lieux

8) Write down the correct French word for 'a' for each of these nouns:
   a) chemise   b) radio   c) chien   d) télévision
   e) stylo   f) gomme   g) fromage

9) For each of these words, swap the 'un' or 'une' for the correct French word for 'the' (le/la/l'):
   a) une maison   b) un professeur   c) une robe   d) un abricot
   e) un jardin   f) une orange   g) un hôpital   h) un hamster

Quick Questions

Quick Questions

10) How would you say in French:
   - a) the cats
   - b) a hotel
   - c) the station
   - d) the pupils
   - e) the holidays
   - f) a car
   - g) the bicycle
   - h) a book

11) All words that begin with 'h' use 'l'' as their definite article. True or false?

12) Using the phrase "Je vais à …", write short sentences to explain that you are going to the following places (NB: You will have to combine the 'à' with the 'le/la/l'/les'):
   - a) le café
   - b) la gare
   - c) l'hôpital
   - d) le collège
   - e) l'office de tourisme
   - f) la pharmacie
   - g) les magasins
   - h) le musée

13) Write down how you would say in French 'to' the following places:
   - a) the bank
   - b) the theatre
   - c) the cinema
   - d) the castle

14) Fill in the gaps in these sentences with the right form of 'à' + 'le/la/l'/les':
   - a) "Je joue ..... football chaque jour."
   - b) "Qu'est-ce que tu fais ..... école?"
   - c) "Le week-end, je vais ..... discothèque."
   - d) "L'été dernier je suis allé ..... États-Unis."

15) Using the phrase "Qu'est que tu penses de …" write short sentences to ask your friend what they think about the following things (NB: this time you need to combine 'de' with the 'le/la/l'/les'):
   - a) la musique pop
   - b) les films américains
   - c) le dernier film de Hugh Grant
   - d) l'Angleterre
   - e) les Français
   - f) la cuisine française
   - g) le football
   - h) le ski

16) Fill in the gaps in these sentences with the right form of 'de' + 'le/la/l'/les':
   - a) "Avez-vous ………. chocolat?"
   - b) "J'ai peur ………. chiens."
   - c) "Je voudrais ………. confiture avec mon croissant."
   - d) "Je joue ………. piano et mon frère joue ………. guitare."
   - e) "Est-ce que tu aimes faire ………. cyclisme?"

17) Translate the following negative sentences into French:
   - a) My father doesn't have any friends.
   - b) My friend Sally doesn't have any animals.
   - c) They don't have any hobbies.

18) Translate this conversation into French:
   - A: 'Have you got any apples?'
   - B: 'Yes, of course. How many would you like?'
   - A: 'Two please. I would also like some bread.'
   - B: 'OK. Would you like some butter as well?'
   - A: 'No thanks, but I would like some cheese.'
   - B: 'I'm sorry but I don't have any cheese today.'
   - A: 'OK. Thanks.'

Adjectives

Gain <u>more marks</u> and show what an interesting person you are by using some <u>juicy describing</u> words.

Adjectives must 'agree' with the thing they're describing

1) In <u>English</u>, the describing word (adjective) stays the <u>same</u> — like <u>big</u> bus, <u>big</u> bananas...

2) In <u>French</u>, the describing word has to <u>change</u> to <u>match</u> whatever it's describing — whether what it's describing is <u>masculine</u> or <u>feminine</u>, and <u>singular</u> or <u>plural</u>.

Look at these examples where 'intéressant' has to change:

> Masculine Singular
> le garçon intéressant
> *(the <u>interesting</u> boy)*
>
> Feminine Singular
> la fille intéressant<u>e</u>
> *(the <u>interesting</u> girl)*
>
> Masculine Plural
> les garçons intéressant<u>s</u>
> *(the <u>interesting</u> boys)*
>
> Feminine Plural
> les filles intéressant<u>es</u>
> *(the <u>interesting</u> girls)*

The rules are:

1)
> Add an '<u>-e</u>' to the describing word if the word being described is <u>feminine</u> (see page 164).

Only if the describing word doesn't already end in an 'e' without an accent.

l'homme intelligent
= the clever man

la femme intelligent<u>e</u>
= the clever woman

2)
> Add an '<u>-s</u>' to the describing word if the word being described is <u>plural</u> (see page 165).

Of course, that means if it's <u>feminine plural</u>, then you usually have to add '<u>-es</u>'.

les hommes intelligent<u>s</u>
= the clever men

les femmes intelligent<u>es</u>
= the clever women

IMPORTANT NOTE: When you look an adjective up in the <u>dictionary</u> it gives the <u>masculine singular</u> form. If you need a feminine or singular form, you'll need to make sure it agrees yourself.

Adjectives never argue — they always agree
Just remember to watch out for those pesky adjective <u>endings</u> so that they <u>always</u> match the gender of the noun. This is really <u>basic</u> stuff but you'll <u>lose marks</u> if your adjectives don't agree with the noun.

Adjectives

Learn the describing words which don't follow the rules

1) Adjectives which end in <u>-x</u>, <u>-f</u>, <u>-er</u>, <u>-on</u>, <u>-en</u>, <u>-el</u>, <u>-il</u> and <u>-c</u> follow different rules:

Group of words ending:	Most important ones in the group	masculine singular	feminine singular	masculine plural	feminine plural
-x	sérieux (serious), ennuyeux (boring), délicieux (delicious), dangereux (dangerous) merveilleux (marvellous) & heureux ➡	heureux (happy)	heureuse	heureux	heureuses
-f	actif (active), négatif (negative), sportif (sporty), vif (lively) & neuf ➡	neuf (new)	neuve	neufs	neuves
-er	dernier (last), fier (proud), cher (dear), étranger (foreign) & premier ➡	premier (first)	première	premiers	premières
-on, -en, -el, -il	mignon (sweet), ancien (old/former), cruel (cruel), gentil (kind) & bon ➡	bon (good)	bonne	bons	bonnes
-c	sec (dry), franc (frank) & blanc ➡	blanc (white)	blanche	blancs	blanches

Adjectives ending in these letters <u>double</u> their <u>last letter</u> before adding 'e' in the feminine.

'<u>Sèche</u>' (f.sing.) and '<u>sèches</u>' (f.pl.) add an accent.

2) There are also some adjectives which are <u>completely irregular</u> — you'll have to learn these ones off by heart.

masculine singular	before a m. sing. noun beginning with a vowel or 'h' which takes 'l'	feminine singular	masculine plural	feminine plural
vieux (old)	vieil	vieille	vieux	vieilles
beau (fine/pretty)	bel	belle	beaux	belles
nouveau (new)	nouvel	nouvelle	nouveaux	nouvelles
fou (mad)	fol	folle	fous	folles
long (long)	—	longue	longs	longues
tout (all)	—	toute	tous	toutes

Quelque and chaque — rule-breakers...

Grammar Fans: '<u>Indefinite Adjectives</u>'.

'Quelque' only changes from singular to plural, by adding an 's'. There is no difference for masculine and feminine.

J'ai acheté quelques bonbons.   = I bought some sweets.

'Chaque' always stays the same.

Chaque personne doit écrire leur nom.   = Each person must write their name.

There are always a few that don't follow the rules

It's one of those <u>annoying</u> little facts of GCSE French that you can make as many rules as you like, but there will always be a few <u>rogue</u> words that don't follow the pattern. Best learn these <u>exceptions</u>.

Adjectives

Details are key to doing well in the exam — so, words to <u>describe</u> things are quite <u>important</u>.

Top 21 Describing Words

Here are 21 <u>adjectives</u> — they're the ones you really <u>have</u> to know.

good:	bon(ne)	*normal:*	normal(e)	*young:*	jeune
bad:	mauvais(e)	*interesting:*	intéressant(e)	*new:*	nouveau / nouvelle
beautiful:	beau / belle	*boring:*	ennuyeux / ennuyeuse	*brand new:*	neuf / neuve
happy:	heureux / heureuse	*terrible:*	affreux / affreuse	*fast:*	rapide
sad:	triste	*long:*	long(ue)	*slow:*	lent(e)
easy:	facile	*small/short:*	petit(e)	*practical:*	pratique
difficult:	difficile	*old:*	vieux / vieille	*strange:*	étrange

Most describing words go after the word they describe

It's the opposite of English — in French <u>most</u> describing words (adjectives) <u>go after</u> the word they're describing (the noun).

EXAMPLES:

J'ai une voiture rapide .   = I have a <u>fast</u> car.

J'ai lu un livre intéressant .   = I read an <u>interesting</u> book.

You can also use describing words in sentences with verbs like '<u>être</u>' (to be) and '<u>devenir</u>' (to become). The adjective still needs to <u>agree</u> with the noun though.

EXAMPLES:

Ils sont prêts .   = They are <u>ready</u>.

> Adjectives are always <u>masculine</u> <u>singular</u> after '<u>ce</u>'. E.g. 'C'est nouveau' (It's new), 'Ce sera cher' (It will be expensive), etc.

Elle est devenue belle .   = She has become <u>beautiful</u>.

It's all in the details

The examiners will be <u>really</u> impressed if you can describe things in loads of detail, and it will make your answers more <u>interesting</u> too. Just remember that the adjectives usually go <u>after</u> the noun.

More Adjectives

Unsurprisingly, there's a few more pages on adjectives for you to get to grips with. See how you get on.

There are some odd ones out that go in front

These describing words almost always go before the noun — a real pain:

good:	bon(ne)	young:	jeune	bad:	mauvais(e)
beautiful:	beau / belle	old:	vieux / vieil(le)	high:	haut(e)
better / best:	meilleur(e)	nice / pretty:	joli(e)	nasty:	vilain(e)
new:	nouveau / nouvel(le)	small:	petit(e)		

EXAMPLES:

Adjectives still have to agree, regardless of whether they come before or after the noun.

J'ai un nouveau chat.   = I have a new cat.

J'ai une petite maison, avec un joli jardin et une belle vue.

= I have a small house, with a pretty garden and a beautiful view.

Some mean different things before and after the noun

Some adjectives change their meaning according to whether they are before or after the noun.
Here are some important ones — learn them carefully.

adjective	meaning if before	meaning if after
ancien	former un ancien soldat (a former soldier)	old/ancient un tableau ancien (an old painting)
cher	dear mon cher ami (my dear friend)	expensive une voiture chère (an expensive car)
propre	own ma propre chambre (my own room)	clean ma chambre propre (my clean room)
grand	great un grand homme (a great man)	grand un homme grand (a big/tall man)

EXAMPLES:

J'ai ma propre voiture.   = I have my own car.

J'ai une voiture propre.   = I have a clean car.

If you're keeping up so far, you're on track for a great grade

By now you're probably thinking you could get through life without adjectives but I'm afraid you'd be wrong. Learn those 11 key words at the top of the page — they'll spice your writing up no end.

More Adjectives

More <u>really</u> important stuff on describing words, including words that show <u>who something belongs to</u>...

My, your, our — words for who it belongs to

You have to be able to <u>use</u> and <u>understand</u> these words to say that something <u>belongs</u> to someone:

Like in English, these go <u>before the noun</u>.
E.g. '<u>mon ami</u>', '<u>notre cousin</u>', etc.

	masculine singular	feminine singular	plural
my	mon	ma	mes
your (informal, sing.)	ton	ta	tes
his/her/its	son	sa	ses
our	notre	notre	nos
your (formal/pl.)	votre	votre	vos
their	leur	leur	leurs

Grammar Fans: These are '<u>Possessive Adjectives</u>'.

You have to choose the <u>gender</u> (masculine, feminine or plural) to match the thing it's <u>describing</u>, and NOT the person it <u>belongs</u> to. So in the example below, it's always 'mon père' even if it's a girl talking.

Mon père est petit, ma mère est grande.   = <u>My</u> father is short, <u>my</u> mother is tall.

This means that <u>son/sa/ses</u> could mean either '<u>his</u>' or '<u>her</u>'. You can usually tell which one it is by the <u>context</u>.

J'ai vu Pierre avec sa sœur .   = I saw <u>Pierre</u> with <u>his sister</u>.

Marie et sa sœur sont inséparables.   = <u>Marie</u> and <u>her sister</u> are inseparable.

Always use 'mon amie' — even if your friend's a girl

Before a noun beginning with a <u>vowel</u> or words beginning with '<u>h</u>' that take '<u>l'</u>', always use the masculine form. You do this because it's easier to <u>say</u>.

Mon amie s'appelle Helen.   = <u>My friend</u>'s called Helen.

Écoutez mon histoire .   = Listen to <u>my story</u>.

My, oh my...

It's so important, all this — especially that the possessive adjectives change according to the <u>thing being described</u>, NOT the owner. You'll need to be able to <u>use</u> and <u>understand</u> this stuff really well.

Quick Questions

Adjectives are all about adding a bit of extra detail to your sentences, and that's where you'll pick up those valuable extra marks. The examiners will only be impressed if you can use adjectives properly though, so make sure you know your stuff by trying these quick questions for size.

Quick Questions

1) Put the correct form of the adjective 'petit' before each of these nouns:
   a) un .... homme
   b) une .... femme
   c) les .... garçons
   d) les .... filles

2) For each of these phrases, write down the correct form of the adjective in brackets:
   a) les (grand) magasins
   b) la voiture (vert)
   c) le chien (méchant)
   d) des questions (difficile)
   e) un homme (fort)
   f) les cheveux (noir)
   g) une femme (intelligent)
   h) les filles (allemand)

3) Turn each of these adjectives from the masculine to the feminine:
   a) heureux
   b) actif
   c) premier
   d) sérieux
   e) bon
   f) gentil
   g) blanc
   h) dangereux
   i) sportif
   j) sec
   k) cher

4) How would you say, "She is really boring" in French?

5) How would you say, "The cakes are delicious" in French?

6) Write a short passage in French to describe your parents. Your father is tall with blue eyes and a big nose. Your mother is short with green eyes and blond hair.

7) Write down the correct form of 'vieux' to use with each of these nouns:
   a) femme
   b) vin
   c) chaussures
   d) homme
   e) journaux

8) Using the adjective 'beau', translate these phrases into French:
   a) a pretty girl
   b) some handsome men
   c) a fine day
   d) some beautiful women
   e) a beautiful bird

9) Using the right form of 'nouveau', how would you say, "I have a new bike" in French?

10) Using the right form of 'nouveau', how would you say, "My Dad has a new car" in French?

11) Fill in the gaps in these sentences with the correct form of 'tout':
   a) "Je regarde la télévision .... les jours."
   b) "Il a plu .... la nuit."
   c) "Il a mangé .... le gâteau."
   d) ".......... les filles anglaises aiment le chocolat."

12) Write a short passage in French to describe your friends. Pierre is tall with short, brown hair, and you think he is mad; Marie is beautiful and has blue eyes and long blond hair; Jean-Paul and Marc are both short and fat, but very kind.

176

Quick Questions

Quick Questions

13) Write down the masculine singular French word for:
   a) interesting   b) strange   c) slow
   d) bad   e) difficult   f) fast

14) How would you say 'happy' in French? (Write the singular form but if the masculine and feminine are different, give both.)

15) How would you say 'sad' in French? (Write the singular form but if the masculine and feminine are different, give both.)

16) Write down the French for "I think homework is easy."

17) Put the describing word in brackets in the right place (before or after the noun), and make sure it agrees in gender and number:
   a) une (rouge) voiture   b) les (bleu) yeux
   c) une (joli) fille   d) une (triste) histoire
   e) un (mauvais) film   f) un (ennuyeux) livre

18) Using the adjective 'neuf', how would you say "I have new shoes" in French?

19) Write a short passage in French to explain that your Maths teacher is old, short and nasty, but your French teacher (a woman) is young, nice and pretty.

20) What is the difference in meaning between these two phrases?
   un ancien professeur   un professeur ancien

21) Translate these sentences into French:
   a) "Amy is a dear friend."   b) "Mark likes expensive wine."
   c) "I have my own room."   d) "Mum likes a clean kitchen."

22) What is the French for:
   a) my dog   b) your house   c) his shoes   d) our parents
   e) their car   f) my friend   g) her brother

23) Translate this conversation into English:
   A: "Est-ce que tu as reçu de jolis cadeaux pour ton anniversaire?"
   B: "Oui. Ma mère m'a donné une robe rouge et des chaussures rouges et noires. Mon père m'a donné un nouveau livre et une grande boîte de chocolats."
   A: "Et ton frère et ta sœur?"
   B: "Ma sœur m'a donné un CD, mais mon frère a perdu tout son argent, donc je n'ai rien reçu de lui."
   A: "C'était un bon anniversaire?"
   B: "Non, pas du tout! La robe est horrible, les chaussures sont trop petites, le livre est ennuyeux, les chocolats sont horribles et le CD est très mauvais."

24) Translate this conversation into French:
   A: "Is that your car?"
   B: "No, that's not my car, it's Pierre's car. His car is fast and expensive. My car is old and slow."

SECTION SEVEN — GRAMMAR

Adverbs

The last few pages were about describing <u>objects</u>, e.g. the bus is <u>red</u>. This page is about describing things you <u>do</u>, e.g. 'I speak French <u>perfectly</u>', and about adding <u>more info</u> — 'I speak French <u>almost</u> perfectly'.

Make your sentences better by saying how you do things

1) In <u>English</u>, you don't say 'I talk slow' — you have to <u>add</u> a '<u>-ly</u>' on the end to say 'I talk slow<u>ly</u>'.
2) In <u>French</u>, you have to <u>add</u> a '<u>-ment</u>' on the end, but first you have to make sure the adjective is in the <u>feminine</u> form (see page 164).

> Grammar Fans:
> these are '<u>Adverbs</u>'.

EXAMPLES:

Il parle lentement *.* = He speaks <u>slowly</u>.

normally: normalement
strangely: étrangement

The French word for 'slow' is '<u>lent</u>', but the feminine form is '<u>lente</u>'. Add '<u>-ment</u>' and you get '<u>lentement</u>' = slowly.

3) <u>Unlike adjectives</u> (pages 170-172) you <u>don't</u> ever have to <u>change</u> these words — they're describing the <u>action</u>, not the person doing it.

Feminine *Elle parle* lentement *.* ← Always the same.

Plural *Nous parlons* lentement *.*

Learn these odd ones out off by heart

Just like in English there are <u>odd ones out</u> — for example, you <u>don't</u> say 'I sing <u>goodly</u>'. The adjective 'good' changes to 'well' when it becomes an adverb. Have a look at the other odd ones out in the table:

ENGLISH	FRENCH
good → well	bon(ne) → bien
bad → badly	mauvais(e) → mal
quick → quickly	rapide → vite

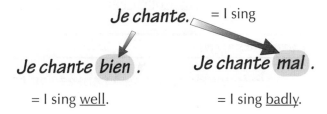

Je chante. = I sing

Je chante bien *.*

= I sing <u>well</u>.

Je chante mal *.*

= I sing <u>badly</u>.

The odd ones are the most common

Adverbs are just like adjectives except they describe the <u>verb</u>. Watch out for the ones that <u>don't</u> fit the pattern, especially as they're the ones that you'll need most <u>often</u>. Learn the <u>regular</u> ones too.

Adverbs

Use one of these fine words to give even more detail

Add any one of these simple <u>words</u> or <u>phrases</u> to make that impressive sentence even more so...

You can use them for sentences saying <u>how something is done</u>:

Je cours **trop** *lentement.*   = I run <u>too</u> slowly.

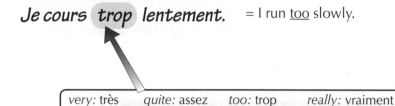

very: très   *quite:* assez   *too:* trop   *really:* vraiment

...and for sentences about <u>what something is like</u>...   *Bob est* **très** *heureux.*

= Bob is <u>very</u> happy.

almost: presque

Il est **peu** *intéressant.*   = He is <u>not very</u> interesting.

...and for saying <u>what you think about something</u>...

too much: trop

J'aime **beaucoup** *la glace.*   = I like ice cream <u>a lot</u>.

...and for saying <u>how often something is done</u>...

sometimes: quelquefois   *often:* souvent

Je joue **de temps en temps** *au football.*   = I play football <u>from time to time</u>.

I eat too quickly and run too slowly

This is a bit like English — you have a set ending (-ment) to learn and stick on, and it's not too tricky either. Make sure you really know the standard rule and all the exceptions.

Comparing Things

Often you don't just want to say that something is <u>tasty</u>, <u>juicy</u> or whatever — you want to say that it's the <u>tastiest</u>, or (to create a nice amount of jealousy) that it's <u>juicier than</u> someone else's...

How to say more strange, most strange

In French you can't say '<u>stranger</u>' or '<u>strangest</u>' — you have to say '<u>more strange</u>' or '<u>the most strange</u>':

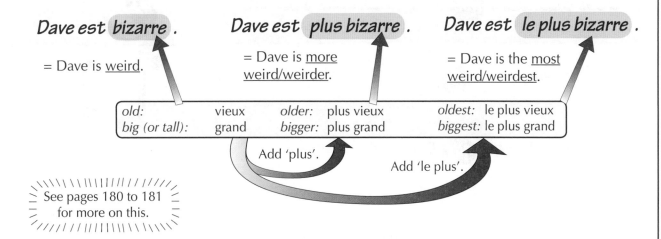

Dave est bizarre .

= Dave is <u>weird</u>.

Dave est plus bizarre .

= Dave is <u>more weird/weirder</u>.

Dave est le plus bizarre .

= Dave is the <u>most weird/weirdest</u>.

old:	vieux	*older:*	plus vieux	*oldest:*	le plus vieux
big (or tall):	grand	*bigger:*	plus grand	*biggest:*	le plus grand

Add 'plus'.

Add 'le plus'.

See pages 180 to 181 for more on this.

Don't forget agreement

See pages 170-172 for more on how adjectives <u>agree</u>.

The adjectives still need to <u>agree</u> as normal:

less pretty: moins jolie

Cette robe est plus jolie . = This dress is <u>prettier</u>.

less strong: moins forts

Ils sont plus forts . = They're <u>stronger</u>.

When you're saying 'the most ...', you need to say '<u>le</u> plus', '<u>la</u> plus' or '<u>les</u> plus' to match the word you're describing (see pages 166-167).

the least funny: la moins amusante

Liz est la plus amusante .

= Liz is <u>the funniest</u>.

the least strong: les moins forts

Ed et Jo sont les plus amusants .

= Ed and Jo are <u>the funniest</u>.

This is the least funny page I've ever seen

If you want to <u>compare</u> something to something else in French then you'll need this page of <u>wonders</u> to see you through. Learn how to turn adjectives into '<u>the most...</u>' or '<u>the least...</u>' by revising this stuff.

Comparing Things

The three ways of comparing things — more, less and as

If you want to say 'less ...' or 'as ... as', you just use the words '<u>moins</u>' and '<u>aussi</u>' instead of '<u>plus</u>'. And the word for '<u>than</u>' is '<u>que</u>'.

Ed est **plus** *grand* **que** *Tom.*   = Ed is tall<u>er</u> <u>than</u> Tom.

Ed est **moins** *grand* **que** *Tom.*   = Ed is <u>less</u> tall <u>than</u> Tom.

Ed est **aussi** *grand* **que** *Tom.*   = Ed is <u>as</u> tall <u>as</u> Tom.

Ed est **le moins** *grand.*

= Ed is <u>the least</u> tall.

To say '<u>the least ...</u>', you just say '<u>le/la/les moins ...</u>':

Pour le meilleur et pour le pire... — For better or worse...

Just like in English, there are some <u>odd ones out</u>, and these tend to be the ones that crop up <u>a lot</u>. With these ones, you don't say '<u>plus ...</u>' or '<u>moins ...</u>'.

good:	bon(ne)(s)	→	*better:*	meilleur(e)(s)	→	*best:*	le meilleur
bad:	mauvais(e)(s)	→	*worse:*	pire(s)	→	*worst:*	le pire
lots:	beaucoup	→	*more:*	plus	→	*most:*	le plus
little:	peu	→	*less:*	moins	→	*least:*	le moins

With these four, the 'le' is replaced with 'la' or 'les' if the thing that's being described is feminine or plural. 'Meilleur' still takes an 'e' in the feminine and an 's' in the plural, and 'pire' still takes an 's' in the plural.

EXAMPLES:

Ce livre est **meilleur** *que le dernier.*   = This book is <u>better</u> than the last (one).

Le vélo bleu est **le pire** .   = The blue bike is <u>the worst</u>.

Make sure you know the stuff on this page inside out
To learn this kind of thing you just need to <u>repeat some examples</u> to yourself about 30 times in a kind of <u>weird chant</u> until it <u>sticks</u>. People might think you're strange, but you'll know <u>lots</u> of French.

Comparing Things

If you thought comparing adjectives was fun, I expect you'll love this page about comparing adverbs.

For 'more' and 'most' use the same rules as before

When you're comparing how people do things, it works pretty much how you'd expect.

Dave parle bizarrement . = Dave talks weirdly.

> 'Bizarrement' is an adverb. See pages 177-178 for more on this.

Dave parle plus bizarrement . = Dave talks more weirdly.

Dave parle le plus bizarrement . = Dave talks the most weirdly.

Adverbs (e.g. 'bizarrement') don't agree, and you always use 'le'.

> DON'T fall into the trap of saying 'vitement' for fast. The adverb is always 'vite' and the adjective is 'rapide'.

Jessica court le plus vite .

= Jessica runs the fastest.

Je chante mieux que toi — I sing better than you

There are some odd ones out you need to know with comparative adverbs:

well:	bien	➡	*better:*	mieux	➡	*best:* le mieux
badly:	mal	➡	*worse:*	pire	➡	*worst:* le pire

Tu joues bien , mais c'est Henri qui joue le mieux .

= You play well, but Henri plays the best.

Il chante mal , mais je chante le pire . = He sings badly, but I sing the worst.

And that's more or less it

This'll help you sound much more sophisticated when you speak French. Instead of saying "It's a good film", you can say "It's a better film than...", or "It's the best film of the year". Loads of possibilities.

Prepositions

It all <u>looks terrifying</u>. But you've got to <u>learn</u> it if you want tip-top marks. It's really only a <u>few words</u>.

TO — à or en

Where we use '<u>to</u>', the French usually use '<u>à</u>': **Il va à Paris.** = He's going <u>to</u> Paris.

But for feminine countries and ones beginning with a vowel, it's usually '<u>en</u>': **Il va en France.** = He's going <u>to</u> France.

For things like <u>to go</u>, <u>to do</u>, just use the <u>infinitive</u> (see page 195); you <u>don't</u> need an extra word for '<u>to</u>'. E.g. aller = <u>to go</u>, faire = <u>to make</u>.

For 'the train to Calais' see 'the train for Calais' on page 183.

ON — sur or à

For '<u>on top</u>' of something, it's '<u>sur</u>':

Sur la table. = <u>On</u> the table.

For days of the week, it's <u>left out</u>:

Je pars lundi. = I'm leaving <u>on</u> Monday.

When it's <u>not</u> 'on top', it's usually '<u>à</u>':

Je l'ai vu à la télé. = I saw it <u>on</u> TV.

J'irai à pied. = I'll go <u>on</u> foot.

IN — dans, à or en

If it's actually <u>inside</u> something, then it's usually '<u>dans</u>': **C'est dans la boîte.** = It's <u>in</u> the box.

If it's <u>in</u> a town, it's '<u>à</u>': **J'habite à Marseille.** = I live <u>in</u> Marseilles.

If you want to say <u>in</u> a feminine country, or one beginning with a vowel, then it's usually '<u>en</u>': **J'habite en France.** = I live <u>in</u> France.

FROM — de or à partir de

Where we use '<u>from</u>', they usually use '<u>de</u>':

De Londres à Paris. = <u>From</u> London to Paris.

Je viens de Cardiff. = I come <u>from</u> Cardiff.

For dates, it's '<u>à partir de</u>':

À partir du 4 juin.

= <u>From</u> the 4th of June.

Tiny but deadly

There's <u>so</u> much on this page that catches people out. Before carrying on, go back over this page and cover up all the <u>coloured boxes</u> with <u>French</u> in them, and translate back all the <u>English</u> sentences.

Prepositions

OF — **de** or **en**

Where we use '<u>of</u>', they usually use '<u>de</u>': *Une bouteille **de** lait.* = A bottle <u>of</u> milk.

Watch out: sometimes it's hard to spot the '<u>de</u>' in a sentence, because '<u>de</u>' + '<u>le</u>' = <u>du</u>, and '<u>de</u>' + '<u>les</u>'= '<u>des</u>' — see page 167.

You don't say 'of' with <u>dates</u> (see page 4):

'<u>Made of</u>' is '<u>en</u>': *C'est **en** cuir.* = It's made <u>of</u> leather. *Le 2 juin.* = The 2nd <u>of</u> June.

FOR — **pour** or **depuis**

Where we use '<u>for</u>', they usually use '<u>pour</u>':   For 'the train for...', it's '<u>pour</u>':

*Un cadeau **pour** moi.* = A present <u>for</u> me.   *Le train **pour** Calais.* = The train <u>for</u> Calais.

To say how long you're going to do something for in the future, use '<u>pour</u>':

*Je vais aller en France **pour** le week-end.*   = I'm going to go to France <u>for</u> the weekend.

To say things like 'I've studied French for 5 years', use the <u>present tense</u> and '<u>depuis</u>':

*J'apprends le français **depuis** cinq ans.*   = I've studied French <u>for</u> 5 years.

AT — **à**

À six heures. = <u>At</u> six o'clock.   *Elle est **à** l'école.* = She is <u>at</u> school.

<u>Watch out</u>: It can be hard to spot the '<u>à</u>' in a sentence, because '<u>à</u>' + '<u>le</u>' = '<u>au</u>' and '<u>à</u>' + '<u>les</u>' = '<u>aux</u>' — see p.167.

Really small but really important words

These pages are chock-full of <u>tiny</u> but <u>vital</u> words. Some words have a few <u>different</u> meanings so you need to make sure you choose the <u>right</u> one, otherwise it might change the meaning of the sentence.

Quick Questions

Take a deep breath and plunge into this double page of Quick Questions. They're the best way of making sure you know everything in this bit of the section, so get going.

Quick Questions

1) Change these describing words into adverbs by adding '-ment' to the feminine form:
   a) lent   b) parfait   c) étrange   d) rapide   e) heureux

2) How would you say the following sentences in French?
   a) "I play piano perfectly"   b) "He talks slowly"

3) Chantal says, "Je chante bien mais je danse mal". What is she telling you?

4) Write a short passage in French to explain that you play table tennis well,
   but you play football badly because you run slowly.

5) Write down the French for: a) too   b) very   c) quite   d) almost

6) How would you say:
   a) I sometimes work faster than Emma.   b) I always work faster than Ed.

7) Translate the following sentence into English: "Je regarde les films d'horreur de temps en
   temps, mais je regarde souvent les films romantiques."

8) "Je parle français" means 'I speak French'. How would you say:
   a) "I speak French well."   b) "I speak French quite well."   c) "I speak French very well."

9) Translate these sentences into French:
   a) "The teacher speaks too quickly."   b) "My feet are very big."
   c) "I've almost finished."   d) "This question is quite easy."

10) "Jack est intelligent" means "Jack is intelligent". How would you say:
    a) "Jack is more intelligent."   b) "Jack is the most intelligent."

11) How would you say the following sentences in French?
    a) "Helen is the tallest."   b) "Robert and Mark are the shortest."

12) Chantal tells you, "La musique jazz est bonne". Tell her that pop music is
    better and rock music is the best.

13) How would you say 'the worst' in French?

14) If "Je cours lentement" means "I run slowly", how would you say:
    a) 'I run more slowly.'   b) 'I run the most slowly.'

15) Write down in French how you would say 'I speak German well,
    I speak French better and I speak English best.'

16) Look at the pictures of the three people on the right and fill
    in the gaps in the sentences with 'plus', 'moins' or 'aussi':
    a) Pierre est .... grand que Jean-Paul.
    b) Céline est .... grande que Pierre.
    c) Jean-Paul est .... grand que Céline.

Céline   Jean-Paul   Pierre

Quick Questions

Quick Questions

17) Write a short passage in French to say that French is less boring than Maths, Biology is more interesting than Chemistry, and Physics is as boring as Geography.

18) Fill in the correct French word for 'to' ('à' or 'en') in each of these sentences:
   a) Je vais .... Manchester.   b) Il va .... France.
   c) Nous allons .... Paris.   d) Elles vont .... Espagne.

19) How would you say the following sentences in French?
   a) "I live in Leeds."   b) "I live in England."

20) Your Mum tells you, "Tes livres sont sur la table et ton déjeuner est dans ton sac." Where are your books and your lunch?

21) Translate these sentences into French, being careful about how you say 'on':
   a) "I went to school on foot."   b) "I saw Wayne Rooney on TV."
   c) "The cat is on the bed."   d) "I'm leaving on Thursday."
   e) "I heard it on the radio."

22) How would you say "I come from London" in French?

23) Tell your friend, in French, that the train goes from London to Paris.

24) Write down how you would tell your French penfriend that you will be in France from the 5th of April.

25) Write down the French for:
   a) a packet of crisps   b) a box of chocolates   c) a group of girls
   d) a bottle of wine   e) a cup of coffee

26) Your friend asks you what your jacket and your bag are made of.
   Tell him that your jacket is made of leather and your bag is made of plastic.

27) How would you say "My birthday is the 10th of June" in French?

28) Using "pour", write short sentences in French to join up these presents with their rightful owners, e.g. "J'ai acheté un poisson pour le chat."
   a) un poisson   le chat
   b) une robe blanche   ma mère
   c) une cravate verte   mon père
   d) un stylo rouge   le professeur

29) How would you say "the train for Lyon" in French?

30) Write a short sentence in French to say that you have been living in Bristol for five years.

31) How would you say in French:
   a) School starts at nine o'clock.   b) He is at the cinema.   c) Mum is at home.

32) You've been grounded, but you really want to go out with your friends. Write out a text message in French saying you'll leave the house at ten o'clock, you'll meet them in the park and you'll stay for an hour.

Conjunctions

Everyone knows <u>long</u> sentences are <u>clever</u> — and clever people are <u>popular</u> when it's exam time. So learn these words to <u>help</u> you make longer sentences, and get <u>more marks</u> for being smart.

Et = And

J'aime jouer au football.   AND   *J'aime jouer au rugby.*

= I like playing football.

= I like playing rugby.

*J'aime jouer au football **et** au rugby.*   = I like playing football <u>and</u> rugby.

ANOTHER EXAMPLE: *J'ai un frère **et** une sœur.*   = I have a brother <u>and</u> a sister.

Ou = Or

This is different from 'où' (with an accent), which means 'where' — see page 8.

For 'nor' see page 219.

Il joue au football tous les jours.   OR   *Il joue au rugby tous les jours.*   OR   *Il joue au football **ou** au rugby tous les jours.*

= He plays football every day.

= He plays rugby every day.

= He plays football <u>or</u> rugby every day.

ANOTHER EXAMPLE: *Je voudrais être médecin **ou** ingénieur.*   = I would like to be a doctor <u>or</u> an engineer.

Mais = But

J'aime jouer au football.   BUT   *Je n'aime pas jouer au rugby.*   =   *J'aime jouer au football **mais** je n'aime pas jouer au rugby.*

= I like playing football.

= I don't like playing rugby.

= I like playing football <u>but</u> I don't like playing rugby.

ANOTHER EXAMPLE: *Je veux jouer au tennis, mais il pleut.*

= I want to play tennis, <u>but</u> it's raining.

I like big buts...

...but I also like these other conjunctions too. They're mighty <u>useful</u> when it comes to constructing <u>longer</u> sentences. You'll find them useful if you're giving <u>opinions</u> or <u>reasons</u> for things too.

Conjunctions

Parce que = Because

This is a really important one you need to use to explain yourself.
There's loads more about it on pages 8-11.

J'aime le tennis parce que c'est amusant.   = I like tennis <u>because</u> it's fun.

J'aime courir parce que c'est facile.   = I like running <u>because</u> it's easy.

Other wee joining words to understand

You don't have to use all of these, but you should <u>understand</u> them all...

See page 11 for more on 'car'.

because:	car
if:	si
with:	avec
as, like:	comme
so, therefore:	donc
while, during:	pendant (que)

EXAMPLES:

Tu peux sortir si tu veux.

= You can go out <u>if</u> you want.

J'ai faim, donc je vais manger.

= I'm hungry, <u>so</u> I'm going to eat.

Il est comme son frère.

= He's <u>like</u> his brother.

Elle joue au hockey pendant qu'il pleut.

= She plays hockey <u>while</u> it's raining.

These are sneaky wee words
The words on the last two pages may seem pretty <u>small</u>, but you really will use them <u>all the time</u> so it's best to learn them now before you move on. Try writing out sentences using each one for <u>practice</u>.

Pronouns

Pronouns are words that <u>replace nouns</u> — things like '<u>you</u>', '<u>she</u>' or '<u>them</u>'.

je, tu, il, elle — I, you, he, she

Paul finally has a new job. (He) shaves poodles at the poodle parlour.

'<u>He</u>' is a <u>pronoun</u>. It means you don't have to say '<u>Paul</u>' again.

The subject pronouns:

I	je	nous	*we*	
you (informal singular)	tu	vous	*you* (informal plural or formal)	
he/it	il	ils	*they* (masc. or masc. & fem.)	
she/it	elle	elles	*they* (all fem.)	
one/we	on			

Le chien mange la brosse. = <u>The dog</u> eats the brush.

(Il) mange la brosse. = <u>He</u> eats the brush.

The French often use 'on' when they're talking about 'we'.
E.g. '<u>On</u> mange' = '<u>We</u> eat', '<u>On</u> va aller au cinéma' = '<u>We</u> are going to go to the cinema.'

me, te, le, la — me, you, him, her

The direct object pronouns:

me	me	nous	*us*
you (inf. sing.)	te	vous	*you* (informal plural or formal)
him/it	le	les	*them*
her/it	la		

*Dave lave **le chien**.* = Dave washes <u>the dog</u>.

Dave (le) lave. = Dave washes <u>it</u>.

Use 'l'' if the verb starts with a vowel.
E.g. if Dave was buying the dog, it would be 'Dave l'achète'.

There are special words for to me, to her, to them

The indirect object pronouns:

to me	me	nous	to us
to you (inf. sing.)	te	vous	to you (informal plural or formal)
to him/her/it	lui	leur	to them

*Le chien donne la brosse **à** Dave.* = The dog gives the brush <u>to</u> Dave.

Le chien (lui) donne la brosse. = The dog gives the brush <u>to him</u>.

Pronouns are really worth learning

You're not going to get very far at all in the exams if you can't understand things like <u>I</u>, <u>you</u>, <u>he</u>, <u>she</u> and <u>we</u>. The good news is that it's fairly <u>easy</u>. Make sure you know <u>all</u> the words on this page.

Pronouns

C'est le mien / la mienne... — It's mine...

Possessive pronouns:

	Singular Masc.	Fem.	Plural Masc.	Fem.
mine:	le mien	la mienne	les miens	les miennes
yours (informal sing.):	le tien	la tienne	les tiens	les tiennes
his / hers:	le sien	la sienne	les siens	les siennes
ours:	le nôtre	la nôtre	les nôtres	les nôtres
yours (plural or formal):	le vôtre	la vôtre	les vôtres	les vôtres
theirs:	le leur	la leur	les leurs	les leurs

You'll only need to <u>recognise</u> these — you won't have to use them.

Donne-lui le ballon; c'est le sien.   = Give him the ball; it's his.

Donne-moi la brosse; c'est la mienne.   = Give me the brush; it's mine.

Special words for me, you, him, her...

In some sentences, you need to <u>emphasise</u> exactly who is being talked about. For example, you can say 'he's taller', but you can make the sentence clearer using an <u>emphatic pronoun</u>, e.g. 'he's taller than <u>you</u>'. There are <u>four occasions</u> when you need to use emphatic pronouns in French:

Emphatic pronouns:

me	moi	nous	*us*
you (informal sing.)	toi	vous	*you* (informal plural or formal)
him/it	lui	eux	*them* (masc. or masc. & fem.)
her/it	elle	elles	*them* (all fem.)
one	soi		

1) Telling people what to do.	*Écoutez-moi!* = Listen to <u>me</u>!	For more, see pages 222-223.
2) Comparing things.	*Il est plus grand que toi.* = He is taller than <u>you</u>.	For more, see pages 179-180.
3) After words like 'with', 'for','from'... (prepositions).	*Nous allons avec eux.* = We're going with <u>them</u>.	For more on prepositions, see pages 182-183.
4) Where the words are on their own, or after 'c'est'.	*Qui parle? Moi! C'est moi!* = Who's speaking? <u>Me</u>! It's <u>me</u>!	

When French people want to be <u>even clearer</u> about who's being talked about, e.g. 'I made this cake <u>myself</u>,' they use one of these words instead of a normal emphatic pronoun. They all mean '...-<u>self</u>' (myself, yourself, himself etc.).

moi-même, toi-même, lui-même, elle-même, soi-même, nous-mêmes, vous-mêmes, eux-mêmes, elles-mêmes

Make sure you know all the different kinds of pronouns

You <u>won't</u> get far without pronouns I'm afraid. Learn this page so you'll know for sure <u>when</u> these pronouns are used and the <u>different forms</u> they take. You'll be really <u>glad</u> you've learnt this stuff.

Pronouns

Two Top Words — 'En' & 'Y'

En — meaning 'of it':

> <u>EN</u> — this pronoun usually translates as '<u>of it</u>',
> '<u>of them</u>', '<u>some</u>' or '<u>any</u>'.
> If a verb needs <u>de</u> after it, like 'avoir besoin de',
> you translate '<u>it</u>' or '<u>them</u>' as '<u>en</u>':
> e.g.: J'ai besoin de la banane.   J'<u>en</u> ai besoin.
>   I need the banana.   I need <u>it</u>.

Y — meaning 'there':

> e.g.: J'<u>y</u> vais.   I'm going there.
> It's also used to mean '<u>it</u>' or '<u>them</u>' after verbs followed
> by <u>à</u>, e.g.: penser à — to think about.
> e.g.:   Je n'<u>y</u> pense plus.
>   I don't think about it any more.
> It's also used in several common expressions.
>   Il <u>y</u> a...   There is / There are...
>   Ça <u>y</u> est!   That's it! — as in 'I've finished!'

Stick all Object Pronouns Before the Verb

These pronouns always go <u>before</u> the verb. If you're using <u>two</u> object pronouns in the same sentence, they <u>both</u> go before the verb, but they go in a <u>special order</u>. This is a bit tricky, so get it learnt:

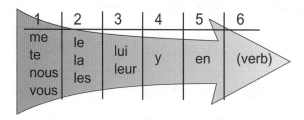

1	2	3	4	5	6
me te nous vous	le la les	lui leur	y	en	(verb)

Examples: Il <u>me les</u> donne.   He gives <u>them to me</u>.
      Je <u>le lui</u> ai donné.   I gave <u>it to him</u>.

If you're using a <u>negative</u>, the '<u>ne</u>' goes <u>before</u> the object pronoun, and the '<u>pas</u>' after the verb.

Example: Je ne <u>les</u> mange pas.   I don't eat <u>them</u>.

I'm not a big fan of nouns myself — I'm an antinoun

Object pronouns can seem a bit <u>terrifying</u> to start with, just because they look <u>similar</u> but mean different things. You'll need to remember the <u>order</u> of pronouns too, so learn all this very well.

Pronouns

Pointing things out in shops, and generally making it clear which thing you're on about, is important.

How to say **this** thing or **these** things

Grammar Fans: these are 'Demonstrative Adjectives'.

Use '<u>ce</u>', '<u>cet</u>', etc. ... in front of a noun where you're saying things like '<u>this man</u>', '<u>these apples</u>' — i.e. when you're using '<u>this</u>' as a <u>describing word</u>.

masculine singular	masculine singular before vowel or 'h' which takes 'l'	feminine singular	plural
ce	cet	cette	ces

EXAMPLES:

this pen: ce stylo	*this bird:* cet oiseau
this house: cette maison	*these apples:* ces pommes

Je veux celui-là — I want that one

Grammar Fans: these are the 'Demonstrative Pronouns'.

When you say 'this is mine', you're using 'this' as a <u>noun</u>.

masculine singular	masculine plural	feminine singular	feminine plural
celui	ceux	celle	celles

If you're <u>not</u> pointing something out, you can use these ones:

ceci = this   cela = that   ça = that

EXAMPLES:
<u>Cela</u> n'est pas vrai. — <u>That</u> isn't true.
Lisez <u>ceci</u>. — Read <u>this</u>.

1) You often use these words with '<u>-ci</u>' or '<u>-là</u>' on the end.
2) Adding '<u>-ci</u>' makes it mean '<u>this one</u>' or '<u>this one here</u>', and '<u>-là</u>' makes it mean '<u>that one</u>' or '<u>that one there</u>'.

J'ai deux chiens. Celui-ci est mignon, mais celui-là est méchant.

= I have two dogs. <u>This one here</u>'s nice, but <u>that one there</u>'s nasty.

3) On their own, these words can mean '<u>the one(s)</u>'.

J'aime bien cette chanson, mais je préfère celle qu'on a écoutée hier soir.

= I like this song, but I prefer <u>the one</u> we listened to yesterday evening.

This and that and these and those

These words pop up <u>all the time</u> in French and you'll be <u>stumped</u> if you don't know what they mean. You need to <u>recognise</u> these words and <u>use</u> them too — especially if you want to <u>compare</u> two things.

Relative Pronouns

Dont — which...

1) 'Dont' can be translated as 'of which' or 'about which'.
2) This is difficult. But don't panic — you only need to recognise it.
3) Dont is used if the verb in the sentence is followed by 'de' e.g. 'avoir peur de', 'avoir besoin de'.

Grammar Fans: this is a 'Relative Pronoun'.

> **Le monstre *dont* j'ai peur est là.**   = The monster which I'm scared of is there.

> **Le livre *dont* j'ai besoin est fantastique.**   = The book which I need is fantastic.

4) You also see it where we would say 'whose'.

> **Le garçon *dont* le père est médecin.**   = The boy whose father is a doctor.
> (Literally 'The boy of whom the father is a doctor.')

Qui and que — Which / who / that...

Grammar Fans: 'Relative Pronouns'.

These are probably the trickiest of the tricky French words. Practise them lots...

1) If the person/thing you are talking about is the subject of the verb, i.e. the person/thing that does the verb, then you use 'qui'.

> **Un professeur qui aime bien sa classe.**   = A teacher who likes his class.
>
> subject   verb   object
>
> *It's the teacher that's doing the liking, so it's QUI.*

2) If the person/thing you are talking about is the object of the verb, i.e. the person/thing that has something done to it, then you use 'que'.

> **Un professeur que sa classe aime bien.**   = A teacher that his class likes.
>
> object   subject   verb
>
> *It's the teacher that is being liked (NOT doing the liking), so it's QUE.*

Examples:

> **Où est le bâtiment qu'on a vu?**   = Where is the building we saw?   → *The building is not doing the seeing — so QUE.*

> **Où est le chien qui courait?**   = Where is the dog that was running?   → *The dog was doing the running — so QUI.*

Des mots que je déteste

Not the easiest stuff in the world, but after a while you should get a feel for qui and que. It's definitely worth learning these examples by heart, and then making up a few of your own.

Quick Questions

What a wonderful feeling — you're just about halfway through the Grammar Section. That is definitely something to be celebrated, and by celebrating I mean... doing these Quick Questions and making sure you know everything there is to know about the last few pages.

Quick Questions

1) Pierre tells you, "Je veux aller à la plage, mais il fait froid." What is he telling you?

2) Translate the following sentences into English:
   a) "Mon père est très fatigué car il travaille tout le temps.
   b) "Prends un chocolat si tu veux."
   c) "Qu'est-ce que tu vas faire pendant les vacances?"
   d) "Je suis fatiguée donc je vais me coucher."
   e) "Je joue au football avec mon frère."

3) For each of these sentences replace the underlined subject (the person doing the action) with the correct subject pronoun:
   a) Amy aime le chocolat.   b) Mark joue au football.
   c) Le chien a mangé mes chaussures.   d) La souris est sous la table.
   e) Les garçons détestent les filles.   f) Emma et Sarah sont allées au cinéma.

4) Ask your friend, in French, what he/she is going to do on Saturday.

5) Ask two of your friends together, in French, if they are going to the park today.

6) For each of these sentences, fill in the correct French direct object pronoun (the thing having the action done to it):
   a) Je regarde la télévision. — Je .... regarde.
   b) Paul lit le journal. — Paul .... lit.
   c) Je déteste les chats et les chiens. — Je .... déteste.
   d) J'ai mangé le gâteau hier soir. — Je .... ai mangé hier soir.

7) How would you say the following sentences in French?
   a) "I love you."   b) "He loves me."

8) What do these mean in English? (Careful, for some there's more than one right answer):
   a) me   b) te   c) lui   d) leur

9) For each of these sentences, fill in the correct French indirect object pronoun (the bit that says 'to someone'):
   a) Je donne le livre à Paul — Je .... donne le livre.
   b) Est-ce que Johnny Depp a parlé avec toi au concert? — Est-ce que
      Johnny Depp .... a parlé au concert?
   c) Je donne le ballon aux enfants. — Je .... donne le ballon.

10) Who is being given a present in each of these sentences?
   a) Je leur donne un cadeau.   b) Il nous a donné un cadeau.
   c) Ma mère m'a donné un cadeau.

11) Using the correct form of 'mien', how would you say "Give me the sweets; they're mine!"?

12) What do these French emphatic pronouns mean?
   a) moi   b) toi   c) eux   d) soi

194

Quick Questions

Quick Questions

13) Translate these phrases into English:
   a) "Écoutez-moi!"
   b) "Asseyez-vous!"
   c) "Il est plus intelligent que toi."
   d) "Je veux le faire moi-même."
   e) "Je t'ai vu avec eux."
   f) "C'est à qui le stylo? — Il est à moi."

14) "J'en prends trois" means "I'll have three of them". For each of the questions below,
   use this phrase to say you will have the number in brackets of each food item.
   The first one is done for you.
   a) Voulez-vous des pommes? (4) — Oui, j'en prends quatre.
   b) Voulez-vous des bananes? (2) — ....
   c) Voulez-vous des oranges? (6) — ....
   d) Voulez-vous du lait? (une bouteille) — ....
   e) Voulez-vous du jambon? (deux tranches) — ....

15) "J'ai besoin de …" means "I need". For each of these sentences, replace the thing
   needed with the pronoun 'en'.
   a) "J'ai besoin d'un stylo."
   b) "J'ai besoin d'une nouvelle voiture."
   c) "J'ai besoin des livres pour faire mes devoirs."
   d) "J'ai besoin de l'argent pour aller au cinéma."

16) Pierre says to you, "Est-ce que tu voudrais un paquet de chips? J'en ai acheté deux
   paquets, et j'en ai mangé seulement un." Why is he offering you some crisps?

17) For each of these sentences, replace the place people are going with 'y'
   (to mean 'there'). The first one has been done for you.
   a) Je vais à la plage – J'y vais.
   b) Vous allez à l'école.
   c) Nous allons au cinéma.
   d) Ils vont à la gare.
   e) Elle va à Paris.

18) What does "il y a" mean in English?

19) If "Je les mange" means "I eat them", how would you say "I don't eat them" in French?

20) Put the correct French word for 'this' or 'these' before each of these nouns:
   a) chien   b) pomme   c) fille   d) chaussettes   e) oiseau
   f) sandwich   g) maison   h) hôpital   i) journaux   j) enfants

21) How would you say in French:
   a) This cake is delicious.
   b) This book is very interesting.
   c) These shoes are too small.
   d) This shirt is green.

22) Translate these sentences into English.
   a) " Je n'aime pas cette robe. Je préfère celle-là."
   b) "As-tu lu ces livres? Celui-ci est très bon, mais celui-là est ennuyeux."
   c) "J'aime les chiens, mais ceux-là sont vraiment méchants."

23) What does "J'ai un cours de français avec le prof dont j'ai peur" mean?

24) Write down the French for:
   a) the rabbit that the children like   b) the rabbit that likes the children

SECTION SEVEN — GRAMMAR

Verbs

You have to know about <u>verbs</u> — you just can't get away from them.
Learn the stuff on this page to make the whole of GCSE French <u>easier</u>.

Verbs are action words — they tell you what's going on

Ethel plays *football every Saturday.*

And so is this.

Alex wished *his grandma* preferred *knitting.*

These are <u>verbs</u>.

Here are two <u>really important</u> things you need to know about verbs...

1) You have different words for different times

You say things <u>differently</u> if they happened last week, or aren't going to happen till tomorrow.

HAS ALREADY HAPPENED
I went to Tibet last year.
I have been to Tibet.
I had been to Tibet.

PAST

HAPPENING NOW
I am going to Tibet.
I go to Tibet.

PRESENT

These are all different <u>tenses</u>, in case you're interested.

HASN'T HAPPENED YET
I go to Tibet on Monday.
I will go to Tibet.
I will be going to Tibet.
I am going to go to Tibet.

FUTURE

2) You have different words for different people

You say 'he plays', but you <u>don't</u> say '<u>I plays</u>' — it'd be daft. You change the verb to fit the person.

ME DOING IT
I <u>am</u> eating parsnips.

YOU DOING IT
You <u>are</u> eating parsnips.

HIM DOING IT
He <u>is</u> eating parsnips.

The word you look up in the dictionary means 'to...'

When you want to say 'I dance' in French, you start by looking up 'dance' in the dictionary.
But you can't just use the first word you find — there's more to it than that...

When you look up a verb <u>in the dictionary</u>, this is what you get:

Grammar Fans: this is called the '<u>Infinitive</u>'.

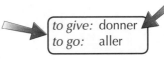
to give: donner
to go: aller

Most of the time you won't want to use the verb in '<u>the infinitive</u>' — you'll have to <u>change</u> it so it's right for the <u>person</u> and <u>time</u> you're talking about. There's more about this on pages 196-231 — learn it all now, and you'll get it right in the assessments.

Verbs are very very vital

The bottom line is — you <u>need</u> verbs in your life if you're going to say even the <u>simplest</u> things in French. There's no getting round this so you may as well <u>accept</u> it. Then you can <u>move on</u>.

Verbs in the Present Tense

You'll probably need to use the present tense more than any other form of the verb, so it's <u>really important</u> to make sure you understand exactly <u>when</u> to use it and <u>how</u> it is formed.

The Present tense describes what's happening now

Present tense verbs describe either something that's happening <u>now</u>, e.g. 'I am brushing my teeth' or something which happens <u>repeatedly</u>, e.g. 'I brush my teeth every day'. There are <u>3 easy steps</u> to put a verb into the present tense:

Examples of Present Tense Stems			
Infinitive	regarder	finir	vendre
Stem	regard	fin	vend

1) Get the <u>infinitive</u> of the verb you want, e.g. 'regarder'.
2) Knock off the <u>last two letters</u>: regard~~er~~ This gives you the <u>stem</u>.
3) Add the new <u>ending</u>. This depends on the kind of verb and the person doing the verb (see below). E.g. Il regar<u>de</u>, vous regar<u>dez</u>, ils regar<u>dent</u>.

Endings for -er verbs

To form the present tense of <u>regular</u> '-er' verbs, add the endings shown to the verb's stem — e.g.:

The first bit ('regard') doesn't change. ➡️ ***regarder = to watch***

See page 6 for when to use '<u>tu</u>' and when to use '<u>vous</u>'.

I watch =	je	regard**e**	*nous*	regard**ons**	*= we watch*
you (informal singular) watch =	tu	regard**es**	*vous*	regard**ez**	*= you (formal & plural) watch*
he/it watches =	il	regard**e**	*ils*	regard**ent**	*= they (masc. or masc. and fem.) watch*
she/it watches =	elle	regard**e**	*elles*	regard**ent**	*= they (fem.) watch*
one watches =	on	regard**e**			

<u>IMPORTANT</u>: 'il', 'elle' and 'on' <u>always</u> have the same ending, and so do 'ils' & 'elles'.

Present tense — learn the endings now

The present tense is really <u>essential</u>. All the tenses are important but this is the one you'll need <u>all</u> the time. Once you know the <u>basics</u> on this page, you should be able to form any <u>regular -er verb</u>.

Verbs in the Present Tense

Endings for -ir verbs

To form the present tense of regular '-ir' verbs, add the endings shown to the verb's stem — e.g.:

The first bit ('fin') doesn't change. ➡️ *finir = to finish*

je	fin**is**	= *I finish*
tu	fin**is**	= *you (inf. sing.) finish*
il/elle/on	fin**it**	= *he/she/it/one finishes*
nous	fin**issons**	= *we finish*
vous	fin**issez**	= *you (formal & plural) finish*
ils/elles	fin**issent**	= *they finish*

Endings for -re verbs

To form the present tense of regular '-re' verbs, add the endings shown to the verb's stem — e.g.:

The first bit ('vend') doesn't change. *vendre = to sell*

je	vend**s**	= *I sell*
tu	vend**s**	= *you (inf. sing.) sell*
il/elle/on	vend	= *he/she/it/one sell*
nous	vend**ons**	= *we sell*
vous	vend**ez**	= *you (formal & plural) sell*
ils/elles	vend**ent**	= *they sell*

NOTE: For il/elle/on you don't need to add an ending — just use the stem.

And learn these present tense endings too

It's <u>very</u> important not to think "the present tense is easy". Think carefully about what endings belong where, then <u>learn</u> them until you don't even need to think about them any more. Do it now.

Verbs in the Present Tense

Verbs that don't follow the same pattern as regular verbs are called 'irregular verbs'.
Most of the really useful verbs are irregular. Anyway, here are a few you'll need most...

Some of the most common verbs are irregular

These are some of the most important verbs in the world, so you really must learn all the bits of them.

① **être** = to be

> I am = je suis
> you (informal singular) are = tu es
> he/she/it/one is = il/elle/on est
> we are = nous sommes
> you (formal & plural) are = vous êtes
> they are = ils/elles sont

② **avoir** = to have

> I have = j'ai
> you (informal singular) have = tu as
> he/she/it/one has = il/elle/on a
> we have = nous avons
> you (formal & plural) have = vous avez
> they have = ils/elles ont

③ **faire** = to make / to do

> I make = je fais
> you (informal singular) make = tu fais
> he/she/it/one makes = il/elle/on fait
> we make = nous faisons
> you (formal & plural) make = vous faites
> they make = ils/elles font

④ **aller** = to go

> I go = je vais
> you (informal singular) go = tu vas
> he/she/it/one goes = il/elle/on va
> we go = nous allons
> you (formal & plural) go = vous allez
> they go = ils/elles vont

⑤ **pouvoir** = to be able to / can

> I can = je peux
> you (informal singular) can = tu peux
> he/she/it/one can = il/elle/on peut
> we can = nous pouvons
> you (formal & plural) can = vous pouvez
> they can = ils/elles peuvent

⑥ **vouloir** = to want

> I want = je veux
> you (informal singular) want = tu veux
> he/she/it/one wants = il/elle/on veut
> we want = nous voulons
> you (formal & plural) want = vous voulez
> they want = ils/elles veulent

⑦ **devoir** = must / to have to

> I must = je dois
> you (informal singular) must = tu dois
> he/she/it/one must = il/elle/on doit
> we must = nous devons
> you (formal & plural) must = vous devez
> they must = ils/elles doivent

⑧ **savoir** = to know

> I know = je sais
> you (informal singular) know = tu sais
> he/she/it/one knows = il/elle/on sait
> we know = nous savons
> you (formal & plural) know = vous savez
> they know = ils/elles savent

Irregular verbs need regular revision

They **really** do. It's no good sitting at home wondering whether or not you'll **need** them in the exam.
The answer's simple — you'll need **all** of them. So MAKE SURE you get learning and do it now.

Verbs in the Present Tense

To say 'we like eating', use 'we like to eat'

To say 'we like eating' you need two verbs. The first verb ('like') needs to be in the right form for the person. The second ('eat'), is just the infinitive.

swimming:	nager
fishing:	pêcher
singing:	chanter

Nous aimons manger .   = We like <u>eating</u>.

I like =	j'aime
you (informal singular) like =	tu aimes
he/she/it/one likes =	il/elle/on aime
we like =	nous aimons
you (formal & plural) like =	vous aimez
they like =	ils/elles aiment

Sometimes the first verb has a <u>preposition</u> — a small but important word that comes before the second verb:

Il arrête de fumer.   = He is stopping smoking.

In the infinitive, you say: 'arrêter de faire quelque chose', 'commencer à faire quelque chose', etc.

Je commence à parler.   = I start speaking.

You can use part of '<u>venir</u>' followed by '<u>de</u>' and the infinitive to mean 'to have just done something':

\\\\|||||////
Prepositions
are on pages
182-183.
//////||||\\\\\

I have just: je viens de	*you (pl.) have just:* vous venez de

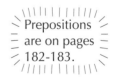

Il vient de parler.   = <u>He has just</u> spoken.

You need two verbs to say you like doing something

This stuff isn't too difficult really — you need to make sure the first verb is in the <u>right form</u> and the second verb is in the <u>infinitive</u>. These combinations of verbs are pretty <u>common</u>, so get them learnt.

Future Tense

You need to be able to talk about things that are <u>going to happen</u> at some point in the future. There are <u>two ways</u> you can do it — and the first one's a piece of cake, so I'd learn that first if I were you.

You can use 'I'm going to' to talk about the Future

This is pretty easy, so there's no excuse for not learning it.

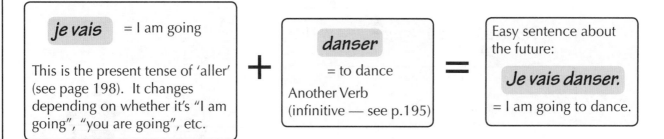

je vais = I am going		Easy sentence about the future:
This is the present tense of 'aller' (see page 198). It changes depending on whether it's "I am going", "you are going", etc.	**+** *danser* = to dance Another Verb (infinitive — see p.195) **=**	*Je vais danser.* = I am going to dance.

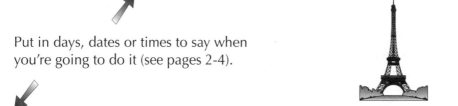

Elle va jouer au tennis **ce soir** *.* = She is going to play tennis <u>this evening</u>.

Put in days, dates or times to say when you're going to do it (see pages 2-4).

Samedi *, on va aller en France.* = <u>On Saturday</u>, we are going to go to France.

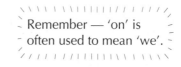

Remember — 'on' is often used to mean 'we'.

Demain, nous allons faire nos devoirs. = Tomorrow, we're going to do our homework.

Ce week-end, ils vont organiser une fête. = This weekend, they're going to organise a party.

Today I am going to revise this page

Lucky lucky you... this future tense isn't really too <u>tricky</u> at all, so you can ramble on about what's going to happen tomorrow, next month etc. Make sure you revise the parts of the verb "<u>aller</u>" really well too.

Future Tense

This page covers the proper future tense. If you're studying for <u>Foundation Level</u> then you only need to <u>recognise</u> this tense, but <u>Higher Level</u> students will need to know how to <u>form it</u> too.

"I will" — the proper Future Tense

The proper future tense in French is the equivalent of '<u>will</u>' in English. It's another one of those tenses where it's all about sticking endings onto something (the '<u>stem</u>').

NOTE: The conditional uses the same 'stems', but different endings. See page 220-221.

Luckily, the 'stems' that you stick the endings onto are pretty easy:

I =	je	**-ai**	*nous*	**-ons**	= *we*
you (informal singular) =	tu	**-as**	*vous*	**-ez**	= *you* (informal plural & formal)
he/she/it/one =	il/elle/on	**-a**	*ils/elles*	**-ont**	= *they*

1) For -er and -ir verbs, you just stick the ending onto the infinitive (see page 195).
   EXAMPLES:

   Je jouerai au tennis. = I will play tennis.

   Tu dormiras. = You will sleep.

2) For -re verbs, you take the 'e' off the end of the infinitive first, then stick on the ending.
   EXAMPLES:

   Il prendra le bus cet après-midi. = He will take the bus this afternoon.

   Nous vendrons le chien la semaine prochaine. = We will sell the dog next week.

3) The verbs below don't follow the pattern. You have to learn them by heart.

These are the most important ones:

aller	ir-	*pouvoir*	pourr-
être	ser-	*devoir*	devr-
avoir	aur-	*venir*	viendr-
faire	fer-	*vouloir*	voudr-

Learn these ones too:

voir	verr-	*falloir*	faudr-
envoyer	enverr-	*mourir*	mourr-
recevoir	recevr-	*tenir*	tiendr-
savoir	saur-		

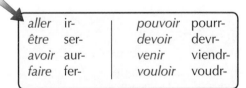

You should know the translations of all these verbs — look them up if you don't.

Two future tenses for the price of one

That's right — there's not just one but <u>two</u> future tenses for you to get your head around. Best learn all this <u>really</u> well so that when the exam comes around, you're familiar with <u>both</u> tenses.

Quick Questions

Take a deep breath and have a go at these Quick Questions. They'll give you lots of practice at the tenses you've met over the last few pages. If you struggle with any of them, go back over the pages again until you know this stuff inside out.

Quick Questions

1) Match up the people on the left with the correct form of the verb 'regarder' on the right.
   a) nous   regardez
   b) vous   regarde
   c) elles   regardent
   d) tu   regardes
   e) on   regardons

2) How would you say the following in French, using the regular -er 'aimer'?
   a) I like   b) you like   c) she likes   d) we like   e) they like

3) How would you say the following in French?
   a) I speak   b) you listen   c) we play   d) they hate   e) he listens

4) Write down the correct present tense form of the verb 'finir' to go with each of these people:
   a) je   b) il   c) vous   d) ils   e) nous   f) tu

5) Put the –ir verbs in brackets into the correct form of the present tense:
   a) "Les cours ………. (finir) à trois heures."   b) "Le film ………. (finir) bien."
   c) "………. (choisir) la robe que vous préférez."

6) Put the correct ending for the present tense on each of these stems of the verb 'vendre':
   a) je vend...   b) nous vend...   c) vous vend...
   d) tu vend...   e) elles vend...   f) on vend...

7) How would you say "The bakery sells bread" in French?

8) Put the verbs in brackets into the correct present tense form:
   a) il (attendre)   b) nous (descendre)   c) je (perdre)
   d) vous (entendre)   e) tu (répondre)   f) ils (correspondre)

9) Write down the French for:
   a) I am   b) you are   c) she is
   d) we are   e) they are

10) Fill in the gaps with the right present tense form of 'être':
    a) "Nous ………. heureux."   b) "Vous ………. anglais."
    c) "Mon père ………. ingénieur."   d) "Je ………. fatigué."
    e) "Les devoirs ………. ennuyeux."   f) "Elle ………. belle."

11) How would you say "I am English" in French?

12) How would you say "Are you happy?" in French?

13) Write down the French for:
    a) I have   b) she has   c) we have   d) they have   e) you have

Quick Questions

Quick Questions

14) How would you say "You have blue eyes" in French to:
   a) your friend?   b) your teacher?

15) How would you say "What are you doing tonight?" in French to:
   a) one friend?   b) three friends?

16) Write a short passage in French explaining that at school you and your best friend
   do Biology and French.

17) Fill in the gaps in these sentences with the correct present tense form of 'aller':
   a) Je ..... au cinéma.   b) Ils ..... à l'école.   c) Vous ..... à la piscine.
   d) Elle ..... à Lille.   e) Nous ..... au musée.   f) Tu ..... à l'office de tourisme.

18) How would you say "Where are you going?" in French to:
   a) your teacher?   b) a friend?

19) Write a short passage explaining that every summer you go to France,
   Mark goes to Spain, and George and Kevin go to Italy.

20) How would you say in French:
   a) we want   b) I want   c) she wants   d) they want   e) you want

21) How would you say in French "What do you want to eat?":
   a) politely?   b) informally to a friend?

22) You're in a restaurant. Write down how you would say in French, "I want a coffee,
   he wants an orange juice, she wants some chips and they want hot chocolate."

23) Fill in the gaps with the right form of 'devoir':
   a) Il .... faire son lit.   b) Nous .... faire la vaisselle.
   c) Tu .... ranger ta chambre.   d) Vous .... débarrasser la table.
   e) Elles .... passer l'aspirateur. f) Je .... lire ce livre.

24) Using 'aller', fill in the gaps to explain what each of these people is going to do:
   a) Liz .... dormir.   b) Pete .... faire ses devoirs.
   c) Je .... aller à la piscine.   d) Dan et Julie .... sortir ce soir.

25) Write a short passage in French explaining what you are going to do during the holidays,
   using 'aller'. Explain that you are going to go to France, you are going to go by train and
   you're going to stay in a hotel. You are going to swim and go for walks, and you are going
   to speak as much French as possible.

26) Put the verb in brackets into the proper future tense:
   a) je (manger)   b) vous (dormir)   c) elle (danser)   d) ils (finir)
   e) tu (penser)   f) on (payer)   g) elles (donner)

27) What do these mean in English:
   a) j'irai   b) vous pourrez   c) il devra   d) tu auras
   e) nous serons   f) ils diront   g) elle voudra   h) je ferai

Perfect Tense

The perfect tense is used for things that happened in the <u>past</u>. It's a bit tricky so we've given you five pages on it. Like most grammar stuff, it's just a question of a few <u>rules</u> to follow, and a few <u>bits and pieces</u> to learn. Nothing you can't handle, I'm sure.

Qu'est-ce que tu as fait? — What have you done?

You have to be able to make and understand sentences like this:

J'ai   joué   au tennis.   = <u>I (have)</u> <u>played</u> tennis.

There are two important bits:

1) You always need a bit to mean 'I have' (or 'you have', etc.). In English, you don't always need the 'have', like in 'last week, I played tennis'. BUT in French you have to have the 'have'.

2) This bit means 'played'. It's a special version of 'jouer' (to play). In English, most of these words end in '-ed'. See the next page.

I have played: for 'have' use 'avoir'

For the '<u>have</u>' bit of these past tense phrases, you use the present tense of '<u>avoir</u>'.

I have =	j'ai
you (informal singular) have =	tu as
he/she/it/one has =	il/elle/on a
we have =	nous avons
you (formal or plural) have =	vous avez
they have =	ils/elles ont

EXAMPLES:

Tu as joué au tennis.   = You have played tennis.

Elle a joué au tennis.   = She has played tennis.

Nous avons joué au tennis.   = We have played tennis.

Elles ont joué au tennis.   = They (female) have played tennis.

Practice makes the perfect tense
The perfect tense is one of the <u>big tenses</u> of the grammatical world. You'll need it often when talking about what happened in the <u>past</u>. Make sure you're up to speed on the present tense of 'avoir'.

Perfect Tense

Joué = played: these are Past Participles

Learn the patterns for making the special past tense words like 'joué' (played).

-er verbs

FORMULA

Remove '-er', then add 'é'

EXAMPLES

jouer	→	joué
to play		played
aller	→	allé
to go		gone

-ir verbs

FORMULA

Remove '-r'

EXAMPLES

partir	→	parti
to leave		left
choisir	→	choisi
to choose		chosen

-re verbs

FORMULA

Remove '-re', then add 'u'

EXAMPLES

vendre	→	vendu
to sell		sold
attendre	→	attendu
to wait		waited

Lots of verbs have irregular past participles

Some verbs don't follow the patterns. It's annoying, because a lot of the most useful verbs are irregular — you just have to learn them by heart:

Verb	Past Participle	Translation
avoir:	eu	had
boire:	bu	drunk
conduire:	conduit	driven
connaître:	connu	known
courir:	couru	run
craindre:	craint	feared
devenir:	devenu	become
devoir:	dû	had to
dire:	dit	said
écrire:	écrit	written
être:	été	been
faire:	fait	done

Verb	Past Participle	Translation
lire:	lu	read
mettre:	mis	put
mourir:	mort	died
naître:	né	been born
ouvrir:	ouvert	opened
pouvoir:	pu	been able
prendre:	pris	taken
rire:	ri	laughed
savoir:	su	known
venir:	venu	come
voir:	vu	seen
vouloir:	voulu	wanted

Irregular verbs — all you can do is learn them

Yes that's right, it's those pesky <u>irregular verbs</u> again, and they happen to be the most <u>common</u> ones that you'll need all the time. If you don't learn these, you could end up being really <u>stuck</u> in the exam.

Perfect Tense

The key to doing <u>well</u> in French GCSE is using a <u>variety</u> of <u>different tenses</u>, so being able to talk about the past is really <u>important</u>. There's a few more pages of stuff on the <u>perfect tense</u> to go, but it's worth having a <u>good look</u> at these example sentences and really getting your head round them before you move on.

Make sure you really get to grips with the perfect tense

J'ai mangé dans un restaurant. = I have eaten / I ate in a restaurant.

Tu as mangé dans un restaurant. = You have eaten / you ate in a restaurant.

Il a mangé dans un restaurant. = He has eaten / he ate in a restaurant.

This would be almost exactly the same if you were talking about a girl except that 'Il' would change to 'Elle'.

Nous avons mangé dans un restaurant. = We have eaten / we ate in a restaurant.

Vous avez mangé dans un restaurant. = You have eaten / ate in a restaurant.

Ils ont mangé dans un restaurant. = They (masc.) have eaten / ate in a restaurant.

This would be almost exactly the same if you were talking about girls except that 'Ils' would change to 'Elles'.

Make sure you know how the perfect tense is formed

These sentences should give you a good idea about <u>how</u> to use the perfect tense. Read over the ones on this page and then have a go at writing your <u>own</u> sentences using the perfect tense.

Perfect Tense

One last thing — there are a handful of verbs which don't use 'avoir' at all in the perfect tense...

A few verbs use **être** instead of avoir

1) A <u>small number</u> of verbs use the present tense of '<u>être</u>' instead of the present tense of '<u>avoir</u>' when forming the perfect tense.
2) Just like with verbs that take 'avoir,' you use the bit of 'être' that <u>matches</u> the person you're talking about. E.g. He went = Il est allé.
3) The <u>only difference</u> with verbs that take 'être' is that the <u>past participle</u> has to <u>agree</u> with the person it's describing. More on this over the page.

être = to be	
I am =	je suis
you (informal singular) are =	tu es
he/she/it/one is =	il/elle/on est
we are =	nous sommes
you (formal or plural) are =	vous êtes
they are =	ils/elles sont

15 verbs, to be precise — learn them

The être verbs are mostly about movement, being born or dying.
You also have to use être with reflexive verbs — see page 217.

Verb	Past Participle	Translation
aller:	allé	*gone*
rester:	resté	*stayed*
venir:	venu	*come*
devenir:	devenu	*become*
arriver:	arrivé	*arrived*
partir:	parti	*left*
sortir:	sorti	*gone out*
entrer:	entré	*entered*
monter:	monté	*gone up*
descendre:	descendu	*gone down*

Verb	Past Participle	Translation
rentrer:	rentré	*gone back*
retourner:	retourné	*returned*
tomber:	tombé	*fallen*
naître:	né	*been born*
mourir:	mort	*died*

EXAMPLES:

See the next page for why this 'e' is there.

Je suis allé(e) au cinéma.   = I have gone to the cinema.

Il est arrivé.   = He has arrived.

Learn which verbs take être instead of avoir

Even though there are only <u>15 verbs</u> that take être in the perfect tense, they're all pretty <u>common</u> ones so they're definitely worth learning. Make sure you know the different parts of <u>être</u> too.

Perfect Tense

With être as the auxiliary verb, the past participle must agree

When you use 'être' to form the perfect tense, the past participle has to agree with the subject of the verb. This means it changes if the subject is feminine or plural, just like an adjective (see p.170-171). The agreements are underlined:

Il est allé en ville.   = He has gone / went into town.

Add **e** if the subject is feminine singular

Elle est allée en ville.   = She has gone / went into town.

Add **s** if the subject is masculine plural

Ils sont allés en ville.   = They (masc.) have gone / went into town.

Add **es** if the subject is feminine plural

Elles sont allées en ville.   = They (fem.) have gone / went into town.

Past participles with être always agree

It's really important to remember that when you form the perfect tense using être, the past participles agree with the person doing the action. It's as simple as that. But make sure you know it.

Imperfect Tense

Another <u>past tense</u> for you. The difference here is that this one's <u>not</u> for actions that were <u>completed</u> in the past — it's for actions that were <u>ongoing</u>. More on that later — first, here's how you form it.

The stem comes from the **nous** form

There are <u>three easy steps</u> to make this past tense:

1) Get the present tense '<u>nous</u>' form of the verb (see p.196-199).
2) Knock the '<u>-ons</u>' off the end.
3) Add on the <u>correct ending</u>:

I:	je	-ais	*we:* nous	-ions
you (informal sing.):	tu	-ais	*you (inf. plu. & formal):* vous	-iez
he/she/it/one:	il/elle/on	-ait	*they:* ils/elles	-aient

The only verb that doesn't make its stem in this way is être (see p. 210).

This bit depends on whether you're saying 'I', 'you', 'he', etc.

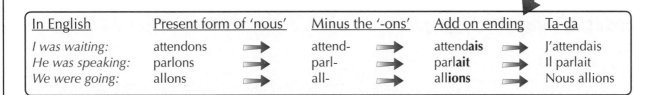

In English	Present form of 'nous'	Minus the '-ons'	Add on ending	Ta-da
I was waiting:	attendons ➡	attend- ➡	attend**ais** ➡	J'attendais
He was speaking:	parlons ➡	parl- ➡	parl**ait** ➡	Il parlait
We were going:	allons ➡	all- ➡	all**ions** ➡	Nous allions

EXAMPLES:

Mon père travaillait dans une banque.   = My dad used to work in a bank.

Mes grands-parents habitaient en France.   = My grandparents used to live in France.

Je faisais de la danse.   = I used to do dance.

Imperfect... but still pretty useful

Forming the imperfect tense is pretty <u>simple</u> — you just have to take the '<u>nous</u>' form in the present tense, take off the '<u>-ons</u>' and add the right <u>ending</u>. See page 210 for more on <u>être</u> in the imperfect tense.

Imperfect Tense

I know all these tenses can seem pretty <u>heavy going</u> at times, but keep going because it will all <u>click</u> eventually — and when it does it'll make a <u>huge difference</u> to the marks you pick up. <u>Chin up</u>.

Être, Avoir and Faire crop up a lot

You're <u>more likely</u> to come up against some verbs than others, so it's a <u>good idea</u> to become really <u>familiar</u> with them.

I'm afraid '<u>être</u>' is a bit <u>different</u> from the others (wouldn't it just be). The endings are the same though — it's just that the <u>stem</u> is '<u>ét-</u>'.

> **être = to be**
>
> | | |
> |---|---|
> | *I was* = | j'étais |
> | *you (informal sing.) were* = | tu étais |
> | *he/she/it/one was* = | il/elle/on était |
> | *we were* = | nous étions |
> | *you (formal & pl.) were* = | vous étiez |
> | *they were* = | ils/elles étaient |

EXAMPLES

Ce roman était magnifique.   = This novel was great.

Vous étiez très petit à l'époque.   = You were very small at the time.

And of course...

C'était...   = It was...

On est allé au Canada — c'était formidable.   = We went to Canada — it was great.

All the other verbs make their imperfect in the normal way.

> '<u>Avoir</u>' is definitely one you'll need, especially because...
>
> **Il y avait...**   = There was / There were...
>
> E.g.   Il y avait deux stylos sur la table.
>   = There were two pens on the table.

> And you'll need '<u>faire</u>' in the imperfect tense too, especially to describe the <u>weather</u>.
>
> E.g.   Il faisait beaucoup trop froid pour
>   faire une promenade.
>   = It was far too cold to go for a walk.

Some verbs are more common than others

The three verbs on this page are really important because they're the ones you'll need <u>all the time</u>. You'll probably want to use "<u>C'était...</u>" pretty often too to <u>describe</u> something in the past.

Imperfect Tense

Use the imperfect for what used to happen

The imperfect is used for talking about what you <u>used to do</u>.

That could be something you did <u>regularly</u>:

J'allais au cinéma tous les jeudis.   = I used to go to the cinema every Thursday.

Or something that was just the <u>general state of affairs</u>:

Je jouais du violon.   = I used to play the violin.

So if you were asked in your speaking and writing
assessments where you used to go on holiday, you might say:

J'allais en Espagne tous les étés.   = I used to go to Spain every summer.

Depuis + imperfect — had been

'<u>Depuis</u>' is always a <u>tricky one</u>. You know how if you want to say
"I <u>have been</u> learning French for three years", you have to use
the present tense: "J'apprends le français depuis trois ans"? Well,
when it's "<u>...had been...</u>", you have to use the <u>imperfect tense</u>.

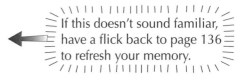

If this doesn't sound familiar,
have a flick back to page 136
to refresh your memory.

*Il pleuvait depuis deux
heures quand...*   = It had been raining
for two hours when...

*J'attendais depuis deux
minutes quand il est arrivé.*   = I had been waiting for two
minutes when he arrived.

*J'étudiais la musique depuis cinq
ans quand j'ai passé l'examen.*   = I had been studying music for
five years when I took the exam.

I remember when revision used to be fun...

This page is about as much fun as being poked in the eye with a <u>blunt stick</u> — but that doesn't mean it's
not <u>really</u> important. The bit about '<u>depuis</u>' and the <u>imperfect tense</u> is a bit tricky but <u>worth learning</u>.

Imperfect Tense

<u>Big question</u> — how do you know <u>when</u> to use the <u>perfect tense</u> (see p.204-208), and when to use the <u>imperfect tense</u>? Well there's no simple answer actually, but here are a few <u>useful pointers</u>.

Use the imperfect for describing the past...
...and the perfect for specific events

Basically, you use the <u>imperfect</u> to describe what <u>was</u> going on, or to <u>set the scene</u>:

> Il était six heures du matin. Il faisait très froid. J'attendais le train.
> = It was six o'clock in the morning. It was very cold. I was waiting for the train.

Description in the imperfect tense

And then, suddenly, <u>something happens</u>. This goes in the <u>perfect tense</u>:

> Tout à coup j'ai vu mon frère sur l'autre quai.
> = All of a sudden I saw my brother on the other platform.

Event in the perfect tense

The French offer presents rather than give them.

More examples

Imperfect

Quand j'avais dix ans, je voulais une console de jeux. Ma mère n'était pas d'accord, donc...

= When I was ten, I wanted a games console. My mother didn't agree, so...

Perfect

...on m'a offert une bicyclette.

= ...they gave me a bike.

Sometimes the <u>event</u> comes <u>first</u>, and then the description:

Perfect

J'ai rencontré une femme...

= I met a woman...

Imperfect

...qui était très amusante.

= ...who was very amusing.

So remember — the imperfect is for description, and the perfect is for events.

Learn by examples

Looking at <u>examples</u> of sentences which use the imperfect and perfect tenses is the only way that you'll learn <u>when</u> to use them. It can seem a bit <u>tricky</u> at first but you'll soon get the <u>hang of it</u>.

Pluperfect Tense

Three more bits to learn — keep at it, you're doing well...

J'avais fait — I had done

1) The pluperfect is like the perfect tense (see p.204-208) — that's for saying what you have done, but this is for what you had done.
2) In English it comes up in sentences like "When I got home, my mum had already made the dinner."
3) It's still made up of a bit of avoir or être + a past participle, but the bit of avoir or être is in the imperfect tense.

> **FORMING THE PLUPERFECT**
>
> Imperfect tense of avoir / être + past participle

For stuff on the imperfect tense, see p.209-212.

imperfect tense of avoir	
I have =	j' avais
you (informal sing.) have =	tu avais
he/she/it/one has =	il/elle/on avait
we have =	nous avions
you (formal & pl.) have =	vous aviez
they have =	ils/elles avaient

imperfect tense of être	
I was =	j'étais
you (informal sing.) were =	tu étais
he/she/it/one was =	il/elle/on était
we were =	nous étions
you (formal & pl.) were =	vous étiez
they were =	ils/elles étaient

J'avais écrit une lettre à mon père.   = I had written a letter to my father.

John avait mangé tout le fromage.   = John had eaten all the cheese.

Nous étions allés voir un film au cinéma.   = We had gone to see a film at the cinema.

The past participle agrees with the subject of the verb when you use 'être' to form the pluperfect tense.

Betty et Sarah étaient arrivées.   = Betty and Sarah had arrived.

Better than perfect

The pluperfect might look a bit daunting at first but it's a handy little tense to know. It's useful when you're talking about something that happened further back in the past than the perfect tense.

214

Quick Questions

Tenses are important to learn. That much is obvious. The last few pages covered three important tenses for talking about the past. You'll be cutting down your options if you can only use the present tense, so make sure you know the perfect, imperfect and pluperfect tenses really well. These questions will help you to pick out the gaps in your knowledge so you can go back over the pages and learn the bits you didn't catch first time round. Good luck...

Quick Questions

1) Write down the past participle of each of these verbs:
   a) finir
   b) manger
   c) regarder
   d) partir
   e) vendre
   f) attendre
   g) aller
   h) dormir

2) Match up the verbs on the left with their irregular past participle on the right.
   a) lire b) craindre
   c) avoir d) devoir
   e) être f) conduire
   g) mourir h) mettre
   i) prendre j) savoir
   k) vouloir l) naître

   eu   mis
   dû   su
   craint   mort
   né   été
   voulu   lu
   pris   conduit

3) Put these verbs into the past tense using the right bit of 'avoir' and the past participle:
   a) je (jouer)
   b) vous (regarder)
   c) il (écouter)
   d) nous (finir)
   e) tu (vendre)
   f) elles (dormir)
   g) je (manger)
   h) on (choisir)

4) How would you say "I did the shopping" in French?

5) Write down how you would say "We watched television all day" in French.

6) Write a short passage in French explaining that yesterday you read a book, played tennis, and helped your mum with the cooking.

7) Complete these sentences by putting the verb in brackets into the past tense (N.B. These ones use 'être' not 'avoir').
   a) Hier je ………. (aller) au théâtre.
   b) Elle ………. (sortir) hier soir.
   c) Vous ………. (devenir) très ennuyeux.
   d) Il ………. (arriver) le 4 septembre.
   e) Nous ………. (monter) dans le train.
   f) Ils ………. (partir) hier.

8) How would you say "He is dead" in French?

9) Hélène tells you, "Pierre n'est pas venu." What is she saying?

10) Write a short passage in French to describe your last holiday. Say that you went to Germany, you arrived on the 4th September and returned on the 20th September, and you stayed in a hotel.

11) Put the verbs in brackets in these sentences into the past tense — be careful to check whether they need 'avoir' or 'être' (and if they use 'être' they need to agree):
   a) "Hier soir mon frère (sortir) avec ses amis et il (rentrer) très tard."
   b) "Je (vouloir) te téléphoner mais je (devoir) faire mes devoirs."
   c) "Le film (finir) à huit heures, donc nous (pouvoir) en voir un autre."
   d) "Quand vous (aller) à la discothèque, est-ce que vous (mettre) votre robe rouge?"

SECTION SEVEN — GRAMMAR

Quick Questions

Quick Questions

12) Translate this conversation into English:
   A: "Salut Pierre! Qu'est-ce que tu as fait hier?"
   B: "Je suis allé à l'école le matin. Les cours ont fini à trois heures, donc je suis allé en ville pour faire des courses."
   A: "Qu'est-ce que tu as acheté?"
   B: "J'ai acheté le nouveau CD de Bon Jovi, c'est chouette! J'ai voulu acheter un tee-shirt, mais je n'ai pas eu le temps."
   A: "Ah, c'est pour cela que tu n'es pas sorti hier avec nous? C'est dommage, nous sommes allés au concert."

13) What do these mean in English?   a) il y avait   b) c'était

14) Turn these sentences from the present tense ('il y a' and 'c'est') to the imperfect:
   a) "Il y a un concert au théâtre."
   b) "C'est trop facile."
   c) "Dans ma chambre il y a un lit et une armoire."

15) Write down the imperfect form of 'regarder' for each of these people:
   a) je   b) il   c) nous   d) tu   e) vous   f) elles

16) Put the verb in brackets into the imperfect tense (was doing):
   a) je (dormir)   b) il (sembler)   c) vous (écouter)
   d) ils (finir)   e) tu (devoir)   f) nous (rester)

17) Complete these sentences by putting the verb in brackets into the imperfect tense:
   a) "Quand j'(être) petit, j'(aller) au parc avec mon père."
   b) "Il (mettre) un jean pour aller à la discothèque, mais maintenant il porte des vêtements plus chics."
   c) "Quand nous (être) plus jeunes nous ne (devoir) pas faire la vaisselle."
   d) "Elles (jouer) au tennis tous les mardis et elles (faire) du cyclisme tous les samedis."

18) How would you say "I used to like sweets" in French?

19) Lisa says, "Pendant mes vacances en Espagne le soleil brillait et il faisait chaud."
   What is she telling you?

20) In each of these sentences there are two verbs. Put the one describing the key event into the perfect tense and the one describing the ongoing situation into the imperfect tense.
   a) "Susie (téléphoner) pendant que tu (faire) tes devoirs."
   b) "Je (manger) tout le gâteau pendant que ma mère (regarder) la télévision."
   c) "Il (se casser) la jambe pendant que nous (jouer) au rugby."
   d) "Pendant que vous (ranger) votre chambre, je (prendre) une douche."

21) Translate these sentences into English:
   a) J'avais fini.   b) Nous avions perdu le chat.
   c) Mark avait oublié de fermer la fenêtre.   d) Vous aviez mangé avant d'arriver.
   e) Michelle et Sharon étaient arrivées.   f) J'étais parti en voiture.
   g) Elle s'était levée à trois heures.

22) Using the pluperfect and perfect tenses, write a short passage in French explaining that you had done your homework but the dog ate it.

Reflexive Verbs

Sometimes you have to talk about things you do to <u>yourself</u> — like washing yourself or getting yourself up in the morning.

Talking about yourself — **me, te, se...**

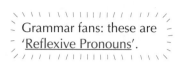

Grammar fans: these are '<u>Reflexive Pronouns</u>'.

Here are all the different ways to say '<u>self</u>':

myself:	me	*ourselves:*	nous
yourself (informal):	te	*yourself (formal), yourselves:*	vous
himself:	se	*themselves, each other:*	se
herself:	se		
oneself:	se		

You can tell which verbs are <u>reflexive</u> by checking in the <u>dictionary</u>. If you look up '<u>to get up</u>', it'll say '<u>se lever</u>'.

Je me lave — I wash myself

You need to be able to talk about '<u>daily routine</u>' and other things which are about what you do to yourself.

se laver = to wash oneself

I wash myself:	je me lave	*one washes oneself:*	on se lave
you wash yourself (informal):	tu te laves	*we wash ourselves:*	nous nous lavons
he washes himself:	il se lave	*you wash yourself (formal) / yourselves:*	vous vous lavez
she washes herself:	elle se lave	*they wash themselves:*	ils/elles se lavent

There are lots of these verbs, but here are the ones you should know for the <u>exams</u>. Learn these:

THE 10 IMPORTANT REFLEXIVE VERBS

to enjoy oneself:	s'amuser	Il s'amuse:	*He's enjoying himself.*
to go to bed:	se coucher	Je me couche à onze heures:	*I go to bed at 11 o'clock.*
to get up:	se lever	Je me lève à huit heures:	*I get up at 8 o'clock.*
to feel:	se sentir	Tu te sens mal?:	*Do you feel ill?*
to be called (literally = to call oneself):	s'appeler	Je m'appelle Bob:	*I'm called Bob.*
			(literally = I call myself Bob)
to excuse oneself / to be sorry / to apologise:	s'excuser	Je m'excuse...:	*I'm sorry / I apologise.*
to be (literally = to find oneself):	se trouver	Où se trouve la banque?:	*Where is the bank?*
			(literally = Where does the bank find itself?)
to be spelt:	s'écrire	Comment ça s'écrit?:	*How is that spelt?*
to be interested in:	s'intéresser à	Je m'intéresse au tennis:	*I'm interested in tennis.*
to happen:	se passer	Qu'est-ce qui se passe?:	*What's happening?*

Reflexive verbs — more grammar to get to grips with

Reflexive verbs are pretty <u>common</u> in French — you'd be <u>silly</u> not to learn them. They're quite straightforward once you get the hang of them, and they really impress examiners if you get them right.

Reflexive Verbs

Je me suis lavé(e) — I have washed myself

1) The perfect tense of these verbs is pretty much the <u>same as normal</u> (see p.204-208) except they all go with '<u>être</u>', not 'avoir'. The only tricky bit is working out <u>where</u> to put the '<u>me</u>' or '<u>te</u>' or '<u>se</u>' or whatever — and it goes <u>right after</u> the '<u>je</u>', '<u>tu</u>' or '<u>il</u>' etc. (In other words, it's <u>before</u> the bit of '<u>être</u>'.)

Je me suis lavé(e)

Stick the 'me' in here.   That's the bit of 'être'.

2) Like other verbs which use 'être' for the perfect tense, you might have to <u>add on</u> an '<u>e</u>' and/or an '<u>s</u>', to match who's doing it. If you're <u>female</u>, make sure you add an '<u>e</u>' when you're talking about yourself.

EXAMPLES:

Je me suis lavé.   = I washed myself.

> Add 'e' if the subject is feminine singular.

Elle s'est lavée.   = She washed herself.

> Add 's' if the subject is masculine plural.

Ils se sont lavés.   = They (masc. or mixed gender) washed themselves.

> Add 'es' if the subject is feminine plural.

Elles se sont lavées.   = They (fem.) washed themselves.

There are quite a few common reflexive verbs to learn

Reflexive verbs are just like normal verbs apart from the small teeny tiny complication of the extra <u>pronoun</u> bit. Make sure you know <u>where</u> the reflexive pronoun goes so you can use it without thinking.

Negatives

You might want to write about something that <u>isn't</u> happening or <u>hasn't</u> happened. To make a sentence <u>negative</u> in English, you would normally use the word '<u>not</u>', but in French it's a bit <u>different</u>.

Use 'ne ... pas' to say not

1) In English you can change a sentence to mean the opposite by adding 'not'.
2) In French, you have to add two little words, 'ne' and 'pas'. They go either side of the verb.

Je suis Bob. = I am Bob. *Je ne suis pas Bob.* = I am <u>not</u> Bob.

This is the verb. The '<u>ne</u>' goes <u>in front</u>, and the '<u>pas</u>' goes <u>after</u>.

3) If the 'ne' part comes <u>before a vowel</u>, you shorten it to '<u>n</u>'':

Vous n'allez pas au cinéma. = You <u>don't</u> go to the cinema.

4) For verbs in the perfect tense (see p.204-208), you stick the 'ne' and 'pas' <u>around</u> the bit of '<u>avoir</u>' or '<u>être</u>'.

Je n'ai pas vu ça. = I have not seen that.

Elle n'est pas arrivée. = She has not arrived.

For an **infinitive**, the **ne** and **pas** go together

The 'ne' and 'pas' usually go either side of the action word (the verb).
BUT if the action word is an infinitive (see page 195) then the 'ne' and the 'pas' both go in front of it.

Je préfère voir un film.  *Je préfère ne pas voir de film.*

= I prefer to see a film.   = I prefer <u>not</u> to see a film.

Just say no

It's really <u>vital</u> that you can say what you <u>don't</u> like or <u>haven't</u> done, especially when you're giving an opinion about something. You just need to get your head around the <u>word order</u> of negative sentences.

Negatives

ne ... jamais — never   ne ... rien — nothing

There are more negatives you need to understand, and for top marks you should use them too.

Je ne vais jamais à York.

Je ne vais plus à York.

= I never go to York.
(I don't ever go to York.)

= I don't go to York any more.
(I no longer go to York.)

Je ne vais ni à York ni à Belfast.

= I neither go to York nor to Belfast.

not any more (no longer): ne ... plus	*not ever (never):* ne ... jamais	*neither ... nor:* ne ... ni ... ni
not anybody (nobody): ne ... personne	*not anything (nothing):* ne ... rien	*not any / not one:* ne ... aucun(e) *(not a single...)*

Il n'y a personne ici.

= There isn't anybody here.
(There is nobody here.)

Il n'y a rien ici.

= There isn't anything here.
(There is nothing here.)

Il n'y a aucune banane.

= There aren't any bananas.
(There is not a single banana.)

'Y' and 'en' go between the 'ne' and the verb.

Je n'ai pas de... — I don't have any...

After a negative, articles such as 'un/une', 'du', 'de la' or 'des' are always replaced by just 'de'.

Je n'ai pas d'argent.   = I haven't got any money.

The 'de' is only shortened if the next word begins with a vowel or an 'h' which takes 'l'', e.g. 'd'argent', 'd'animaux'.

Elle n'a plus de chocolat.   = She hasn't got any more chocolate.

Learn how to say nobody, nothing, not and never

Here are some more negative words for you — it's not the <u>cheeriest</u> page in the world but it could be handy if you want to tell your teacher that you <u>never</u> want to study French ever again. Or maybe <u>not</u>...

The Conditional

The conditional tense is used for saying things like 'I would...' or 'they would...'.
It's a handy little tense if you're talking about things that <u>might</u> happen.

Je voudrais et j'aimerais... — I would like...

These two verbs are really useful in the conditional —
you can use them lots in your speaking assessment.

---

vouloir = to want

I would like =	je voudrais
you (informal singular) would like =	tu voudrais
he/she/it/one would like =	il/elle/on voudrait
we would like =	nous voudrions
you (formal & plural) would like =	vous voudriez
they would like =	ils/elles voudraient

Je voudrais aller à l'hôpital.   = I would like to go to hospital.

Tu voudrais voir ce film?   = Would you like to see this film?

---

aimer = to like

I would like =	j'aimerais
you (informal singular) would like =	tu aimerais
he/she/it/one would like =	il/elle/on aimerait
we would like =	nous aimerions
you (formal & plural) would like =	vous aimeriez
they would like =	ils/elles aimeraient

J'aimerais du lait.   = I would like some milk.

Ils aimeraient manger.   = They would like to eat.

Would you like to revise this page...?

I'm guessing the answer is probably <u>no</u>, but you never know. You'll see these two verbs in the
<u>conditional tense</u> all the time so you'd be <u>foolish</u> not to learn them now. You'll be <u>glad</u> you did.

The Conditional

You only need this page if you're studying for the <u>Higher Level</u> exam.

The conditional = future stem + imperfect endings

The <u>conditional</u> (for saying '<u>would</u>', '<u>could</u>', '<u>should</u>') is simple to form, but you have to be <u>on the ball</u> to spot it if it comes up in the reading or listening exams — it's easy to mistake it for the <u>imperfect tense</u> (because the endings are the same) or the <u>future tense</u> (because the stem is the same). This is how you form it:

1) Take the stems from the future tense (see p.200-201).

2) Add the endings from the imperfect tense (see page 209).

FUTURE	IMPERFECT	CONDITIONAL
Vous <u>pourrez</u> chanter.	*Vous pouviez chanter.*	*Vous <u>pourriez</u> chanter.*
= You will be able to sing.	= You were able to sing.	= You would be able to / could sing.
Tu <u>devras</u> m'écrire.	*Tu devais m'écrire.*	*Tu <u>devrais</u> m'écrire.*
= You will have to write to me.	= You had to write to me.	= You should write to me.
Elle <u>ira</u> en France.	*Elle all<u>ait</u> en France.*	*Elle <u>irait</u> en France.*
= She will go to France.	= She was going to France.	= She would go to France.
Je <u>manger</u>ai du pain.	*Je mange<u>ais</u> du pain.*	*Je <u>mangerais</u> du pain.*
= I will eat some bread.	= I was eating some bread.	= I would eat some bread.

The 'je' one ('<u>-ais</u>') can be hard to spot when you're <u>listening</u>, because it sounds exactly the same to the future ending ('<u>-ai</u>'). You have to think about what the <u>rest</u> of the sentence means and work out whether the person's saying what they <u>would do</u>, or what they <u>will do</u>.

This is tricky but Higher Level students need to know it

You often use the conditional when you have 'if' followed by the <u>imperfect tense</u>, so watch out for this in the exam. This is a really <u>useful</u> tense but rather <u>difficult</u> to form I'm afraid. Best get going with it...

Imperatives

How to boss people around — the quicker you learn it, the quicker you can get on with your life...

You need this for giving orders

Grammar Fans: this is called the '<u>Imperative</u>'.

It looks like the present tense (see p.196-199) but without the 'tu', 'vous' or 'nous' bits.

For when to choose 'tu' or 'vous' see page 6.

You need this one for <u>suggesting</u> doing something — like 'Let's go' or 'Let's dance'.

	you (inf sing.): tu	you (formal & plu.): vous	let's: nous
sortir (to go out)	sor<u>s</u>! (get out!)	sort<u>ez</u>! (get out!)	sort<u>ons</u>! (let's go out!)

Look at these endings. They're all the same as the present tense. Easy.

The odd one out is any 'tu' form that ends in 'es' (e.g. all 'er' verbs). See next page for more.

EXAMPLES:

Écoute ceci! = Listen to this!

Vendons la voiture! = Let's sell the car!

Finissez vos devoirs! = Finish your homework!

Allez dormir! = Go to sleep!

Attends! = Wait!

Tell people what to do using imperatives

The imperative is just a fancy word for a <u>command</u> — this stuff is what you'll <u>need</u> if you want to tell someone to do something. Have a look at the next page too for <u>more</u> on forming the imperative.

Imperatives

Take off the 's' from the 'tu' form of '-er' verbs

As mentioned on the previous page, the odd one out is any 'tu' form that ends in 'es'.
That means you have to be careful with regular '-er' verbs. You just have to lose the final '-s':

Regarde Jean-Paul!   Arrête de m'énerver!

= Look at Jean-Paul!   = Stop annoying me!

The ones below are irregular. They're nothing like the present tense, so you have to learn them by heart.

	you (inf. sing.): tu	you (formal & plu.): vous	let's: nous
to be: être	sois (be)	soyez (be)	soyons (let's be)
to have: avoir	aie (have)	ayez (have)	ayons (let's have)
to know: savoir	sache (know)	sachez (know)	sachons (let's know)

Negatives work normally, except for reflexives

Put 'ne' in front of the verb and 'pas' after, like normal (see p.218-219). Add the noun at the end.

EXAMPLES: *N'écoute pas!*   = Don't listen!

               Ne vendez pas la voiture!   = Don't sell the car!

In sentences with a reflexive verb (see p.216-217) you have to use an emphatic pronoun (p.189), and fiddle the word order...

E.g.   *Tu te lèves.*   = You get up.   ➡   *Lève-toi!*   = Get up!

WATCH OUT though — in negative sentences, you use normal pronouns and normal word order.

E.g.   *Tu ne te lèves pas.*   = You don't get up.   ➡   *Ne te lève pas!*   = Don't get up!

Watch out for negative or reflexive imperatives

Hopefully you haven't found this page too horrendous. But do be careful about dropping the 's' from the 'tu' form of '-er' verbs — that catches out many a weary GCSE student. Don't be one of them.

Quick Questions

I have some good news for you... this is almost the last set of questions in the whole book. Don't just skip through these because you're so near the end. This stuff is just as important as stuff at the beginning of the section, so make sure you do them properly.

Quick Questions

1) What is the French reflexive pronoun that means:
   a) himself?　　　　b) ourselves?　　　　c) myself?　　　d) themselves?

2) Write down the French for:
   a) to get up　　　　b) to go to bed　　　　c) to wash oneself

3) Fill in the correct reflexive pronoun for each person (or people) feeling ill below:
   a) Je ..... sens mal.　　　　b) Nous ..... sentons mal.　　　c) Elle ..... sent mal.
   d) Vous ..... sentez mal.　　　　e) Ils ..... sentent mal.　　　f) Tu ..... sens mal.

4) How would you say the following sentences in French?
   a) "I'm interested in science-fiction."　　　　b) "He's enjoying himself."

5) Mary asks you, "Ton nom? Comment ça s'écrit?" What is she asking?

6) Write a short passage in French describing your daily routine. You get up at 7 o'clock, wash yourself at 7.30, have breakfast at 8 o'clock, go to school at 9 o'clock, come home at 4 o'clock and go to bed at 10 o'clock.

7) Someone phones and wants to leave a message for your mum. They say their surname is 'Blanche'. How would you ask how it's spelt?

8) Put the reflexive verbs in these sentences into the past tense, making sure they agree with the person they are talking about. The first one has been done for you:
   a) Je me lave à huit heures. — Je me suis lavé(e) à huit heures.
   b) Nous nous sentons mal.　　　　c) Elle se trouve devant la gare.
   d) Vous vous couchez à onze heures.　　　e) Tu te lèves à neuf heures.
   f) Ils s'amusent au concert.　　　　g) Elles s'intéressent au problème.

9) Now translate the past tense versions of the above sentences into English.

10) Change these sentences to say the opposite, i.e. 'not', by adding 'ne' and 'pas':
    a) Je mange de la viande.　　　　b) Tu as beaucoup d'argent.
    c) Elle aime faire les courses.　　　d) Nous allons au cinéma ce soir.

11) Now change these sentences by adding 'ne' and 'pas' to say that something didn't happen (N.B. These are in the past tense, be careful):
    a) Elle a fait ses devoirs.　　　　b) Je suis allé à la banque.
    c) Nous avons vu Paul au parc.　　　d) Ils sont arrivés.

12) Dave says "Je préfère aller au théâtre." Using 'préfère + infinitive', tell him that you would not like to go to the theatre.

13) Jenny can't stop complaining. Translate what she is saying into English:
    "Je ne vais plus au cinéma parce que je n'ai pas assez d'argent; je ne vais jamais à la discothèque parce que je n'aime pas danser; je ne fais rien le week-end parce que je ne connais personne."

Quick Questions

14) How would you say 'I neither eat peas nor carrots' in French?

15) A shop assistant tells you, "Il n'y a plus de pommes et il n'y a aucune banane."
What did she say?

16) Your worst enemy asks if you'd like to go to the cinema. How would you say in
French that you don't have any: a) money? b) time?

17) One way to say "I would like" in French is "je voudrais". What is the other way?

18) Write down how you would say the following sentences in French:
a) "I would like a ham sandwich." b) "I would like to go to France this summer."

19) The conditional has the same... a) stem as which tense? b) endings as which tense?

20) Translate these sentences into English:
a) Est-ce que tu pourrais m'aider?
b) Il devrait m'écrire plus souvent.
c) Je sortirais ce soir si je ne devais pas faire mes devoirs.
d) Elles iraient en vacances si elles avaient plus d'argent.

21) Write down what these commands mean in English:
a) Viens-ici! b) Ouvre la fenêtre! c) Écoutez-moi! d) Levez la main!

22) Turn these phrases into informal commands (using 'tu'):
a) Faire la vaisselle b) Ranger ta chambre
c) Regarder le tableau noir d) Finir tes devoirs

23) Now turn these phrases into commands using 'vous':
a) Manger votre déjeuner b) Lire ce livre
c) Aller à l'école d) Prendre la première rue à gauche

24) How would you say the following sentences to your little brother in French?
a) "Let's go to the park." b) "Be careful!"

25) a) Your teacher tells your class 'Soyez gentils.' What does she mean?
b) Your friend says 'Aie peur!' What is he telling you?
c) Mark says, 'Sachez que je suis plus intelligent que vous.' What did he say?

26) Add 'ne' and 'pas' to these commands to tell people NOT to do something:
a) Écoute la radio! b) Prenez la deuxième rue à droite!
c) Vendez le chien! d) Mange mes chocolats!

27) Change these sentences containing pronouns into commands.
The example has been done for you. e.g. Tu te lèves. — Lève-toi!
a) Tu te tais. b) Vous vous asseyez. c) Vous vous taisez. d) Tu te souviens.

28) Now change these negative sentences into negative commands,
being very careful with the pronouns: e.g. Tu ne te lèves pas. — Ne te lève pas!
a) Tu ne te perds pas. b) Vous ne vous lavez pas. c) Tu ne te couches pas.

Know and Can

So many people get these verbs confused — so learn them right now.

'To know information' is 'Savoir'

1) 'Savoir' means 'to know' in the sense of knowing information (e.g. knowing what time the bus leaves).

Different forms of savoir

I know =	je sais
you (informal singular) know =	tu sais
he/she/it/one knows =	il/elle/on sait
we know =	nous savons
you (formal and plural) know =	vous savez
they know =	ils/elles savent

Elle sait cuisiner.   = She knows how to cook.

Je ne sais pas si nous avons des bananes.

= I don't know if we have any bananas.

2) 'Savoir' followed by an infinitive means 'to know how to do something', in the sense of a skill...

EXAMPLES:

Je sais conduire.   = I can drive.   *Elle ne sait pas lire.*   = She can't read.

'To be familiar with' is 'Connaître'

Connaître means to know a person or place — to 'be familiar with'.
If someone asks you whether you know their mate Bob, this is the one to use.

Different forms of connaître

I know =	je connais
you (informal singular) know =	tu connais
he/she/it/one knows =	il/elle/on connaît
we know =	nous connaissons
you (formal and plural) know =	vous connaissez
they know =	ils/elles connaissent

Connais-tu mon ami?   = Do you know my friend?

Je connais bien Paris.   = I know Paris well.

You need to know this page

If you're in a pickle and you don't know which verb to choose, just remember that you need 'savoir' for information and 'connaître' for knowing people and places. Try learning some examples too.

Know and Can

'Pouvoir' — to be able to

Different forms of pouvoir

I can =	je peux
you (informal singular) *can* =	tu peux
he/she/it/one can =	il/elle/on peut
we can =	nous pouvons
you (formal and plural) *can* =	vous pouvez
they can =	ils/elles peuvent

'Pouvoir' (to be able to/can) has <u>three</u> very important meanings:

1) Being <u>able</u> to do <u>something</u> (not knowing how, but just being able — like 'Yes, I can come tomorrow').

Je peux porter les bagages, si tu veux.   = I can carry the luggage, if you like.

Elle ne peut pas venir ce matin.   = She cannot come this morning.

2) <u>Permission</u> to do something.

On peut prendre des photos ici.   = You can take photos here.

Tu ne peux pas rester demain.   = You can't stay tomorrow.

3) <u>Possibility</u> — something <u>could</u> or <u>might</u> be the case.

Cela peut arriver.   = That can happen.

You need to be able to use 'pouvoir'

This verb is so <u>important</u> that it gets a page all to itself. Lucky old verb. Learn the <u>three</u> meanings on this page so you won't be surprised when you see '<u>pouvoir</u>' in the exam. You'll need it all the time.

Present Participles & Après Avoir/Être

Present participles are the '-ing' form of the verb, like 'speaking' or 'writing'.

Doing, saying, thinking are present participles

En + the present participle means 'while doing something':

Il lit le journal en déjeunant. = He reads the paper while having lunch.

This is how you form the present participle:

> imperfect stem + '-ant'

Remember — the imperfect stem is made from the 'nous' form of the present minus the '-ons'. See p.209.

Examples:

> PLAYING: jou~~ons~~ + ant = jouant   SAYING: dis~~ons~~ + ant = disant   BLUSHING: rougiss~~ons~~ + ant = rougissant

CAREFUL THOUGH — you translate things like 'I am doing' with the present tense, e.g. "je fais" and things like 'I like doing' with the present tense followed by the infinitive (see page 196).

Après avoir mangé... — After having eaten...

This could easily crop up in the exam/assessments. 'Après avoir + past participle' means 'after having done something'. The verbs which go with 'être' in the perfect tense (p.207-208) take 'être' here too.

Après avoir joué au foot, j'ai mangé. = After having played football, I ate.

Après être arrivé(e), j'ai... = After having arrived, I...

Learn this stuff really well

Don't translate sentences like 'I am speaking' or 'I am writing' with the present participle because most of the time you'll just need the present tense. Make sure you know when you should use it though.

The Passive

The stuff on this page all sounds quite grammary, but in fact the passive in French is not very different from how we form it in English. And you only really need to recognise this stuff, not use it.

La tasse est cassée — The cup is broken

1) In most sentences, there's a person or thing <u>doing</u> the action that's described by the verb. In a <u>passive</u> sentence, the person or thing is having <u>something done to it</u>.
2) The passive in French is made up of a <u>person</u> or <u>thing</u> + <u>être</u> + <u>past participle</u>.
3) The <u>past participle</u> has to <u>agree</u> with the <u>person</u> or <u>thing</u> that is having the <u>action done to it</u>.

Elle est renversée par la voiture.   = She is run over by the car.

'est' is a present tense form of the verb 'être' — to see the rest of it in the present, go to p.198

See p.204-208 for more past participles.

In the past and future, only the 'être' bit changes...

1) You also need to <u>recognise</u> the passive when it's describing what happened in the <u>past</u> or what will happen in the <u>future</u>.
2) Don't worry though — the passive in the different tenses is formed in basically the same way as in the <u>present</u>. The only thing that changes is the <u>tense</u> of 'être'.

The <u>imperfect passive</u> describes what happened to someone in the past. It's formed using the imperfect tense of être and a past participle:

L'homme était blessé.   = The man was injured.   **Ils étaient tués.**   = They were killed.

The <u>perfect passive</u> tells you about an event in the past that lasted for a fixed amount of time. It's formed using the perfect tense of être and a past participle:

Les chiens ont été volés par le voisin.   = The dogs have been stolen by the neighbour.

The <u>future passive</u> is made up of part of the future tense of être + past participle:

Elles seront tuées.

= They (fem.) will be killed.

Don't forget that with all tenses of the passive, if it's talking about something feminine or plural the past participle has to agree.

One last thing — there's a reason why you'll need to recognise this but not use it. French doesn't use the passive as much as it's used in English. In French, they often use an active sentence with 'on' instead.

I wasn't seen.

= On ne m'a pas vu(e).

You need to know the passive tense

Though this stuff looks <u>complicated</u>, you only need to be able to <u>understand</u> most of it so this page isn't as bad as it looks. Just read through this stuff so you're sure that you've totally <u>got to grips</u> with it.

Impersonal Verbs

Some pretty <u>meaty</u> stuff on this page. But don't despair, you've <u>almost finished</u> this section.

Impersonal verbs only work with '**il**'

<u>Impersonal verbs</u> always have '<u>il</u>' as the subject. For example:

Il faut aller au collège tous les jours.   = It is necessary to go to school every day.

You also use impersonal verbs to talk about the <u>weather</u>:

Il a plu hier, et aujourd'hui il neige.   = It rained yesterday, and today it's snowing.

Some impersonal verbs <u>combine</u> with <u>other verbs</u> in the <u>infinitive</u>:

Il est nécessaire de courir.   = It is necessary to run.

> For more on infinitives,
> see page 195 and page 199.

Il me semble raisonnable d'arrêter.   = It seems reasonable to me to stop.

> See p.188 for indirect object pronouns.

Il s'agit d'argent.   = It's a question of money.

It's nothing personal — you've just got to know it

Impersonal verbs do exactly what they say on the tin. They only work with the '<u>il</u>' form because they're <u>never</u> used to talk about a specific person doing an action. That's the <u>main thing</u> to remember.

The Subjunctive

I won't lie, this page isn't too easy. If you're studying for <u>Foundation Level</u>, you don't need to worry about any of this and if you're studying for <u>Higher Level</u>, you only need to <u>recognise</u> and <u>understand</u> it.

You may see the subjunctive instead of the infinitive

Not all <u>impersonal verbs</u> are followed by the <u>infinitive</u> — some are followed by the <u>subjunctive</u> instead. You just need to <u>understand</u> what common verbs <u>look and sound like</u> in the subjunctive in case they come up in your <u>listening</u> or <u>reading</u> exam.

The expressions that use the subjunctive that you're most likely to see are:

Il faut qu 'il parte demain. = <u>It is necessary that</u> he leaves tomorrow.

Il semble qu 'il ne vienne pas. = <u>It seems that</u> he's not coming.

Bien qu 'elle ait deux enfants. = <u>Although</u> she has two children.

Pour qu 'il fasse ses devoirs. = <u>So that</u> he does his homework.

Avant que vous partiez. = <u>Before</u> you leave.

And these are the verbs you really need to recognise in the subjunctive:

'Avoir' and 'être' in the subjunctive are pretty much the same as the imperative (those command words you met on p.222-223).

Subjunctive forms					
Avoir	j'aie	tu aies	il/elle/on ait	nous ayons	vous ayez	ils/elles aient
Être	je sois	tu sois	il/elle/on soit	nous soyons	vous soyez	ils/elles soient
Faire	je fasse	tu fasses	il/elle/on fasse	nous fassions	vous fassiez	ils/elles fassent
Pouvoir	je puisse	tu puisses	il/elle/on puisse	nous puissions	vous puissiez	ils/elles puissent

Make sure you can spot the subjunctive

Basically, if you see a <u>funny-looking</u> verb after the word '<u>que</u>', it's probably the <u>subjunctive</u>. You won't be expected to use it, but don't let it throw you if it comes up in the exam. Best get it <u>learnt</u>.

Quick Questions

Guess what — these are the final pages of Quick Questions, both in this section AND in the whole book. Hooray, the end is in sight. You should give yourself a mighty good pat on the back for getting this far. But first work your way through these questions and make sure you can answer every one.

Quick Questions

1) How would you say the following sentences in French?
   a) "I know how to cook."   b) "I know how to drive."
   c) "I don't know how to ski but I know how to swim."

2) Someone asks you, "Est-ce qu'il y a une banque près d'ici?" Tell him you don't know.

3) Freddy boasts, "Je connais la reine d'Angleterre."
   a) What is he claiming?   b) Ask Freddy, in French, if he knows the President of America.

4) Tell your French penfriend that you know London quite well.

5) Emma says, "Je ne sais pas faire mes devoirs." Tell her, in French, that you can help her if she wants.

6) A policeman tells you, "Vous ne pouvez pas entrer dans l'église sans chapeau."
   What did he say?

7) Ask your mum, in French, if you can go out tonight.

8) Write a short passage in French explaining that you could go to France this summer and you know France very well. You could also go to Spain, but you don't know how to speak Spanish.

9) What do these mean in English?
   a) chantant   b) mangeant   c) partant   d) courant

10) Turn these infinitives into the present participle (the –ing form):
    a) dire   b) jouer   c) parler   d) dormir
    e) lire   f) boire   g) faire   h) descendre

11) Translate these sentences into English:
    a) Je fais mes devoirs en regardant la télévision.
    b) Il reste en forme en jouant au tennis.
    c) Je me suis cassé le bras en jouant au football.
    d) Nous nous amusons en lisant des bandes dessinées.

12) Translate these sentences into French:
    a) We watch television while having lunch.   b) She is enjoying herself playing tennis.
    c) He entered the church while singing.   d) You arrive quicker going by train.

13) Read the extract from your friends blog below and answer the questions that follow.

> Ce matin, j'ai pris mon petit déjeuner en regardant la télé. Malheureusement, j'ai remarqué qu'il y avait un insecte dans mes céréales seulement en le mangeant. Tout de suite, j'ai couru voir ma mère en pleurant.

a) Why was he not concentrating while making his breakfast?
b) When did he notice there was an insect in his cereal?
c) What was he doing when he ran to find his mum?

Quick Questions

Quick Questions

14) You would translate the sentence "I am eating" into French using the present participle. True or false?

15) Translate these sentences into French:
    a) After having slept, I ate three croissants.   b) After having worked, I watched television.

16) Now translate these sentences into English:
    a) Après être monté, je suis resté là pendant trois heures.
    b) Après être tombée, je suis allée chez le médecin.

17) All of these sentences are missing an agreement. For each one, add the correct ending:
    a) Après être sorti, Mike et Paul ont mangé une pizza.
    b) Après être devenu célèbre, Emma mangeait au restaurant tous les jours.
    c) Après être arrivé, Sarah et Katie se sont couchées tout de suite.

18) Translate this sentence into English: "Nous sommes aimés par notre grand-mère."

19) These sentences are also in the passive. Translate them into English:
    a) J'ai été employé par un café en ville.
    b) Mes devoirs ont été mangés par mon petit frère.

20) Now for the future passive. Translate this sentence into English too: "Les journaux seront recyclés la semaine prochaine."

21) Your French friend tells you, "On ne m'a pas offert de cadeau pour mon anniversaire." What is he telling you?

22) What does "Chaque jour, il faut manger cinq fruits et légumes" mean?

23) Impersonal verbs are often used to talk about the weather. How would you say "It snowed yesterday, but today it's warm" in French?

24) You arrive at a French person's house for dinner. There's a sign on the door that says "Il est nécessaire de laisser vos chaussures ici." What does it mean?

25) What do the following phrases mean?
    a) il faut que   b) bien que   c) il semble que   d) avant que

26) One of the verbs in this sentence is underlined: "Je ne veux pas qu'il <u>vienne</u>." What type of verb is it?

27) Translate the following sentences into English:
    a) Je vais te donner de l'argent pour que tu ranges ta chambre.
    b) Je ne crois pas qu'il soit aussi beau que moi.

28) For each of these verbs in the subjunctive, say what the infinitive form of the verb would be: a) soyez   b) fasse   c) aies   d) puissions

Revision Summary

This is the <u>last Revision Summary</u> of the book, so there's no excuse for being lazy and skipping through it. Understanding grammar is <u>crucial</u> in GCSE French so you'd be <u>foolish</u> to ignore these questions.

1) What are the words for both 'the' and 'a/some' which have to accompany these:
   a) maison   b) chien   c) chaussure   d) soleil   e) travail   f) jeu
   g) jeux   h) journaux

2) "Je vais à la maison." Change this sentence to tell people you're going to:
   a) le cinéma   b) l'église   c) la banque   d) le stade   e) les magasins   f) les Alpes

3) What is the French for: a) my horse   b) our house   c) his clothes   d) her house

4) "Janie is cool. Janie is cooler than Jimmy. She is the coolest." Translate these three sentences into French, then swap "cool" for each of the following words and write them out all over again:
   a) formidable   b) intelligent(e)   c) célèbre   d) pratique   e) bavard(e)

5) Write six French sentences each using one of the following words.
   a) à   b) en   c) dans   d) pour   e) depuis   f) de

6) Place the missing <u>qui</u>'s and <u>que</u>'s in the following text and then translate it, please...
   "J'ai rencontré un homme __ adorait les sports. Cet homme __ j'ai rencontré, __ adorait les sports, n'aimait pas les escargots __ je lui avais achetés, surtout ceux __ venaient de France."

7) What are the French words for:
   a) and   b) or   c) but   d) because
   e) with   f) while   g) therefore

8) Replace the underlined parts of these sentences with either 'y' or 'en':
   a) J'ai besoin <u>du chocolat</u>. b) Je vais aller <u>au cinéma</u>. c) Je prends six kilos <u>de bonbons</u>.

9) How do you say the following in French:
   a) I have   b) she has   c) we have   d) they have   e) I am   f) he is   g) we are   h) they are

10) What does each of these French phrases mean in English: a) je mange un gâteau
    b) j'ai mangé un gâteau   c) je mangeais un gâteau   d) j'avais mangé un gâteau
    e) je vais manger un gâteau   f) je mangerai un gâteau   g) je mangerais un gâteau

11) Use reflexive verbs to say:
    a) We wash ourselves.   b) She went to bed.   c) They had fun.   d) I'm interested in French.

12) How do you say these in French:
    a) I don't go out.   b) I never go out.   c) I don't go out any more.

13) Turn these sentences from the present tense to the imperative:
    a) Tu arrêtes de faire ça.   b) Vous êtes tranquille.   c) Nous allons au Portugal.
    d) Tu te lèves.   e) Vous ne vous inquiétez pas.   f) Nous ne regardons pas le film.

14) Translate: a) He reads the paper while taking a shower.   b) I talk after having eaten.
    c) They play Scrabble while walking the dog.   d) We work after having listened to the radio.

15) Final question. What does "Il faut que tu apprennes toutes les choses dans ce livre avant de le jeter" mean?

Do Well in Your Exam

Here are some little gems of advice, whichever exam board you're studying for.

Read the questions carefully

<u>Don't</u> go losing <u>easy marks</u> — it'll break my heart.
Make sure you <u>definitely</u> do the things on this list:

1) <u>Read all the instructions</u> properly.

2) <u>Read the question</u> properly.

3) <u>Answer the question</u> — don't waffle.

Don't give up if you don't understand

If you don't understand, <u>don't panic</u>. The <u>key thing</u> to remember is that you can still <u>do well</u> in the exam, even if you <u>don't understand</u> every French word that comes up.

If you're reading or listening — look for lookalikes:

1) Some words <u>look</u> or <u>sound</u> the <u>same</u> in French and English — they're called <u>cognates</u>.
2) These words are <u>great</u> because you'll recognise them when you see them in a text.
3) Be careful though — there are some <u>exceptions</u> you need to watch out for.
    Some words <u>look</u> like an English word but have a totally <u>different meaning</u>:

sensible:	*sensitive*	la journée:	*day*	le car:	*coach*
grand(e):	*big*	la pièce:	*room, coin or play*	le crayon:	*pencil*
large:	*wide*	la cave:	*cellar*	les affaires:	*business*
mince:	*slim*	la veste:	*jacket*	le pain:	*bread*
joli(e):	*pretty*	le médecin:	*doctor*	les baskets:	*trainers*

Words like these are called 'faux amis' — false friends.

Always keep your eyes peeled for false friends

Don't get caught out by words that <u>look</u> like English words, but in fact mean something <u>different</u>. Generally speaking, if a word <u>doesn't</u> seem to <u>fit</u> into the context of the question, have a <u>rethink</u>.

Do Well in Your Exam

Make use of the context

You'll likely come across the odd word that you don't know, especially in the <u>reading exam</u>. Often you'll be able to find some <u>clues</u> telling you what the text is all about.

> 1) The <u>type of text</u>, e.g. newspaper article, advertisement, website
> 2) The <u>title</u> of the text
> 3) Any <u>pictures</u>
> 4) The <u>verbal context</u>

Say you see the following in the reading exam, and don't know what any of these words mean:

"...des vêtements en polyester, en soie, en laine et en coton."

Use these steps to work out what the sentence means:

> 1) The fact that this is a list of things all starting with '<u>en ...</u>' coming after the French word for '<u>clothes</u>' suggests they're all <u>things</u> that <u>clothes</u> can be <u>made out of</u>.
> 2) You can guess that '<u>polyester</u>' means '<u>polyester</u>', and '<u>coton</u>' means '<u>cotton</u>'.
> 3) So it's a pretty good guess that the two words you don't know are different types of <u>fabric</u>. (In fact, '<u>soie</u>' means '<u>silk</u>' and '<u>laine</u>' means '<u>wool</u>'.)
> 4) Often the questions <u>won't</u> depend on you understanding these more difficult words. It's important to be able to understand the <u>gist</u> though, and not let these words <u>throw</u> you.

Take notes in the listening exam

1) You'll have <u>5 minutes</u> at the start of the listening exam to have a <u>quick look</u> through the paper. This'll give you a chance to see <u>how many questions</u> there are, and you might get a few clues from the questions about what <u>topics</u> they're on, so it won't be a horrible surprise when the recording starts.

2) You'll hear each extract <u>twice</u>. Different people have different strategies, but it's a good idea to jot down a few details that you think might come up in the questions, especially things like:

> Dates
> Numbers
> Names

3) But... don't forget to <u>keep listening</u> to the gist of the recording while you're making notes.

4) You won't have a <u>dictionary</u> — but you probably wouldn't have time to use it anyway.

Try and stay calm and think logically in the exams

The examiners aren't above sticking a few tricky bits and pieces into the exam to see how you <u>cope</u> with them. Using all your <u>expert knowledge</u>, you should stand a pretty <u>good chance</u> of working it out.

Do Well in Your Exam

These pages could <u>improve</u> your grade — they're all about exam technique.

Look at how a word is made up

You may read or hear a sentence and not understand <u>how the sentence works</u>. You need to remember all the <u>grammar bits</u> in Section Seven to give you a good chance at <u>piecing it all together</u>.

1) A word that ends in '<u>-é</u>', '<u>-u</u>' or '<u>-i</u>' may well be a <u>past participle</u>. Look for a bit of '<u>avoir</u>' or a bit of '<u>être</u>' nearby to work out who's done what.

2) A word that ends in '<u>r</u>' or '<u>er</u>' might be an <u>infinitive</u>. If you take off the 'er', it might look like an English word which may tell you what the verb means.

> E.g. 'confirm ~~er~~' = *to confirm*

3) If you see '<u>-ment</u>' at the end of a word, it could well be an <u>adverb</u> (see p.177-178). Try replacing the '-ment' with '<u>-ly</u>' and see if it makes sense.

> E.g. 'général~~ement~~' ➔ 'généralely' = *generally*

4) '<u>Dé-</u>' at the beginning of a word is often '<u>dis-</u>' in the equivalent word in English.

> E.g. '~~dé~~courage~~r~~' = *to discourage*

5) Sometimes <u>letters with accents</u> show that there may have been an '<u>s</u>' at some point in the past. This may help you find the corresponding English word.

> E.g. 'tempête' = *tempest*   'mât' = *mast*   'forêt' = *forest*

6) A word beginning with '<u>in-</u>' might be a <u>negative prefix</u>.

> E.g. 'inconnu' = 'in+connu = *unknown*

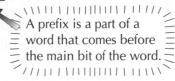
A prefix is a part of a word that comes before the main bit of the word.

Piece together all the parts of a sentence to find the meaning

Breaking down a French sentence into <u>little bits</u> can help you work out what the <u>whole thing</u> means. Now would be a good time to look over the <u>grammar section</u> to make sure you know what's what.

How to Use Dictionaries

Don't go mad on dictionaries — it's the path to <u>ruin</u>. However, you're allowed to use one in the writing task, so it's good to know how to make the <u>most</u> of it.

Don't translate word for word — it DOESN'T work

If you turn each word of this phrase into English, you get <u>rubbish</u>.

Il y a une pomme.   *It there has an apple.*

NO!

I am reading.   *Je suis lisant.*

It's the <u>same</u> the other way round — turn English into French word by word, and you get <u>balderdash</u> — <u>don't do it</u>.

If it doesn't make sense, you've got it wrong

Some words have several meanings — don't just pick the first one you see.
Look at the <u>meanings</u> listed and <u>suss out</u> which one is what you're looking for.

If you read this... *J'ai mal à l'oeil droit.*

...you might look up '<u>droit</u>' and find this:

So the sentence could mean:

My straight eye hurts. ✘

My right eye hurts. ✔

This is the only one that sounds sensible.

My law eye hurts. ✘

> **droit, e**
> <u>adj</u> upright; straight;
> // right, right-hand
> // <u>adv</u> straight
> <u>tiens-toi droit</u>: stand up straight
> // <u>nm</u> law; justice
> // droits; rights; taxes, duties
> <u>droits d'auteur</u>: royalties

Verbs change according to the person

When you look up a <u>verb</u> in the dictionary, you'll find the <u>infinitive</u> (the 'to' form, like '<u>to</u> run', '<u>to</u> sing' etc.). But you may need to say '<u>I</u> run', or '<u>we</u> sing' –– so you need to change the verb <u>ending</u>.

Say you need to say '<u>I work</u>'.

For the low-down on verbs and all their different endings, see the grammar section.

1) If you looked up '<u>work</u>', you'd find the word '<u>travailler</u>', meaning 'to work'.
2) But '<u>travailler</u>' is the <u>infinitive</u> — you can't put 'je travailler'.
3) You need the '<u>I</u>' (je) form of the verb — 'je <u>travaille</u>'.
4) Check the <u>tense</u> — e.g. you might want the future: 'je travaillerai'.

If you're looking up a <u>French</u> verb, look for its <u>infinitive</u> (it'll probably end in 'er', 'ir' or 're'). If you want to know what 'nous poussons' means, you'll find '<u>pousser</u>' (to push, or to grow) in the dictionary. So 'nous poussons' must mean '<u>we push</u>' or '<u>we grow</u>'.

Don't stop thinking just because you've got a dictionary

Don't get <u>put off</u> dictionaries by this page. They're <u>lovely</u> really. Just make sure your writing technique isn't to look up every single word and then write them down in order. Because it won't make sense.

Hints for Writing

Here are a few <u>general hints</u> about how you should approach the writing tasks.

Write about what you know

1) You will <u>need</u> to cover things that the question asks you to talk about, but there'll be plenty of scope to be <u>imaginative</u>.
2) Usually the writing tasks will give you some <u>flexibility</u> so you can base your answer on something you know about.

You get marks for saying when and why...

1) Saying <u>when</u> and <u>how often</u> you did things gets you big marks. Learn <u>times</u>, <u>dates</u> and <u>numbers</u> carefully (pages 1-4).
2) Make sure you talk about what you've done <u>in the past</u> (see pages 204-212) or what you will do <u>in the future</u> (p.200-201).
3) Give <u>descriptions</u> where possible, but keep things <u>accurate</u> — a short description in <u>perfect French</u> is better than a longer paragraph of nonsense.
4) <u>Opinions</u> (pages 10-12) also score highly. Try to <u>vary them</u> as much as possible.

...and where and who with...

Most teachers are really quite nosy, and love as many details as you can give. It's a good idea to ask yourself all these 'wh-' questions, and write the bits that show your French off in the <u>best light</u>. Also, it doesn't matter if what you're writing isn't strictly true — as long as it's <u>believable</u>.

Use your dictionary, but sparingly

1) The time to use the dictionary is <u>not</u> to learn a completely new, fancy way of saying something.
2) Use it to look up a particular word that you've <u>forgotten</u> — a word that, when you see it, you'll <u>know</u> is the right word.
3) Use it to check <u>genders</u> of nouns — that's whether words are <u>masculine</u> (le/un) or <u>feminine</u> (la/une).
4) Check any <u>spellings</u> you're unsure of.

> Most importantly, don't use the dictionary to delve into the unknown. If you don't know what you've written is right, it's probably wrong.

Take your time

1) Don't <u>hurtle</u> into writing about something and then realise halfway through that you don't actually know the French for it.
2) <u>Plan</u> how you can cover all the things that the task mentions, and then think about the extra things you can slip in to show off your French.

And lastly, don't forget your pen

I suppose the key is <u>variety</u> — lots of different <u>tenses</u>, plenty of meaty <u>vocabulary</u> and loads of <u>details</u>. This is your only chance to show what you can do, so don't waste all your <u>hard work</u>.

Hints for Writing

<u>Accuracy</u> is important in the writing assessment.

Start with the Verb

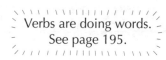
Verbs are doing words.
See page 195.

1) Verbs really are the <u>cornerstone</u> of every French sentence.
   If you get the verb right, the rest of the sentence should <u>fall into place</u>.
2) Don't translate the verb without reading the <u>whole sentence</u> first —
   you're likely to end up with the wrong verb.

<u>EXAMPLE</u>: Say you want to write the following sentence in French:

> *On Sundays, we <u>go for a walk</u>, if <u>the weather is nice</u>.*

Don't see 'go' and jump in with 'aller'.
The expression for 'go for a walk' is 'faire une promenade'.

You know that 'the weather
is nice' is 'il fait beau'.

Make sure your <u>tenses</u> and the <u>endings</u> of the verbs are right, then piece it all together:

> *Le dimanche, nous faisons une promenade, s'il fait beau.*

Check and re-check

No matter how careful you think you're being, <u>mistakes</u> can easily creep into your work.

Go through the <u>checklist</u> below for every sentence <u>straight after</u> you've written it.

1) Are the verbs in the right <u>tense</u>?
   Demain, je <u>travaillais</u> dans le jardin. ✖   Demain, je <u>travaillerai</u> dans le jardin. ✓

2) Are the <u>endings</u> of the verbs right?
   Tu n'<u>aime</u> pas les carottes? ✖   Tu n'<u>aimes</u> pas les carottes? ✓

3) Do your adjectives <u>agree</u> as they should?
   Elle est <u>grand</u>. ✖   Elle est <u>grande</u>. ✓

4) Do your past participles <u>agree</u>?
   Ils sont <u>parti</u>. ✖   Ils sont <u>partis</u>. ✓

5) Do your adjectives come in the <u>right place</u>?
   Une <u>rose</u> chemise ✖   Une chemise <u>rose</u> ✓

6) Have you used <u>tu / vous</u> correctly?
   Madame, <u>peux-tu</u> m'aider, s'il vous plaît? ✖ Madame, <u>pouvez-vous</u> m'aider, s'il vous plaît? ✓

Then when you've finished the whole piece of work, have <u>another</u> read through with <u>fresh eyes</u>.
You're bound to pick up one or two more mistakes.

Do nothing without a verb

I know there's loads to remember, and French verbs are a pain, but checking over your work is a real <u>must</u>. Reread your work <u>assuming there are errors</u> in it, rather than assuming it's fine as it is.

Hints for Speaking

The speaking assessment fills many a student with <u>dread</u>. Remember though — it's your chance to show what you can <u>do</u>. It won't be nearly as bad as you think it's going to be. <u>Honest</u>.

Be Imaginative

There are two tricky things about the speaking assessment — one is <u>what to say</u>, and the other is <u>how to say it</u>. No matter how good your French is, it won't shine through if you can't think of anything to say.

Say you're asked to talk about your <u>daily routine</u> (or to imagine someone else's daily routine). It would be easy to give a list of things you do when you get in from school:

"Je fais mes devoirs. Je regarde la télé. Je mange. Je vais au lit."   = I do my homework. I watch TV. I eat. I go to bed.

It makes sense, but the problem is, it's all a bit <u>samey</u>...

1) Try to think of when this <u>isn't</u> the case, and put it into a <u>different tense</u>:

    "Mais demain ce sera différent, parce que je jouerai au hockey après le collège."

      = But tomorrow it will be different, because I will play hockey after school.

2) Don't just talk about yourself. Talk about <u>other people</u> too.

    "J'ai regardé la télé avec mon frère, mais il n'aime pas les mêmes émissions que moi."

      = I watched TV with my brother, but he doesn't like the same programmes as me.

3) Give loads of <u>opinions</u> and <u>reasons</u> for your opinions.

    "J'aime finir mes devoirs avant de manger. Alors je peux me détendre plus tard."

      = I like to finish my homework before eating. Then I can relax later on.

A couple of 'Don't's...

1) <u>DON'T</u> try to <u>avoid</u> a topic if you find it difficult — that'll mean you won't get <u>any</u> marks at all for that bit of the assessment. You'll be surprised what you can muster up if you stay calm and concentrate on what you <u>do</u> know how to say.
2) <u>DON'T</u> make up a word in the hope that it exists in French unless you're really, really stuck. Try one of the tricks on the next page first. However, if it's your <u>last resort</u>, it's worth a try.

Have Confidence

1) Believe it or not, the teacher isn't trying to catch you out. He or she <u>wants</u> you to do <u>well</u>, and to be dazzled by all the excellent French you've learnt.
2) Speaking assessments can be pretty <u>daunting</u>. But remember it's the same for <u>everyone</u>.
3) <u>Nothing horrendous</u> is going to happen if you make a few slip-ups. Just try and focus on showing the teacher how much you've <u>learnt</u>.

Make sure you speak clearly and don't mumble

They won't be able to give you any marks if they can't hear you. Remember that it's better to have <u>too much</u> to say than <u>too little</u>. Try to use your <u>imagination</u> and show off your beautiful French.

Hints for Speaking

Nothing in life ever goes completely according to plan, so it's a good idea to prepare yourself.

Try to find another way of saying it

There may be a particular word or phrase that trips you up. There's always a way round it though.

1) If you can't <u>remember</u> a French word, use an <u>alternative</u> word or try <u>describing it</u> instead.

2) E.g. if you can't remember that '<u>grapes</u>' are '<u>les raisins</u>' and you really need to say it, then describe them as 'the small green or red fruits', or 'les petits fruits verts ou rouges'.

3) You can avoid words you can't remember — if you can't remember the word for '<u>dog</u>' then just say you've got a <u>cat</u> instead. Make sure what you're saying makes <u>sense</u> though — saying you've got a <u>pet radio</u> isn't going to get you any marks, trust me.

4) If you can't remember the word for a <u>cup</u> (la tasse) in your speaking assessment, you could say '<u>glass</u>' (le verre) instead — you'll still make yourself <u>understood</u>.

If the worst comes to the worst, ask for help in French

1) If you can't think of a way around it, you <u>can</u> ask for help in the speaking assessment — as long as you ask for it in <u>French</u>.

2) If you can't remember what a chair is, ask your teacher; "Comment dit-on 'chair' en français?" It's <u>better</u> than wasting time trying to think of the word.

You may just need to buy yourself some time

If you get a bit <u>stuck</u> for what to say, there's always a <u>way out</u>.

1) If you just need some <u>thinking time</u> in your speaking assessment or you want to check something, you can use these useful phrases to help you out:

Um... :	Ben...	*Can you repeat, please?:*	Pouvez-vous répéter, s'il vous plaît?
Well... :	Eh bien...	*I don't understand:*	Je ne comprends pas.
I'm not sure:	Je ne suis pas sûr(e).	*That's a good question:*	Ça, c'est une bonne question.

2) Another good tactic if you're a bit stuck is to say what you've <u>just said</u> in a <u>different way</u>. This shows off your <u>command of French</u>, and also it might lead onto something else, e.g.:

Saying the same thing a different way...

"On mange en famille... Je ne mange pas seul, sauf quand mes parents travaillent tard."

= We eat as a family... <u>I don't eat on my own</u>, <u>except when my parents work late</u>.

... leading on to another idea.

And don't be afraid to make mistakes — even native French speakers make them. Don't let a silly error shake your concentration for the rest of the assessment.

One last thing — don't panic

Congratulations...you've <u>almost</u> made it to the end of the book without accident or injury. <u>Read</u> these pages, <u>take on board</u> the information, <u>use it</u> in your GCSE, <u>do well</u> and then <u>celebrate</u> in style.

Practice Exam

Once you've been through all the questions in this book, you should feel pretty confident about the exam. As final preparation, here's a **practice exam** to prepare you for the real thing. It's designed to give you the best exam practice possible, whichever exam specification you're following.

General Certificate of Secondary Education

CGP   Practice Exam Paper
GCSE French

GCSE
French

Centre name					
Centre number					
Candidate number					

Listening Paper

Surname	
Other names	
Candidate signature	

Time allowed: 40 minutes approximately
+ 5 minutes reading time before the test.

Instructions
- Write in black or blue ink.
- Before the CD is started you will be given **5** minutes during which you may read through the questions and make notes.
- Answer **all** questions in the spaces provided.
- Answer all questions in **English**.
- Give all the information you are asked for, and **write neatly**.

This is what you should do for each item:
- Before each new question, read through all the question parts and instructions carefully.
- Listen carefully to the recording. There will be a pause to allow you to reread the question, make notes or write down your answers.
- Listen to the recording again. There will be another pause to allow you to complete or check your answers.
- You may write at any point during the exam.
- Each item on the CD is repeated once.
- You are **not** allowed to ask questions or interrupt during the exam.

Information
- The number of marks are shown by each question.
- The maximum mark for this paper is **40**.
- You are **not** allowed to use a dictionary.

Instructions for playing the CD.
- There are 16 questions, covered on the CD by tracks 27 – 38.

Question No.	1	2	3	4	5	6	7-8	9	10-11	12-13	14-15	16
CD Track No.	27	28	29	30	31	32	33	34	35	36	37	38

- Play the CD, one track at a time, pausing the CD after each track.

Answer ALL questions

Track 27

1   Caroline is talking about her holiday. Answer the following questions.

   a)   Caroline is going to stay:

| A | in a youth hostel.

| B | with a host family.

| C | at a campsite.   Write the correct letter in the box.   ☐

   b)   Caroline would like to visit:

| A | museums.

| B | art galleries.

| C | a theme park.   Write the correct letter in the box.   ☐

   c)   She wants to go on an excursion to see:

| A | churches.

| B | castles.

| C | a market.   Write the correct letter in the box.   ☐

(3 marks)

Track 28

2   You're going to hear some announcements about shop opening hours.
     Fill in the gaps to complete these sentences.

   a)   The .... and the pharmacy shut at 18:30.

   b)   The .... and the sweetshop shut at 18:15.

   c)   The bookshop and the .... shut at 19:00.

(3 marks)

Track 29

You're being told about the flat that you've rented for your holiday. Answer the questions.

Example: There are: | A | three bedrooms.

| B | two bedrooms.

| C | two bathrooms. Write the correct letter in the box. | B |

3 a) The living room is: | A | nice.

| B | small.

| C | pretty. Write the correct letter in the box. ☐

b) The kitchen has a: | A | modern table.

| B | small table.

| C | green table. Write the correct letter in the box. ☐

c) In the bedroom, there is a: | A | wardrobe.

| B | carpet.

| C | armchair. Write the correct letter in the box. ☐

(3 marks)

Track 30

In the Tourist Information Office, you're given the telephone number for three hotels.
Write down the three numbers.

Remember that French telephone numbers are always given in pairs. E.g. they would say 'twenty-three' rather than 'two three'.

Example L'Hôtel de la Gare **02.64.34.41.13**

4 a) Le Commerce ....

b) Le Royal ....

c) Le Lion d'Or ....

(3 marks)

Turn over

Track 31

You have two messages on your answering machine. Fill in the grid with the missing details.

5

	Message 1	Message 2
Who has phoned?	**Mrs Durocq**	c)
Why?	**have you received her packet?**	d)
Date?	a)	**Saturday 11th May**
Time?	b)	e)

(5 marks)

Track 32

Céline is talking about methods of transport. Fill in the gaps.

6 a) She thinks that taking the bus is ....

b) She says that buses pollute the environment .... than cars.

c) On days when there aren't any buses, it can be ....

d) At night, she has to check the time so she doesn't ....

(4 marks)

Track 33

A group of friends are talking about health.

What problems do the following people have?

How long have they had them?

	Name	Problem	Since
Example	Charlotte	**flu**	**a week and a half ago**
7	Marc-Olivier		**yesterday morning**
8	Ariane	**headaches**	

(2 marks)

Track 34

9   Aurélie is talking about pocket money. Answer the questions below.

a)   How much pocket money does she receive each month?

....

b)   What does she spend her money on? Give **two** details.

....

....

(2 marks)

248

Track 35

Some young people are talking about their future careers. What is their favourite subject?

What career would they like? Choose the **two** pictures which represent what each person says.

Example

A   B   C   D   A C

10

A   B   C   D

11

A   B   C   D

(4 marks)

Track 36

David, Camille and Alice are talking about work experience.

Fill in the table to say where they did their placement and why they did / didn't like it.

	Where?	Why did / didn't they like it?
Example	**Renault in Lyon**	**didn't like town**
12		
13		

(4 marks)

Track 37

For each of these young people, write down what they worry about.

Example: exhaust fumes (or pollution)

14 ....

15 ....

(2 marks)

Track 38

16 These people are talking about their life at home.

For each person, choose the correct sentence from the list and write the letter in the box.

A "I do chores around the house and earn money."

B "I regularly do the shopping."

C "I help on the farm a lot."

D "A woman comes to do the housework."

E "I don't have to do anything to help."

a) Marie

b) Erwan

c) Laëtitia

d) Stéphanie

e) Nicolas

(5 marks)

END OF TEST

General Certificate of Secondary Education

GCSE
French

Reading Paper

Centre name					
Centre number					
Candidate number					

Surname	
Other names	
Candidate signature	

Time allowed: 50 minutes

Instructions
- Write in black or blue ink.
- Answer **all** questions in the spaces provided.
- Answer all questions in **English**.
- Give all the information you are asked for, and **write neatly**.

Information
- The marks are shown next to each question.
- The maximum mark for this paper is **40**.
- You are **not** allowed to use a dictionary.

Answer ALL questions

1 These people are talking about the cinema.

> Moi je suis fan des comédies musicales. Je pense que je dois les avoir toutes vues! Je suis allé à New York en voyage scolaire et j'ai vu mon histoire préférée qui s'appelle "West Side Story" au théâtre. Le spectacle a duré trois heures! Les acteurs ont très bien joué et j'en étais très impressionné. – *David*

> Je suis journaliste à Paris et ma spécialité est le cinéma. Mon travail me permet d'assister aux premières et à donner mon point de vue sur les films qui sortent. Je viens de rentrer de Cannes où j'ai rencontré Robert de Niro et Gérard Depardieu. – *Alexia*

> Le week-end dernier j'ai vu un film classique britannique au cinéma. Il n'était pas en noir et blanc mais il était vieux quand même. Il s'agit d'un homme qui a dû quitter sa ville et sa maison pour échapper à la police parce qu'il est accusé d'un crime. On sait dès le debut qu'il est innocent et je trouve ça génial. – *Jasmine*

For each of the following sentences, write **T** (true), **F** (false) or **N** (not in text) in the box.

a) David starred in a production of West Side Story. ☐

b) Alexia has recently returned from a film festival. ☐

c) Jasmine watched a film about a man being falsely accused of a crime. ☐

d) David was disappointed that there was no interval in his favourite musical. ☐

(4 marks)

Turn over

2   Elisa has written you an email about how she celebrates Christmas.

J'adore les fêtes de Noël parce que mes grands-parents, mon oncle, ma tante et mes cousins viennent nous rendre visite. Nous avons déjà préparé le sapin et mis les décorations de Noël aux portes et aux fenêtres pour leur arrivée la veille de Noël.

Pour le repas du réveillon nous allons manger de la dinde avec des haricots verts et des champignons. Comme entrée nous allons manger des escargots — j'adore les escargots et nous n'en mangeons qu'à Noël. Cependant, ce que j'aime même plus que les escargots, c'est la bûche au chocolat. J'adore ça et j'aimerais pouvoir en manger tous les jours!

Après le repas je suis sûre que ma mère mettra de la musique et nous danserons tous dans la salle à manger. Ce sera chouette!

Finalement, nous irons à la messe de minuit pour chanter, comme tous les ans. Il fait toujours très froid mais après la messe nous boirons un chocolat chaud pour nous réchauffer avant de nous coucher.

Au réveil nous irons tous nous asseoir autour du sapin pour ouvrir les cadeaux. J'aime bien recevoir des cadeaux mais j'adore les offrir — cette année j'ai dépensé tout mon argent de poche en cadeaux pour ma famille. Selon moi, Noël, c'est le meilleur jour de l'année!

Choose the **four** sentences that are correct and write the letters in the boxes below.

A │ Elisa has already put up the decorations this year.

B │ This year they will not be going to Mass.

C │ They will be eating snails this year as a starter.

D │ Elisa will go for a walk on Christmas morning with the family.

E │ Elisa will open her presents in her bedroom.

F │ Elisa has spent all her pocket money on presents.

G │ Elisa's mum dances in the lounge.

H │ Elisa loves to eat chocolate log at Christmas.

Write the correct letters in the boxes. ☐ ☐ ☐ ☐

(4 marks)

3   You've received an email from your friend Tom.

Salut,

Ça va? Merci pour ton **D** . Tu m'as demandé de te parler de mes

qualités et mes défauts.

En général je suis une personne agréable. J'ai beaucoup d'[ ] et

je suis très amical. Cependant de temps en [ ] je peux être [ ]

mais ce n'est pas souvent.

Au collège je suis travailleur et j'ai un bon sens de l'humour. Je

m'[ ] bien avec tous mes profs et je sais faire rire les gens.

Mon petit frère m'[ ] quelquefois à la maison parce qu'il prend mes

vêtements, mais à part ça il est sympa.

À plus, Tom

Fill in the gaps using the words below. Write the correct letter in each box above.

A respect	**E** impatient
B temps	**F** pleurer
C énerve	**G** amis
Example: **D** email	**H** entends

(5 marks)

---

4   Five teenagers are talking about the environment.

1. J'habite à Poitiers, c'est une ville au centre de la France. J'aime ma ville et je pense qu'il y a d'excellents transports en commun dans ma région. Il y a une gare et nous avons beaucoup de trains rapides pour Paris. Il y a aussi de nombreuses pistes cyclables, ce qui rend le trajet au collège en bicyclette plus pratique et surtout beaucoup moins dangereux.

2. Selon moi le plus grand problème environnemental, c'est la pollution. Il y a toujours trop de circulation en ville et les gaz d'échappement entraînent des problèmes. Je pense que ma ville doit investir dans de nouvelles routes pour les bus ou ouvrir plus de zones piétonnes.

3. À la maison nous faisons très attention à notre consommation d'eau. C'est vrai qu'il faut être vigilant à ne pas consommer trop d'eau dans la vie quotidienne. Alors, ma famille et moi nous prenons tous des douches au lieu de prendre des bains. Mon père a aussi maintenant la meilleure excuse pour ne pas laver la voiture! Il dit qu'il fait des economies d'eau!

4. À l'école j'ai beaucoup appris sur l'environnement et avec mes amis nous faisons partie d'un groupe qui aide à faire le recyclage du papier et du plastique dans notre collège. Je pense que c'est très important de faire attention à ce qu'on jette et aussi de recycler nos déchets. Il faut que tout le monde essaie de recycler plus.

5. Que ce soit à la maison ou au lycée, je fais très attention à éteindre la lumière quand je quitte une pièce ou bien à éteindre l'ordinateur ou tout autre appareil électrique après l'avoir utilisé. Comme ça je fais des economies d'énergie et je ne gaspille pas l'électricité.

Choose a title for each paragraph. Write the number of the paragraph in each box.

a)   Recycling ☐

b)   Saving electricity ☐

c)   Saving water ☐

d)   Pollution ☐

e)   Public transport ☐

(5 marks)

5   Six teenagers are talking about work.

1. L'été dernier j'ai fait mon stage dans un bureau. Mon rôle principal était de répondre aux clients au téléphone. J'ai passé beaucoup de temps à envoyer des emails. J'ai trouvé mon stage ennuyeux.

4. Après le lycée j'espère continuer à étudier les sciences parce que je voudrais devenir médecin et soigner les gens. Je rêve de travailler dans un cabinet dans une station de ski.

2. L'année dernière j'ai passé une année sabbatique au Sénégal. J'ai travaillé dans un centre educatif où je jouais au foot tous les jours. J'adorais travailler avec les jeunes et j'ai été très triste de les quitter.

5. Je n'aime pas travailler seul parce que je suis sociable et dynamique. Mon travail idéal serait de travailler pour un journal et écrire des articles au sujet du sport.

3. Je travaille dans un supermarché tous les samedis au rayon poissonnerie. Je sers les clients et je nettoie les crustacés. J'adore mon job parce qu'il me permet de rencontrer des gens.

6. Depuis tout petit j'ai toujours aimé les animaux. L'année dernière je suis allé en safari en Afrique. J'ai tellement adoré mon voyage que quand je suis rentré j'ai decidé de travailler dans un parc zoologique.

Choose a title for each paragraph. Write the number of the paragraph in each box.

a)   Working with animals   ☐

b)   Voluntary work   ☐

c)   Work experience   ☐

d)   Working in a team   ☐

e)   Working to help people   ☐

f)   Part-time job   ☐

(6 marks)

Turn over

6   Your friend Sabine has written you a letter about shopping.

J'aime faire du shopping parce que j'ai le droit d'acheter ce que je veux et aussi ça me donne l'occasion de sortir avec mes amies et d'avoir de leurs nouvelles.

Pour moi, pouvoir dépenser mon argent de poche comme je veux me donne de l'indépendance et aussi beaucoup de liberté, et j'aime ça. Ce que je n'apprécie pas du tout c'est de faire les courses au supermarché parce que je trouve ça très ennuyeux.

J'habite dans une petite ville qui s'appelle Mulsanne où il y a quelques magasins comme une boulangerie et une papeterie. C'est très avantageux d'avoir de petits magasins près de chez moi car je peux y aller à pied pour chercher du pain ou un magazine. Mais, malheureusement pour trouver des magasins intéressants il faut aller au Mans. Là, il y a un grand centre commercial où on peut trouver toutes sortes de magasins, comme par exemple des magasins de vêtements et d'électroniques.

Il n'y a aucun doute, je préfère les centres commerciaux aux petits magasins car il y a énormément de choix maintenant et on peut tout y acheter. Par contre faire les achats sur internet ne m'intéresse pas parce qu'on ne peut pas essayer les choses avant de les acheter.

Je dépense presque tout mon argent en achetant des vêtements, car j'aime être à la mode. Mais ce week-end, j'ai dû acheter des livres pour mon frère parce que c'est son anniversaire demain.

Si j'avais un peu plus d'argent de poche je m'achèterais un baladeur mp3 parce que le mien est cassé. Il va falloir que je fasse des économies!

Sabine

Answer the following questions in English.

a)   Give **one** reason why Sabine likes shopping.

        ....

b)   Why does she like buying clothes?

        ....

c)   Where does she prefer shopping and why?

        ....

d)   Why doesn't internet shopping appeal to her?

        ....

e)   What did Sabine buy for her brother and why?

        ....

f)   What would she buy if she had more pocket money and why?

        ....

(6 marks)

Turn over

7   Some French people are talking about health.

Jean Paul

Quand j'étais à l'école je n'étais pas très sportif. Je détestais le sport et c'était un énorme effort pour moi. Mais, maintenant ma vie a complètement changé parce que je fais du sport tous les jours. Cela me permet de rester en forme et en bonne santé et donc j'aurai une vie plus longue.

Sara

Je suis étudiante au lycée et j'ai énormément de travail. Mes amis sont stressés et ils ont commencé à fumer parce qu'ils disent que la cigarette les aide à se détendre. Je ne fumerai jamais et je continuerai à essayer de convaincre mes amis que le tabac c'est vraiment mauvais, mais j'ai peur qu'ils ne puissent pas arrêter.

Monsieur Legrand

Je suis prof de sport et je pense que l'obésité chez les jeunes est devenue un grand problème. Beaucoup d'élèves ne peuvent pas faire de l'exercice sans être vite fatigués. Je crois qu'ils devraient regarder moins de télé et faire plus de sport. En plus, les parents devraient faire plus attention à ce que mangent leurs enfants.

Madame Laporte — Je travaille dans un supermarché et je dirais que beaucoup de gens ont de mauvaises habitudes en ce qui concerne la nourriture. Ils achètent trop de plats préparés et de plats surgelés quand ils devraient plutôt acheter des fruits et des légumes. Je pense que c'est un fait de société, on travaille trop et on n'a plus le temps de cuisiner.

Luc — J'ai toujours aimé le fast-food! J'habite près du centre ville et il est très facile pour moi d'acheter des pizzas à emporter ainsi que des burgers à l'américaine avec des frites. Je devrais faire un effort pour manger moins de matières grasses parce qu'on me dit que je suis un peu trop gros en ce moment.

Choose the correct person and write the letter(s) in the box. Write **JP** (Jean Paul), **S** (Sara), **LG** (Monsieur Legrand), **LA** (Madame Laporte) or **L** (Luc).

a) Who thinks that more should be done at home to educate young people? ☐

b) Who believes they are now destined for a longer and healthier life? ☐

c) Who fears for their friends' health? ☐

d) Who feels they should eat less fatty foods? ☐

e) Who thinks that people buy the wrong types of food? ☐

(5 marks)

Turn over

8 Nadine's penfriend has written her a letter about her holiday.

> Chère Nadine,
>
> Tu m'as demandé de te parler de mes vacances. Alors voilà, l'année dernière, au mois d'août, je suis allée en vacances au bord de la mer. Je suis allée à Pluduno, en Bretagne dans l'ouest de la France. Mes parents y avaient loué un gîte. Il était très grand et très confortable et j'avais ma propre chambre.
>
> Pendant la deuxième semaine, des amis de mes parents sont venus nous voir avec leurs enfants Rémi et Charlotte. Nous nous sommes bien entendus et nous avons fait beaucoup d'activités. Nous sommes allés à la plage tous les jours pour nous baigner. Quelquefois il pleuvait un peu, mais il ne faisait pas froid. Pendant les vacances j'ai pris des cours pour apprendre à faire de la planche à voile, mais j'ai trouvé ça très difficile!
>
> J'ai vraiment aimé mes vacances et l'année prochaine je vais retourner en Bretagne mais cette fois-ci avec mes amies Laure et Lydia. Elles sont jumelles et nous nous amusons très bien ensemble. Je préfère les vacances entre amis, c'est plus amusant qu'avec les parents! Nous avons l'intention de passer deux semaines à Roscoff près de la plage. On m'a dit que Roscoff est joli et il y a beaucoup de petites boutiques chics où on peut dépenser beaucoup d'argent.
>
> Pendant mes vacances j'espère pouvoir manger plein de fruits de mer et la spécialité bretonne — les crêpes. J'adore faire des crêpes et surtout les manger, avec du beurre de caramel.
>
> À mon avis, pouvoir passer de bonnes vacances c'est très important et j'attends avec impatience mon séjour en Bretagne. Et toi, où comptes-tu aller en vacances après tes examens?
>
> Aurélie

For each of the following sentences, write **T** (true), **F** (false) or **N** (not in text) in the box.

a) Aurélie stayed in Brittany with friends. ☐

b) She didn't go to the beach every day because of the weather. ☐

c) She really enjoyed the food. ☐

d) During her holiday she took some scuba diving lessons. ☐

e) She thinks holidays are very important. ☐

(5 marks)

END OF TEST

General Certificate of Secondary Education

GCSE
French

Speaking Paper

Centre name				
Centre number				
Candidate number				

Surname
Other names
Candidate signature

Instructions
- Find a friend or parent to read the teacher's part for you.
- You may read over the questions before you start each task.
- You may prepare a plan of up to 40 words for each task.
- Your plan cannot include full sentences.
- You may use dictionaries and other resource materials while planning your answer.
- You may not use a dictionary or any other resource material during the actual task.
- There will be one unseen question in each task.

Instructions to teachers
- It is essential that you give the student every opportunity to use the material they have prepared.
- You may alter the wording of the questions as printed in this test. However you must remember not to provide students with any key vocabulary.
- Choose one of the suggested unseen questions for each task.

Information
- This paper contains 2 speaking tasks.
- Each task is worth **30** marks.

SPEAKING TASK 1

CANDIDATE'S ROLE

Task: Television

You are going to have a conversation with your teacher about television.
Your teacher will start the conversation and ask you the following questions:

- How many times a week do you watch television?
- Tell me about one of your favourite television programmes:
  When is it on? What is it about? Which characters do you like?
- What don't you like watching?
- What sort of programmes would you like to see more often on television?
- What do you think is the future of television?
- !

!   Remember that the exclamation mark means you'll have to answer a
     question that you won't have prepared an answer to.

The whole conversation should last about five minutes.

(30 marks)

SPEAKING TASK 1

TEACHER'S ROLE

You need to ask the student the following questions. You should speak first.

1   Tu regardes la télé combien de fois par semaine?

2   Parle-moi d'une émission que tu aimes:

Quand est-ce qu'elle passe? De quoi s'agit-il? Tu aimes quels personnages?

3   Qu'est-ce que tu n'aimes pas regarder?

4   Quel genre d'émissions est-ce que tu voudrais voir plus souvent à la télé?

5   À ton avis, comment sera l'avenir de la télévision?

6   !

!   The unpredictable question could be:

Est-ce que tu aimes regarder la télé en famille?

Qu'est-ce que tu fais quand tu ne regardes pas la télé?

Quels sont les avantages et les inconvénients de la télé, à ton avis?

Turn over

SPEAKING TASK 2

CANDIDATE'S ROLE

Task: Where You Live

You are going to have a conversation with your teacher about where you live. Your teacher will start the conversation and ask you the following questions:

- Where do you live? Where is it in Britain?
- What is there to do in your town?
- Do you like living there?
- What are the advantages and disadvantages of living there?
- What is there for visitors to do?
- What sort of house do you live in?
- !

! Remember that the exclamation mark means you'll have to answer a question that you won't have prepared an answer to.

The whole conversation should last about five minutes.

(30 marks)

SPEAKING TASK 2

TEACHER'S ROLE

You need to ask the student the following questions. You should speak first.

1   Où habites-tu?
    Où est-ce que ça se trouve exactement?

2   Qu'est-ce qu'il y a à faire?

3   Tu aimes y habiter?

4   Quels sont les avantages et les inconvénients d'y habiter?

5   Qu'est-ce qu'il y a à faire pour les visiteurs?

6   Comment est ta maison?

7   !

!   The unpredictable question could be:
       Est-ce que tu y as toujours habité?
       Qu'est-ce que tu voudrais changer dans ta ville?
       Où est-ce que tu voudrais vivre à l'avenir?

END OF TEST

General Certificate of Secondary Education

CGP Practice Exam Paper GCSE French

GCSE
French

Writing Paper

Centre name				
Centre number				
Candidate number				

Surname	
Other names	
Candidate signature	

Time allowed: 60 minutes for each task
+ planning time.

Instructions
- Write in black or blue ink.
- Give all the information you are asked for and **write neatly**.
- You may prepare a plan of up to 40 words for each task.
- Your plan cannot include full sentences.
- You may use dictionaries and other resource materials while planning your answer.
- You may not use a dictionary during the actual task.

Information
- This paper contains 2 writing tasks.
- Each task is worth **30** marks.

Task 1: Famous People

Your French partner school has asked for an article about a famous person. You should write 250-300 words.

You could include:

- A description of the person you have chosen,
- Details of how he/she became famous,
- What successes or problems they have had,
- Reasons why you admire them,
- How they have influenced people's lives,
- What you hope will happen to them in the future.

Remember that to score the highest marks you need to answer the task as fully as possible, expanding on the points above when it is relevant to do so.

(30 marks)

Task 2: Work Experience

Write a letter to your French penfriend describing your recent work experience placement. You should write 250-300 words.

You could include:

- Reasons why you have to do work experience,
- A description of where you worked,
- What sort of tasks you had to do and what you thought of them,
- An example of something you particularly enjoyed doing,
- An example of something you found boring,
- How the work has affected your decision about your future career.

Remember that to score the highest marks you need to answer the task as fully as possible, expanding on the points above when it is relevant to do so.

(30 marks)

Page 5 (Quick Questions)

1) a) trente et un
   b) vingt-huit
   c) cinquante-six
   d) soixante-trois
   e) vingt-neuf
   f) quarante et un
2) onze, douze, treize, quatorze, quinze, seize, dix-sept, dix-huit, dix-neuf, vingt.
3) a) soixante-quinze
   b) quatre-vingt-cinq
   c) quatre-vingt-quinze
4) cent un
5) mille onze
6) trois cent soixante-cinq
7) 4376
8) a) first b) tenth c) third d) twenty-first
9) On the third floor
10) The fourth street on the left
11) b) Il est douze heures / Il est midi / Il est minuit.
    c) Il est dix heures et quart.
    d) Il est neuf heures et demie.
    e) Il est huit heures moins le quart.
12) Wednesday
13) Je joue au football le lundi et je vais au cinéma le jeudi.
14) e.g. Mon anniversaire est le trente et un janvier.
15) a) mille neuf cent quatre-vingt-quinze
    b) deux mille
    c) deux mille dix
16) a) always b) sometimes c) often d) rarely
17) a) yesterday
    b) tomorrow
    c) this autumn around November 5th
    d) go to school
18) Qu'est-ce que tu fais ce soir?

Page 13 (Quick Questions)

1) bonjour / salut
2) Bon week-end!
3) a) Comment allez-vous?
   b) Comment ça va? / Comment vas-tu?
4) Your teacher is so-so and your best friend feels good.
5) a) Entre. Assieds-toi.
   b) Entrez. Asseyez-vous.
   c) Entrez. Asseyez-vous.
6) Est-ce que je peux vous présenter Paul?
7) Je voudrais de l'eau.
8) a) s'il vous plaît
   b) merci
   c) de rien
9) a) Pardon.
   b) Je suis désolé(e).
10) Excusez-moi.
11) May I have something to drink?
12) a) comment? b) quand? c) pourquoi? d) qui? e) où?
13) a) Est-ce que tu aimes le football?
    b) Est-ce que vous avez vu ce film?
14) a) Qu'est-ce que tu manges pour le petit déjeuner?
    b) Qu'est-ce que tu as fait en vacances?

15) a) As-tu mangé mon sandwich?
    b) Est-elle allée à l'école?
16) She likes your trousers but she thinks your shoes are awful.
17) a) Qu'est-ce que tu penses de ma maison?
    b) Quel est ton opinion sur le football?
18) quelqu'un
19) a) amical b) beau c) intéressant d) mauvais e) affreux
20) a) car / parce que
21) I don't like this book. I think it's awful. Do you like this book?

Page 16 (Quick Questions)

1) a) Chère Barbara
   b) Cher Dave
2) Merci pour ta lettre.
3) I was very pleased to hear from you.
4) Amitiés
5) At the top right-hand corner of the letter
6) I hope to hear from you soon.
7) b) See you soon.
8) a) Top left-hand corner
   b) Below your address, on the right-hand side
9) Monsieur / Madame
10) a) I spent five nights at your hotel.
    b) The staff were kind.
    c) My room was clean.
11) Malheureusement, je ne suis pas satisfait(e).
12) a) Je vous prie d'agréer, Monsieur, l'expression de mes sentiments distingués.
13) Je vous remercie d'avance.

Page 17 (Listening Questions)

1) 16th August
2) 1st July
3) 31st January
4) Tomorrow morning
5) Saturday afternoon
6) a) 3:40 / 15:40 / three forty / twenty to four
   b) 1:55 / 13:55 / one fifty-five / five to two

Page 18 (Reading Question)

5	match
7	billet
1	**formidable**
4	buts
2	fana
6	copains
8	argent
3	télé

Page 19 (Speaking Question)

Sample conversation:

1 Quelle est ton émission préférée? Pourquoi?
Mon émission préférée est "Doctor Who" parce que les personnages sont géniaux et j'adore la science-fiction.

2 Qui est ton acteur préféré à la télé? Décris le/la.
Mon acteur préféré est Kiefer Sutherland, qui joue dans "24". Il a les cheveux blonds et les yeux bleus, et il est très doué comme acteur.

3 Combien d'heures de télévision regardes-tu chaque semaine?
Je regarde environ dix heures de télévision chaque semaine.

4 Est-ce que tu aimerais être vedette de télévision? Pourquoi/pourquoi pas?
Je n'aimerais pas être vedette de télévision car je ne suis pas fort(e) en art dramatique.

5 Crois-tu que les gens regardent trop de télévision?
Non, les gens ne regardent pas trop de télévision. Regarder la télévision est un bon passe-temps parce qu'il y a plein d'émissions intéressantes et c'est gratuit.

6 Est-ce que tu aimes les mêmes émissions que tes ami(e)s?
Oui, nous aimons tous les feuilletons et nous passons souvent vendredi soir ensemble devant la télé.

7 Qu'est-ce que tu vas regarder ce week-end?
Je vais regarder un documentaire samedi soir et puis je vais regarder aussi un film avec ma famille dimanche après-midi.

Page 20 (Writing Questions)

Sample answer for Task 1:

Chère Isabelle,

Je te remercie de ton email où tu m'as demandé si j'aime aller au cinéma.

Je vais au cinéma au moins deux fois par mois, avec mes copains, ou, de temps en temps, avec ma famille. Le cinéma dans notre ville a trois écrans et c'est très moderne et confortable. Je préfère y aller le samedi soir, mais quelquefois, quand il fait mauvais temps, on y va le dimanche après-midi aussi.

Nous préférons les films comiques comme, par exemple, 'Nacho Libre' avec Jack Black. J'ai vu presque tous ses films parce que je l'adore. Il n'est pas très beau mais je le trouve très rigolo.

Est-ce que tu as vu son film 'School of Rock'? Il parle d'une rock star qui est obligé de travailler dans une école très stricte pour gagner de l'argent. Ses élèves l'adorent et l'aident à gagner un concours de rock. Je n'ai pas arrêté de rire. Si tu ne l'as pas encore vu je te le conseille.

Cependant, je déteste les films d'action, surtout quand il y a beaucoup de violence. Je vais au cinéma pour me détendre, pas pour me rendre malade!

Samedi soir, j'irai au cinéma avec ma famille pour fêter l'anniversaire de ma petite sœur. Nous verrons le nouveau 'Shrek'. Je sais que c'est un film animé pour les enfants, mais je trouve Shrek très drôle. Après, nous mangerons dans un restaurant tout près du cinéma. J'espère que ce sera une sortie amusante.

J'aimerais beaucoup voir un film français qui me ferait rire, mais ils ne passent jamais de films français dans notre cinéma. Je devrais donc en acheter sur l'internet. Est-ce que tu pourrais me conseiller un film comique que tu as aimé?

À la prochaine,

Emma

Sample answer for Task 2:

Susan Morgan
1 Cherry Lane
Warrington
WA5 7HR

Chez François
17, rue de Paris
Paris
France

le 20 mai

Monsieur,

Vendredi dernier j'ai mangé dans votre restaurant avec ma famille. C'était l'anniversaire de mariage de mes parents, alors nous avons voulu le fêter avec un bon repas français. Malheureusement, la soirée s'est très mal passée.

J'avais réservé une table mais, en arrivant au restaurant, nous avons dû attendre presque une heure avant d'être assis. Personne n'est venu nous expliquer pourquoi il fallait attendre si longtemps.

Quand nous nous sommes assis, la serveuse nous a donné la carte. Cependant, elle n'a pas rangé les plats sales qui restaient sur la table. Je lui ai demandé d'enlever les plats et elle était très impolie avant de le faire.

Ma mère a choisi le poulet aux amandes, mais elle l'a trouvé trop cuit et ne pouvait pas le manger. Mon père a eu la truite mais elle sentait mauvais, alors il ne l'a pas mangée non plus. Mon frère a commandé de l'agneau; on lui a donné du porc, qu'il déteste! Mes légumes étaient brûlés et tout noirs. Nous avons tout dit à la serveuse, mais elle a dit qu'elle ne voyait pas de problème!

À la fin, nous avons décidé de partir sans commander ni fromage ni dessert. L'addition n'était pas juste parce qu'ils avaient mis trop de boissons. Nous étions quatre, et nous avions commandé une seule bouteille de vin blanc et de l'eau du robinet. On a essayé de nous faire payer deux bouteilles de vin et quatre bouteilles d'eau minérale. Évidemment, nous n'avons pas laissé de pourboire.

Nous retournerons chez nous en Angleterre samedi et nous ne mangerons jamais plus dans votre restaurant. Je vous demande donc de nous rembourser le prix de nos repas.

En attendant votre réponse, veuillez agréer, Monsieur, l'expression de mes sentiments distingués,

Susan Morgan

Page 28 (Quick Questions)

1) a) apricots
   b) tea
   c) potatoes
   d) butter
   e) a leg of lamb
   f) prawns/shrimps
   g) a lemon
   h) wine

2) a) les desserts
   b) les légumes
   c) les fruits de mer
   d) les boissons

3) a) les escargots
   b) le croque-monsieur
   c) le gratin dauphinois

4) Voudriez-vous l'eau?

5) Est-ce que je peux vous passer le beurre?

6) Would you like to eat?

7) Est-ce que tu as faim?

8) I'm hungry but I'm not thirsty.

9) a) Pourriez-vous me passer le sel, s'il vous plaît?
   b) Pourriez-vous me passer une serviette, s'il vous plaît?

10) Je ne mange ni les légumes ni les fruits mais j'adore les hamburgers.

11) Je mange souvent des pommes mais je ne mange jamais de champignons.

12) They're vegan.

13) We always eat as a family except on Tuesdays because my father goes to the gym.

14)a) Je voudrais un peu de gâteau.
   b) Je voudrais un gros morceau de gâteau.

15) Did you like it?

16) Sample answers:
   a) Je me lève à sept heures moins le quart.
   b) Je me douche à sept heures.
   c) Je m'habille à sept heures et demie.
   d) Je me couche à onze heures.

17) Le lundi je mets la table et le vendredi je fais la vaisselle. Je gagne de l'argent de poche quand j'aide à la maison.

18) Can you help me wash the car?

19) As-tu besoin de quelque chose?

Page 36 (Quick Questions)

1) Where do you live?
2) J'ai quinze ans.
3) J'ai les yeux bleus et les cheveux longs et blonds.
4) I am tall and I have green eyes. I have short, red hair.
5) What are you called? And how is that spelt?
6) Sample answer: Paul: Pay, ah, ue, ell.
7) J'ai deux frères et une sœur. Ils s'appellent John, James et Kathryn.
8) I have a girlfriend.
9) a) père b) sœur c) grand-mère d) tante e) beau-père
10) a) Do you have any pets?
   b) J'ai un frère et il a dix ans.
   c) He has some male cousins and some female cousins.
11) He is funny, chatty and generous.
12) I am well-behaved and nice but a bit lazy.
13) Mon frère a treize ans. Il est vraiment méchant et égoïste.
14) I always have a positive attitude and I'm often in a good mood. I am amazing.
15) Je sais comment faire rire les gens.
16) a) to be trustworthy
   b) to be kind
   c) to be like me
17) À mon avis, un(e) bon(ne) ami(e) doit être amusant(e).
18) On s'entend bien ensemble.
19) a) I get on well with Camille.
   b) I fancy Michel.
20) a) I've fallen in love.
   b) We always argue.
   c) She doesn't listen to me.
21) À l'avenir, je voudrais me marier et avoir des enfants.

Page 43 (Quick Questions)

1) Ce n'est pas juste de discriminer à cause de l'âge.
2) Some people are mean because I'm a Muslim.
3) Il y a beaucoup de pauvreté dans ma ville.
4) On the way home once I was threatened. It was terrifying.
5) a) les chômeurs
   b) la crainte
   c) les personnes sans abri / les SDF
6) Mon oncle est au chômage depuis trois ans.
7) It's difficult to find housing without work.
8) a) Where does it hurt?
   b) Can you give me something?
9) J'ai mal à l'estomac et je dois aller voir le médecin.
10) a) mal à l'oreille
   b) mal à la gorge
   c) mal à la tête
11) I have a cold and a cough. And I also have a temperature.
12) a) le nez
   b) le pied
   c) le bras
   d) le doigt
   e) les dents
   f) l'épaule
13) Pour rester en bonne santé, je ne mange que de la nourriture saine.
14) Je ne fais pas de sport parce que faire de l'exercice, c'est ennuyeux.
15) Je pense que la drogue est un problème dans le football. Ce n'est pas juste parce que la majorité des joueurs ne trichent pas.
16) It's depressing to see really fat children. It's the fault of advertising.

17) Alain smokes all the time and I find smoking disgusting. I don't like it when Alain smokes.
18) J'ai arrêté de fumer il y a un an.

Page 44 (Listening Questions)

1) white wine and beer
2) bread and cheese
3) coffee and sugar
4) a) experience
   b) do a work experience placement (at an IT company)
   c) the company offered him a job

Page 45 (Reading Question)

1) F
2) F
3) T
4) ?
5) F
6) T

Page 46 (Reading Question)

1) B
2) D
3) F
4) A

Page 47 (Speaking Question)

Sample conversation:

1) Qu'est-ce que tu fais pour rester en bonne santé?
Pour rester en bonne santé, j'essaie de manger cinq fruits ou légumes par jour et de faire du sport au moins trois fois par semaine.

2) Quel est ton sport préféré? Pourquoi?
Mon sport préféré est la natation parce que je peux en faire tout(e) seul(e) et il y a une piscine à deux pas de chez moi.

3) Quand était la dernière fois que tu étais malade? Qu'est-ce que tu avais?
J'étais malade il y a trois mois. J'avais la grippe et c'était affreux.

4) Qu'est-ce que tu manges à midi au collège?
Normalement, je n'ai pas beaucoup de temps pour manger à midi, donc je prends un sandwich ou une salade.

5) Qu'est-ce que tu vas manger ce soir?
Ce soir, ma mère va préparer mon repas préféré, du poulet rôti avec des légumes et des pommes de terre. J'adore ce repas parce que c'est sain mais délicieux aussi.

6) Penses-tu qu'il existe des mannequins qui sont trop maigres?
Oui, je crois que les mannequins sont beaucoup plus maigres que les gens normaux et donc les gens pensent qu'ils ont besoin de faire un régime même s'ils ont un poids normal.

7) Qu'est-ce que tu penses du tabagisme?
Je pense que le tabagisme est dégoûtant. Moi, je ne fume pas parce que je ne veux pas avoir les dents jaunes et les vêtements qui sentent la fumée.

Page 48 (Writing Questions)

Sample answer for Task 1:
Chère Manon,

Ma mère m'a donné de tes nouvelles hier, et je voulais te féliciter sur tes fiançailles. Je sais que tu as très envie de te marier avec Luc, et j'imagine que tu dois être très contente.

Cependant, je crois que tu es un peu trop jeune pour te fiancer — pendant que tu es encore adolescente, c'est le moment de t'amuser avec tes copines et ne pas t'inquièter en choisissant une robe et en essayant de louer une maison avec ton copain. J'aime bien Luc, mais vous êtes ensemble depuis seulement dix-huit mois, et c'est trop rapide pour savoir si tu veux vraiment passer le reste de ta vie avec lui.

Est-ce que tu as pensé à lui dire que tu as très envie de te marier un jour, mais que tu n'es pas encore prête? Tu pourrais aussi lui dire qu'il vaut mieux dépenser votre argent en achetant une maison, plutôt qu'une bague. Comme ça tu seras encore plus sûre qu'il est sans doute l'homme de tes rêves.

Moi, je ne suis pas contre le mariage en général — en fait je pense qu'il vaut mieux être marié si on veut avoir d'enfants. Mais si, comme tu m'as dit, tu ne veux pas avoir d'enfants avant l'âge de vingt ans, il n'y a pas de raison de te marier encore.

À ta place, j'attendrais encore quelques années. J'économiserais mon argent pour avoir assez d'argent pour me payer une grande noce. Je pense que c'est mieux que d'en avoir une plus petite aujourd'hui.

Caroline est du même avis que moi — elle dit que s'il est vraiment ton partenaire idéal il comprendra et il pourra attendre. J'espère que tu n'es pas fâchée avec moi à cause de ce que je t'ai dit et j'espère aussi qu'on restera bonnes amies.

Louise

Sample answer for Task 2:

Mike est vendeur du 'Big Issue'. La semaine dernière il a parlé aux étudiants de notre collège de sa vie comme SDF.

Il habite dans un centre pour les sans-abri depuis deux ans. Il a sa propre petite chambre mais il partage une salle de bains. Le matin il se lève à sept heures et demie et il prend du café et du pain grillé pour le petit déjeuner. Après avoir mangé, il va au centre de distribution dans la cité industrielle où il achète au moins vingt journaux pour la moitié du prix qu'il les vend. Puis il s'installe devant le grand supermarché en ville où il passe la journée à vendre. À midi, il va à une église où il peut prendre un repas chaud gratuitement. L'après-midi il continue à vendre devant le supermarché. Il rentre 'chez lui' vers cinq heures et quart. Le soir, il reste dans sa chambre, regarde la télé ou joue aux cartes avec les autres. Dans le passé il a eu des problèmes d'alcool mais il sait que, s'il arrivait au centre après avoir bu de l'alcool, il serait mis dehors.

Il est sans-abri depuis trois ans, après la mort de sa mère. Avant, il habitait dans un HLM avec elle. Il ne travaillait pas parce qu'il s'occupait d'elle. Quand elle est décédée il ne pouvait plus y habiter parce que sa mère était la locataire. Il a passé un an à dormir dans les rues et il a commencé à trop boire. Puis un jour, ivre, il a été renversé par un bus en traversant la rue. À l'hôpital on a offert de l'aider et après trois mois sans alcool il est allé habiter au centre.

Il est content dans le centre, mais quelquefois les résidents se disputent et il y a toujours trop de bruit. À l'avenir il aimerait travailler comme jardinier et trouver un petit appartement.

J'ai beaucoup aimé Mike. Il était calme et gentil, et il fait des efforts pour améliorer sa vie. J'ai compris qu'on peut être sans-abri sans avoir fait d'erreurs dans la vie et j'ai l'intention d'acheter le 'Big Issue' toutes les deux semaines.

Page 56 (Quick Questions)

1) a) Je fais du ski.
   b) Je fais du cyclisme / du vélo.
   c) Je vais à la pêche.
2) The leisure centre
3) J'aime regarder le sport mais je préfère participer parce que j'adore m'entraîner.
4) Do you have a hobby?
5) a) the drums b) every day
6) He is a member of a swimming club.
7) Je n'aime pas jouer aux échecs parce que c'est ennuyeux.
8) a) skiing b) rugby c) ice skating
9) a) Je trouve faire de la randonnée intéressant.
   b) Je trouve le surf des neiges passionnant.
10) She likes watching documentaries but she doesn't like watching adverts.
11) Mon émission préférée commence à dix-neuf heures trente et finit à vingt heures quinze.
12) I heard the new song by John Bonne two weeks ago.
13) a) a play
   b) a show
   c) a comic strip
14) It's about a woman who had lots of money and loved to travel.

Page 62 (Quick Questions)

1) Qu'est-ce que tu aimes comme musique?
2) a) Pop music
   b) She likes them.
   c) Their songs are really great/cool.
3) lecteur mp3 / baladeur mp3
4) Je joue de la batterie dans un groupe de rock.
5) a) She is a famous English singer.
   b) She sings like an angel.
   c) His/Her clothes are so cool.
6) Ma mère m'a beaucoup influencé(e).
7) My greatest achievement is the support I've been able to give to international organisations.
8) J'aime la vie de vedette parce que je peux voyager et j'ai beaucoup d'argent.
9) a) un site internet
   b) une console de jeux
   c) un écran tactile
   d) une pile
   e) un réseau
10) Mon frère est toujours sur l'ordinateur. Il a créé un site internet pour son orchestre.
11) I'll put it on my blog.
12) un courrier électronique / un courriel / un email
13) a) to send
    b) to reply
    c) to copy
    d) to forward
14) Je vérifie ma boîte email tous les jours.
15) tu
16) Children should be playing sport instead of being in front of a monitor all the time — it's not very healthy.

Page 73 (Quick Questions)

1) a) Où est le kiosque à journaux / le tabac?
   b) Où est la librairie?
   c) Où est la boucherie?
2) All the shops close at 7pm except the supermarket. The supermarket closes at 9pm.
3) Je préfère faire du shopping sur internet parce que c'est plus rapide et il y a toujours des soldes.
4) essayer des vêtements
5) Can I help you?
6) Je voudrais un litre d'eau et un kilo de pommes de terre. Est-ce que vous avez du fromage?
7) I would like some cherries and a slice of ham.
8) a) des espèces
   b) la carte de crédit
9) On me donne quinze livres d'argent de poche par mois.
10) I'm saving up. I would like to buy a handbag.
11) a) le chapeau
    b) le pantalon
    c) le pull
    d) la robe
    e) l'imperméable
    f) la cravate
12) a) Je voudrais un portefeuille rouge.

272

b) Je voudrais une chemise bleu clair.

c) Je voudrais un foulard violet foncé.

13) Je prends la taille quarante-deux.

14) This summer all the girls are wearing shorts and a white blouse. At the moment, ties are really fashionable for boys.

15) Allons au cinéma ce soir.

16) J'organise une surprise-partie. Est-ce que tu peux amener des films et des bonbons?

17) Is there a sports field near here?

18) Quand est-ce que la piscine ouvre? Combien coûte l'entrée à la piscine?

19) I watched a film with my girlfriend. It was a comedy and it was really good.

20) Who won the match?

Pages 74-75 (Listening Questions)

1) at the sports centre   12 o'clock / midday

2) at the ice rink   4.45pm / quarter to five

3) in front of the theatre   6.30pm / half past six

4) a) 3.35 pm

   b) 5.55 pm

   c) 7.20 euros

   d) 5.70 euros

5) singing   every day

6) going for a walk   three times a week

7) going fishing   twice a month

8) a) two days ago

   b) in front of the station

   c) no

   d) the guitarist

9) guitar   from time to time

10) dance/ballet   Tuesday and Thursday evenings / twice a week

11) jogging/running   every morning / every day

12) 6.50 euros a week   clothes, books

13) 42 euros a month   computer games, drinks

Page 76 (Reading Question)

1) A

2) F

3) N

4) F

Page 77 (Reading Question)

1) Amélie

2) Élodie

3) Marc

4) Naomie

5) Marc

Page 78 (Speaking Question)

Sample conversation:

1) **Est-ce que tu écoutes souvent de la musique?**
J'écoute de la musique tout le temps, du matin au soir. J'adore ça.

2) **Où est-ce que tu aimes l'écouter?**
Je l'écoute dans ma chambre pendant que je fais mes devoirs et en allant au collège sur mon baladeur mp3. Quelquefois je vais aux concerts mais ça coûte très cher.

3) **Quelle genre de musique aimes-tu?**
Je préfère la musique pop, comme par exemple Take That et The Sugababes. Mais j'aime aussi la musique des années soixante, comme The Beatles.

4) **Où est-ce que tu achètes ta musique?**

Je l'achète dans des magasins spécialisés, et sur l'internet.

5) **Tu écoutes de la musique à la radio?**
J'écoute la radio le matin de temps en temps, quand je prends mon petit déjeuner, mais je n'aime pas beaucoup ça.

6) **Est-ce que tu joues d'un instrument?**
Quand j'étais jeune je jouais du piano, mais maintenant j'apprends à jouer de la guitare électrique parce que j'espère faire partie d'un groupe.

7) **Quel genre de musique est-ce que tu n'aimes pas?**
Je n'aime pas le rap, parce que je le trouve trop ennuyeux, et je déteste la musique classique. Mon père aime Schubert; mais je trouve sa musique horrible!

Page 79 (Writing Questions)

Sample answers:

Task 1: Pocket Money

On n'a jamais assez d'argent de poche. Moi, mes parents me donne vingt livres par mois de mes parents, mais seulement si je lave la voiture deux fois par mois. Je fais du baby-sitting quelquefois et, pour ça, on me donne quinze livres par soirée.

J'économise l'argent que je gagne parce que j'aime acheter des vêtements assez chers. En ce moment, je voudrais acheter une veste en cuir marron — elle est magnifique. Je l'ai vue dans un grand magasin le mois dernier et je pourrai l'acheter dans cinq ou six semaines.

Plus on économise son argent, plus on peut acheter des choses chères. Par exemple, la semaine dernière, ma grande sœur a acheté une petite voiture avec toutes ses économies. C'est formidable!

Je crois que les parents doivent donner de l'argent à leurs enfants jusqu'à ce qu'ils trouvent un travail. L'année prochaine, je veux trouver un emploi dans un magasin de vêtements.

Heureusement, j'habite dans un petit village où il n'y a pas beaucoup de magasins. Alors, je ne peux pas très souvent dépenser mon argent. Mais, il y a une librairie et j'aime bien acheter des livres de temps en temps — la dernière fois que j'ai fait les magasins, j'en ai acheté trois!

Alors, n'oublie pas de faire des économies; ça en vaut la peine!

Task 2: Leisure Activities

J'ai beaucoup de passe-temps, mais je ne suis pas très sportif / sportive. Je trouve le football ennuyeux. Le seul sport qui me plaît, c'est le ski. J'adore descendre les pistes à toute vitesse. J'adore jouer aux échecs: je suis membre d'un club d'échecs et nous jouons tous les vendredis. J'aime faire du théâtre aussi.

Samedi dernier, je suis allé(e) au cinéma pour voir le nouveau film de Harry Potter. Les scènes d'action étaient passionnantes, mais j'ai préféré le livre. J'aime mieux imaginer les personnages moi-même. J'aime la télévision et la radio: je n'ai pas de préférence. J'adore regarder les dessins animés à la télé, mais j'aime écouter les nouvelles chansons à la radio quand je fais mes devoirs.

Samedi après-midi, je vais faire une randonnée dans la forêt avec ma copine et sa famille, et dimanche soir nous irons au concert en ville. Ce sera un week-end formidable!

Cependant, je m'ennuie un peu pendant les vacances. Je n'ai pas assez d'argent pour sortir tous les jours et mes amis habitent loin de chez moi. Je pense que c'est difficile pour les jeunes en Grande-Bretagne de s'amuser surtout parce qu'on ne peut pas souvent être dehors à cause du temps. Je serais content s'il y avait un café dans ma ville où je pouvais discuter avec mes copains.

Page 90 (Quick Questions)

1) Je suis gallois(e) et je viens du pays de Galles.

2) a) une Irlandaise

   b) un Français

   c) une Italienne

   d) une Allemande

3) I am English-speaking.

4) a) l'Allemagne

   b) l'Espagne

   c) la Suisse

d) l'Angleterre

e) l'Écosse

5) Is there a train to Lyons?

6) a) un aller simple, en première classe

b) deux aller-retours

c) un aller simple, en deuxième classe

7) a) Where is the platform, please?

b) When does the train leave for Paris?

c) When are you travelling?

8) It's the national French train network.

9) l'horaire

10) a) by bus

b) she goes into town on the underground

c) she walks

11) Quel bus va à l'aéroport?

12) In Brittany you'll be staying with a host family, but in Paris you'll stay in a youth hostel.

13) a) la salle à manger

b) la note

c) l'ascenseur

d) l'escalier

e) la demi-pension

14) Avez-vous des chambres libres?

15) Je voudrais rester ici une semaine, s'il vous plaît.

16) a) Est-ce que je peux camper ici?

b) Est-ce que je peux allumer un feu ici?

c) Où est-ce que je peux trouver un sac de couchage?

17) Do you want to see proof of identity?

18) I'd like to hire some sleeping bags.

Page 96 (Quick Questions)

1) Où est la salle de jeu?

2) Où sont les toilettes?

3) The telephone is on the ground floor.

4) It's on the fourth floor, at the end of the corridor.

5) a) à droite   b) à gauche   c) tout droit

6) À quelle heure est-ce que le petit déjeuner est servi?

7) Il n'y a pas de serviettes dans la chambre et l'eau est trop froide.

8) The shower doesn't work.

9) There's too much noise and I can't sleep. I would like another room.

10) Il me faut des lits supplémentaires.

11) a) Service included

b) Wait here

c) Tips

12) Est-ce que vous avez une table libre?

13) There are two of us and we would like to sit outside.

14) Est-ce que je peux avoir la carte, s'il vous plaît?

15) a) Je voudrais le gâteau au chocolat.

b) Je préférerais le porc.

c) J'aimerais goûter les escargots.

16) There's no more lamb.

17) Je prendrai la soupe à la place des frites.

18) Le bœuf n'est pas assez cuit.

19) The service here is awful and I found a hair in my soup.

20) Est-ce que le service est compris?

Page 104 (Quick Questions)

1) A: Where did you go on holiday? Did you go abroad?

B: Of course, I went to Spain last month.

A: And who did you go on holiday with?

B: With my friends. We went to the beach every day. I enjoyed myself.

A: Cool! In the summer, I went to Ireland for two weeks with my family. The holiday was great.

2) Je me suis détendu(e).

3) We went there by boat.

4) Comment était le voyage?

5) a) a week

b) (skiing in) Italy

c) her family

d) her father fell and broke his arm

6) une station balnéaire

7) In France, it was sunnier than in England. In Italy, it rained less than in Switzerland.

8) a) Where will you go?

b) What are you going to take?

9) Je vais aller en Écosse en train et je vais prendre un magazine et beaucoup de vêtements.

10) My dream holiday would be to stay in a five-star hotel in the countryside.

11) a) Demain, il neigera / il va neiger.

b) Demain, il y aura des éclairs / il va y avoir des éclairs.

c) Demain, il fera du soleil / il va faire du soleil.

12) la météo aujourd'hui

13) Quel temps fera-t-il demain? / Quel temps va-t-il faire demain?

14) It rained every day.

Page 105-106 (Listening Questions)

1) Belgium   fine   windy

2) Switzerland   raining   thunder

3) a) 4th floor

b) 75 euros

4) youth hostel   brothers   a week

5) campsite   friend   a month

6) D

7) A

8) a) true   b) true   c) false   d) false

9) b) lamb

10) a) strawberries

c) raspberries

11) b) honey

c) chocolate

Page 107 (Reading Question)

1 a) F   b) F   c) F   d) T   e) T   f) T   g) F

Page 108 (Speaking Question)

Sample conversation:

1 **Où êtes vous allé(e) en vacances l'année dernière?**
L'année dernière je suis allé(e) en Espagne avec ma famille.

2 **Vous y êtes allé(e) comment? Comment était le voyage?**
Nous y sommes allés en avion. Le vol était assez bien mais il est arrivé avec du retard.

3 **Est-ce que vous êtes resté(e) dans un hôtel? C'était comment?**
Non, nous sommes restés dans un camping. C'était très bien. J'ai rencontré beaucoup de jeunes et il y avait une piscine et un bowling.

4 **Est-ce que vous avez eu des problèmes pendant votre séjour?**
Nous n'avons pas eu de grands problèmes mais le deuxième jour nous n'avons pas pu nous doucher car les douches étaient très sales.

5 **Vous vous êtes plaint(e)? Qu'est-ce qu'il s'est passé?**
Oui, on s'est plaint au propriétaire et il s'est excusé.

6 **Est-ce que vous y retourneriez un jour?**
Bien sûr. En fait, nous avons déjà fait une réservation pour y retourner l'année prochaine.

7   Comment était la nourriture?

Au camping, la nourriture n'était pas trop bonne et on mangeait des frites presque tous les jours, mais nous avons mangé dans un restaurant en ville plusieurs fois où la nourriture était délicieuse.

Page 109 (Writing Questions)

Sample answers:

Task 1: Holidays

Salut!

Je suis en vacances en Normandie avec mes parents et mon frère. Nous avons loué un gîte à Jonville, près de Saint-Vaast, sur la côte, à une demi-heure de Cherbourg. Nous sommes allés de chez nous à Portsmouth en voiture, puis nous avons pris le ferry jusqu'à Cherbourg et continué en voiture.

Tu sais que c'est ma première visite en France? J'aime beaucoup le paysage près d'ici et la plage est super. Le village de Jonville est très petit et il n'y a pas de magasins, mais je peux aller à la plage tous les jours.

Près de Saint-Vaast il y a une île; on peut y aller à pied le matin alors hier nous avons fait la traversée. Après avoir visité l'île nous avons voulu repartir. Il y avait un peu d'eau sur le sol mais pas trop et mon père a dit qu'il fallait continuer. Mais après quelques minutes la mer arrivait jusqu'à nos genoux! C'était horrible et j'avais très peur. Heureusement quelqu'un est venu en bateau pour nous sauver.

Nous sommes sortis manger au restaurant à Barfleur un autre jour. Le repas était super! Nous nous sommes assis sur la terrasse, qui donnait sur la mer, et nous avons tous pris les moules marinières. J'espère qu'on y retournera avant de partir.

J'aime bien le gîte parce qu'il est à deux pas de la mer, mais il n'y a qu'une seule pièce en bas, avec coin cuisine et je ne suis jamais seul(e).

Demain je vais à l'école de voile et après-demain je ferai de l'équitation. J'aimerais aussi aller au centre commercial à Cherbourg faire des courses, mais je ne pense pas que mes parents m'y amèneront.

On va repartir samedi. Je ne veux pas retourner en Angleterre parce que j'ai bien aimé mon séjour ici, même si c'était un peu trop tranquille quelquefois.

Task 2: Tourist Information

Vous êtes en vacances dans le Leicestershire? Ou vous passez quelques jours à Warwick? Pourquoi pas venir à Foxton Locks, à quinze kilomètres de Leicester?

Vous pourrez visiter le canal très calme et voir le célèbre 'escalier' où les bateaux descendent la colline. Foxton Locks se trouve en pleine campagne et vous aurez de belles vues de la région agricole et de jolis petits villages qui l'entourent. Laissez votre voiture dans le parking et promenez-vous au bord du canal. Les enfants peuvent apprendre un peu de notre histoire industrielle et voir les canards.

Il y a un petit musée très intéressant qui montre la vie dure des personnes qui vivaient et travaillaient sur les canaux dans le passé. Et en plus on commence à reconstruire l'autre système que les bateaux utilisaient pour monter et descendre les collines. C'est incroyable.

Après avoir tout vu, vous pourrez vous détendre en prenant une boisson ou en mangeant une glace dans le petit café, ou manger dans le restaurant célèbre. Si vous choisissez une table sur la terrasse vous pouvez regarder les bateaux, les oiseaux et les habitants du canal. Mais, si vous préférez, vous pouvez apporter un pique-nique et vous asseoir sur l'herbe.

Et, si vous avez envie de vous détendre sur le canal, vous pouvez de faire un petit tour à la campagne en bateau.

Avant de partir, allez au petit magasin pour acheter un souvenir de votre belle journée tranquille et passionnante à Foxton Locks.

Si vous voulez organiser une visite ou si vous avez besoin de plus d'informations, téléphonez au 07 16 23 71 55.

Page 115 (Quick Questions)

1) a) la gare
   b) la boucherie
   c) la boulangerie
   d) la bibliothèque
   e) l'église
2) les bâtiments

3) a) the shop
   b) the travel agent
   c) the town hall
   d) the tourist information office
4) Where is the bus station?
5) Où est le centre de recyclage?
6) Est-ce qu'il y a un commissariat près d'ici?
7) The swimming pool is at the end of the road, next to the market.
8) Le terrain de sport est en face de la banque.
9) a) La cathédrale est entre la pâtisserie et le tabac / kiosque à journaux.
   b) La banque est au-dessus de la poste.
   c) La pharmacie est par ici, au coin.
   d) L'auberge de jeunesse est devant l'école.
10) Is it far from here?
11) C'est à deux pas d'ici. / Ce n'est pas loin.
12) Pour aller à l'université, s'il vous plaît?
13)a) The police station? Go straight on and take the first road on the left.
   b) I think the police station is near here. Turn right at the traffic lights and go past the butcher's.
   c) OK, turn left. The police station is below the bank.

Page 122 (Quick Questions)

1) a) I come from the south of France.
   b) Me? I come from Corsica.
   c) I come from the Massif Central.
2) J'habite dans le Cumbria.
3) a) Londres   b) Édimbourg   c) Douvres
4) la Manche
5) J'habite dans une ville située sur l'Avon.
6) J'habite à Bristol. Bristol se trouve dans le sud-ouest de l'Angleterre.
7) Do you like living in Manchester?
8) a) The west of France
   b) There are lots of restaurants. / There's a pretty river in the town centre.
   c) There's a lot of industry.
9) J'habite avec mes parents, ma sœur et mes grands-parents.
10) J'aime habiter en famille parce que je n'ai pas besoin de cuisiner, mais mon frère m'énerve.
11) J'habite une jolie maison jumelée près des magasins.
12) My flat is on the ground floor.
13) Comment est ta maison?
14) Ma cuisine est grande et laide / moche. La salle à manger est ma pièce préférée parce que c'est grand.
15) We have a lawn, a swimming pool and lots of flowers in our garden.
16) J'ai une chambre à moi. / J'ai ma propre chambre.
17) In my bedroom, there's a wardrobe, a red armchair, a bed and white curtains.
18) Les murs dans ma chambre sont bleus.

Page 129 (Quick Questions)

1) a) la veille de Noël
   b) le réveillon
   c) Pâques
2) We celebrate Valentine's day on 14th February.
3) Où est-ce que vous fêtez / tu fêtes Noël?
4) I'm going to celebrate my birthday with my friends.
5) Je voudrais organiser une fête dans un restaurant.
6) a) on s'amuse
   b) on offre des cadeaux
   c) on chante ensemble
   d) on danse
7) Pour Noël, on va à la messe de minuit et on a un sapin de Noël.

8) She lights eight candles and plays games, and she eats with her family.

9) a) la surpopulation

b) le réchauffement de la terre / de la planète.

c) l'effet de serre

10) We don't pay enough attention to endangered species. There's too much deforestation and it endangers the environment.

11) Je crois que l'environnement est très important et je pense qu'on ne recycle pas comme on devrait.

12) L'environnement ne m'intéresse pas parce qu'il y a d'autres choses qui sont plus importantes.

13) I'm worried about the environment. We could switch off the light and heating. We should sort our rubbish and buy products with recyclable packaging.

14) a) We should use public transport to travel to school.

b) We can recycle bottles, cardboard boxes and plastic bags.

c) We should build more cycle lanes.

15) a) À l'avenir, on n'aura plus de pétrole.

b) Le monde sera surpeuplé.

c) Il faudra réduire les émissions de gaz carbonique.

Page 130 (Listening Questions)

1)	station	E
2)	police station	A
3)	currency exchange / bank	D
4)	Yes	There's lots to do **or** it's calm
5)	No	It's dirty **or** there's nothing to do
6)	Yes	They live near the park **or** they live near the swimming pool

7)	Far	Office	Motorbike
8)	Near	School	Bike
9)	Far	Stadium	Coach

Page 131 (Reading Question)

1) B, C, F, H

Page 132 (Reading Question)

1) A, C, F, D

Page 133 (Speaking Question)

Sample conversation:

1. **Est-ce que l'environnement est important pour toi?**

Oui, je m'intéresse beaucoup à l'environnement parce que je m'inquiète pour le futur de la planète.

2. **À ton avis, quels sont les problèmes les plus graves dans ta région?**

J'habite à la campagne où tout le monde a une voiture parce qu'il n'y a pas de transports en commun.

3. **Est-ce que tu fais du recyclage?**

Je recycle le papier et le verre. Mes parents ont toujours essayé de ne pas gaspiller l'eau et l'électricité, donc j'éteins l'ordinateur quand je ne l'utilise pas, et je me douche au lieu de prendre un bain.

4. **Comment est-ce que tu penses qu'on pourrait améliorer les taux de recyclage?**

Dans notre ville on ne peut pas recycler les emballages en plastique, alors les magasins pourraient en utiliser moins. Trier les déchets prend beaucoup de temps; cela devrait être plus simple.

5. **Comment penses-tu qu'on pourrait réduire la pollution entraînée par les transports?**

On pourrait créer plus de zones piétonnes et de pistes cyclables pour encourager les gens à ne pas utiliser leur voiture. Les bus et les trains devraient coûter moins chers.

6. **Qu'est-ce que tu pourrais faire chez toi pour aider l'environnement?**

Je pourrais acheter moins de choses. Mes parents aimeraient cultiver des légumes dans le jardin, ce qui serait super. Mais je n'aimerais pas arrêter de voyager à l'étranger parce que j'adore les vacances.

7. **À ton avis, quel est le futur pour l'environnement?**

À mon avis, si nous ne faisons pas beaucoup plus d'efforts aujourd' hui, les gens dans les pays pauvres souffriront encore plus à l'avenir.

Page 134 (Writing Questions)

Sample answers:

Task 1: Promoting Your Town

Visitez Market Harborough pour voir la vie animée mais calme d'une petite ville de campagne. Elle se trouve en plein centre de l'Angleterre, à quinze kilomètres de la ville multiculturelle de Leicester, et à une centaine de kilomètres de Londres.

Vous pouvez passer quelques heures à chercher un cadeau original dans les magasins indépendants dans le joli centre. Il y a un marché le mardi, le vendredi et le samedi; et le premier jeudi du mois, il y a le marché où les fermiers de la région vendent leurs produits. Là vous pouvez trouver une grande sélection de choses intéressantes à manger. Pour ceux qui préfèrent la culture, il y a trois librairies et un musée qui montre l'histoire de la région.

Et quand vous voulez vous reposer un peu, nous avons beaucoup de petits cafés et restaurants où vous pouvez goûter toutes sortes de bons plats anglais, indiens, chinois ou italiens. Vous pouvez aussi essayer le célèbre 'pork pie' fait dans la région ou nos savoureux fromages anglais, comme par exemple 'le Stilton'. De nombreux touristes disent que nous avons la meilleure nourriture d'Angleterre!

Si vous visitez Market Harborough pendant l'été il y a beaucoup de fêtes de village dans les environs ou on peut visiter les jardins privés ouverts au public une ou deux fois par an. Là vous verrez la vraie vie de la campagne anglaise. Nous avons notre propre fête en juin avec beaucoup d'activités pour tous les âges et un festival d'arts au mois de septembre. Il y a toujours quelque chose à faire.

Venez passer une journée paisible chez nous avant d'aller visiter les villes plus célèbres comme Stratford, Oxford ou Cambridge. Vous ne le regretterez pas.

Task 2: Festivals and Celebrations

Je voudrais vous parler de comment nous fêtons Noël chez nous. Moi, j'habite avec mes parents et mes deux petites sœurs, alors dans notre maison il y a beaucoup à faire avant Noël.

Les magasins commencent très tôt à vendre des cartes de vœux et d'autres choses pour Noël. On peut les acheter même en août. Mais mes parents commencent leurs préparations au début de novembre. Ils commandent une dinde du fermier près de chez nous, et ma mère fait le gâteau de Noël. Le gâteau est plein de fruits secs et il est très bon.

À l'école primaire mes petites sœurs commencent à apprendre des chansons pour leur concert de Noël. Au collège on ne fait rien, sauf passer des examens. C'est horrible!

Le week-end avant le vingt-cinq décembre mon père achète un sapin de Noël et nous le décorons ensemble. Le jour de Noël tout le monde se lève très tôt et va dans la chambre de mes parents pour ouvrir leurs cadeaux. Mes sœurs reçoivent beaucoup de petites choses, mais mes parents m'offrent toujours des CD ou des vêtements que j'ai déjà choisis. Je préfère ça.

Après le petit déjeuner mon père va chercher mes grands-parents en voiture, mes sœurs jouent avec leurs cadeaux et moi, j'aide ma mère à préparer le grand repas traditionnel. Nous mangeons toujours le saumon fumé, suivi de la dinde avec légumes et pommes de terre rôties. Comme dessert nous avons une glace spéciale parce que nous n'aimons pas le pudding traditionnel.

L'après-midi, s'il fait beau nous sortons nous promener un peu et puis nous retournons chez nous pour jouer aux cartes et, plus tard, regarder la télé.

Mes grands-parents partent vers neuf heures et à onze heures je peux finalement me coucher après une belle journée traditionnelle en famille. J'adore ça.

Page 142 (Quick Questions)

1) a) le dessin

b) la chimie

c) les travaux manuels

d) l'éducation physique / l'EPS / le sport

2) What is your favourite subject?

3) Je déteste les mathématiques / les maths mais j'adore l'anglais.

4) Ma matière préférée est la géographie.

5) a) How long have you been learning French?

   b) e.g. J'apprends le français depuis trois ans.

6) Je vais au collège en voiture.

7) Pendant la récré, je joue au football ou je vais dans la salle d'informatique. Je mange toujours un fruit.

8) At school, each class lasts fifty minutes and we have six classes each day. Break is at half past eleven. We have three terms.

9) J'aime la rentrée parce que j'ai hâte de voir mes ami(e)s, mais je ne veux pas porter l'uniforme.

10) Notre uniforme est une chemise blanche, une cravate rouge, un pull vert et un pantalon noir.

11) In France, we don't wear uniform. We don't go to school on Wednesday afternoons but we have to go there on Saturday mornings and the school day is very long.

12) Les règles au collège sont strictes. On n'a pas le droit de parler dans les couloirs ou de porter des bijoux.

13)a) rubber

   b) exercise book

   c) felt-tip pen

14)a) j'ai de bonnes notes

   b) je suis sous pression

   c) je ne veux pas échouer

   d) on me brutalise

15) I work quite hard but I talk to my friends in class and the teachers don't like me. They always put me in detention.

Page 150 (Quick Questions)

1) As-tu fait un stage?

2) Je n'ai jamais fait de stage.

3) I worked at Renault in Paris for a month.

4) a) The work was stressful

   b) I felt lonely

   c) It's not very well paid

   d) The hours are fantastic

5) J'ai un travail à mi-temps et je gagne six livres par heure.

6) Je voudrais préparer le bac et je veux aller à l'université.

7) I've made the decision to leave school because I'd like to take a year out and travel.

8) Je vais chercher un emploi.

9) Je voudrais étudier les maths parce que je veux devenir professeur de maths.

10)a) l'acteur / l'actrice

   b) le boucher / la bouchère

   c) le comptable / la comptable

   d) l'hôte d'accueil / l'hôtesse d'accueil

11)a) hairdresser

   b) plumber

   c) nurse

   d) writer

12) Je voudrais travailler avec les gens. Je n'aimerais pas être avocat(e) parce que les horaires seraient trop longs. Je préférerais être journaliste parce que j'aurais l'occasion de voyager.

13) Would you like to work abroad?

14) Je voudrais aller en France pour travailler dans une station de ski ou dans un bar. Je voudrais voir le pays et rencontrer des gens.

15) une année sabbatique

16) Une année en France sera une bonne chose pour ma carrière.

17) I would like to do some professional training because I would like to be a lawyer.

Page 156 (Quick Questions)

1) Je cherche un emploi dans un bureau.

2) a) un emploi à mi-temps

   b) un emploi temporaire

3) Je serais idéal(e) pour ce poste parce que j'aime travailler avec les enfants et je parle français.

4) a) I'm bilingual

   b) I'm full of life

   c) I'm never impolite

5) Do you like working with the public? Do you speak English? We are looking for a waiter or waitress. 15 hours a week. Call Pierre on 034 23 34 12 34.

6) Hello, can you come for an interview on Monday 31st January at 9am with the boss? Bring a copy of your CV and your driving licence, please.

7) a) licence de français

   b) expérience professionnelle

   c) programme de formation d'informatique

   d) autres renseignements

8) Hello, this is Jean-Paul. I have a message for Marie. Can she call me back at around 8pm tonight? My telephone number is 53-21-44. Thanks a lot. Goodbye.

9) a) Do you know where I can find a hairdresser?

   b) I advise you to look in the phone book.

10) J'ai trouvé votre commande. On a eu des problèmes de fournisseur. Je suis désolé(e). Je peux vous l'envoyer la semaine prochaine.

Page 157-158 (Listening Questions)

1) Brother: Policeman

   Person speaking: Mechanic

2) Mother: Journalist

   Person speaking: Salesperson / Shop assistant

3) Lessons start at **8.30** and finish at **5.35**.

   On Monday morning, he has **Art**, English, **Chemistry** and Maths.

   His favourite subject is **Biology** because it's **interesting**.

4) Lessons start at **8.10** and finish at **5.20**.

   On Monday morning, she has **P.E.**, Geography, **Music** and IT.

   Her favourite subject is **English** because it's **easy**.

5) café   8.75 euros an hour

6) restaurant   9.90 euros an hour

7) swimming pool   75 euros a week

8) a) Maths

   b) He has an excellent teacher.

   c) a gap year (maybe in England)

9) a) A b) B

10) E

11) A

Page 159 (Reading Question)

1 a) She thinks it's important.

  b) doctor

  c) Yes — he's given her lots of encouragement.

  d) Work very hard to pass her exams.

  e) She works in a shoe shop.

Page 160 (Reading Question)

1 a) A b) C c) Y d) L e) A f) Y

Page 161 (Speaking Question)

Sample conversation:

1 **Comment vas-tu au collège?**

   D'habitude je prends le car pour aller au collège, mais de temps en temps mon père m'y amène en voiture.

2 **Quelles sont tes matières préférées? Pourquoi?**

J'aime l'anglais et la géographie aussi. L'anglais me plaît parce que j'adore lire et j'aime la géographie car j'aime apprendre des choses sur les pays étrangers.

3 **Comment était ton école primaire?**

Mon école primaire était très petite. Il n'y avait que cinquante élèves et trois profs. Cependant, j'y étais très content(e) parce que tout le monde était très gentil.

4 **Est-ce que tu as des problèmes au collège?**

En général, tout va bien au collège. Le seul problème que j'ai, c'est que j'ai quelques difficultés en maths. Souvent j'ai trop de travail et je n'arrive pas à tout finir avant la fin du cours.

5 **Si tu pouvais changer une chose au collège, qu'est-ce que tu changerais?**

Il y a plein de choses que j'aimerais changer au collège, mais la chose que je ferais en premier, c'est de construire un terrain de sport où nous pourrions jouer au football pendant l'hiver.

6 **Qu'est-ce que tu voudrais faire l'année prochaine?**

L'année prochaine je vais commencer à préparer mon bac. Je veux étudier l'anglais, la géographie, l'histoire et la chimie.

7 **Qu'est-ce que tu voudrais faire après avoir quitté l'école?**

Après avoir quitté l'école, je voudrais prendre une année sabbatique et faire du travail pour une organisation caritative à l'étranger. Puis je voudrais étudier l'anglais à l'université de Durham.

Page 162 (Writing Questions)

Task 1: Sample Answer

Monsieur/Madame,

Je voudrais réserver trois places pour votre conférence sur le Commerce Éthique qui aura lieu à partir du 15 septembre à Compiègne. Les membres de notre équipe qui aimeraient venir sont:

Madame Julie Felton, qui est notre Chef de Marketing

Monsieur Mark Jones, notre acheteur de jouets

Mademoiselle Mary Gilbertson, notre acheteuse de bijoux.

Notre entreprise est assez nouvelle. Nos produits sont faits en Inde et dans plusieurs pays en Afrique, et, en ce moment, nous avons trois magasins: à Londres, à Birmingham et à Manchester.

Est-ce que vous pourriez me donner quelques renseignements? Si nos employés arrivent à l'aéroport Charles de Gaulle comment est-ce qu'ils iront à Compiègne? Est-ce qu'il y a des trains fréquents? Ils partent de quelle gare à Paris? Ou, à votre avis, serait-il plus simple de prendre l'Eurostar™ et descendre à Calais ou à Lille? Votre conférence aura lieu à quelle distance du centre-ville? Est-ce qu'ils devront prendre un taxi de la gare?

J'ai vu qu'on restera à l'Hôtel de l'Armistice. Où se trouve cet hôtel? Pourriez-vous m'envoyer une carte de la ville? Est-ce que nos employés auront des chambres individuelles ou est-ce qu'ils devront partager? Est-ce que tous les repas seront compris et est-ce qu'il y aura un choix de menus? Madame Felton est végétarienne et ne mange ni viande ni poisson. Est-ce que les chambres ont une salle de bains ou une douche?

Veuillez agréer l'expression de mes sentiments distingués,

Jack Thompson

Task 2: Sample Answer

Je vais parler des différences entre l'éducation en France et en Grande-Bretagne.

En Angleterre, on commence le matin entre huit heures et demie et neuf heures — ça dépend de l'école individuelle. Pendant la matinée il y a une récréation de quinze ou vingt minutes et puis on s'arrête une heure pour la pause-déjeuner vers midi et demie. Dans beaucoup d'établissements la pause-déjeuner ne dure que quarante minutes. Il n'y a pas de récréation dans l'après-midi, sauf dans les écoles primaires, mais notre journée scolaire se termine entre trois et quatre heures. Nous allons à l'école du lundi au vendredi mais on n'y va jamais le samedi.

Je pense que nous étudions presque toutes les mêmes matières que les Français, mais à l'âge de quinze ans nous avons plus de choix en Angleterre. Après les examens GCSE, nous étudions entre trois et cinq matières seulement. En France les élèves doivent continuer à étudier certaines matières comme les maths et le français, avec un groupe de sujets comme les sciences ou les langues, par exemple.

Nous passons des examens importants en seconde, en première et en terminale: c'est un peu trop, à mon avis. Mais nous ne sommes pas obligés d'avoir de bonnes notes pour pouvoir continuer dans la classe suivante, comme en France.

Dans la plupart des écoles et des collèges en Grande-Bretagne nous sommes obligés de porter un uniforme scolaire. On dit que c'est plus simple si tout le monde porte les mêmes vêtements, et meilleur pour la discipline, mais je n'en suis pas certain(e).

À mon avis, la journée scolaire est mieux en Grande-Bretagne parce que nous finissons tôt et nous avons toute la soirée libre pour se détendre ou faire nos devoirs. Je suis très content(e) de ne pas aller à l'école le samedi! Si je devais porter un uniforme j'en préférerais un plus simple, sans cravate. Mais, finalement, je préfère le système scolaire en Grande-Bretagne.

Pages 168-169 (Quick Questions)

1) a) m b) f c) m d) m e) m f) f g) m h) f i) f j) m k) f l) f m) f n) m o) f p) m

2) a) l'aéroport (m) b) la musique (f) c) le gâteau (m) d) le cinéma (m) e) la plage (f) f) l'œuf (m) g) la fraise (f) h) le tennis (m) i) le rugby (m) j) la biologie (f)

3) a) f b) f c) m d) f e) m f) f g) f h) m i) m j) f k) m l) f m) f n) f o) m

4) masculine

5) a) fromages b) poires c) hommes d) enfants e) maisons f) poissons g) tables h) chaises i) crayons

6) a) journaux b) tableaux c) os d) chevaux e) oiseaux f) yeux g) nez h) jeux i) châteaux j) drapeaux

7) a) travail (m) b) chou (m) c) bureau (m) d) cadeau (m) e) femme (f) f) œil (m) g) feu (m) h) bras (m) i) gâteau (m) j) lieu (m)

8) a) une b) une c) un d) une e) un f) une g) un

9) a) la maison b) le professeur c) la robe d) l'abricot e) le jardin f) l'orange g) l'hôpital h) le hamster

10) a) les chats b) un hôtel c) la gare d) les élèves e) les vacances f) une voiture g) le vélo h) un livre

11) false

12) a) Je vais au café. b) Je vais à la gare. c) Je vais à l'hôpital. d) Je vais au collège. e) Je vais à l'office de tourisme. f) Je vais à la pharmacie. g) Je vais aux magasins. h) Je vais au musée.

13) a) à la banque b) au théâtre c) au cinéma d) au château

14) a) Je joue au football chaque jour. b) Qu'est-ce que tu fais à l'école? c) Le week-end, je vais à la discothèque. d) L'été dernier je suis allé aux États-Unis.

15) a) Qu'est-ce que tu penses de la musique pop? b) Qu'est-ce que tu penses des films américains? c) Qu'est-ce que tu penses du dernier film de Hugh Grant? d) Qu'est-ce que tu penses de l'Angleterre? e) Qu'est-ce que tu penses des Français? f) Qu'est-ce que tu penses de la cuisine française? g) Qu'est-ce que tu penses du football? h) Qu'est-ce que tu penses du ski?

16) a) Avez-vous du chocolat? b) J'ai peur des chiens. c) Je voudrais de la confiture avec mon croissant. d) Je joue du piano et mon frère joue de la guitare. e) Est-ce que tu aimes faire du cyclisme?

17) a) Mon père n'a pas d'amis. b) Mon amie Sally n'a pas d'animaux. c) Ils n'ont pas de passe-temps.

18) A: Avez-vous des pommes?

B: Oui, bien sûr. Vous en voulez combien?

A: Deux, s'il vous plaît. Je voudrais du pain aussi.

B: D'accord. Voulez-vous du beurre aussi?

A: Non merci, mais je voudrais du fromage.

B: Je suis désolé(e) mais je n'ai pas de fromage aujourd'hui.

A: D'accord. Merci.

Pages 175-176 (Quick Questions)

1) a) un petit homme   b) une petite femme   c) les petits garçons

   d) les petites filles.

2) a) les grands magasins   b) la voiture verte   c) le chien méchant

   d) des questions difficiles   e) un homme fort   f) les cheveux noirs

   g) une femme intelligente   h) les filles allemandes

3) a) heureuse   b) active   c) première   d) sérieuse   e) bonne   f) gentille

   g) blanche   h) dangereuse   i) sportive   j) sèche   k) chère

4)   Elle est très ennuyeuse.

5)   Les gâteaux sont délicieux.

6)   e.g. Mon père est grand avec les yeux bleus et un grand nez. Ma mère est petite avec les yeux verts et les cheveux blonds.

7) a) vieille femme   b) vieux vin   c) vieilles chaussures   d) vieil homme

   e) vieux journaux

8) a) une belle fille   b) de beaux hommes   c) une belle journée

   d) de belles femmes   e) un bel oiseau

9)   J'ai un nouveau vélo.

10)   Mon père a une nouvelle voiture.

11)a) Je regarde la télévision tous les jours.   b) Il a plu toute la nuit.

   c) Il a mangé tout le gâteau.   d) Toutes les filles anglaises aiment le chocolat.

12)   e.g. Pierre est grand avec les cheveux bruns et courts. Je pense qu'il est fou. Marie est belle. Elle a les yeux bleus et les cheveux longs et blonds. Jean-Paul et Marc sont tous les deux petits et gros, mais ils sont très gentils.

13)a) intéressant   b) étrange   c) lent   d) mauvais   e) difficile   f) rapide

14)   heureux / heureuse

15)   triste

16)   e.g. Je pense que les devoirs sont faciles.

17)a) une voiture rouge   b) les yeux bleus   c) une jolie fille
   d) une histoire triste   e) un mauvais film   f) un livre ennuyeux

18)   J'ai des chaussures neuves.

19)   e.g. Mon prof de maths est vieux, petit et méchant, mais mon prof de français est jeune, gentille et jolie.

20)   A former teacher; an old teacher.

21)a) Amy est une chère amie.   b) Mark aime le vin cher.   c) J'ai ma propre chambre.   d) Maman aime une cuisine propre.

22)a) mon chien

   b) ta maison / votre maison

   c) ses chaussures

   d) nos parents

   e) leur voiture

   f) mon ami(e) / mon copain / ma copine

   g) son frère

23)   Sample answer:
      A: Did you get any nice presents for your birthday?
      B: Yes. My mother gave me a red dress and some red and black shoes. My father gave me a new book and a big box of chocolates.
      A: And your brother and sister?
      B: My sister gave me a CD, but my brother has lost all his money, so I didn't get anything from him.
      A: Was it a good birthday?
      B: No, not at all! The dress is horrible, the shoes are too small, the book is boring, the chocolates are horrible and the CD is very bad.

24)   Sample answer:
      A: C'est ta voiture?
      B: Non, ce n'est pas ma voiture, c'est la voiture de Pierre. Sa voiture est rapide et chère. Ma voiture est vieille et lente.

Pages 184-185 (Quick Questions)

1) a) lentement   b) parfaitement   c) étrangement   d) rapidement

   e) heureusement

2) a) Je joue du piano parfaitement.

   b) Il parle lentement.

3)   She sings well but she dances badly.

4)   e.g. Je joue bien au tennis de table, mais je joue mal au football parce que je cours lentement.

5) a) trop   b) très   c) assez   d) presque

6) a) Quelquefois je travaille plus vite qu'Emma.

   b) Je travaille toujours plus vite qu'Ed.

7)   I watch horror films from time to time, but I often watch romantic films.

8) a) Je parle bien français.   b) Je parle assez bien français.

   c) Je parle très bien français.

9) a) Le professeur parle trop rapidement.

   b) Mes pieds sont très grands.

   c) J'ai presque fini.

   d) Cette question est assez facile.

10)a) Jack est plus intelligent.   b) Jack est le plus intelligent.

11)a) Helen est la plus grande.

   b) Robert et Mark sont les plus petits.

12)   La musique pop est meilleure. La musique rock est la meilleure.

13)   le pire

14)a) Je cours plus lentement.   b) Je cours le plus lentement.

15)   Je parle bien l'allemand, je parle mieux le français et je parle l'anglais le mieux.

16)a) Pierre est plus grand que Jean-Paul.

   b) Céline est moins grande que Pierre.

   c) Jean-Paul est aussi grand que Céline.

17)e.g. Le français est moins ennuyeux que les maths. La biologie est plus intéressante que la chimie et la physique est aussi ennuyeuse que la géographie.

18) a) Je vais à Manchester.   b) Il va en France.   c) Nous allons à Paris.

   d) Elles vont en Espagne.

19) a) J'habite à Leeds.

   b) J'habite en Angleterre.

20)   Your books are on the table, and your lunch is in your bag.

21)a) Je suis allé(e) à l'école à pied.

   b) J'ai vu Wayne Rooney à la télé.

   c) Le chat est sur le lit.

   d) Je pars jeudi.

   e) Je l'ai entendu à la radio.

22)   Je viens de Londres.

23)   Le train va de Londres à Paris.

24)   e.g. Je serai en France à partir du 5 avril.

25) a) un paquet de chips   b) une boîte de chocolats   c) un groupe de filles

   d) une bouteille de vin   e) une tasse de café

26)   Ma veste est en cuir et mon sac est en plastique.

27)   Mon anniversaire est le dix juin.

28)   a) J'ai acheté un poisson pour le chat.   b) J'ai acheté une robe blanche pour ma mère.   c) J'ai acheté une cravate verte pour mon père.   d) J'ai acheté un stylo rouge pour le professeur.

29)   le train pour Lyon

30)   J'habite à Bristol depuis cinq ans.

31) a) L'école commence à neuf heures.   b) Il est au cinéma.

   c) Maman est à la maison.

32)   Je vais quitter la maison à dix heures, je vais vous rencontrer dans le parc et je vais rester une heure. / Je quitterai la maison à dix heures, je vous rencontrerai dans le parc et je resterai une heure.

Pages 193-194 (Quick Questions)

1) He wants to go to the beach but it's cold.
2) a) My father is very tired because he works all the time.
   b) Take a chocolate if you want.
   c) What are you going to do during the holidays?
   d) I'm tired so I'm going to go to bed.
   e) I play football with my brother.
3) a) Elle aime le chocolat.
   b) Il joue au football.
   c) Il a mangé mes chaussures.
   d) Elle est sous la table.
   e) Ils détestent les filles.
   f) Elles sont allées au cinéma.
4) e.g. Qu'est-ce que tu vas faire samedi?
5) e.g. Est-ce que vous allez au parc aujourd'hui?
6) a) Je la regarde.
   b) Paul le lit.
   c) Je les déteste.
   d) Je l'ai mangé hier soir.
7) a) Je t'aime. (or 'Je vous aime.')
   b) Il m'aime.
8) a) me/to me   b) you/to you   c) to him/her/it   d) to them
9) a) Je lui donne le livre.
   b) Est-ce que Johnny Depp t'a parlé au concert?
   c) Je leur donne le ballon.
10) a) them   b) us   c) me
11) Donne-moi les bonbons, ce sont les miens!
12) a) me   b) you   c) them   d) one
13) a) Listen to me!
   b) Sit down!
   c) He is more intelligent than you.
   d) I want to do it myself.
   e) I saw you with them.
   f) Whose pen is it? – It's mine.
14) b) Oui, j'en prends deux.
   c) Oui, j'en prends six.
   d) Oui, j'en prends une bouteille.
   e) Oui, j'en prends deux tranches.
15) a) J'en ai besoin.
   b) J'en ai besoin.
   c) J'en ai besoin pour faire mes devoirs.
   d) J'en ai besoin pour aller au cinéma.
16) He bought two packets of crisps but only ate one.
17) b) Vous y allez.
   c) Nous y allons.
   d) Ils y vont.
   e) Elle y va.
18) there is / there are
19) Je ne les mange pas.
20) a) ce chien   b) cette pomme   c) cette fille   d) ces chaussettes
   e) cet oiseau   f) ce sandwich   g) cette maison   h) cet hôpital
   i) ces journaux   j) ces enfants
21) a) Ce gâteau est délicieux.
   b) Ce livre est très intéressant.
   c) Ces chaussures sont trop petites.
   d) Cette chemise est verte.
22) a) I don't like this dress. I prefer that one.
   b) Have you read these books? This one is very good, but that one is boring.
   c) I like dogs, but those ones are really nasty.
23) I have a French lesson with the teacher that I'm scared of.
24) a) le lapin que les enfants aiment
   b) le lapin qui aime les enfants

Pages 202-203 (Quick Questions)

1) a) nous regardons   b) vous regardez   c) elles regardent   d) tu regardes
   e) on regarde
2) a) j'aime
   b) tu aimes/vous aimez
   c) elle aime
   d) nous aimons
   e) ils/elles aiment
3) a) je parle
   b) tu écoutes/vous écoutez
   c) nous jouons
   d) ils/elles détestent
   e) il écoute
4) a) je finis   b) il finit   c) vous finissez   d) ils finissent   e) nous finissons
   f) tu finis.
5) a) Les cours finissent à trois heures.
   b) Le film finit bien.
   c) Choisissez la robe que vous préférez.
6) a) je vends   b) nous vendons   c) vous vendez   d) tu vends
   e) elles vendent   f) on vend
7) La boulangerie vend du pain.
8) a) il attend   b) nous descendons   c) je perds   d) vous entendez
   e) tu réponds   f) ils correspondent
9) a) je suis   b) tu es / vous êtes   c) elle est   d) nous sommes
   e) ils / elles sont
10) a) Nous sommes heureux.
   b) Vous êtes anglais.
   c) Mon père est ingénieur.
   d) Je suis fatigué.
   e) Les devoirs sont ennuyeux.
   f) Elle est belle.
11) Je suis anglais(e).
12) Êtes-vous/Es-tu heureux/heureuse(s)?
13) a) j'ai   b) elle a   c) nous avons   d) ils/elles ont   e) vous avez/tu as
14) a) Tu as les yeux bleus.
   b) Vous avez les yeux bleus.
15) a) Qu'est-ce que tu fais ce soir?
   b) Qu'est-ce que vous faites ce soir?
16) e.g. À l'école moi et mon meilleur ami (ma meilleure amie) faisons de la biologie et du français.
17) a) Je vais au cinéma.
   b) Ils vont à l'école.
   c) Vous allez à la piscine.
   d) Elle va à Lille.
   e) Nous allons au musée.
   f) Tu vas à l'office de tourisme.
18) a) e.g. Où allez-vous?   b) e.g. Où vas-tu?
19) e.g. L'été je vais en France, Mark va en Espagne, et George et Kevin vont en Italie.
20) a) nous voulons   b) je veux   c) elle veut   d) ils/elles veulent
   e) tu veux/vous voulez
21) a) Qu'est-ce que vous voulez manger?
   b) Qu'est-ce que tu veux manger?
22) e.g. Je veux un café, il veut un jus d'orange, elle veut des frites et ils/elles veulent du chocolat chaud.
23) a) Il doit faire son lit.
   b) Nous devons faire la vaisselle.

c) Tu dois ranger ta chambre.

d) Vous devez débarrasser la table.

e) Elles doivent passer l'aspirateur.

f) Je dois lire ce livre.

24) a) Liz va dormir.

b) Pete va faire ses devoirs.

c) Je vais aller à la piscine.

d) Dan et Julie vont sortir ce soir.

25) e.g. Je vais aller en France. Je vais y aller en train et je vais rester dans un hôtel. Je vais nager et faire des promenades. Je vais parler français autant que possible.

26) a) je mangerai

b) vous dormirez

c) elle dansera

d) ils finiront

e) tu penseras

f) on payera / on paiera

g) elles donneront

27) a) I will go

b) you will be able to

c) he will have to

d) you will have

e) we will be

f) they will say

g) she will want

h) I will do/make

Pages 214-215 (Quick Questions)

1) a) fini b) mangé c) regardé d) parti e) vendu f) attendu g) allé
h) dormi

2) a) lire – lu b) craindre – craint c) avoir – eu d) devoir – dû
e) être – été f) conduire – conduit g) mourir – mort h) mettre – mis
i) prendre – pris j) savoir – su k) vouloir – voulu l) naître – né

3) a) j'ai joué

b) vous avez regardé

c) il a écouté

d) nous avons fini

e) tu as vendu

f) elles ont dormi

g) j'ai mangé

h) on a choisi

4) J'ai fait les courses.

5) Nous avons regardé la télé(vision) toute la journée.

6) e.g. Hier j'ai lu un livre, j'ai joué au tennis et j'ai aidé ma mère à faire la cuisine.

7) a) Hier je suis allé(e) au théâtre.

b) Elle est sortie hier soir.

c) Vous êtes devenu(s) très ennuyeux.

d) Il est arrivé le 4 septembre.

e) Nous sommes monté(e)s dans le train.

f) Ils sont partis hier.

8) Il est mort.

9) Pierre did not come.

10) e.g. Je suis allé(e) en Allemagne. Je suis arrivé(e) le 4 septembre, et je suis rentré(e) le 20 septembre. Je suis resté(e) dans un hôtel.

11) a) Hier soir mon frère est sorti avec ses amis et il est rentré très tard.

b) J'ai voulu te téléphoner mais j'ai dû faire mes devoirs.

c) Le film a fini à huit heures, donc nous avons pu en voir un autre.

d) Quand vous êtes allée à la discothèque, est-ce que vous avez mis votre robe rouge?

12) e.g.:

A: Hi Pierre! What did you do yesterday?

B: I went to school in the morning. Lessons finished at three o'clock, so I went into town to do some shopping.

A: What did you buy?

B: I bought the new Bon Jovi CD, it's great! I wanted to buy a T-shirt, but I didn't have time.

A: Ah, is that why you didn't come out with us yesterday? It's a shame, we went to the concert.

13) a) there was b) it was

14) a) Il y avait un concert au théâtre.

b) C'était trop facile.

c) Dans ma chambre il y avait un lit et une armoire.

15) a) je regardais b) il regardait c) nous regardions d) tu regardais
e) vous regardiez f) elles regardaient.

16) a) je dormais

b) il semblait

c) vous écoutiez

d) ils finissaient

e) tu devais

f) nous restions

17) a) Quand j'étais petit, j'allais au parc avec mon père.

b) Il mettait un jean pour aller à la discothèque, mais maintenant il porte des vêtements plus chics.

c) Quand nous étions plus jeunes nous ne devions pas faire la vaisselle.

d) Elles jouaient au tennis tous les mardis et elles faisaient du cyclisme tous les samedis.

18) J'aimais les bonbons.

19) During her holidays in Spain the sun shone and it was hot.

20) a) Susie a téléphoné pendant que tu faisais tes devoirs.

b) J'ai mangé tout le gâteau pendant que ma mère regardait la télévision.

c) Il s'est cassé la jambe pendant que nous jouions au rugby.

d) Pendant que vous rangiez votre chambre, j'ai pris une douche.

21) a) I had finished.

b) We had lost the cat.

c) Mark had forgotten to close the window.

d) You had eaten before you arrived.

e) Michelle and Sharon had arrived.

f) I had left by car.

g) She had got up at three o'clock.

22) e.g. J'avais fait mes devoirs mais le chien les a mangés.

Pages 224-225 (Quick Questions)

1) a) se b) nous c) me d) se

2) a) se lever b) se coucher c) se laver

3) a) Je me sens mal.

b) Nous nous sentons mal.

c) Elle se sent mal.

d) Vous vous sentez mal.

e) Ils se sentent mal.

f) Tu te sens mal.

4) a) Je m'intéresse à la science-fiction.

b) Il s'amuse.

5) How do you spell your name?

6) e.g. Je me lève à sept heures. Je me lave à sept heures et demie. Je mange le petit déjeuner à huit heures. Je vais à l'école à neuf heures. Je rentre à la maison à quatre heures et je me couche à dix heures.

7) Comment ça s'écrit?

8) b) Nous nous sommes senti(e)s mal.

c) Elle s'est trouvée devant la gare.

d) Vous vous êtes couché(e)(s) à onze heures.

e) Tu t'es levé(e) à neuf heures.

f) Ils se sont amusés au concert.

g) Elles se sont intéressées au problème.

9) a) I washed myself at eight o'clock.

b) We felt ill.

c) She found herself in front of the station. / She was in front of the station.

d) You went to bed at eleven o'clock.

e) You got up at nine o'clock.

f) They enjoyed themselves at the concert.

g) They were interested in the problem.

10)a) Je ne mange pas de viande.

b) Tu n'as pas beaucoup d'argent.

c) Elle n'aime pas faire les courses.

d) Nous n'allons pas au cinéma ce soir.

11)a) Elle n'a pas fait ses devoirs.

b) Je ne suis pas allé à la banque.

c) Nous n'avons pas vu Paul au parc.

d) Ils ne sont pas arrivés.

12) Je préfère ne pas aller au théâtre.

13) I don't go to the cinema any more because I don't have enough money; I never go to the disco because I don't like dancing; I don't do anything at the weekend because I don't know anybody.

14) Je ne mange ni petits pois ni carottes.

15) There are no more apples and there isn't a single banana.

16)a) Je n'ai pas d'argent.

b) Je n'ai pas le temps.

17) j'aimerais

18)a) Je voudrais un sandwich au jambon.

b) Je voudrais aller en France cet été.

19)a) future tense

b) imperfect tense

20) a) Would you be able to help me? / Could you help me?

b) He should write to me more often.

c) I would go out this evening if I didn't have to do my homework.

d) They would go on holiday if they had more money.

21)a) Come here!

b) Open the window!

c) Listen to me!

d) Put your hand up!

22)a) Fais la vaisselle!

b) Range ta chambre!

c) Regarde le tableau noir!

d) Finis tes devoirs!

23)a) Mangez votre déjeuner!

b) Lisez ce livre!

c) Allez à l'école!

d) Prenez la première rue à gauche!

24)a) Allons au parc!

b) Fais attention!

25)a) Be kind.

b) Be afraid!

c) Know that I am more intelligent than you.

26)a) N'écoute pas la radio!

b) Ne prenez pas la deuxième rue à droite!

c) Ne vendez pas le chien!

d) Ne mange pas mes chocolats!

27)a) Tais-toi!

b) Asseyez-vous!

c) Taisez-vous!

d) Souviens-toi.

28)a) Ne te perds pas!

b) Ne vous lavez pas!

c) Ne te couche pas!

Pages 232-233 (Quick Questions)

1) a) Je sais cuisinier.

b) Je sais conduire.

c) Je ne sais pas faire du ski mais je sais nager

2) Je ne sais pas.

3) a) He knows the Queen of England.

b) e.g. Est-ce que tu connais le président des États-Unis?

4) Je connais assez bien Londres.

5) Je peux t'aider si tu veux.

6) You can't go into the church without a hat.

7) Est-ce que je peux sortir ce soir?

8) e.g. Je pourrais aller en France cet été, mais je connais très bien la France. Je pourrais aller en Espagne aussi, mais je ne sais pas parler espagnol.

9) a) singing b) eating c) leaving d) running

10) a) disant b) jouant c) parlant d) dormant e) lisant f) buvant g) faisant h) descendant

11)a) I do my homework while watching the television.

b) He stays fit by playing tennis.

c) I broke my arm playing football.

d) We entertain ourselves by reading comics.

12)a) Nous regardons la télévision en déjeunant.

b) Elle s'amuse en jouant au tennis.

c) Il est entré dans l'église en chantant.

d) On arrive plus vite en prenant le train.

13)a) He was watching TV.

b) when he was eating it

c) crying

14) False

15)a) Après avoir dormi, j'ai mangé trois croissants.

b) Après avoir travaillé, j'ai regardé la télévision.

16)a) After having gone up, I stayed there for three hours.

b) After having fallen, I went to the doctor's.

17)a) Après être sortis, Mike et Paul ont mangé une pizza.

b) Après être devenue célèbre, Emma mangeait au restaurant tous les jours.

c) Après être arrivées, Sarah et Katie se sont couchées tout de suite.

18) We are loved/liked by our grandmother.

19)a) I was employed by a café in town.

b) My homework was eaten by my little brother.

20) The newspapers will be recycled next week.

21) e.g. I didn't get a present for my birthday.

22) e.g. It's necessary to eat five pieces of fruit and vegetables every day.

23) Il a neigé hier, mais aujourd'hui il fait chaud.

24) It's necessary to leave your shoes here.

25)a) it's necessary that b) although c) it seems that d) before

26) subjunctive

27)a) I'm going to give you money so that you tidy your room.

b) I don't believe he is as attractive as me.

28)a) être b) faire c) avoir d) pouvoir

EXAM PAPER ANSWERS

Listening Exam

Q. no.	Answer:	Marks
1 a)	A	1 mark
b)	B	1 mark
c)	B	1 mark
2 a)	department store	1 mark
b)	cake shop	1 mark
c)	newsagent / newspaper kiosk / newsstand	1 mark
3 a)	B	1 mark
b)	C	1 mark
c)	A	1 mark
4 a)	02.98.75.16.21	1 mark
b)	02.62.21.15.36	1 mark
c)	02.77.85.19.55	1 mark
5 a)	Tuesday 31st October	1 mark
b)	15:20	1 mark
c)	Mr Grosjean	1 mark
d)	to confirm his reservation	1 mark
e)	11:45	1 mark
6 a)	cheap / not expensive	1 mark
b)	less	1 mark
c)	difficult	1 mark
d)	miss the last bus	1 mark
7	sore arm / pain in the arm	1 mark
8	3 days	1 mark
9 a)	30 euros a month	1 mark
b)	going to the cinema / going to the café *(Half a mark for each answer.)*	1 mark
10	A	1 mark
	D	1 mark
11	B	1 mark
	C	1 mark
12	newspaper office	1 mark
	the people weren't nice	1 mark
13	library (in her town)	1 mark
	she was working with people, which is important to her	1 mark
14	unemployment	1 mark
15	racism	1 mark
16 a)	C	1 mark
b)	E	1 mark
c)	A	1 mark
d)	D	1 mark
e)	B	1 mark

(Total marks available for the Listening Paper = 40 marks.)

Reading Exam

Q. no.	Answer:	Marks
1 a)	F	1 mark
b)	T	1 mark
c)	T	1 mark
d)	N	1 mark
2	A	1 mark
	C	1 mark
	F	1 mark
	H	1 mark
3	G	1 mark
	B	1 mark
	E	1 mark
	H	1 mark
	C	1 mark
4 a)	4	1 mark
b)	5	1 mark
c)	3	1 mark
d)	2	1 mark
e)	1	1 mark
5 a)	6	1 mark
b)	2	1 mark
c)	1	1 mark
d)	5	1 mark
e)	4	1 mark
f)	3	1 mark
6 a)	She can buy whatever she wants. / It gives her a chance to go out with friends. *(One mark for either answer.)*	1 mark
b)	She likes being fashionable.	1 mark
c)	Shopping centres because you can get everything there / there's lots of choice.	1 mark
d)	Because you can't try clothes on before buying them.	1 mark
e)	She bought him books because it's his birthday.	1 mark
f)	She would buy an MP3 player because hers is broken.	1 mark
7 a)	LG	1 mark
b)	JP	1 mark
c)	S	1 mark
d)	L	1 mark
e)	LA	1 mark
8 a)	F	1 mark
b)	F	1 mark
c)	N	1 mark
d)	F	1 mark
e)	T	1 mark

(Total marks available for the Reading Paper = 40 marks.)

Speaking Assessment Mark Scheme

It's very difficult to mark the speaking exam yourself because there isn't one 'right' answer for any of the questions. To make it easier to mark, you need to record the whole exam. Then you can use a dictionary or get someone who's really good at French to go back over it to mark how well you did. Use the mark schemes below to help you, but bear in mind that they'll only be a rough guide. You really need a teacher who knows the exam board's mark scheme well and has a very good knowledge of the French language to mark it properly.

The speaking tasks don't have a specific mark scheme because each person will say different things, so you can't just have one set of acceptable answers. Instead, they're marked against a series of criteria, which will be something like the ones below. Answers are marked for 'Communication', 'Range and Accuracy of Language', and 'Pronunciation and Intonation'. In this mark scheme, 'Communication' is marked out of 15, 'Range and Accuracy of Language' is marked out of 10, and 'Pronunciation and Intonation' is marked out of 5.

Each of your two speaking tasks should be marked using these criteria, to give you a total mark out of 60 for the two tasks.

Communication	
13-15	You answer all the questions, including unpredictable and open-ended ones, fully and confidently. You speak clearly and fluently, with little or no hesitation, and interact very well with the teacher. You give detailed information, and develop and explain your ideas and points of view. You can give relevant information without being prompted, and sometimes take control of the conversation.
10-12	You answer the questions fully, and give extra information for most of them, without going off-topic. You speak confidently, with little hesitation, and interact well. You explain and justify some of your opinions without difficulty.
7-9	You answer most of the questions, giving the required information. You at least attempt to answer any unpredictable questions. You give some opinions, but don't explain them all. You sometimes hesitate or have some trouble keeping the conversation going.
4-6	You mainly give only simple pieces of information and basic opinions, without developing many answers. You hesitate quite a lot, particularly on the unpredictable questions. You need a lot of prompting from the teacher.
1-3	You only give a small amount of relevant information. You answer slowly, hesitate a lot and don't connect your ideas. You need prompting for nearly all the questions.
0	You don't say anything that's relevant to the topic.

Range and Accuracy of Language	
9-10	You use a wide range of vocabulary. You use different tenses correctly and use complex sentences. Any mistakes you make are small, and mainly only when you're using more complex language.
7-8	You use a good range of vocabulary and sentence structures, and you use different tenses. You make a few mistakes, but always get your meaning across clearly.
5-6	Most of your sentences are simple, but you do attempt some more complicated language. Your vocabulary is straightforward and mostly predictable. You might get some of your tenses mixed up. You make mistakes, but get more right than wrong and usually get your basic message across.
3-4	Almost all your sentences are simple and your vocabulary is limited and repetitive. You make a lot of mistakes, but can still usually make yourself understood.
1-2	You mainly use simple, short phrases or individual words. Your range of vocabulary is poor. You make a lot of mistakes, which often make what you're saying hard to understand.
0	You don't say anything that makes sense or could be easily understood.

Pronunciation and Intonation	
5	Your accent and intonation are consistently good for someone who doesn't speak French as their first language, with only minor errors.
4	Your pronunciation and intonation are generally good with occasional errors.
3	Your pronunciation and accent are mainly accurate, but there are several mistakes. You sometimes sound quite English.
2	There are a lot of pronunciation errors that sometimes make it difficult to tell what you're saying.
1	You sound very English — most of your pronunciation is wrong, and it's hard to understand what you're trying to say.
0	You don't pronounce anything clearly and can't be easily understood.

Speaking Task 1

Sample answer:

1 Tu regardes la télé combien de fois par semaine?

Je regarde la télé pendant au moins trois heures chaque soir, quand je suis à la maison. J'ai une télé dans ma chambre que je regarde en faisant mes devoirs.

2 Parle-moi d'une émission que tu aimes:
Quand est-ce qu'elle passe? De quoi s'agit-il?
Tu aimes quels personnages?

Mon émission préférée est un feuilleton qui passe le lundi, mardi, jeudi et vendredi soir. Il s'agit des vies d'un groupe de personnes qui habitent un quartier de Londres. Les histoires sont intéressantes et dramatiques aussi. Récemment un homme a tué sa première femme et l'a laissée dans un jardin. On a découvert son corps à cause de l'odeur horrible et des mouches. C'était choquant. J'aime beaucoup le propriétaire du café, qui est vraiment bizarre. Il est égoïste et un peu stupide, et il ne comprend pas sa femme. Mais quand sa fille a disparu il a montré qu'il était comme tous les autres pères.

3 Qu'est-ce que tu n'aimes pas regarder?

J'aime aussi les autres feuilletons et les émissions sur les animaux, mais je déteste les comédies qui sont pour les gens de l'âge de mes grands-parents.

4 Quel genre d'émissions est-ce que tu voudrais voir plus souvent à la télé?

J'aimerais voir plus d'émissions pour les jeunes de mon âge; sur la musique, par exemple. Mon père parle des émissions qu'il regardait quand il avait mon âge et elles ont l'air bien.

5 À ton avis, comment sera l'avenir de la télévision?

À mon avis il y a trop d'émissions de télé réalité maintenant, ainsi que des programmes de cuisine. Je pense que la télévision devra changer à l'avenir ou bien les jeunes arrêteront de la regarder. Avec l'internet on peut choisir ce qu'on regarde et c'est beaucoup mieux.

Sample answers to unexpected questions:

6 Est-ce que tu aimes regarder la télé en famille?

Je regarde la télé avec ma famille de temps en temps mais mes parents aiment les émissions que je n'aime pas. Mon petit frère aime les dessins animés et je les regarde avec lui quelquefois.

Qu'est-ce que tu fais quand tu ne regardes pas la télé?

Je sors assez souvent pour voir mes copains. Nous allons au cinéma ou en boîte de nuit. Et le samedi je travaille dans un supermarché toute la journée.

Quels sont les avantages et les inconvénients de la télé, à ton avis?

À mon avis, la télé est très bonne pour les personnes âgées qui ne peuvent pas sortir; et il y a des émissions très éducatives, comme les documentaires, par exemple. Mais beaucoup de membres d'une même famille ne se parlent pas et ne font rien ensemble parce qu'ils regardent la télé tout le temps.

Speaking Task 2

Sample answer:

1 Où habites-tu? Où est-ce que ça se trouve exactement?

J'habite dans un petit village dans le Nord-Est de l'Angleterre, pas loin de York. Il y a environ deux cent habitants et le village est très isolé. Il n'y a pas de bus pour aller en ville alors je dois demander à mes parents de m'y amener. Quelquefois, en hiver, les routes sont fermées par la neige et je ne peux pas aller au collège.

2 Qu'est-ce qu'il y a à faire?

Dans le village il n'y a presque rien sauf un magasin avec une poste, un bar-restaurant et un terrain de sport; c'est tout.

3 Tu aimes y habiter?

J'aime y habiter parce que c'est très calme et le paysage est vraiment joli.

4 Quels sont les avantages et les inconvénients d'y habiter?

Malheureusement, je ne peux pas voir mes copains de classe quand je veux et c'est difficile de trouver un petit job, alors je m'ennuie souvent. Mais j'aime lire et écouter de la musique et je m'entends bien avec ma famille!

5 Qu'est-ce qu'il y a à faire pour les visiteurs?

Les visiteurs viennent pour faire des randonnées dans les collines derrière le village. Ils vont à York pour voir la belle cathédrale et les jolies rues étroites. Il y a aussi plusieurs châteaux dans la région qui sont intéressants si on aime l'histoire.

6 Comment est ta maison?

Ma famille et moi, nous habitons une assez grande maison avec un jardin énorme. Il y a cinquante ans tous les habitants du village avaient des animaux dans leurs jardins, et ils cultivaient tous leurs fruits et légumes. Maintenant nous avons une pelouse où nous jouions quand nous étions plus jeunes.

Sample answers to unexpected questions:

7 Est-ce que tu y as toujours habité?

Avant j'habitais dans le Sud de l'Angleterre mais nous avons déménagé à cause du travail de mon père quand j'étais bébé.

Qu'est-ce que tu voudrais changer dans ta ville?

J'aimerais avoir plus à faire. S'il y avait un bus le samedi je pourrais travailler à York et gagner un peu d'argent. Il n'y a pas assez de jeunes de mon âge dans le village: ils sont tous plus jeunes que moi.

Où est-ce que tu voudrais vivre à l'avenir?

À l'avenir j'aimerais habiter dans une grande ville avec des cinémas, des magasins et des boîtes de nuit. Je pourrais sortir tous les soirs avec mes copains et nous serions contents.

Writing Assessment Mark Scheme

Like the speaking assessment, it's difficult to mark the writing assessment yourself because there isn't one 'right' answer for any of the questions. Make sure that you complete both tasks in exam conditions and stick to the time limit. Afterwards, you can use a dictionary or get someone who's good at French to mark how well you did. Use the mark schemes below to help you, but bear in mind that they'll only be a rough guide. You really need a teacher who knows the exam board's mark scheme well and has a very good knowledge of the French language to mark it properly.

The writing tasks don't have a specific mark scheme because each person will write different things, so you can't just have one set of acceptable answers. Instead, they're marked against a series of criteria, which will be something like the ones below. Answers are marked for 'Communication and Content', 'Range and Use of Language', and 'Accuracy'. In this mark scheme, 'Communication and Content' is marked out of 15, 'Range and Use of Language' is marked out of 10, and 'Accuracy' is marked out of 5.

Each of your two writing tasks should be marked using these criteria, to give you a total mark out of 60 for the two tasks.

Communication and Content	
13-15	You've answered the question fully, and your meaning is always clear. You can describe things, write about what happened, give your own opinions and justify them. Your writing has a clear structure and all your ideas are linked together. Overall, it's a nice piece of writing to read.
10-12	You've answered the question, giving lots of information. You've only left out minor things and almost everything you've written is relevant. You can explain your ideas and give and justify your own point of view. Overall, your answer might be either a bit simplistic or over-ambitious.
7-9	You've mainly answered the question, although you may have missed a few things out or written some things that are irrelevant. You can describe things and give and develop your opinions, and you've tried to link your ideas together. It might be hard to understand some of what you've written when you've tried to use complex language.
4-6	You mainly give only simple pieces of information and basic opinions, such as likes/dislikes, although you've tried to develop some of your ideas. You haven't fully answered the question, and lots of what you've written is irrelevant or repeated. It's just about possible to understand what you've written.
1-3	You've only given a very small amount of relevant information, and your sentences aren't linked together. A native French person wouldn't really be able to understand what you've written.
0	You haven't written anything that's relevant to the topic.

Range and Use of Language	
9-10	You use a wide range of vocabulary and structures, and you write longer sentences accurately. You use different tenses correctly, and can also use things like superlatives, negatives and object pronouns.
7-8	You use a good range of vocabulary and sentence structures, and most of your longer sentences are accurate. You've tried to use a variety of tenses and object pronouns.
5-6	You've used some variety of words and structures, including some correctly linked and/or longer sentences. You've included a range of adjectives and adverbs.
3-4	You've used simple structures and pre-prepared sentences to give a basic answer to the question. You've used some adjectives, but have often made mistakes when using different tenses.
1-2	Most of the language you've used is not relevant to the question. You don't really understand sentence structure, but some of the words you've written are correct.
0	You don't write anything that makes sense or could be easily understood.

Accuracy	
5	Your writing is very accurate, although it might have occasional, minor errors. Nearly all of your spellings, verb forms, genders and agreements are correct.
4	Your writing is generally accurate. Most spellings, verb forms and genders correct. Most mistakes are in longer sentences.
3	Your writing is quite accurate, except in more complex sentences. Most of your verb forms are correct, and it's usually easy to understand what you mean.
2	There are a few correct phrases, but also lots of misspelt words, and errors with genders and verb forms which can make it hard to understand what you're trying to say.
1	Very few, if any, of your verb forms are correct, and there are many incorrect spellings and genders. The large number of mistakes makes your work very hard to understand.
0	You don't write anything that makes sense or could be easily understood.

Writing Task 1

Sample answer:

Je vais vous parler d'une jeune femme qui est très connue en Grande Bretagne. Elle s'appelle Gladys Higginbottom. Est-ce que vous la connaissez en France?

Elle est née en 1980 à Leeds, une grande ville dans le Nord de l'Angleterre. Elle est petite et mince, et elle a les cheveux marron. Elle a toujours voulu danser et chanter et elle a toujours été très jolie.

Pendant son enfance elle a gagné beaucoup de concours de beauté et de talent. Elle a même été choisie parmi neuf mille autres pour étudier gratuitement à l'École Royale de Ballet.

Après ses études elle a travaillé comme serveuse avant de chanter dans un concours à la télé, qu'elle a gagné avec quatre autres filles! Ces cinq filles ont commencé à chanter ensemble dans un groupe qui s'appelle 'Beautiful Girls'. Elles ont eu vingt chansons dans le 'Hit Parade'. J'adore leur musique et j'ai toujours voulu ressembler à Gladys parce qu'elle est très belle et elle porte des vêtements super.

Elle a aussi été dans plusieurs émissions de télé comme présentatrice et elle vient de commencer à chanter seule avec beaucoup de succès.

En 2004 elle s'est mariée avec un joueur de foot. C'est un couple très beau et très riche, mais récemment ils ont eu des problèmes.

Gladys est généreuse et elle fait beaucoup de travail pour les organisations caritatives comme 'Comic Relief'.

Je l'adore parce qu'elle montre que n'importe qui peut avoir du succès si on travaille beaucoup. Elle a eu des difficultés pendant sa vie, mais elle a toujours essayé de s'améliorer. J'espère qu'elle continuera à réussir dans sa carrière.

Writing Task 2

Sample answer:

Cher Paul,

Dans mon collège, tous les étudiants en troisième doivent faire un stage en entreprise. Cela nous aide à comprendre le monde du travail et comment il faut se comporter.

Moi, j'ai passé une semaine à travailler dans un magasin de vêtements dans notre ville. La mode m'intéresse et je voudrais peut-être travailler comme chef des achats dans un grand magasin à l'avenir.

J'ai dû commencer le matin à neuf heures moins le quart, ce qui est plus tard qu'au collège. Mais le magasin fermait à cinq heures et demie et j'étais enfin de retour chez moi vers six heures. C'était une journée longue et fatigante!

Chaque jour je vérifiais les étagères et je les remplissais si nécessaire. J'ouvrais le courrier et je repassais les vêtements. Quelquefois j'ai servi les clients mais je n'ai pas pu utiliser la caisse. Certains clients étaient très gentils et j'ai aimé les aider à choisir quelque chose à porter.

Un jour la propriétaire m'a demandé de faire la vitrine. J'ai donc choisi un pantalon et un chemisier que j'aimais beaucoup et je les ai mis dans la vitrine. La propriétaire en était très contente et nous avons vendu cinq pantalons et dix chemisiers le même jour!

Mais j'ai dû aussi préparer le café pour les autres vendeurs et faire la vaisselle, ce qui était très ennuyeux. Et à la fin de la journée on m'a demandé de balayer. J'ai détesté cette tâche!

Amitiés,
David

Turn over the page to work out which grade you've got.

Working Out Your Grade

- Add up your marks from the Listening, Reading, Speaking and Writing exams.

- Look up your total in the table to see what grade you got. If you're borderline, don't push yourself up a grade — the real examiners won't.

- These grades will only give you a rough guide — they're no guarantee that you'll get this grade in the real exam. It's really important that you do as much practice and revision as possible to help you get the grade you want.

Mark (out of 200)	180+	160 – 179	140 – 159	120 – 139	100 – 119	80 – 99	60 – 79	40 – 59	under 40
Average %	90+	80 – 89	70 – 79	60 – 69	50 – 59	40 – 49	30 – 39	20 – 29	under 19
Grade	A*	A	B	C	D	E	F	G	U

Important:

- This is a higher level paper, but it's still good practice if you're preparing for a foundation level exam. Don't be put off if you found some of the questions really difficult — they'll be more straightforward in the actual foundation exam.

Track 1

Example Je m'appelle Louise, et mon anniversaire est le 7 juin.

1 Je m'appelle Marc, et mon anniversaire est le 16 août.

2 Je m'appelle Élodie, et mon anniversaire est le premier juillet.

3 Je m'appelle Sylvie, et mon anniversaire est le 31 janvier.

Track 2

Example Alors, cette semaine, je suis libre mercredi soir.

4 Moi, je suis libre demain matin.

5 Et moi, je suis libre samedi après-midi.

Track 3

Example Le film commence à trois heures cinq.

6 Bon, je pense que le film commence à deux heures et quart, et finit à quatre heures moins vingt. Alors Pierre, tu dois arriver au cinéma à deux heures moins cinq.

Track 4

Example Pardon, pourriez-vous me passer le sel et le poivre, s'il vous plaît?

1 Pourriez-vous me passer le vin blanc et la bière?

2 Est-ce que je peux avoir le pain et le fromage, s'il vous plaît?

3 Pourriez-vous me passer le café et le sucre, s'il vous plaît?

Track 5

Example Je suis resté au chômage un an après avoir quitté l'université.

4 Les entreprises cherchent toujours les gens qui ont de l'expérience, et bien sûr ce n'était pas mon cas. J'ai donc décidé de faire un stage dans une société d'informatique. Au début je répondais au téléphone, j'écrivais des lettres et faisais des photocopies – rien de très excitant, mais j'étais content d'être là et d'avoir la chance de gagner de l'expérience. Enfin après six mois la société était si contente de moi, qu'ils m'ont proposé un vrai travail d'employé.

Track 6

Example OK, on se retrouve devant la piscine à 2h.

1 D'accord, on se retrouve au centre sportif à midi.

2 Entendu, on se retrouve à la patinoire à 4h45.

3 OK, on se retrouve devant le théâtre à six heures et demie .

Track 7

4 Vous écoutez les détails de nos films au cinéma Rex pour aujourd'hui, lundi. Le premier film commence à 15h35 et il finit à 17h55.

Le prix des billets: pour un adulte, un billet coûte 7,20€, et pour les jeunes, il y a une réduction d'un euro 50. C'est-à-dire, ça va coûter 5,70€.

Track 8

Example Moi j'aime nager le week-end.

5 Et moi chaque jour j'adore chanter.

6 J'aime faire une promenade trois fois par semaine.

7 Je vais à la pêche deux fois par mois.

Track 9

8 Il y a 2 jours, je suis allée au concert au stade. J'ai retrouvé mes amis devant la gare, puis on est allé au stade ensemble. Comme tu sais c'est mon groupe préféré et d'habitude j'aime leur musique, mais il faut dire que le concert n'était pas très bon. Cependant, celui qui jouait de la guitare était excellent.

Track 10

Example Après le collège je rentre chez moi avec quelques amis pour jouer aux jeux électroniques. Je n'aime pas le sport et préfère réfléchir en jouant à un jeu stratégique.

9 Mon hobby c'est la guitare. Je joue de la guitare depuis 6 ans, et j'aime en jouer pour me détendre. Dans le passé, j'en jouais tous les jours, mais maintenant c'est juste de temps en temps.

10 Le mardi et le jeudi soir je suis des cours de danse. J'apprends le ballet, et j'adore. Si j'avais le temps j'aimerais en faire plus souvent, mais ça coûte assez cher.

11 Tous les jours je me lève à 5h30 pour faire du jogging. Je cours dans la ville presque une heure avant de rentrer à la maison pour le petit déjeuner. J'aime commencer ma journée avec de l'exercice.

Track 11

Example Je reçois 8 euros par semaine et je dépense mon argent en achetant des CD et des magazines.

12 Quelle chance. Moi je reçois 6,50€ par semaine et je dépense mon argent en achetant des vêtements et des livres.

13 Je reçois 42€ par mois, et je dépense mon argent en achetant des jeux électroniques et des boissons.

Track 12

Example Voici la météo pour aujourd'hui et demain pour l'Europe. En France, aujourd'hui il fait chaud, et demain il fera très chaud.

1 En Belgique aujourd'hui il fait beau, mais demain il fera du vent.

2 En Suisse aujourd'hui il pleut, et demain il tonnera.

Track 13

3 Bon, voici votre clef. Votre chambre est au 4ème étage au bout du couloir. Ici au rez-de-chaussée vous avez le salon et le restaurant. En ce qui concerne le prix, ça coûte 75€ par nuit pour la chambre, d'accord?

Track 14

Example Moi, je suis restée dans un hôtel avec ma famille pendant 10 jours.

4 Moi, je suis resté dans une auberge de jeunesse avec mes frères pendant une semaine.

5 Moi, je suis restée dans un camping avec mon ami pendant un mois.

Track 15

6 L'année dernière j'avais gagné une compétition à la télé. Le prix était un vol en première classe pour New York — on a passé une semaine formidable.

7 Ma femme est autrichienne. Alors on essaie de rentrer en Autriche au moins une fois par an. J'aime bien le pays, et surtout y aller pour faire du ski.

Track 16

8 Je dépends de ma voiture pour aller partout. Au travail, au supermarché, chez mes amis, pour tout. C'est plus facile en voiture. Les femmes peuvent être en danger si elles sortent toutes seules la nuit. Avec une voiture je suis libre de sortir quand je veux, et être en sécurité. Mais c'est aussi vrai que les voitures sont très polluantes. Je sais aussi que je fais beaucoup moins d'exercice depuis que j'ai une voiture, et ma santé doit en souffrir.

Track 17

Example Comme légumes, on a pommes de terre, choux-fleurs et carottes.

9 Comme viandes, on vous propose du porc, de l'agneau ou du bœuf.

10 Comme fruits, il y a fraises, pommes ou framboises.

11 Ah oui, les crêpes, on les sert à la confiture, au miel ou au chocolat.

Track 18

Example Bon, pour aller au cinéma, allez tout droit et vous verrez le cinéma.

1 Alors pour aller à la gare, tournez à gauche aux feux, et vous verrez la gare.

2 OK, pour aller au commissariat, prenez la troisième rue à droite, et vous verrez le commissariat.

3 Bon, pour changer de l'argent, allez tout droit, et tournez à droite à l'église, et voilà.

Track 19

Example Moi j'aime bien ma ville car il y a un cinéma et j'adore voir des films.

4 Moi j'aime bien vivre ici, car il y a beaucoup à faire et c'est calme.

5 Et moi je n'aime pas du tout ma ville, parce qu'elle est sale, et aussi il n'y a rien à faire.

6 Quant à moi, j'aime vivre ici, car j'habite près du parc et de la piscine.

Track 20

Example Moi j'habite près de l'université. Alors j'y vais à pied.

7 Moi j'habite loin de mon bureau, alors j'y vais d'habitude en moto.

8 Et moi j'habite à deux pas de mon collège, et j'y vais en vélo.

9 Moi j'habite loin du stade, alors je vais aux matchs en car.

Track 21

Example Mon père, il est coiffeur, et ma sœur, elle est étudiante. Moi je suis secrétaire.

1 Mon frère est gendarme, et ma sœur aussi. Moi je suis mécanicien.

2 Alors, ma mère est journaliste, et mon frère est prof. En ce moment, je suis vendeuse.

Track 22

Example Dans mon collège les cours commencent à 8h05 et finissent à 4h55. Lundi matin j'ai espagnol, histoire, maths et français. Ma matière préférée est le français. J'aime ça parce que c'est facile.

3 Mon collège est un peu différent. Les cours commencent à 8h30 et finissent à 5h35. Lundi matin, j'ai dessin, anglais, chimie et maths. Ma matière préférée est la biologie. J'aime ça parce que c'est intéressant.

4 Dans mon collège les cours commencent à 8h10 et finissent à 5h20. Lundi matin j'ai sport, géographie, musique et informatique. Ma matière préférée est l'anglais. J'aime ça parce que c'est facile.

Track 23

Example Ah oui, j'ai un travail à mi-temps dans un magasin, et je gagne neuf euros par heure.

5 Moi je travaille dans un café et je gagne 8,75€ par heure.

6 Et moi j'ai un boulot dans un restaurant et je gagne 9,90€ par heure.

7 Je travaille à mi-temps à la piscine et je gagne 75€ par semaine.

Track 24

8 Bon, je suis assez sûr de ce que je vais faire après mon bac. Ma matière préférée est les maths — oui c'est bizarre mais j'ai un excellent prof. Alors je voudrais étudier les maths à l'université après une année sabbatique en Angleterre peut-être.

Track 25

9 Une fois le bac passé, j'aimerais continuer mes études dans la médecine. J'aime écouter les gens, les aider, et c'est pour cela que je voudrais devenir infirmière. C'est une carrière intéressante et j'ai toujours eu un énorme respect pour ces gens qui soignent les malades. Par contre, tout le monde n'est pas d'accord avec moi. Mes parents préféreraient me voir suivre une autre piste. Ma mère dit que les infirmières sont mal payées, et elle voudrait me voir devenir pharmacienne. Mais moi, je me sentirais beaucoup plus utile dans un hôpital que dans une boutique à vendre des médicaments.

Track 26

10 Je me plais bien au collège. Les matières que j'aime le plus sont l'histoire et le français. Ce que je déteste absolument, ce sont les sciences. C'est si ennuyeux. On a huit heures de science par semaine, et personnellement, je trouve ça beaucoup trop.

11 On a des devoirs pratiquement tous les jours. Je passe à peu près 2 heures par soir à travailler dans ma chambre, et les jeudis soirs sont affreux. J'ai toujours des maths à finir, et j'ai souvent du mal à les comprendre.

Track 27

1 Tu sais après mes examens je vais aller en avion en Grande-Bretagne et je vais rester dans une auberge. Je voudrais bien visiter Londres, surtout les galeries, car j'adore l'art moderne. Si possible je vais faire une excursion dans la région pour voir les châteaux — ce sera chouette.

Track 28

2 Le grand magasin et la pharmacie vont fermer à 18h30 ce soir.

La pâtisserie et la confiserie vont fermer à 18h15.

La librairie et le kiosque à journaux vont fermer à 19h ce soir.

Track 29

Example Alors cet appartement est ancien. Vous avez 2 chambres. Je vais décrire l'intérieur.

3 Le salon est petit et dedans il y a un canapé noir et rouge. Et la cuisine est moderne avec une grande table verte. Votre chambre est jolie avec une petite armoire bleue.

Track 30

Example Je peux recommander des hôtels. Il y a l'Hôtel de la Gare, au 02 64 34 41 13.

4 Il y a aussi le Commerce, au 02 98 75 16 21.

Et puis il y a le Royal, au 02 62 21 15 36.

Et enfin il y a le Lion d'Or au 02 77 85 19 55.

Track 31

5 Message numéro 1: Allô, ici Mme Durocq à l'appareil. Ça s'écrit DUROCQ. Je vous téléphone parce que je voudrais savoir si vous avez reçu mon paquet. Aujourd'hui c'est le mardi 31 octobre, il est maintenant 15h20.

Message numéro 2: Allô, ici Monsieur Grosjean à l'appareil. Ça s'écrit GROSJEAN. Je vous téléphone parce que je voulais confirmer ma réservation. Aujourd'hui c'est le samedi 11 mai, et il est maintenant midi moins le quart. Rappelez-moi s'il vous plaît.

Track 32

6 Voyager en autobus n'est pas cher. Les bus sont fréquents, et coûtent beaucoup moins qu'une voiture. En plus, ça pollue moins l'environnement. Cependant, les jours de grève, quand il n'y a pas de bus, ça peut être difficile. Ça m'énerve parfois d'attendre les bus, spécialement quand ils sont en retard. C'est frustrant, lorsqu'on est pressé. La nuit, il y a moins de bus en service, donc on ne peut pas rentrer tard d'une soirée. Il faut toujours regarder l'heure, pour ne pas manquer le dernier bus.

Track 33

Example Au début j'étais contente de ne pas aller au collège, mais ça fait une semaine et demie que je dois rester au lit avec cette grippe, et j'en ai assez.

7 Je jouais au rugby dans un match hier matin, quand je suis tombé par terre en courant. J'avais très mal au bras toute la soirée et je vais chez le médecin aujourd'hui.

8 Je pense que j'ai besoin de changer mes lunettes. Ça fait trois jours que j'ai des maux de tête quand j'essaie de travailler ou de lire tout simplement.

Track 34

9 Mon argent de poche, c'est une somme misérable — 30€ par mois. Qu'est-ce qu'on peut faire avec 30€? J'aime sortir au cinéma et au café, mais mon argent est toujours vite dépensé.

Track 35

Example Pour moi ce sont les langues et la musique qui me fascinent le plus, et je voudrais une carrière dans les médias, peut-être.

10 Moi j'adore voyager, et au collège je préfère les langues. Alors j'espère trouver un emploi dans le tourisme, si possible.

11 Pour moi mes matières préférées sont les sciences, et je veux une carrière où je peux améliorer la pollution dans les villes. Et ça, c'est une priorité.

Track 36

Example J'ai fait mon stage en entreprise chez Renault, à Lyon. Ce n'était pas bien parce que je n'ai pas aimé la ville.

12 Bon, moi j'ai fait mon stage dans le bureau d'un journal. C'était affreux, car les gens n'étaient pas du tout sympathiques.

13 Alors moi j'ai eu de la chance de faire mon stage dans la bibliothèque de ma ville. C'était excellent parce que j'ai travaillé avec les gens et ça c'était important pour moi.

Track 37

Example Vu que j'habite au centre-ville, et que je fais beaucoup de sport, ce sont les gaz d'échappement qui m'inquiètent le plus.

14 Et pour moi je trouve que le chômage est le plus grand problème. Mon père ne travaille pas depuis longtemps — on n'a pas assez d'argent.

15 Moi et ma famille on est souvent victimes de racisme, et c'est presque impossible pour nous. Les gens dans mon village ne sont pas sympathiques, et moi je me sens très isolé.

Track 38

16 Je m'appelle Marie. J'habite dans une ferme, ça veut dire qu'il y a toujours du travail à faire. Moi je fais un peu de tout. Je donne la nourriture aux animaux, je cherche les œufs des poulets et je suis toujours en train de nettoyer — j'aide beaucoup mes parents.

Je m'appelle Erwan. Parfois je fais la vaisselle à la maison. Parfois je passe l'aspirateur. En général je suis propre et je range bien mes affaires dans ma chambre, mais mes parents ne m'obligent pas à les aider.

Je m'appelle Laëtitia. Je suis la fille aînée donc je travaille pas mal à la maison. Je fais le babysitting pour mes frères et sœurs, avant que mes parents ne rentrent du travail. Quelquefois je fais la cuisine aussi. C'est comme ça que je gagne un peu d'argent de poche.

Je m'appelle Stéphanie. On habite dans un appartement au centre-ville. Mes parents payent une dame qui vient nettoyer chez nous 3 fois par semaine. Tant mieux — comme ça je n'ai pas besoin d'aider à la maison, et j'en suis heureuse.

Je m'appelle Nicolas. Ma mère me demande régulièrement de faire les courses pour elle quand elle n'a pas le temps. Ça ne me plaît pas trop, mais je préfère ça au ménage.

French — English Dictionary

KEY

m:	masculine noun
f:	feminine noun
pl:	plural
v:	verb
vr:	reflexive verb
a:	adjective (describes a noun)
ad:	adverb (describes a verb/adjective)
prep:	preposition (connects the verb to a place, thing or person: e.g. 'to', 'for')
pron:	pronoun (replaces noun: e.g. 'he', 'me')
interj:	interjection (stands alone: e.g. 'Hello!')
conj:	conjunction (connects two parts of a sentence: e.g. 'and', 'because')
art:	article (e.g. 'the', 'a')

A

la A6 f *A6 motorway*
à prep (à la, à l', au, aux) *at, to, in*
abîmer v *to damage*
l' abricot m *apricot*
absent(e) a *absent*
absolument ad *absolutely*
accepter v *to accept*
accompagner v *to accompany*
accro a *addicted*
accueillir v *to welcome*
l' achat m *purchase*
acheter v *to buy*
l' acteur/actrice m/f *actor/actress*
les actualités fpl *news, current affairs*
l' addition f *bill (restaurant)*
l' adolescent(e) m/f *adolescent, teenager*
adorer v *to adore*
l' adresse f *address*
l' adulte m/f *adult*
l' aéroport m *airport*
les affaires fpl *business*
l' affiche f *poster, sign*
affreux/affreuse a *awful*
l' Afrique f *Africa*
agacer v *to annoy*
l' âge m *age*
âgé(e) a *old, aged*
l' agence de voyages f *travel agency*
l' agent de police m *policeman/ woman*
agité(e) a *restless*
agréable a *pleasant*
agresser v *to attack*
agricole a *agricultural*
aider v *to help*
l' ail m *garlic*
aimable a *likeable, friendly*
aimer v *to like, love*
aîné(e) a *older (e.g. sister)*
ainsi ad *in this way*
l' air m *air, appearance*
  avoir l'air (de) *to seem*
  en plein air ad *outdoors*
l' aire de repos f *motorway services*
ajouter v *to add*
l' alcool m *alcohol*
les alentours mpl *surroundings*
l' Algérie f *Algeria*
(l') algérien(ne) a/m/f *Algerian*
l' alimentation f *food, groceries*
l' Allemagne f *Germany*
l' allemand m *German (language)*
(l') allemand(e) a/m/f *German*
aller v *to go*
aller bien/mieux *to be well/better*
l' aller-retour m *return ticket*
l' aller simple m *single ticket*
allô interj *hello (when answering phone)*
alors ad *then*
les Alpes fpl *Alps*
l' alpinisme m *mountaineering*
l' ambiance f *atmosphere*
l' ambulance f *ambulance*
améliorer v *to improve*
aménagé(e) a *flexible (e.g. working hours)*
l' amende f *fine*
(l') américain(e) a/m/f *American*
l' Amérique f *America*
l' ami(e) m/f *friend*
amical(e) a *friendly, amicable*
amicalement ad *in a friendly way*
l' amitié f *friendship*
amitiés *best wishes*
l' amour m *love*
amoureux/amoureuse a *in love*
amusant(e) a *amusing, fun*
amuser v *to amuse*
  s'amuser vr *to enjoy oneself*
l' an m *year*
l' ananas m *pineapple*
ancien(ne) a *old, former*
l' anglais m *English (language)*
(l') anglais(e) a/m/f *English, English person*
l' Angleterre f *England*
l' animal m *animal*
l' animateur/animatrice m/f *presenter*
animé(e) a *lively, animated*
l' année f *year*
l' anniversaire m *birthday*
l' annonce f *advertisement*
l' annuaire m *phone book*
annuler v *to cancel*
l' anorak m *anorak*
l' antenne f *aerial*
l' antenne parabolique f *satellite dish*
(l') août m *August*
à l' appareil *on the telephone*
l' appareil-photo m *camera*
l' appartement m *flat, apartment*
l' appel m *call*
appeler v *to call*
  s'appeler vr *to be called*
l' appétit m *appetite*
apporter v *to bring*
apprécier v *to appreciate*
apprendre v *to learn*
l' apprenti(e) m/f *apprentice*
l' apprentissage m *apprenticeship*
(s')approcher v(r) *to approach*
après prep *after*
après-demain ad *the day after tomorrow*
l' après-midi m/f *afternoon*
l' arbitre m *referee*
l' arbre m *tree*

l' argent m *money*
l' argent de poche m *pocket money*
l' armoire f *wardrobe*
l' arrêt m *stop*
l' arrêt d'autobus m *bus stop*
arrêter v *to stop (something)*
  s'arrêter vr *to stop*
les arrhes fpl *deposit (money)*
l' arrivée f *arrival*
arriver v *to arrive*
l' arrondissement m *district (e.g. in Paris)*
arroser v *to water*
l' art dramatique m *drama*
l' artisan m *craftsman*
l' ascenseur m *lift*
l' assassin m *murderer*
s' asseoir vr *to sit down*
  assieds-toi! *sit down! (informal)*
  asseyez-vous! *sit down! (polite)*
assez ad *quite, enough*
l' assiette f *plate*
l' assurance f *insurance*
l' atelier m *workshop*
l' athlétisme m *athletics*
(l')Atlantique a/m *Atlantic*
attaquer v *to attack*
attendre v *to wait*
l' attention f *attention*
  faire attention *to be careful*
atterrir v *to land*
au = à le — *see à*
au bord de ad *alongside*
au bout de ad *at the end of*
au dehors de ad *outside of*
au fond de ad *at the bottom of*
au milieu de ad *in the middle of*
au revoir interj *goodbye*
au secours! interj *help!*
l' auberge de jeunesse f *youth hostel*
aucun(e) *any*
  ne ... aucun(e) a *no .../ none...*
augmenter v *to increase*
aujourd'hui ad *today*
auparavant ad *before*
aussi ad *too, as well, as*
aussi ... que ad *as ... as*
l' Australie f *Australia*
(l') australien(ne) a/m/f *Australian*
l' auto f *car*
l' autobus m *bus*
l' automne m *autumn*
l' automobiliste m/f *motorist*
l' autoroute f *motorway*
autour (de) prep *around*
autre a *other*
autrement dit *in other words*
l' Autriche f *Austria*
(l') autrichien(ne) a/m/f *Austrian*
aux = à les — *see à*
avaler v *to swallow*
en avance ad *early*
  à l'avance ad *in advance*
avant prep *before, in front of*
l' avantage m *advantage*
avant-hier ad *the day before yesterday*
avec prep *with*
  avec plaisir *gladly*
l' avenir m *future*
  à l'avenir ad *in the future*
l' aventure f *adventure*
l' avenue f *avenue*
l' averse f *shower (of rain)*
l' avion m *plane*
  en avion ad *by plane*
l' avis m *opinion*
avoir v *to have*
  avoir besoin de *to need*
  avoir hâte de *to be eager to*
  avoir lieu *to take place*
  avoir raison *to be right*
  avoir tort *to be wrong*
(l') avril m *April*

B

le baby-sitting m *babysitting*
  faire du baby-sitting *to babysit*
le bac(calauréat) m *baccalauréat (equivalent of A-levels)*
les bagages mpl *luggage*
la bague f *ring*
la baguette f *baguette, stick*
se baigner vr *to bathe*
la baignoire f *bath*
le bain m *bath*
le bal m *ball (dancing)*
la balade f *walk*
le balcon m *balcony, circle (at theatre)*
la balle f *ball*
le ballon m *ball (big, e.g. football)*
la banane f *banana*
la bande f *group*
la bande dessinée f *comic strip*
la banlieue f *suburbs*
la banque f *bank*
le bar m *bar*
barbant(e) a *boring*
la barbe f *beard*
bas(se) a *low*
  en bas ad *downstairs*
  en bas de prep *at the bottom of*
le basket m *basketball*
les baskets fpl *trainers*
le bateau m *boat*
le bâtiment m *building*
la batterie f *drum kit*
battre v *to beat*
bavard(e) a *talkative*
bavarder v *to chat / gossip*
beau/belle a *beautiful*
  il fait beau *it's nice weather*
beaucoup ad *a lot*
beaucoup (de) a *lots of, many*
le beau-fils m *son-in-law, stepson*
le beau-frère m *brother-in-law, stepbrother*
le beau-père m *father-in-law, stepfather*
le bébé m *baby*
(le/la) belge a/m/f *Belgian*
la Belgique f *Belgium*
la belle-fille f *daughter-in-law, stepdaughter*
la belle-mère f *mother-in-law, stepmother*
la belle-sœur f *sister-in-law, stepsister*
les béquilles fpl *crutches*
le besoin m *need*
  avoir besoin de *to need*
bête a *stupid*
la bêtise f *mistake*
le béton m *concrete*
le/la beur m/f *second generation North African immigrant*
le beurre m *butter*
la bibliothèque f *library*
le bic m *biro*
bien ad *well*
  bien cuit a *well done (meat)*
  bien payé(e) a *well paid (job)*
  bien sûr ad *of course*
bientôt ad *soon*
  à bientôt interj *see you soon*
la bienvenue f *welcome*
la bière f *beer*
le bifteck m *steak*
le bijou m *jewel, gem*
la bijouterie f *jewellery*
le billet m *ticket, banknote*
la biologie f *biology*
le biscuit m *biscuit*
la bise f *kiss*
  faire la bise *to kiss someone on both cheeks*
blaguer v *to joke*
blanc(he) a *white*
blessé(e) a *wounded*

bleu(e) a *blue*
blond(e) a *blond(e)*
le blouson m *jacket*
le bœuf m *beef*
bof! interj *huh! (shrug)*
boire v *to drink*
le bois m *wood*
  en bois a *made of wood*
la boisson (gazeuse) f *drink (fizzy)*
la boîte f *tin, can, box*
la boîte aux lettres f *postbox*
le bol m *bowl*
bon(ne) a *good*
bon anniversaire interj *happy birthday*
bon appétit interj *enjoy your meal*
bon marché a *cheap*
bon voyage interj *have a good journey*
bon week-end interj *have a good weekend*
le bonbon m *sweet*
le bonheur m *happiness*
bonjour interj *good day, hello*
bonne année interj *Happy New Year*
bonne chance interj *good luck*
la bonne couleur *the right colour*
bonne fête interj *have a good party*
bonne idée interj *good idea*
bonne nuit interj *good night*
bonnes vacances interj *enjoy your holiday*
bonsoir interj *good evening*
le bord m *edge*
  au bord de la mer *by the sea*
la bouche f *mouth*
le/la boucher/bouchère m/f *butcher*
la boucherie f *butcher's*
le bouchon m *cork, traffic jam*
bouclé(e) a *curly*
la boucle d'oreille f *earring*
le/la boulanger/boulangère m/f *baker*
la boulangerie f *baker's*
les boules fpl *bowls (ball game)*
le boulevard m *boulevard*
bouleverser v *to disrupt*
le boulot m *work, job*
la boum f *party*
la bouteille f *bottle*
la boutique f *small shop*
le bowling m *bowling*
le bras m *arm*
bravo interj *bravo, well done*
le brevet (BEPC) m *equivalent of GCSEs*
le bricolage m *DIY*
briller v *to shine*
la brique f *brick*
  en brique a *made out of brick*
britannique a *British*
la brochure f *booklet, brochure*
se bronzer vr *to sunbathe*
la brosse à dents f *toothbrush*
se brosser les dents/les cheveux vr *to brush one's teeth/hair*
le brouillard m *fog*
  faire du brouillard *to be foggy*
le bruit m *noise*
brûler v *to burn*
la brume f *mist*
brun(e) a *brown*
Bruxelles *Brussels*
bruyant(e) a *noisy, loud*
le buffet m *sideboard, buffet*
le bureau m *office, desk*
le bureau de change m *bureau de change, money exchange*
le bureau des objets trouvés m *lost property office*
le bureau des renseignements m *information service*
le bureau de tabac m *tobacconist's*
le bus m *bus*

*nouns — **m**: masculine*   ***f**: feminine*   ***pl**: plural*   ***v**: verb*   ***vr**: reflexive verb*   ***a**: adjective*

French — English Dictionary

C

c'est *it is*
c'est-à-dire conj *that is to say*
c'est quoi? *what is it?*
c'était *it was*
ça pron *that*
ça dépend *that depends*
ça fait combien?
　how much does that come to?
ça me fait rire *that makes me laugh*
ça ne me dit rien
　that doesn't mean anything to me
ça s'écrit comment?
　how do you spell that?
ça va(?) *I'm okay, how are you?*
ça ne va pas *I'm not great*
ça vaut *it's worth*
la cabine téléphonique f *phone box*
le cadeau m *present*
cadet(te) a *younger (e.g. sister)*
le cadre m *frame*
le café m *coffee, café*
le café-crème m *white coffee*
le cahier m *notebook, exercise book*
la caisse f *counter, checkout*
le/la caissier/caissière m/f *cashier*
le calcul m *calculation, arithmetic*
la calculatrice f *calculator*
calme a *calm*
le camion m *lorry*
cambrioler v *to burgle*
la caméra f *camera*
　(used for filming TV programmes or films)
le caméscope m *video camera*
la campagne f *countryside, campaign*
le camping m *campsite*
　faire du camping
　to go camping
le Canada m *Canada*
(le/la) canadien(ne) a/m/f *Canadian*
le canapé m *sofa, open sandwich*
le cancer m *cancer*
le/la candidat(e) m/f *candidate*
la cantine f *canteen, dining hall*
car conj *because, since*
le car m *coach*
le car de ramassage m *school bus*
la caravane f *caravan*
le carnet m *notebook, book of tickets*
la carotte f *carrot*
carré(e) a *square*
à carreaux a *squared, checked*
le carrefour m *crossroads*
la carrière f *career*
le cartable m *schoolbag, satchel*
la carte f *map, card, menu*
　la carte bancaire f *bank card*
　la carte de crédit f
　　credit card
　la carte d'identité f *ID card*
　la carte postale f *postcard*
　la carte routière f *road map*
le carton m *cardboard*
la case f *square, box*
le casier m *locker*
le casque m *helmet*
la casquette f *baseball cap*
le casse-croûte m *snack, lunch*
casse-pieds a *pain in the neck*
casser v *to break*
la casserole f *saucepan*
la cassette f *cassette tape*
le cassis m *blackcurrant*
la cathédrale f *cathedral*
causer v *to cause, to chat*
la caution f *guarantee (money), deposit*
la cave f *cellar*
le CD m *CD*
le CDI (centre de documentation et d'information) m *school library*

ce, celle, cet, cette, ces pron *this*
la ceinture de sécurité f *safety belt*
cela pron *that (i.e. that thing)*
célèbre a *famous*
célibataire a *single (not married)*
(le) cent a/m *hundred, a (Euro) cent*
le centime m *centime (French equivalent of penny)*
le centimètre m *centimetre*
le centre m *centre*
　le centre commercial m
　　shopping centre
　le centre de loisirs m
　　leisure centre
　le centre de recyclage m
　　recycling centre
　le centre sportif m
　　sports centre
le centre-ville m *city centre*
cependant conj *however*
les céréales fpl *cereal*
la cerise f *cherry*
certainement ad *certainly*
le certificat m *certificate*
le CES = collège d'enseignement secondaire m *secondary school*
ceux pron *these — see ce*
la chaîne m *TV channel*
la chaîne stéréo f *hi-fi system*
la chaise f *chair*
la chaleur f *heat*
la chambre f *bedroom*
　la chambre individuelle/ double/de famille f
　　single/double/family room
　la chambre pour une personne f *room for one person*
　la chambre d'hôte f
　　bed and breakfast
le champ m *field*
le champignon m *mushroom*
la chance f *luck, chance*
　avoir de la chance *to be lucky*
　par chance ad *luckily*
changer v *to change*
la chanson f *song*
chanter v *to sing*
le/la chanteur/chanteuse m/f *singer*
le chapeau m *hat*
chaque a *each*
la charcuterie f *delicatessen, pork butcher's*
chargé(e) a *loaded, laden*
le chariot m *trolley*
le chat m *cat*
châtain(e) a *chestnut coloured*
le château m *castle, palace*
chaud(e) a *warm, hot*
　avoir chaud *to be hot*
　il fait chaud *it's warm*
le chauffage central m
　central heating
chauffé(e) a *heated*
le chauffeur m *driver, chauffeur*
la chaussette f *sock*
la chaussure f *shoe*
le/la chef m/f *boss/chef*
　le/la chef de cuisine m/f
　　head chef
le chemin de fer m *railway*
la chemise f *shirt*
le chèque (de voyage) m
　(traveller's) cheque
cher/chère a, cher ad
　dear, expensive
chercher v *to search for, to look for*
le cheval m *horse*
les cheveux mpl *hair*
la cheville f *ankle*
chez prep *chez moi/toi at my/your house*
chic a *stylish*
le chien m *dog*
les chiffres mpl *numbers, figures*

la chimie f *chemistry*
la Chine f *China*
(le/la) chinois(e) a/m/f
　Chinese (person)
les chips mpl *crisps*
le chocolat m *chocolate*
le chocolat chaud m *hot chocolate*
choisir v *to choose*
le choix m *choice*
le chômage m *unemployment*
la chose f *thing*
le chou m *cabbage*
le chou-fleur m *cauliflower*
(le/la) chrétien(ne) a/m/f *Christian*
le cidre m *cider*
le ciel m *sky, heaven*
la cigarette f *cigarette*
le cinéma m *cinema*
(le) cinq a/m *five*
　cinquante a/m *fifty*
　cinquième a *fifth*
　en cinquième *in year 8*
la circulation f *traffic*
le cirque m *circus*
la cité f *housing estate, city*
le citron m *lemon*
la civière f *stretcher*
clair(e) a *light (colour), clear*
la classe f *class*
classer v *to file*
le clavier m *keyboard*
la clé, clef f *key*
le/la client(e) m/f *customer*
le climat m *climate*
cliquer v *to click*
le club m *club*
　le club des jeunes m *youth club*
le coca m *Coca-Cola®*
cocher v *to tick*
le cochon d'Inde m *guinea-pig*
la cochonnerie f *disgusting food*
le code postal m *postal code*
le cœur m *heart*
le/la coiffeur/coiffeuse m/f
　hairdresser
le coin m *corner*
la colère f *anger*
le colis m *parcel*
collectionner v *to collect*
le collège m *school (secondary)*
le/la collègue m/f *colleague*
la colline f *hill*
la colonie de vacances f *holiday camp*
combien ad *how much, how many*
　c'est combien? *how much is it?*
la comédie f *comedy*
comique a *funny*
commander v *to order*
comme prep *like*
　comme ci comme ça ad *so-so*
commencer v *to start*
　pour commencer *to start with, to begin with*
comment ad *how*
comment dit-on ... en français?
　how do you say ... in French?
le commerce m *business*
le/la commerçant(e) m/f *shopkeeper*
commercial(e) a *commercial*
le commissariat m *police station*
comparer v *to compare*
complet/complète a *full, complete*
compléter v *to complete*
compliqué(e) a *complicated*
comporter v *to consist of*
composer v *to compose*
composé(e) de *composed of*
composter v *to stamp (ticket)*
compréhensif/compréhensive a *understanding*
comprendre v *to understand*

le comprimé m
　tablet (to swallow)
compris(e) a *inclusive*
　non compris(e) a
　　not included
le/la comptable m/f *accountant*
le compte m *account*
compter (sur) v *to count (on)*
concerner v *to concern*
　en ce qui concerne...
　　as far as ... is concerned
le concert m *concert*
le concours m *competition*
le/la conducteur/conductrice m/f
　driver
conduire v *to drive*
la confiance f *confidence*
confirmer v *to confirm*
la confiserie f *sweetshop*
la confiture f *jam*
le confort m *comfort*
confortable a *comfortable*
le congé m *holiday*
congeler v *to freeze*
la connaissance f *knowledge*
connaître v *to know (e.g. a person)*
se consacrer à vr *to devote oneself to*
le conseil m *advice*
le conseiller (d'orientation) m
　(careers) advisor
la consigne (automatique) f
　left luggage (lockers)
la consommation f *consumption*
construire v *to build*
contacter v *to contact*
content(e) a *happy*
le contenu m *contents*
continuer v *to continue*
(le) contraire a/m *opposite*
le contrat m *contract*
contre prep *against*
le contrôle m *test*
convenir à v *to suit*
le/la copain/copine m/f *friend*
copier v *to copy*
le corps m *body*
correct(e) a *correct*
la correspondance f *connection*
le/la correspondant(e) m/f
　correspondent, penfriend
corriger v *to correct*
la Corse f *Corsica*
la côte f *coast*
le côté m *side*
　à côté de prep *next to*
le coton m *cotton*
　en coton a *made of cotton*
le cou m *neck*
la couche d'ozone f *ozone layer*
se coucher vr *to go to bed*
la couleur f *colour*
le couloir m *corridor*
le coup m *knock, blow*
　le coup de feu m *(gun)shot*
　le coup de poing m *punch*
　le coup de soleil m *sunburn*
　le coup de téléphone m
　　phone call
couper v *to cut*
la cour f *yard, playground*
couramment ad *fluently*
courir v *to run*
le courrier (électronique) m *post, (email)*
le courrier du cœur m *problem page*
le cours m *lesson*
le cours de change m *exchange rate*
la course f *running*
les courses fpl *shopping*
　faire les courses *to go shopping*
court(e) a *short*
le/la cousin(e) m/f *cousin*

le couteau m *knife*
coûter v *to cost*
la couture f *sewing*
couvert(e) a *overcast (weather)*
couvrir v *to cover*
la cravate f *tie*
le crayon m *pencil*
la crème f *cream*
　la crème solaire f *suncream*
la crêpe f *pancake*
crevé(e) a *burst, punctured*
la crise cardiaque f *heart attack*
critiquer v *to criticize*
croire v *to believe*
le croissant m *croissant*
le croque-monsieur m
　cheese and ham toastie
cru(e) a *raw*
les crudités fpl *raw salad items*
la cuiller, cuillère f *spoon*
la cuillerée f *spoonful*
le cuir m *leather*
la cuisine f *kitchen*
la cuisinière f (à gaz / électrique)
　stove, cooker (gas / electric)
la cuisse f *thigh*
cultiver v *to cultivate, to grow*
le cyclisme m *cycling*

D

d'abord ad *first (of all)*
d'accord inter *OK, I agree*
d'habitude ad *normally, usually*
d'occasion a *used, secondhand*
d'origine (africaine) f *native, of (African) origin*
la dame f *lady*
le danger m *danger*
dangereux/dangereuse a
　dangerous
dans prep *in, into*
　dans le bon ordre *in the right order*
danser v *to dance*
la date f *date (of year)*
de prep (du, de la, de l', des)
　of, from, some
　de bonne heure ad *early*
　de chaque côté ad *from each side*
　de l'autre côté *on the other side*
　de la part de qui? *Who's it from?*
　de rien *don't mention it*
　de temps en temps ad
　　from time to time
　de tous côtés ad *from all sides*
débarquer v *to get off (e.g boat)*
débarrasser v *to clear*
se débrouiller vr *to get on with, to manage*
le début m *start, début*
(le) décembre m *December*
les déchets mpl *rubbish*
déchiré(e) a *torn*
décider v *to decide*
décoller v *to take off*
décrire v *to describe*
décrocher v *to pick up (telephone)*
déçu(e) a *disappointed*
dedans ad *inside*
défense (f) de fumer *no smoking*
le défilé m *procession*
dégoûtant(e) a *disgusting*
le degré m *degree*
dehors ad *outside*
déjà ad *already*
le déjeuner m *lunch,*
déjeuner v *to have lunch*
délicieux/délicieuse a *delicious*
demain ad *tomorrow*
　à demain interj *see you tomorrow*
demander v *to ask*
déménager v *to move house*
demi(e) a *half*
　deux heures et demie
　　half past two

ad: adverb　　**prep**: preposition　　**pron**: pronoun　　**interj**: interjection　　**conj**: conjunction

French — English Dictionary

le demi-frère m *half-brother*
la demi-pension f *half-board*
le/la demi-pensionnaire m/f *day pupil*
la demi-sœur f *half-sister*
démodé(e) a *old-fashioned*
démuni(e) a *destitute*
le denim m *denim*
la dent f *tooth*
le dentifrice m *toothpaste*
le/la dentiste m/f *dentist*
dépanner v *to fix, repair*
le départ m *departure*
le département m *department (equivalent of county)*
dépassé(e) a *old-fashioned*
dépasser v *to go past*
dépêcher v *to send*
se dépêcher vr *to hurry*
dépenser v *to spend*
le dépliant m *leaflet*
déposer v *drop off, put down*
depuis prep *since, for*
déranger v *to disturb*
dernier/dernière a *last, previous*
derrière prep *behind*
des = de les — *see de*
dès prep *from*
désagréable a *unpleasant, disagreeable*
le désavantage m *disadvantage*
descendre v *to go down*
se déshabiller vr *to get undressed*
désirer v *to desire*
désolé(e) a *sorry*
le dessert m *dessert*
le dessin m *art, drawing*
le dessin animé m *cartoon*
dessiner v *to draw*
la destination f *destination*
le détail m *detail*
détester v *to hate*
le détritus m *litter*
détruire v *to destroy*
(le) deux a/m *two*
deuxième a *second*
devant prep *in front of*
devenir v *to become*
la déviation f *diversion*
devoir v *to have to*
les devoirs mpl *homework*
le dialogue m *dialogue*
la différence f *difference*
différent(e) a *different*
difficile a *difficult*
la difficulté f *difficulty*
(le) dimanche m *Sunday*
dîner v *to dine*
le dîner m *supper*
le diplôme m *degree*
dire v *to say*
ça (te/vous) dit quelque chose? *does that mean anything to you?*
direct(e) a *direct*
le/la directeur/directrice m/f *headteacher, manager*
la direction f *direction, management*
la discipline f *discipline*
la disco(thèque) f *disco*
discuter v *to discuss, to talk*
disparaître v *to disappear*
la disparition f *disappearance*
en voie de disparition a *endangered (e.g. species)*
disponible a *available*
la dispute f *quarrel*
se disputer vr *to argue*
le disque m *record*
le disque compact m *compact disc*
la distance f *distance*
distribuer v *to distribute*
le distributeur (automatique) de billets m *cashpoint*
divorcé(e) a *divorced*
(le) dix a/m *ten*

(le) dix-sept a/m *seventeen*
(le) dix-huit a/m *eighteen*
(le) dix-neuf a/m *nineteen*
la dizaine f *about ten, ten or so*
le docteur m *doctor*
le documentaire m *documentary*
le doigt m *finger*
le domicile m *home*
le dommage m *damage*
donc ad *therefore*
donner v *to give*
donner un coup de main *to lend a hand*
dont pron *of which, of whom*
dormir v *to sleep*
le dortoir m *dormitory*
le dos m *back*
la douane f *customs*
doubler v *to repeat a year, to overtake*
la douche f *shower*
doué(e) a *gifted*
la douleur f *pain*
Douvres *Dover*
doux, douce a *soft, mild (weather)*
la douzaine f *dozen, about twelve*
(le)douze a/m *twelve*
le drapeau m *flag*
la drogue f *drug(s)*
drogué(e) a *drugged, on drugs*
se droguer vr *to take drugs*
droit(e) a *straight, right*
tout droit ad *straight on*
la droite f *right*
tournez à droite *turn right*
drôle a *funny*
du = de le — *see de*
dur(e) a/ad *hard, harsh*
à durée déterminée ad *for a fixed period of time*
durer v *to last*

E

l' eau f *water*
l'eau minérale f *mineral water*
l'eau potable / non potable f *drinking water / non-drinking water*
l' échange m *exchange*
échanger v *to exchange, to swap*
les échecs mpl *chess*
échouer (à) v *to fail (at)*
l' éclaircie f *sunny spell*
l' école f *school*
l'école primaire f *primary school*
les économies fpl *savings*
faire des économies *to save money*
(l')écossais(e) a/m/f *Scottish, Scot*
l' Écosse f *Scotland*
écouter v *to listen*
l' écran m *screen*
écraser v *to crush*
écrire v *to write*
s'écrire vr *to write to each other, to be spelt*
comment ça s'écrit? *how is that spelt?*
Édimbourg *Edinburgh*
l' éducation physique f *P.E.*
l' effet de serre m *greenhouse effect*
effrayant(e) a *frightening*
égal(e) a *equal*
ça m'est égal *I don't mind*
l' égalité f *equality*
l' église f *church*
égoïste a *selfish*
l' électricien(ne) m/f *electrician*
électrique a *electric*
électronique a *electrical, electronic*
l' élève m/f *pupil*
l' emballage m *package, packaging*

embarquer v *to embark*
l' embouteillage m *traffic jam*
l' émission f *programme (e.g. TV)*
l'émission jeunesse f *children's programme*
l'émission musicale f *music programme*
l'émission sportive f *sports programme*
emmener v *to take (along)*
empêcher (de faire) v *to prevent (from doing)*
l' emplacement m *pitch (for tent)*
l' emploi m *job*
l' emploi du temps m *timetable, schedule*
l' employé(e) m/f *employee*
emprunter v *to borrow*
en prep *in, to, by (e.g. by plane), made of (e.g. of wool)*
enchanté(e) a *delighted (e.g. to meet someone)*
encore ad *still, yet, another*
encore du/de la a *more*
encore une fois ad *once more*
pas encore ad *not yet*
encourager v *to encourage*
s'endormir vr *to go to sleep*
l' endroit m *place, area*
l' énergie f *power*
l'énergie nucléaire f *nuclear power*
énerver v *to annoy*
s'énerver vr *to get annoyed*
l' enfant m/f *child*
enfin ad *at last*
ennuyeux/ennuyeuse a *boring, annoying*
enregistrer v *to record*
enrichissant(e) a *enriching*
enrhumé(e) a *having a cold*
l' enseignement m *teaching*
ensemble a *together*
l'ensemble m *whole*
dans l'ensemble *on the whole*
ensoleillé(e) a *sunny*
ensuite ad *next*
entendre v *to hear*
s'entendre vr *to get on*
entendu(e) a *understood, agreed*
enthousiaste a *enthusiastic*
l' entorse f *sprain*
entre prep *between*
l' entrée f *entrance, admission, first course*
entrer v *to go in*
l' entrevue f *interview, discussion*
l' enveloppe f *envelope*
l' envie f *want, desire*
avoir envie de *to want to*
environ ad *around*
l' environnement m *environment*
envoyer v *to send*
l' épaule f *shoulder*
épeler v *to spell*
l' épicerie f *grocery*
l' épicier/épicière m/f *grocer*
éplucher v *to peel*
épouser v *to marry*
l' épouvante f *fear, terror*
l' épreuve f *test*
l' EPS = éducation physique et sportive f *P.E.*
épuiser v *to exhaust*
équilibré(e) a *balanced*
l' équipe f *team*
l' équitation f *riding (horses)*
l' erreur f *mistake*
l' escalier m *staircase*
l' escrime f *fencing (sport)*
l' espace m *space*
l' Espagne f *Spain*
l' espagnol m *Spanish (language)*
(l')espagnol(e) a/m/f *Spanish, Spaniard*
l' espèce f *species*

espérer v *to hope*
l' espoir m *hope*
essayer (de) v *to try (to)*
l' essence f *petrol*
essuyer v *to wipe*
l' est m *east*
est-ce que...? *is ... ?*
l' estivant(e) m/f *summer holidaymaker*
l' estomac m *stomach*
et conj *and*
l' établissement m *establishment*
l' étage m *storey, floor*
l' étagère f *shelf*
l' état m *state*
les États-Unis mpl *United States*
l' été m *summer*
éteindre v *to turn off, put out*
l' étoile f *star*
étonné(e) a *surprised*
étonner v *to surprise*
à l'étranger ad *abroad*
être v *to be*
étroit(e) a *narrow*
l' étude f *study*
l' étudiant(e) m/f *student*
étudier v *to study*
l' euro m *euro*
l' Europe f *Europe*
l' événement m *event*
l' évier m *sink*
éviter v *to avoid*
exact(e) a *exact*
exactement ad *exactly*
l' examen m *exam*
excellent(e) a *excellent*
l' excursion f *trip, excursion*
l'excursion scolaire f *school trip*
s'excuser vr *to apologise*
l' exemple m *example*
par exemple *for example*
expérimenté(e) a *experienced*
expliquer v *to explain*
l' exposition f *exhibition*
exprès ad *on purpose*
extra a *fantastic*

F

fabriquer v *to make*
la fac f *university*
en face (de) ad/prep *opposite*
fâché(e) a *angry*
facile a *easy*
le/la facteur/factrice m/f *postman/ woman*
facultatif/facultative a *optional*
la faculté f *faculty, department*
faible a *weak*
la faim f *hunger*
avoir faim *to be hungry*
faire v *to do, make*
faire correspondre *to match up*
faire du lèche-vitrine *to go window-shopping*
faire le ménage *to do the housework*
le fait divers m *(short) news item*
familial(e) a *family, domestic*
la famille f *family*
(le/la) fana a/m/f *fanatical, fan*
fantastique a *fantastic*
la farine f *flour*
fatigant(e) a *tiring*
fatigué(e) a *tired*
faut *see il faut*
la faute f *fault*
le fauteuil m *armchair*
faux/fausse a *false, wrong*
favori(e) a *favourite*
les félicitations fpl *congratulations*
féliciter v *to congratulate*
la femme f *woman*
la femme de chambre f *chambermaid, housekeeper*
la fenêtre f *window*

le fer m *iron*
férié *see jour férié*
la ferme f *farm*
fermé(e) a *closed*
fermer v *to shut*
la fermeture (annuelle) f *closing, closure (for holidays)*
la fermeture éclair f *zip*
le/la fermier/fermière m/f *farmer*
la fête f *party, feast, saint's day*
fêter v *to celebrate*
le feu m *fire*
le feu d'artifice m *firework*
le feu rouge m *red light*
les feux mpl *traffic lights*
le feuilleton m *soap opera*
(le) février m *February*
les fiançailles fpl *engagement*
la fiche f *sheet, form*
se fier v *to trust*
fier / fière a *proud*
la fièvre f *fever*
la filière (scientifique) f *(scientific) course of study*
la fille f *girl, daughter*
le film m *film*
film d'aventures m *adventure film*
film comique m *comedy*
film d'amour m *love story*
film d'épouvante m *horror film*
film de guerre m *war film*
film d'horreur m *horror film*
film policier m *detective film*
film de science-fiction m *science fiction film*
le fils m *son*
la fin f *end*
finir v *to finish*
la Finlande f *Finland*
(le/la) finlandais(e) a/m/f *Finnish, Finn*
le flash m *flash, news flash*
le fléau m *curse, pest*
la flèche f *arrow*
la fleur f *flower*
le fleuve m *river*
le flic m *cop, police officer*
la foire f *fair, market*
la fois f *time*
foncé(e) a *dark*
le fond m *bottom*
au fond de prep *at the bottom, back of*
le foot(ball) m *football*
la forêt f *forest*
la formation f *training*
formation continue f *further (vocational) education*
formation permanente f *continuing education*
la forme f *shape*
être en forme *to be fit*
formidable a *great*
le formulaire m *form*
fort(e) a *strong, loud*
le four m *oven*
le four à micro-ondes m *microwave*
la fourchette f *fork*
fournir v *to supply*
le fournisseur m *supplier*
frais/fraîche a *fresh*
la fraise f *strawberry*
la framboise f *raspberry*
le franc m *franc*
le français m *French (language)*
(le/la) français(e) m/f *French, French person*
la France f *France*
franchement ad *frankly, honestly*
francophone a *French-speaking*
frapper v *to hit, strike*
le frein m *brake*
le frère m *brother*
le frigo m *fridge*
frisé(e) a *curly (e.g. hair)*

nouns — **m**: masculine **f**: feminine **pl**: plural **v**: verb **vr**: reflexive verb **a**: adjective

French — English Dictionary

les frites fpl *chips*
froid(e) a *cold*
   avoir froid *to be cold*
   il fait froid *it's cold*
le fromage m *cheese*
le fruit m *fruit*
les fruits de mer mpl *seafood*
la fumée f *smoke*
fumer v *to smoke*
le/la fumeur/fumeuse m/f *smoker*
fumeur/fumeuse a *smoking*

G

gâcher v *to spoil, to waste*
gagner v *to win, to earn*
le gallois m *Welsh (language)*
(le/la) gallois(e) a/m/f
   Welsh, Welsh person
la gamme f *range, scale*
le gant m *glove*
le garage m *garage*
le garçon m *boy, waiter*
   Garçon! interj *Waiter!*
le garçon de café m *waiter*
garder v *to keep*
la gare f *station*
   la gare routière f
       coach station
   la gare maritime f *port*
garer v *to park*
le gâteau m *cake*
gâter v *to spoil*
(la) gauche f/a *left*
   tournez à gauche *turn left*
le gaz m *gas*
   le gaz carbonique m
       carbon dioxide
   les gaz d'échappement mpl
       exhaust fumes
le gazon m *grass, lawn*
geler v *to freeze*
le/la gendarme m/f
   policeman/woman
gêner v *to bother*
en général ad *generally, usually*
généralement ad *generally*
généreux/généreuse a *generous*
génial(e) a *great, of genius*
le genou m *knee*
le genre m *type, kind, sort*
les gens mpl *people*
gentil(le) a *nice, kind*
la géographie f *geography*
le gigot d'agneau m *leg of lamb*
le gîte m *self-catering cottage*
la glace f *ice cream*
le golf m *golf*
la gomme f *rubber*
la gorge f *throat*
le gosse m *kid*
le goût m *taste*
goûter v *to taste*
le goûter m *tea, snack*
les graffiti mpl *graffiti*
le gramme m *gram*
grand(e) a *big, great*
   le grand magasin m
       department store
   la grande surface f
       hypermarket
   les grandes vacances fpl
       summer holidays
la Grande-Bretagne f
   Great Britain
la grand-mère f *grandmother*
le grand-père m *grandfather*
les grands-parents mpl *grandparents*
gras(se) a *fatty*
le gratin dauphinois m *potatoes*
   with cheese topping
gratuit(e) a *free (no cost)*
grave a *serious*
(le/la) grec/grecque a/m/f *Greek*
la Grèce f *Greece*
le grenier m *attic*
la grève f *strike (industrial)*
griffé(e) a *scratched, designer*
la grille f *gate, grid*
la grippe f *flu*

gris(e) a *grey*
gros(se) a *fat, big*
le groupe m *group*
guérir v *to cure*
la guerre f *war*
le guichet m *ticket office*
la guitare f *guitar*
le gymnase m *gymnasium*
la gymnastique f *gymnastics*

H

habile a *skilful*
s'habiller vr *to get dressed*
l' habitant(e) m/f *inhabitant*
habiter v *to live in*
l' habitude f *habit*
   d'habitude *usually*
   comme d'habitude *as usual*
s' habituer vr *to get used to*
haïr v *to hate, to detest*
le hamburger m *hamburger*
le hamster m *hamster*
le handball m *handball*
le haricot vert m *green bean*
haut(e) a *high*
   en haut ad *upstairs*
   en haut de prep
       at the top of
la hauteur f *height*
hélas interj *alas*
hésiter v *hesitate*
l' heure f *hour*
   à l'heure ad *on time*
   à quelle heure?
       at what time?
   de bonne heure ad *early*
   l'heure d'affluence f
       rush hour
   l'heure du déjeuner f
       dinner time
heurter v *to collide*
heureux/heureuse a *happy*
hier ad *yesterday*
la hi-fi f *hi-fi, stereo*
l' histoire f *history, story*
historique a *historical*
l' hiver m *winter*
le HLM m = habitation à
   loyer modéré *council flat*
le hockey m *hockey*
(le/la) hollandais(e) a/m/f
   Dutch, Dutch person
la Hollande f *Holland*
l' homme m *man*
la honte f *shame*
l' hôpital m *hospital*
l' horaire m *timetable*
l' horreur f *horror*
   avoir horreur de
       to loathe, to detest
l' hors-d'œuvre m *starter*
l' hospitalité f *hospitality*
l' hôtel m *hotel*
l' hôtel de ville m *town hall*
l' hôtesse de l'air f *air hostess*
l' huile f *oil*
(le) huit a/m *eight*
humide a *damp (weather)*
l' hypermarché m *hypermarket*

I

ici ad *here*
l' idée f *idea*
identifier v *to identify*
idiot(e) a *idiot, idiotic*
il faut *(we) must,*
   it is necessary to
il manque (un bouton)
   (a button) is missing
il me faut *I need*
il me reste *I've got ... left*
il me reste 3 euros *I've got 3*
   euros left
il n'y a pas *there isn't/aren't*
il s'agit de *it's about, it's a*
   question of
il y a *there is, there are*
il y a trois ans *three years ago*

il y avait *there was, there were*
l' île f *island*
l' illustration f *illustration*
l' image f *picture*
l' immatriculation f
   registration, enrolment
l' immeuble m *building, flats*
l' immigré(e) m/f *immigrant*
impatient(e) a *impatient*
l' imper(méable) m *raincoat*
impoli(e) a *impolite*
important(e) a *important*
importer v *to import, to matter*
   n'importe quel(le) a *any*
   n'importe qui pron *any*
   person
l' imprimante f *printer*
imprimer v *to print*
inadmissible a *intolerable,*
   unacceptable
l' incendie m *fire*
l' inconnu(e) m/f *stranger,*
   unknown (person)
l' inconvénient m *disadvantage*
l' Inde f *India*
l' indicatif m *indicative (verb form)*
(l') indien(ne) a/m/f *Indian*
indiquer v *to indicate*
individuel(le) a *individual*
industriel(le) a *industrial*
l' infirmier/infirmière m/f *nurse*
l' informaticien(ne) m/f *computer*
   scientist
les informations (les infos) fpl *news*
l' informatique f *computer science*
l' ingénieur m *engineer*
l' inondation f *flood*
inquiet/inquiète a *worried*
s' inquiéter vr *to worry*
l' insolation f *sunstroke*
l' insonorisation f *sound-proofing*
l' instant m *moment*
l' instituteur/institutrice m/f
   primary school teacher
l' instruction civique f *citizenship*
intelligent(e) a *intelligent*
interdit(e) a *prohibited*
intéressant(e) a *interesting*
intéresser v *to interest*
s' intéresser à vr
   to be interested in
introduire v *to introduce*
inutile a *useless*
l' invitation f *invitation*
inviter v *to invite*
(l') irlandais(e) a/m/f *Irish, Irish*
   person
l' Irlande f *Ireland*
l' Irlande du Nord f *Northern*
   Ireland
l' Italie f *Italy*
(l') italien(ne) a/m/f *Italian*
l' IUT m *polytechnic,*
   technical school
ivre a *drunk*

J

j'en ai marre
   I've had enough, I'm fed up
jaloux/jalouse a *jealous*
jamais — ne...jamais ad *never*
la jambe f *leg*
le jambon m *ham*
(le) janvier m *January*
le Japon m *Japan*
(le/la) japonais(e) a/m/f
   Japanese, Japanese person
le jardin m *garden*
le jardin zoologique m
   zoological garden
le jardinage m *gardening*
jaune a *yellow*
je ne sais pas *I don't know*
je veux bien *I'm happy to*
le jean m *jeans*
jeter v *to throw (away)*
le jeu m *game*
jeu de cartes m *card game*

jeu de société m *board game*
jeu vidéo m *video game*
(le) jeudi m *Thursday*
jeune a *young*
le job m *job*
le jogging m *tracksuit, jogging*
joli(e) a *pretty*
jouer v *to play*
   jouer + à *to play a sport*
   jouer + de *to play an*
       instrument
le jouet m *game, toy*
le jour m *day*
le jour de congé m *day off (leave)*
le jour férié m *public holiday*
le journal m *newspaper*
la journée f *day*
joyeux/joyeuse a *happy*
le judo m *judo*
le/la juge m/f *judge*
juif/juive a *Jewish*
(le) juillet m *July*
(le) juin m *June*
jumelé(e) a *twin, twinned*
la jupe f *skirt*
le jus m *juice*
   le jus de fruit m *fruit juice*
   le jus d'orange m *orange*
       juice
jusqu'à prep *until, as far as*
juste a *just, fair*

K

le kilo m *kilo(gram)*
le kilomètre m *kilometre*
   à ... kilomètres *...kilometres*
   away

L

là ad *there*
   là-bas ad *over there*
le laboratoire m *laboratory*
le lac m *lake*
laid(e) a *ugly*
la laine f *wool*
laisser v *to leave*
le lait m *milk*
laitier/laitière a *dairy*
la laitue f *lettuce*
la lampe f *lamp*
la langue f *language, tongue*
   les langues vivantes fpl
       modern languages
le lapin m *rabbit*
large a *wide, broad*
le lavabo m *washbasin*
laver v *to wash*
   se laver vr *to wash oneself*
le lave-vaisselle m *dishwasher*
la leçon f *lesson*
le lecteur m *reader, scanner*
   le lecteur DVD m *DVD*
       player
   le lecteur mp3 m *MP3 player*
la lecture f *reading*
léger/légère a *light*
le légume m *vegetable*
le lendemain m *the next day*
lent(e) a *slow*
lentement ad *slowly*
les lentilles de contact fpl *contact*
   lenses
la lessive f *washing powder,*
   washing
la lettre f *letter*
la levée f *collection (postal)*
lever v *to raise*
   se lever vr *to get up*
la librairie f *bookshop*
libre a *free*
licencier v *to dismiss,*
   to make redundant
le lieu m *place*
   avoir lieu *to take place*
la ligne f *line*
la limonade f *lemonade*
lire v *to read*
la liste f *list*

le lit m *bed*
   le grand lit m *double bed*
   faire le lit *to make the bed*
le litre m *litre*
le livre m *book*
la livre sterling f *pound sterling*
livrer v *to deliver*
le local m *premises*
la location f *rental, hire*
   la location de voitures f
       car rental
le logement m *accommodation*
loger v *to stay*
loin (de) ad/prep *far (from)*
le loisir m *leisure*
Londres *London*
long(ue) a *long*
   le long de prep *along*
   longtemps ad *for a long time*
la longueur f *length*
le look m *look, image, style*
louer v *to hire*
le loyer m *rent*
la lumière f *light*
(le) lundi m *Monday*
les lunettes fpl *glasses*
   les lunettes de soleil fpl
       sunglasses
lutter (contre) v *to fight (against)*
le lycée m *secondary school*
   le lycée technique m
       secondary school for
       vocational training

M

le machin m *thing, contraption*
la machine f *machine*
la machine à laver f *washing*
   machine
Madame f *Mrs, Madam*
Mademoiselle f *Miss*
   Mademoiselle! interj
       Waitress!
le magasin m *shop*
le magazine m *magazine*
(le/la) maghrébin(e) a/m/f *North*
   African
le magnétoscope m *video recorder*
magnifique a *magnificent*
(le) mai m *May*
maigre a *thin*
le maillot m *vest*
le maillot de bain m
   swimming costume
la main f *hand*
maintenant ad *now*
la mairie f *town hall*
mais conj *but*
la maison f *house*
   la maison des jeunes (MJC —
      la maison des jeunes et de la
      culture) f *youth club*
   la maison individuelle f
      detached house
   la maison jumelée f
      semi-detached house
   la maison de la presse f
      newsagent's
le maître nageur m *swimming*
   instructor
le mal m *pain, evil*
   avoir mal à *to have a pain in*
mal ad *badly*
   mal payé(e) a *badly paid*
(le/la) malade a/m/f *ill, ill person*
la maladie f *illness*
malheureusement ad
   unfortunately
malheureux/malheureuse a
   unhappy, unlucky
la maman f *mum*
la Manche f *the Channel*
manger v *to eat*
la manifestation f *demonstration*
le mannequin m *model (person),*
   mannequin
manquer v *to miss*
le manteau m *coat*

---

ad: adverb   **prep**: preposition   **pron**: pronoun   **interj**: interjection   **conj**: conjunction

French — English Dictionary

le maquillage m *make-up*
le/la marchand(e) m/f *shopkeeper*
le marché m *market*
marcher v *to walk, to work*
(le) mardi m *Tuesday*
la marée f *tide, flood*
le mari m *husband*
le mariage m *marriage*
marié(e) a *married*
se marier vr *to get married*
le marketing m *marketing*
le Maroc m *Morocco*
(le/la) marocain(e) a/m/f *Moroccan*
la marque f *brand, label*
marquer v *to mark, write down*
marron a *brown (eyes, hair)*
(le) mars m *March*
le Massif Central m *mountainous region near the centre of France*
le match m *match (sport)*
la maternelle f *reception class*
les maths fpl *maths*
la matière f *subject*
les matières grasses fpl *fat content*
le matin m *morning*
matinal(e) a *morning*
être matinal(e)
    to be a morning person
la matinée f *morning*
    faire la grasse matinée
        to have a lie-in
mauvais(e) a *bad*
    il fait mauvais
        the weather's bad
    la mauvaise taille f *the wrong size*
le/la mécanicien(ne) m/f *mechanic*
méchant(e) a *nasty, naughty*
le médecin m *doctor*
le médicament m *medicine*
la Méditerranée f *Mediterranean Sea*
meilleur(e) a *better*
    meilleurs vœux *best wishes*
le membre m *member*
même ad *even*
même a *same*
le ménage m *household, housework*
mener v *to lead*
la mentalité f *mentality, attitude*
mentir v *to lie*
le menu m *set menu*
    menu à 15 euros m
        set menu at 15 euros
    menu à prix fixe m
        fixed-price menu
    menu touristique m
        tourist menu
la mer f *sea*
merci interj *thank you*
(le) mercredi m *Wednesday*
la mère f *mother*
la merguez f *spicy sausage*
merveilleux/merveilleuse a *marvellous*
le message m *message*
mesurer v *to measure*
le métal m *metal*
la météo f *weather forecast*
le métier m *job, profession*
le mètre m *metre*
    à ... mètres *... metres away*
le métro m *underground (tube)*
le metteur en scène m *director (of a play or film)*
mettre v *to put*
    mettre à la poste *to post*
    mettre dans le bon ordre
        to put in the right order
    se mettre en route
        to take to the road
le meuble m *piece of furniture*
(le) midi m *midday*
le Midi m *South of France*
mieux ad *better*
mignon(ne) a *cute, sweet, nice*
le milieu m *middle*

au milieu de prep
    in the middle of
le million m *million*
mi-long(ue) a *shoulder-length (hair)*
mince a *slim*
(le) minuit m *midnight*
la minute f *minute*
    à ... minutes *in ... minutes' time*
le miroir m *mirror*
la mi-trimestre f *half-term*
mixte a *mixed (e.g. school)*
la mobylette f *moped*
moche a *ugly, rotten*
la mode f *fashion*
    à la mode a *in fashion, fashionable*
moderne a *modern*
à moi a *mine*
moins ... que *less ... than*
    au moins *at least*
le mois m *month*
la moitié f *half*
le/la môme m/f *kid*
le moment m *moment, time*
    en ce moment ad *at the moment*
mon Dieu! interj *my God!*
le monde m *world*
le moniteur m *instructor, computer monitor*
la monnaie f *change (money)*
monoparental(e) a *single-parent (family)*
Monsieur m *Mr / Sir*
la montagne f *mountain*
monter v *to rise*
la montre f *watch*
montrer v *to show*
le monument m *monument*
la moquette f *fitted carpet*
le moral m *morale, spirit*
le morceau m *piece*
la mort f *death*
    mort(e) a *dead*
le mot m *word*
le moteur m *motor*
la moto f *motorbike*
le/la motocycliste m/f *motorcyclist*
le mouchoir v *handkerchief*
mouillé(e) a *wet*
mouiller v *to get wet*
mourir v *to die*
la moutarde f *mustard*
le mouton m *sheep*
moyen(ne) a *medium*
la moyenne f *average*
le mur m *wall*
le musée m *museum*
la musique f *music*
    musique pop/rock/classique f
        pop/rock/classical music
(le/la) musulman(e) a/m/f *Muslim*

N

la N7 f *the N7 (French A-road)*
nager v *to swim*
la naissance f *birth*
la natation f *swimming*
la nationalité f *nationality*
nautique a *nautical*
né(e) le *born on*
ne ... jamais *never*
ne ... pas *not*
ne ... personne *no one*
ne ... plus *no longer*
ne ... rien *nothing*
nécessaire a *necessary*
négatif/négative a *negative*
la neige f *snow*
neiger v *to snow*
nettoyer v *to clean*
(le) neuf a/m *nine*
neuf/neuve a *new*
le neveu m *nephew*
le nez m *nose*
ni... ni... conj *neither... nor...*

la nièce f *niece*
le niveau m *level*
les noces fpl *wedding*
(le) Noël m *Christmas*
noir(e) a *black*
le nom m *name*
le nombre m *number*
non interj *no*
non plus ad *neither, either (e.g. I haven't any either)*
non-fumeur/non-fumeuse a *non-smoking*
le nord m *north*
normalement ad *normally*
la Normandie m *Normandy*
la note f *mark, grade*
noter v *to note*
la nourriture f *food*
nouveau/nouvelle a *new*
le Nouvel An m *New Year*
(le) novembre m *November*
le nuage m *cloud*
nuageux/nuageuse a *cloudy*
la nuit f *night*
nul(le) a *useless*
le numéro m *number*
le numéro de téléphone m *telephone number*

O

l' obésité f *obesity*
les objets trouvés mpl *lost property*
obligatoire a *compulsory*
l' occasion f *opportunity (to)*
occupé(e) a *engaged, busy*
(l') octobre m *October*
l' odeur f *smell, fragrance*
l' œil m (pl. les yeux) *eye*
l' œuf m *egg*
l' office de tourisme m *tourist office*
l' offre f *offer*
l' offre d'emploi f *job offer*
l' oignon m *onion*
l' oiseau m *bird*
    ombragé(e) a *shaded*
l' omelette f *omelette*
on pron *one, you*
    on se retrouve à quelle heure?
        what time shall we meet?
l' oncle m *uncle*
(l') onze a/m *eleven*
l' opinion f *opinion*
    optimiste a *optimistic*
l' option f *option*
l' or m *gold*
l' orage m *storm*
    orageux/orageuse a *stormy*
    orange a *orange (colour)*
l' orange f *orange (fruit)*
l' orangina m *orangina*
l' orchestre m *orchestra*
    ordinaire a *ordinary*
l' ordinateur m *computer*
l' ordonnance f *prescription*
les ordures fpl *rubbish*
l' oreille f *ear*
    organiser v *to organise*
l' os m *bone*
    ou conj *or*
    où pron/ad *where*
        d'où? *where from?*
    oublier v *to forget*
l' ouest m *west*
    oui interj *yes*
    ouvert(e) a *open*
    ouvrir v *to open*

P

la page f *page*
le pain m *bread*
le pain grillé m *toast*
la paire f *pair*
    paisible a *quiet, peaceful*
en panne a *broken down*
le panneau m *sign, notice*
le pantalon m *trousers*

le papa m *dad*
le papier m *paper*
    en papier a *made of paper*
    le papier peint m *wallpaper*
(les) Pâques m/fpl *Easter*
le paquet m *parcel, packet*
par prep *by, per*
    par chance ad *luckily*
    par contre ad *on the other hand*
    par hasard ad *by chance, on the off-chance*
    par ici/là ad *this way/that way*
    par terre *on the ground*
paraître v *to appear*
le parapluie m *umbrella*
le parc m *park*
    le parc d'attractions m *amusement park*
parce que conj *because*
pardon interj *excuse me*
le pare-brise m *windscreen*
pareil(le) a *the same*
les parents mpl *parents*
paresseux/paresseuse a *lazy*
parfait(e) a *perfect*
parfois ad *sometimes*
le parfum m *flavour, perfume*
la parfumerie f *perfume shop*
le parking m *car park*
parler v *to talk*
la parole f *word*
à part *on one side, separately, except for*
partager v *to share*
le/la partenaire m/f *partner*
la partie f *part*
partir v *to depart, leave*
    à partir de prep *from*
partout ad *everywhere*
pas — ne...pas ad *(...) not*
pas de — je n'ai pas de...
    I have no ...
pas du tout ad *not at all*
pas encore ad *not yet*
pas grand-chose *not much*
pas mal de a *quite a few*
passable a *acceptable*
le passage à niveau m *level crossing*
le/la passant(e) m/f *passer-by*
le passé m *past*
le passeport m *passport*
passer v *to pass*
    passer l'aspirateur *to vacuum*
    passer un examen
        to take an exam
    passer le temps à
        to spend time doing
se passer vr *to happen*
le passe-temps m *hobby*
la passion f *passion*
passionnant(e) a *exciting*
les pastilles fpl *lozenges*
le pâté m *pâté*
les pâtes fpl *pasta*
patient(e) a *patient*
patienter v *to wait*
le patin à roulettes m *roller skate*
le patinage m *skating*
patiner v *to skate*
la patinoire f *ice rink*
la pâtisserie f *cake/pastry shop*
le/la patron(ne) m/f *boss*
la pause f *break, pause*
    la pause-café f *coffee break*
    la pause de midi f
        lunch break
    la pause-déjeuner f
        lunch break
    la pause-thé f *tea break*
pauvre a *poor*
payer v *to pay*
le pays m *country*
le paysage m *countryside*
le pays de Galles m *Wales*

le PC m *computer*
le PDG (président-directeur général) m *chairman and managing director*
le péage m *toll*
la peau f *skin*
la pêche f *fishing, peach*
se peigner vr *to comb one's hair*
la peine f *sadness, difficulty*
    ce n'est pas la peine
        don't bother, there's no point
    à peine a *barely*
la peinture f *painting*
la pellicule f *(camera) film*
la pelouse f *lawn*
pendant (+ que) prep (conj)
    during, while
pénible a *hard, tiring*
penser v *to think*
la pension f *board*
la pension complète f *full board*
perdre v *to lose*
le père m *father*
perfectionner v *to perfect, to improve*
le périphérique m *ring road*
permettre v *to allow*
le permis (de conduire) m *permit, (driving) licence*
la permission f *permission*
la personnalité f *personality*
la personne f *person*
la perte f *loss*
peser v *to weigh*
pessimiste a *pessimistic*
petit(e) a *small, short*
le/la petit(e)-ami(e) m/f *boyfriend/girlfriend*
le petit déjeuner m *breakfast*
le petit-fils m *grandson*
la petite-fille m *granddaughter*
les petits pois mpl *peas*
le pétrole m *oil, petroleum*
peu ad *little, few*
    un peu de a *a little*
la peur f *fear*
    avoir peur *to be scared*
peut-être ad *perhaps*
le phare m *lighthouse, headlight*
la pharmacie f *pharmacy*
le/la pharmacien(ne) m/f *pharmacist*
la photo f *photo*
la photocopie f *photocopy*
la phrase f *sentence*
la physique f *physical appearance*
le piano m *piano*
la pièce f *piece, coin, room*
la pièce de théâtre f *play*
la pièce d'identité f *proof of identity*
le pied m *foot*
    à pied ad *on foot*
(le/la) piéton(ne) m/f/a *pedestrian*
piquant(e) a *spicy*
le pique-nique m *picnic*
piquer v *to sting*
la piqûre f *bite, sting*
la piscine f *swimming pool*
la piste f *track, trail*
    la piste cyclable f
        cycle lane, cycle track
pittoresque a *picturesque, vivid*
la pizza f *pizza*
le placard m *cupboard*
la place f *square, room, space, seat*
le plafond m *ceiling*
la plage f *beach*
se plaindre vr *to complain*
plaire (+ à) v *to please*
le plaisir m *pleasure*
le plan m *plan, map*
le plan de la ville m *map of the town*
la planche à voile f *windsurfing*
la plante f *plant*
le plastique m *plastic*
    en plastique a *made of plastic*

---

nouns — **m**: *masculine*   **f**: *feminine*   **pl**: *plural*   **v**: *verb*   **vr**: *reflexive verb*   **a**: *adjective*

French — English Dictionary

le plat m *dish*
le plat du jour m *dish of the day*
le plat principal m *main course*
la platine laser f *laser disc player*
plein(e) a *full*
faire le plein *to fill the car up*
plein de vie a *full of life*
pleurer v *to cry*
pleuvoir v *to rain*
le plombier m *plumber*
plonger v *to dive*
le/la plongeur/plongeuse m/f *diver*
la pluie f *rain*
plus ad *more*
plus tard ad *later*
plus ... que *more ...*
plusieurs pron *several*
pluvieux/pluvieuse a *rainy*
le pneu m *tyre*
la poche f *pocket*
le poids (lourd) m *(heavy) weight*
à point a *medium (cooked)*
la pointure f *size (of shoe)*
la poire f *pear*
le poisson m *fish*
le poisson rouge m *goldfish*
le poivre m *pepper*
poli(e) a *polite*
la police f *police*
la police-secours f *emergency services*
le/la policier/policière m/f *policeman/woman*
pollué(e) a *polluted*
la pollution f *pollution*
la Pologne f *Poland*
(le/la) polonais(e) a/m/f *Polish, Polish person*
la pomme f *apple*
la pomme de terre f *potato*
le pont m *bridge*
populaire a *popular*
le porc m *pork, pig*
le port m *harbour, port*
le portable m *mobile phone*
la porte f *door*
la porte d'entrée f *front door*
le portefeuille m *wallet*
le porte-monnaie m *purse*
porter v *to carry, wear*
la portière f *door (of car, train)*
(le/la) portugais(e) a/m/f *Portuguese, Portuguese person*
le Portugal m *Portugal*
poser v *to pose, to place*
poser des questions *to ask questions*
poser sa candidature *to apply (for a position)*
positif/positive a *positive*
possible a *possible*
la poste f *post office*
le poster m *poster*
le pot m *jar, pot, carton*
potable/non potable a *drinkable/ undrinkable*
le potage m *soup, broth*
la poubelle f *dustbin*
le poulet m *chicken*
le poumon m *lung*
pour prep *for*
le pourboire m *tip*
pourquoi ad/conj *why*
pousser v *to push*
pouvoir v *to be able to*
pratique a *practical*
pratiquer v *to practise*
la préférence f *preference*
préférer v *to prefer*
premier/première ad *first*
au premier étage ad *on the first floor*
en premier a *first of all*
prendre v *to take*
le prénom m *first name*
préparer v *to prepare*
près (+ de) ad (prep) *near, close (to)*

tout près *very near*
présent(e) a *present (here)*
présenter v *to present*
le préservatif m *contraception, protection*
presque ad *almost*
pressé(e) a *busy*
la pression f *pressure*
prêt(e) a *ready*
prêter v *to lend*
la prévention routière f *road safety*
les prévisions fpl *weather forecast*
prévu(e) a *expected*
le printemps m *spring (season)*
priorité à droite *give way to the right (on road signs)*
la prise f *catch, hold*
privé(e) a *private*
le prix m *price*
le prix fixe m *fixed price (e.g. menu)*
le problème m *problem*
prochain(e) a *next*
proche a *near, close*
le produit m *product*
le professeur m *teacher*
la profession f *profession*
profiter de v *to profit from, to take advantage of*
profond(e) a *deep*
le programme m *programme*
le/la programmeur/programmeuse m/f *programmer*
le progrès m *progress*
le projet m *project*
la promenade f *walk*
faire une promenade *to go for a walk*
promener v *to walk (e.g. a dog)*
se promener vr *to go for a walk*
la promotion f *promotion*
en promotion ad *on sale*
proposer v *to propose, suggest*
propre a *clean, own (e.g. my own room)*
le/la propriétaire m/f *owner*
la protection f *protection*
protéger v *to protect*
en provenance de a *coming from*
la Provence m *Provence*
la proximité f *closeness*
à proximité a *close, nearby*
la prune f *plum*
public/publique a *public*
la publicité f *publicity, advertisement(s)*
puis ad *then, next*
le pull (over) m *jumper*
la purée f *mashed potato*
le pyjama m *pyjamas*
les Pyrénées fpl *Pyrenees*

Q
le quai m *platform*
la qualité f *quality*
quand conj/ad *when*
la quantité f *quantity*
(le) quarante a/m *forty*
le quart m *quarter*
le quartier m *district, part of town*
(le) quatorze a/m *fourteen*
(le) quatre a/m *four*
quatre-vingts a/m *eighty*
quatre-vingt-dix a/m *ninety*
quatrième a *fourth*
en quatrième *in year 9*
que conj/pron *that, than*
le Québec m *Quebec*
quel, quelle, quels, quelles pron *which*
quelque(s) a *some*
quelque chose pron *something*
quelqu'un pron *someone*
quelquefois ad *sometimes*
qu'est-ce que / qu'est-ce qui pron *what, who (in questions)*

qu'est-ce que c'est? *what is it?*
qu'est-ce qu'il y a? *what is there, what is it?*
la question f *question*
la queue f *tail, queue*
que veut dire ... en anglais? *what does ... mean in English?*
qui pron *who, that*
(le) quinze a/m *fifteen*
(les) quinze jours mpl *fortnight*
quitter v *to leave (e.g. a place)*
quoi pron *what*
le quotidien m *everyday life, the daily newspaper*
quotidien(ne) a *daily*

R
raccrocher v *to hang up (e.g. phone)*
raconter v *to tell*
la radio f *radio*
raid(e) a *straight*
le raisin m *grape*
le raisin sec m *raisin*
la raison f *reason*
avoir raison *to be right*
ralentir v *slow down*
la randonnée f *hike*
ranger v *to tidy (e.g. a bedroom)*
(le) rapide a/m *quick, express train*
rapidement ad *quickly*
le rappel m *recall, reminder*
rappeler v *to call back*
se rappeler vr *to recall, to remember*
les rapports mpl *relationships*
rare a *rare*
se raser vr *to shave*
ravi(e) a *delighted*
rayé(e) a *striped*
le rayon m *shelf, department (of a department store)*
la réaction f *reaction*
le/la réalisateur/réalisatrice m/f *director (of film)*
récemment ad *recently*
récent(e) a *recent*
la réception f *reception*
recevoir v *to receive*
être reçu(e) *to be received*
le réchaud m *stove*
le réchauffement m *warming (up)*
le réchauffement de la planète m *global warming*
recommander v *to recommend*
reconnaissant(e) a *grateful*
la récréation f *leisure, recreation, break(time)*
le reçu m *receipt*
recycler v *to recycle*
le/la rédacteur/rédactrice m/f *editor*
redoubler v *to repeat a year*
la réduction f *reduction*
réduit(e) a *reduced*
réfléchir v *to reflect, think*
refuser v *to refuse*
regarder v *to look at*
le régime m *diet*
la région f *region*
la règle f *rule, ruler*
le règlement m *ruling, guideline*
regretter v *to be sorry*
se relaxer vr *to relax*
religieux/religieuse a *religious*
la religion f *religion*
remarquer v *to notice*
rembourser v *to reimburse, to give back*
remercier v *to thank*
la remise f *discount*
remplir v *to fill (in)*
remporter (un prix) v *win (a prize)*
rencontrer v *to meet*
se rencontrer vr *to meet up*
le rendez-vous m *meeting*
renoncer à v *to give up*
renouvelable a *renewable*

les renseignements mpl *information*
la rentrée f *start of school year*
rentrer v *to return*
renverser v *to knock over*
le repas m *meal*
repasser v *to iron*
répéter v *to repeat*
le répondeur m *answerphone*
répondre v *to reply*
la réponse f *reply*
se reposer vr *to rest*
reprendre v *to start again*
le RER (réseau express régional) m *regional train network*
la réservation f *reservation*
réserver v *to reserve*
respecter v *to respect, to observe*
respiratoire a *breathing*
la responsabilité f *responsibility*
ressembler v *to look like, resemble*
se ressembler vr *to look alike*
la ressource f *resource*
les ressources naturelles fpl *natural resources*
le restaurant m *restaurant*
rester v *to stay*
le résultat m *result*
le retard m *delay*
en retard a *late*
la retenue f *deduction, detention*
retirer v *to take out*
le retour m *return (journey)*
retourner (à) v *to return (to)*
la retraite f *retirement*
rétrécir v *to shrink, to make narrower*
la réunion f *meeting, gathering*
réussir v *to succeed*
le réveil m *alarm clock*
se réveiller vr *to wake up*
revenir v *to come back*
rêver v *to dream*
réviser v *to revise*
revoir v *to see/meet again*
au revoir interj *goodbye*
la revue f *magazine*
le rez-de-chaussée m *ground floor*
le Rhin m *Rhine (river)*
le Rhône m *Rhone (river)*
le rhume m *cold*
riche a *rich*
le rideau m *curtain*
ridicule a *ridiculous*
rien pron *nothing*
rigolo a *funny*
rire v *to laugh*
le risque m *risk*
la rivière f *river*
le riz m *rice*
la robe f *dress*
le robinet m *tap*
le rock m *rock (music)*
le roman m *novel*
le roman-photo m *graphic novel, comic*
rond(e) a *round*
le rond-point m *roundabout*
rose a *pink*
rôti(e) a *roast*
la roue f *wheel*
rouge a *red*
le rouge à lèvres m *lipstick*
rouler v *to go (car)*
la route f *road*
la route nationale f *A-road*
le routier m *lorry driver*
roux/rousse a *red (hair)*
le Royaume-Uni m *United Kingdom*
la rue f *street*
le rugby m *rugby*

S
s'il te plaît/s'il vous plaît *please*
le sable m *sand*
le sac m *bag*

le sac à main m *handbag*
le sac de couchage m *sleeping bag*
le sac en plastique m *plastic bag*
sage a *wise, good (child)*
saignant(e) a *bleeding, rare (meat)*
sain(e) a *healthy*
la Saint-Sylvestre f *New Year's Eve*
la Saint-Valentin f *Valentine's Day*
la saison f *season*
la salade f *salad*
le salaire m *salary*
sale a *dirty*
salé(e) a *salted*
la salle f *room*
la salle à manger f *dining room*
la salle d'attente f *waiting room*
la salle de bain(s) f *bathroom*
la salle de classe f *classroom*
la salle de séjour f *living room*
le salon m *living room*
salut interj *hi, bye*
(le) samedi m *Saturday*
le SAMU m *mobile emergency medical service*
la sandale f *sandal*
le sandwich m *sandwich*
le sang m *blood*
sans prep *without*
sans doute a *without doubt*
sans plomb a *unleaded*
sans-souci a *carefree*
sans travail a *unemployed*
la santé f *health*
en bonne santé a *in good health*
les sapeurs-pompiers mpl *fire service*
satisfaire v *to satisfy, to live up to*
la sauce f *sauce*
la saucisse f *sausage*
le saucisson m *cold sausage*
sauf prep *except (for)*
le saumon m *salmon*
sauter v *to jump*
sauvage a *wild, undomesticated*
sauvegarder v *to protect, to save*
sauver v *to save*
savoir v *to know (e.g. how to do something)*
je ne sais pas *I don't know*
le savon m *soap*
la science-fiction f *science fiction*
les sciences fpl *science*
scolaire a *school*
la scolarisation f *schooling*
le/la SDF (sans domicile fixe) m/f *homeless person*
la séance f *showing (e.g. of film)*
sec/sèche a *dry*
secondaire a *secondary*
la seconde f *second (period of time)*
en seconde *in year 11*
le secours m *help*
au secours! interj *help!*
le/la secrétaire m/f *secretary*
la section (d'anglais) f *(English) section, department*
la sécurité f *security*
séduisant(e) a *attractive*
(le) seize a/m *sixteen*
le séjour m *stay*
le sel m *salt*
la semaine f *week*
sembler v *to seem*
le sens de l'humour m *sense of humour*
à sens unique a *one-way*
sensass a *sensational*
sensible a *sensitive*
sentir v *to feel, smell*
se sentir vr *to feel*

ad: *adverb*   **prep**: *preposition*   **pron**: *pronoun*   **interj**: *interjection*   **conj**: *conjunction*

French — English Dictionary

se sentir bien/mal *to feel good/ill*
séparé(e) a *separated*
(le) sept a/m *seven*
(le) septembre m *September*
la série f *set, series*
sérieux/sérieuse a *serious*
serré(e) a *tight*
le/la serveur/serveuse m/f *waiter/ waitress*
le service m *service*
la serviette f *towel, napkin*
servir v *to serve*
seul(e) a/ad *only, alone*
tout(e) seul(e) *all alone*
à moi seul(e) *by myself*
seulement ad *only*
sévère a *strict*
le shampooing m *shampoo*
le shopping m *shopping*
le short m *shorts*
si conj *if*
le sida m *AIDS*
signer v *to sign*
le silence m *silence*
simple a *simple, single*
le sirop m *syrup (medicine)*
le site m *site*
situé(e) a *situated*
(le) six a/m *six*
sixième a *sixth*
en sixième *in year 7*
le skate m *skateboarding*
le ski m *skiing*
faire du ski *to go skiing*
faire du ski nautique *to go water skiing*
SNCF (Société nationale des chemins de fers français) f *French national railway*
la sœur f *sister*
la soif f *thirst*
avoir soif *to be thirsty*
soigner v *to care for*
le soin m *care*
le soir m *evening*
la soirée f *evening*
(le) soixante a/m *sixty*
(le) soixante-dix a/m *seventy*
le/la soldat(e) m/f *soldier*
les soldes mpl *sales*
le soleil m *sun*
il fait du soleil *it's sunny*
le son (et lumière) m *sound and lighting, a type of show*
le sondage m *survey*
sonner v *to ring*
la sorte f *sort, kind (of)*
la sortie f *exit*
la sortie de secours f *emergency exit*
sortir v *to go out*
le souci m *worry*
soudain ad *suddenly*
souffrir v *to suffer*
souhaitable a *desirable*
souligner v *to underline*
la soupe f *soup*
sourire v *to smile*
la souris f *mouse*
sous prep *under*
sous-marin(e) a *underwater*
le sous-sol m *basement*
sous-titré(e) a *subtitled*
souterrain(e) a *underground*
le souvenir m *souvenir, memory*
souvent ad *often*
les spaghettis mpl *spaghetti*
le sparadrap m *sticking plaster*
spécial(e) a *special*
la spécialité (locale) f *(local) speciality*
le spectacle m *show*
le/la spectateur/spectatrice m/f *spectator*
splendide a *splendid*
le sport m *sport*
faire du sport *to do sport*

les sports d'hiver mpl *winter sports*
les sports nautiques mpl *water sports*
sportif/sportive a *sporty*
le stade m *stadium*
le stage (en entreprise) m *work experience*
la station f *station, stop*
la station balnéaire f *seaside resort*
la station de ski f *ski resort*
le stationnement m *parking*
stationner v *to park*
la station-service f *petrol station, service station*
le steak m *steak*
strict(e) a *strict*
le studio m *studio apartment*
stupide a *stupid*
le stylo m *pen*
le sucre m *sugar*
sucré(e) a *sweetened*
le sud m *south*
suffisamment a *sufficiently, enough*
la Suisse f *Switzerland*
(le/la) suisse a/m/f *Swiss*
suivant(e) a *following, next*
suivre v *to follow*
super a *great*
le supermarché m *supermarket*
le supplément m *extra, supplement*
supporter v *to put up with*
sur prep *on, on top of*
sur le point de *about to*
sur (vingt) *out of (twenty)*
sûr(e) a *sure*
surcharger v *to overload*
le surf m *surfing*
le surf des neiges m *snowboarding*
la surpopulation f *overpopulation*
la surprise f *surprise*
la surprise-partie f *surprise party*
surtout ad *especially*
le/la surveillant(e) m/f *guard, supervisor*
surveiller v *to watch*
le sweat-shirt m *sweatshirt*
sympa(thique) a *nice, friendly*
le syndicat m *union, association*
le syndicat d'initiative m *tourist information office*

T

le tabac m *newsagent, tobacco*
la table f *table*
le tableau m *picture*
la taille f *size*
se taire vr *to be quiet*
la Tamise f *Thames*
tant ad *(so) much*
tant mieux *good, that's better*
tant pis *never mind, too bad*
la tante f *aunt*
taper v *to type, to knock*
taper à la machine *to type*
le tapis m *carpet*
tard ad *late*
le tarif m *tarif, rate*
le tarif réduit m *reduced tarif*
la tarte au citron f *lemon tart*
la tasse f *cup*
le tatouage m *tattoo*
le taux (d'alcool) m *(alcohol) percentage, level (of alcohol)*
le taxi m *taxi*
le/la technicien(ne) m/f *technician*
la technologie f *technology*
la télécarte f *phonecard*
le téléphone m *telephone*
le téléphone portable m *mobile telephone v to phone*
le/la téléspectateur/téléspectatrice m/f *television viewer*

la télévision f *television*
le témoin m *witness*
la température f *temperature*
la tempête f *storm*
le temps m *weather, time*
de temps en temps ad *from time to time*
en même temps ad *at the same time*
à temps partiel a *part-time*
le tennis m *tennis*
la tente f *tent*
en terminale *in upper 6th*
terminer v *to terminate, end*
le terrain m *ground*
la terrasse f *terrace*
terrible a *terrible, dreadful*
la tête f *head*
le texte m *text*
le texto m *text message*
le TGV (train à grande vitesse) m *high-speed train*
le thé m *tea*
le théâtre m *theatre*
faire du théâtre *to act, be a stage actor*
le ticket m *ticket*
à la tienne interj *cheers!*
le timbre m *stamp*
timide a *shy*
tirer v *to pull*
le (gros) titre m *headline*
le toast m *toast*
les toilettes fpl *toilets*
le toit m *roof*
la tomate f *tomato*
tomber v *to fall*
tomber amoureux (de) *to fall in love (with)*
la tonalité f *dialling tone*
tondre v *to cut, to mow*
le tort m *fault, wrong*
avoir tort *to be wrong*
tôt ad *early*
la touche f *key, button, touch*
toucher v *to touch*
toujours ad *always*
la tour f *tower*
le tourisme m *tourism*
le/la touriste m/f *tourist*
touristique a *touristy*
la tournée f *tour, round*
tourner v *to turn*
tourner un film *to shoot a film*
tous m *everyone*
tous les jours ad *every day*
la Toussaint f *All Saints' Day, November 1st*
tousser v *to cough*
tout, toute, tous, toutes pron *all*
tout à coup ad *all of a sudden*
à toute à l'heure interj *see you later*
tout de suite ad *immediately*
tout droit ad *straight ahead*
tout le monde pron *everyone*
tout près m *close by*
toutes directions fpl *all directions (on road sign)*
toutes les cinq minutes *every five minutes*
le train m *train*
être en train de faire quelque chose *to be in the process of doing something*
le train-train m *daily routine*
le traitement de texte m *word-processing*
traiter de v *to deal with*
le trajet m *journey*
la tranche f *slice*
tranquille a *quiet*
les transports en commun mpl *public transport*
le travail m (pl. les travaux) *work*
travailler v *to work*

travailleur/travailleuse a *hard-working*
traverser v *to cross (e.g. street)*
(le) treize a/m *thirteen*
le tremblement de terre m *earthquake*
tremper v *to soak*
la trentaine f *about thirty, thirty or so*
(le) trente a/m *thirty*
très ad *very*
le tricot m *jumper, knitting*
le trimestre m *term*
triste a *sad*
(le) trois a/m *three*
troisième a *third*
en troisième *in year 10*
le troisième âge m *retirement years*
se tromper vr *to make a mistake*
se tromper de numéro *to dial the wrong number*
trop ad *too, too much*
le trottoir m *pavement*
le trou m *hole*
la trousse de premiers secours f *first-aid kit*
trouver v *to find*
se trouver vr *to be (situated)*
le truc m *thing, trick*
la truite f *trout*
le T-shirt m *T-shirt*
le tube m *tube, hit song*
tuer v *to kill*
la Tunisie f *Tunisia*
(le/la) tunisien(ne) a/m/f *Tunisian*
typique a *typical*

U

l' UE (Union européenne) m *EU (European Union)*
un/une/des art/a *a, one, some*
la une f *the front page*
l' uniforme m *uniform*
uni(e) a *plain, smooth*
unique a *only*
l' université f *university*
l' usine f *factory*
utile a *useful*
utiliser v *to use*

V

les vacances fpl *holiday, vacation*
la vache f *cow*
la vague f *wave*
la vaisselle f *washing-up*
faire la vaisselle *to wash up*
valable a *valid*
la valeur f *value*
la valise f *suitcase*
la vallée f *valley*
le vandalisme m *vandalism*
la vanille f *vanilla*
varié(e) a *varied*
variable a *variable, unsettled*
le veau m *veal*
la vedette f *star (e.g. film star)*
(le/la) végétarien(ne) a/m/f *vegetarian*
le véhicule m *vehicle*
le vélo m *bike*
le/la vendeur/vendeuse m/f *shop assistant*
vendre v *to sell*
(le) vendredi m *Friday*
venir v *to come*
le vent m *wind*
il fait du vent *it's windy*
le ventre m *stomach*
le verglas m *(black) ice*
vérifier v *to check, verify*
la vérité f *truth*
le verre m *glass*
en verre a *made of glass*
vers prep *around, about, towards*
la version française f *film dubbed into French*

la version originale f *film in the original language, with subtitles*
vert(e) a *green*
la veste f *jacket*
les vêtements mpl *clothes*
le/la veuf/veuve m/f *widower, widow*
la viande f *meat*
vide a *empty*
le vide-grenier m *car-boot sale, garage sale*
la vie f *life*
vieux/vieille a *old*
le village m *village*
la ville f *town*
en ville a *in town*
le vin m *wine*
le vinaigre m *vinegar*
(le) vingt a/m *twenty*
la vingtaine f *about twenty, twenty or so*
la violence f *violence*
violet(te) a *purple*
le visage m *face*
la visite f *visit*
visiter v *to visit (a place)*
la vitamine f *vitamin*
vite ad *quickly*
la vitesse f *speed*
à toute vitesse ad *at full speed*
la vitrine f *window*
vivre v *to live*
le vocabulaire m *vocabulary*
voici prep *here is, here are*
la voie f *way, route*
voilà prep *there is, there are*
la voile f *sailing, sail*
voir v *to see*
se voir vr *to see each other*
voisin(e) a *neighbouring*
le/la voisin(e) m/f *neighbour*
la voiture f *car*
la voix f *voice*
le vol m *flight*
le volant m *steering wheel*
voler v *to fly, to steal*
le volet m *shutter, section*
le volley m *volleyball*
volontiers ad *gladly, willingly, with pleasure*
vomir v *to vomit*
à la vôtre interj *cheers!*
vouloir v *to want*
vouloir bien *to not mind, be happy to*
je veux bien *I'll be happy to*
le voyage m *journey*
voyager v *to travel*
le/la voyageur/voyageuse m/f *traveller*
vrai(e) a *true*
vraiment ad *really*
le VTT (vélo tout-terrain) m *mountain bike*
la vue f *sight, view*

W

le wagon-lit m *sleeping car*
le wagon-restaurant m *restaurant car*
le W.C. m *W.C., toilet*
le web m *web*
le web mail m *webmail*
le week-end m *weekend*

X,Y

y pron *there, to it etc.*
le yaourt m *yoghurt*
les yeux mpl *eyes (plural of l'oeil)*

Z

(le) zéro a/m *nought*
la zone f *zone*
la zone piétonne f *pedestrian zone*
le zoo m *zoo*
zut! interj *dash it!*

nouns — **m**: masculine   **f**: feminine   **pl**: plural   **v**: verb   **vr**: reflexive verb   **a**: adjective

Index

Index

Make sure you're not missing out on another superb
CGP revision book that might just save your life...

...order your **free** catalogue today.

CGP customer service is second to none

We work very hard to despatch all orders the **same day** we receive them, and our success rate
is currently 99.9%. We send all orders by **overnight courier** or **First Class** post.
If you ring us today you should get your catalogue or book tomorrow. Irresistible, surely?

- Phone: 0870 750 1252   (Mon-Fri, 8.30am to 5.30pm)
- Fax: 0870 750 1292
- e-mail: orders@cgpbooks.co.uk
- Post: CGP, Kirkby-in-Furness, Cumbria, LA17 7WZ
- Website: www.cgpbooks.co.uk

...or you can ask at any good bookshop.